Representing Mass Violence

Conflicting Responses to Human Rights Violations in Darfur

Joachim J. Savelsberg

D1457349

UNIVERSITY OF CALIFORNIA PRESS

University of California Press, one of the most distinguished university presses in the United States, enriches
lives around the world by advancing scholarship in the
humanities, social sciences, and natural sciences. Its activities are supported by the UC Press Foundation and by
philanthropic contributions from individuals and institutions. For more information, visit www.ucpress.edu.

University of California Press
Oakland, California

© 2015 by The Regents of the University of California

This work is licensed under a Creative Commons CC-BY
license. To view a copy of the license, visit
http://creativecommons.org/licenses.

Suggested citation: Savelsberg, Joachim, J. *Representing
Mass Violence: Conflicting Responses to Human Rights
Violations in Darfur*. Oakland, University of California
Press, 2015. doi: http://dx.doi.org/10.1525/luminos.4

Library of Congress Cataloging-in-Publication Data

Savelsberg, Joachim J., 1951–.
    Representing mass violence : conflicting responses
to human rights violations in Darfur / Joachim J.
Savelsberg.
        p.   cm.
    Includes bibliographical references and index.
    isbn 978-0-520-28150-9 (pbk. : alk. paper)
    isbn 978-0-520-96308-5 (ebook)
    1. Sudan—History—Darfur Conflict, 2003—Foreign
public opinion. 2. Sudan—History—Darfur Conflict,
2003—Press coverage. 3. Sudan—History—Darfur
Conflict, 2003—Mass media and the conflict.
4. Violence—Sudan—Darfur al-Janubiyah (Province)—
Public opinion. 5. Violence—Press coverage—Sudan—
Darfur al-Janubiyah (Province) 6. Human rights—
Sudan—Darfur al-Janubiyah (Province)—Public opinion.
7. Human rights—Press coverage—Sudan—Darfur
al-Janubiyah (Province) I. Title.
    DT159.6.D27S2548   2015
    962.404'3—dc23

                                          2015017231

24 23 22 21 20 19 18 17 16 15
10 9 8 7 6 5 4 3 2 1

Representing Mass Violence

*Dedicated to those who strive for
justice, humanitarianism, and peace
and to those who keep us informed—
with all their constraints and
all the tensions between their fields*

Contents

Illustrations

TABLES

Acknowledgments

I owe great thanks to interviewees—Africa correspondents from eleven major European and North American newspapers, as well as Sudan and Darfur specialists at foreign ministries and with sections of Amnesty International and Doctors Without Borders in most of the eight countries I examined. They must remain unnamed as I promised anonymity. In some cases I may even have manipulated their gender attribution to inhibit identification. Many others—scholars, administrators, librarians, and archivists—contributed valuable information.

I thank my research team, a hardworking group of then–graduate students from the sociology (Abby Hagel, Ryan Moltz, Hollie Nyseth Brehm), political science (Brooke Coe, Henry Thomson), and history departments (Ed Snyder) at the University of Minnesota. They diligently coded 3,387 media articles. Reliability tests show how solidly they worked. Precious undergraduate student assistance, supported by the University of Minnesota's Undergraduate Research Opportunity Program, was provided by Patrick Alcorn, Victoria Dutcher, Taylor Yess, and Meghan Zacher (Meghan with the support of a National Science Foundation Research Experiences for Undergraduates grant). Graduate student Suzy Maves McElrath, supported by the University of Minnesota's Center for German and European Studies, coded foreign ministry press releases and helped coordinate the undergraduate work. Erez Garnai, also a graduate student in sociology at Minnesota, contributed to artwork as well as the front matter. Within the research assistant team,

Hollie Nyseth Brehm stood out. A (by now former) doctoral co-advisee, since fall 2014 on the sociology faculty of The Ohio State University, she helped develop the code book, coordinate the work of the coder team, and organize the data set, and contributed to data collection and analysis with great skill and seemingly unlimited energy. Collaboration with Hollie resulted in a coauthored article in the *American Journal of Sociology* (Vol. 121, No. 2, 2015), where we apply advanced statistical methods to some of the data presented in this book.

Research underlying this book is based primarily on funding by the National Science Foundation, Law and Social Science Program (Grant No. SES-0957946). The University of Minnesota and its College of Liberal Arts granted me supplemental funding during a 2010–11 sabbatical year and a Faculty Development Leave in 2013–14. The sabbatical allowed me to travel across seven European countries to conduct field research and interviews, while the Institute for Social Sciences at Humboldt Universität in Berlin hosted me generously. I am indebted to Klaus Eder, the institute's director at the time, and Hans Bertram, who provided office space and made his infrastructure available. During the Faculty Development Leave, I was a Fellow at the Käte Hamburger Center for Advanced Study in the Humanities "Law as Culture" at the Friedrich-Wilhelm Universität in Bonn. I owe great thanks to Werner Gephart, its director; to Raja Sakrani, its academic program director; to its academic and support staff; and to my fellow Fellows from five disciplines, eight countries, and six continents. They shielded me against many risks of parochialism in academic work. A German version of this book is forthcoming in the Käte Hamburger Center's series with Vittorio Klostermann Publisher, Frankfurt am Main. Finally, the Rockefeller Foundation funded a 2010 collaborative fellowship, with John Hagan and Jens Meierhenrich, and a 2012 conference, Representations of Darfur, that our trio organized at its Bellagio Center. The conference allowed us to bring together scholars, journalists, Sudanese opposition activist-journalists, ICC staff, and leading diplomats from the Bill Clinton and George W. Bush administrations.

I presented parts of this work at numerous places, including annual meetings of the American Sociological Association; the Law & Society Association; the American Society of Criminology; the Research Council for the Sociology of Law at its 2013 Toulouse meetings; the 2013 Legal Frames of Memory conference in Warsaw; the 2012 Rockefeller Bellagio conference; the 2013 conference "The Memory of Trauma: After the Holocaust and an Era of Genocides," organized by the Humanities Institute and the Department for Jewish Studies at the University of California, Davis; the 2013 Representations of Genocide conference, which I coorganized with Alejandro Baer, Director of the Center for Holocaust and Genocide Studies at the University of Minnesota; workshops in the sociology departments of Johannes-Gutenberg Universität in Mainz, Karl-Franzens-Universität Graz, and the University of Minnesota; the Institute for Diaspora and Genocide Research at the Ruhr Universität Bochum; All Souls College and the Institute of Criminology at Oxford University; a Punishment & Society conference at the University of Edinburgh; the Käte Hamburger Center for Advanced Study in the Humanities "Law as Culture" in Bonn; and the Käte Hamburger Centre for Global Cooperation Research in Duisburg. Everywhere I received deserved critiques and helpful suggestions. My expression of gratitude for inspiration or hospitality has to be selective, but I will at least mention Martin Albrow, Alejandro Baer, Marta Bucholc, Mirhan Dabag, Nina Dethloff, Noemi Gal-Or, David Garland, Werner Gephart (again), John Hagan, Marina Hennig, Matthias Herdegen, Philipp Kuntz, Ian Loader, Jens Meierhenrich, Mark Osiel, Leigh Payne, Devin Pendas, Kristin Platt, Birgit Schwelling, Kathryn Sikkink, Richard Sparks, Natan Sznaider, Annette Weber, and Diane Wolf. A number of colleagues and friends read all or part of the manuscript: Shai Dromi, Erez Garnai, Shannon Golden, Matthias Herdegen, Ryan D. King, Matthias Revers, Rebecca Savelsberg, and Philip Smith. Anonymous reviewers for the University of California Press read the prospectus as well as the manuscript; each provided helpful suggestions. My profound thanks go to all of them and to others who contributed in manifold ways. Any remaining mistakes, of course, are mine.

At Minnesota, I thank Jim Parente, who, as Dean of the College of Liberal Arts and, jointly with Michal Kobialka, as Associate Dean for Faculty, supported several of the initiatives mentioned above. I was honored when Dean Parente offered me, in 2013, the Arsham and Charlotte Ohanessian Chair, dedicated to research and service in the name of human rights. I gratefully accepted, and work on judicial and legislative struggles over the history of the Armenian genocide is under way. My gratitude goes to the Ohanessian Fund and family.

At the University of California Press, Maura Roessner and her team, including Glynnis Koike, Elena McAnespie, Jessica Moll, and Jack Young, helped with enthusiasm and great professionalism. Steven B. Baker did outstanding work as copyeditor.

Finally, as always, Pamela Feldman-Savelsberg accompanied me through the process of researching and writing. I can never count the conversations, moments of frank critique, and precious advice that accumulate along the way. The last year of writing was accompanied by new life, by saved life, and by death among those closest to us. Millions of distant lives, saved and destroyed, of those who suffer from the greatest human rights violations, unnamed and unknown to us and the readers, and the struggle over their acknowledgment and representation are what this book is about.

Abbreviations

ABF	American Bar Foundation
ADS	Atrocities Documentation Survey
AEC	Assessment and Evaluation Commission
AI-IS	Amnesty International—International Secretariat
AI-USA	Amnesty International—USA section
AJWS	American Jewish World Service
ASC	American Society of Criminology
AU	African Union
AUHIP	African Union High Level Implementation Panel for Sudan
CARE	Cooperative for Assistance and Relief Everywhere
CBC	Congressional Black Caucus
CFSP	Common Foreign and Security Policy
CLG	Center on Law and Globalization
CPA	Comprehensive Peace Agreement
CSI	Christian Solidarity International
DFA	Department of Foreign Affairs
DPA	Deutsche Presse-Agentur
EPD	Evangelischer Pressedienst
FAZ	*Frankfurter Allgemeine Zeitung*
FCO	Foreign and Commonwealth Office

FDP	Free Democratic Party
FIDH	Fédération Internationale des Ligues des Droits de l'Homme
GNI	Gross National Income
GoNU	Government of National Unity for Sudan
HRW	Human Rights Watch
IAI	International African Institute
ICID	International Commission of Inquiry on Darfur
ICRC	International Committee of the Red Cross
ICTJ	International Center for Transitional Justice
ICTR	International Criminal Tribunal for Rwanda
ICTY	International Criminal Tribunal for the former Yugoslavia
IDP	internally displaced person
IGAD	Intergovernmental Authority for Development
IMT	International Military Tribunal (Nuremberg)
INGO	international nongovernmental organization
IRB	Institutional Review Board
JEM	Justice and Equality Movement
MFA	Ministry of Foreign Affairs
MSF	Médecins Sans Frontières (Doctors Without Borders)
NCP	National Congress Party
NGO	nongovernmental organization
NPWJ	No Peace Without Justice
NYT	*New York Times*
Oxfam	Oxford Committee for Famine Relief
PAA	Population Association of America
PDF	Popular Defense Forces
RAS	Royal African Society
REU	Research Experiences for Undergraduates
RTE	Radió Teilifís Éireann (Ireland)
R2P	Responsibility to Protect
SAF	Sudanese Armed Forces
SCSL	Special Court for Sierra Leone
SLA	Sudan Liberation Army
SLM/A	Sudan Liberation Movement/Army
SOAS	School of Oriental and African Studies

SPLA	Sudan People's Liberation Army
SSRC	Social Sciences Research Council
SZ	*Süddeutsche Zeitung*
TAN	transnational advocacy network
UNAMID	African Union–United Nations hybrid operation in Darfur
UNAMIS	United Nations Advance Mission in Sudan
UNOCHA	United Nations Office for the Coordination of Humanitarian Affairs
UNSC	United Nations Security Council
USHMM	United States Holocaust Memorial Museum
WFP	World Food Program
WSJ	*Wall Street Journal*

Questions, Theory, Darfur, Data

"Imagine . . ."

"If men define situations as real, they are real in their consequences."
These famous words, coined by W. I. Thomas (1928), the classical
Chicago School sociologist, have particular weight when mass violence
and atrocities are at stake. Politicians, diplomats, military leaders, NGO
activists, jurists, journalists, and citizens define such situations. Their
definitions codetermine how the world responds to events such as those
in Cambodia in the 1970s, in Rwanda and the former Yugoslavia in the
1990s, or in Darfur in the 2000s. It has often been argued for the case of
Rwanda that the United Nations' and the US government's reluctance
to call the 1994 mass killings genocidal prevented an appropriate response and cost hundreds of thousands of additional lives. It thus matters whether we define mass violence as a form of genocide specifically,
as criminal violence generally, or as something else altogether.

Definitions of mass violence as crime, some argue, have advanced
fast in the late twentieth and early twenty-first century, an era characterized by a "justice cascade" according to some scholars (Sikkink
2011). But actors may define mass violence differently, for example,
as an insurgency or counterinsurgency, a civil war, or a complex humanitarian emergency, and each of these definitions will support a distinct response. In the radical alternative, we may refuse to register the
suffering and practice denial (Cohen 2001). In this book I explore the
struggles over recognition and over competing definitions of the mass
violence that befell the Darfur region of Sudan in the first decade of the

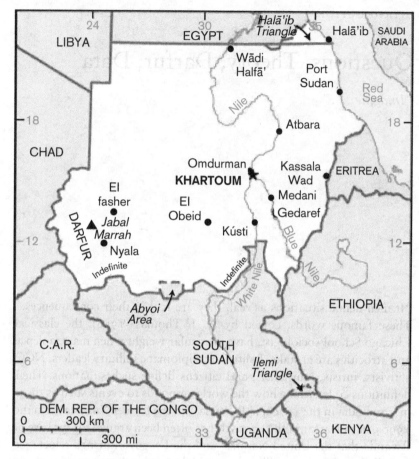

FIGURE 1. Darfur within Sudan and neighboring countries.

twenty-first century (see figure 1). I focus on the fields of human rights and criminal law, humanitarianism, and diplomacy, as they generate at least partially competing representations of the mass violence, and on the journalistic field and its contribution to the diffusion of competing narratives to a wide public. I invite the reader to accompany me on this journey.

Imagine you enter the light-filled foyer and modern extension of Germany's foreign ministry in Berlin. You then cross an expansive courtyard and finally reach the massive Nazi-era building, survivor of the destructions of the final stages of World War II, and once home to Joseph Goebbels's Ministry of Propaganda. There you learn from the Sudan specialist of the *Auswärtige Amt,* as the foreign ministry is called in Germany, about this country's diplomatic efforts toward advancing peace in Sudan. You listen to skeptical comments regarding the use of penal law, a tool deemed at least partially incompatible with diplomacy. Now envision a lecture room at Georgetown University's Law School in Washington, DC, where you meet a young Amnesty International activist. She tells you vivid tales about her and her organization's efforts to help bring those to (criminal) justice who bear primary responsibility for the suffering of the people of Darfur. Finally, imagine a small conference room in the Geneva operational center of Doctors Without Borders (MSF), where the interviewee, himself witness to horrific suffering in many areas of mass violence, including Darfur, speaks eloquently about impediments that criminal justice interventions create for those who seek to alleviate the pain on the ground and to save lives. He is especially critical of the work of human rights activists and the International Criminal Court (ICC) with its interventions in Darfur.

You travel beyond Berlin, Washington, and Geneva to London, Dublin, Paris, Frankfurt, Munich, Vienna, New York City, The Hague, and Bern, and finally arrange for a collaborator to visit Nairobi and Johannesburg. You speak with foreign policy makers, workers for international NGOs (INGOs)—both those with rights agendas and those with humanitarian aid orientations, and Africa correspondents of prominent newspapers. You are impressed by many of your interviewees. Most have left the stability of their home countries to instead devote crucial chapters of their lives and careers to responding to catastrophic situations. They have traded comfort for danger and hardship. You encounter intense engagement, profound belief in the mission to which your conversation partners are devoted. And you are exposed to distinct narratives, representations, and knowledge repertoires about what occurred in Darfur. Suggestions of appropriate remedies are aligned with these narratives and they diverge just as profoundly. Significant differences also appear among respondents within the same sector but with different national backgrounds. How, then, do we make sense of the varieties of stories we hear about the same event, each presented with passion and conviction? This book seeks to answer that question.

Imagine further the reader of some 3,400 news reports and opinion pieces about Darfur, all published by leading newspapers in eight Western countries. That reader would encounter amalgams of the narratives we heard in interviews and conversations while traveling to the homes of governments, media organizations, and INGOs. But this reader wants to go further and identify patterns of reporting, hoping to find out, for example, which newspapers (or papers from which countries) are how likely to report about the rapes in Darfur or to term the killings genocidal or to cite the ICC and apply a criminal justice frame to the violence—as opposed to a civil war or humanitarian emergency frame. Our reader then convinces the National Science Foundation to support such effort and engages a team of PhD students to code the content of all of these articles along a systematic set of analytic dimensions. Coders document the place and timing of each article, what it reports, and how.

This is in fact what I did. As I began to analyze the resulting Darfur media data set, fascinating patterns emerged. I realized, for example, that criminal justice actors and their supporters do affect how media report about the Darfur conflict. Applications of the crime frame to the violence in Darfur, as opposed to the civil war or humanitarian emergency frames, have increased substantially in all eight countries at crucial (but not all) intervention points. They did so, for example, after the International Commission of Inquiry on Darfur, established by the UN Security Council, released its report on Darfur on January 25, 2005; when the ICC issued its first arrest warrants—against Ahmed Harun, a Sudanese minister, and Ali Kushayb, a Janjawiid militia leader—on April 27, 2007; and, eventually, when the prosecutor applied for and the court issued an arrest warrant against Omar al-Bashir, the president of Sudan, charging him initially with war crimes and crimes against humanity (March 4, 2009) and ultimately with genocide (July 12, 2010).

It would be a grave error to mistake such effects of court activity on the public representation of mass violence as trivial. First, much constructivist research has shown that media foci are not necessarily—and at times not at all—related to events (and institutional responses to them) in the real world. It is thus not to be taken for granted that media will pay attention to actions by the ICC, despite intense efforts by its press office. Second, the fact that categories of criminal law are being applied to the actions of political and military leaders and resulting mass violence is a revolutionary achievement of the twentieth century (Giesen 2004b). Third, variation across countries shows that the type of representation of mass violence is not a matter of course but something to be explained. For example, news media of different countries vary in their willingness to subscribe to the crime frame as an appropriate lens through which to interpret the events in Darfur.

The Darfur media data set similarly shows that media in the eight countries are not evenly willing to refer to the violence in Darfur as genocidal. German news reporters are particularly reluctant to use the "G-word," and Irish reports are generally cautious in the use of both the crime and genocide frames. Interviews in these countries show that such caution is not limited to news media. US papers, on the other hand, liberally refer to the violence as criminal and call genocidal the killings, rapes, destruction of livelihood and displacements in Darfur. American editorial writers go even further. They do not shy away from building rhetorical bridges between Darfur and the Holocaust. Nicholas Kristof stands out when he argues in the *New York Times*: "The Sudanese authorities, much like the Turks in 1915 and the Nazis in the 1930's, apparently calculated that genocide offered considerable domestic benefits—like the long-term stability to be achieved by a 'final solution' of conflicts between Arabs and non-Arabs—and that the world would not really care very much" (*NYT* 6/19/04, sec. A, p. 17). Elsewhere Kristof asserts: "As in Rwanda and even during the Holocaust, racist ideologies sometimes disguise greed, insecurity and other pathologies. Indeed, one of the genocide's aims is to drive away African tribes to achieve what Hitler called Lebensraum: 'living space' for nomadic Arabs and their camels" (NYT 3/14/06, sec. A, p. 27).

By now you have begun to ask: Why such differences? Why do we find an array of affinities, varying by societal field and country, toward applying the crime frame to Darfur and to calling the atrocities genocide? Why do some actors instead prefer to describe the violence as a case of civil war or as a humanitarian emergency? And why do such preferences vary over time?

Answers to such questions matter in scholarly and in policy terms. We know that whether and how we acknowledge and name instances of mass violence, and whom we blame, has consequences for the willingness of the international community to intervene, and to do so either with diplomatic, judicial, humanitarian, or military means. The history of Rwanda is a case in point. US president Bill Clinton later considered as a low point of his presidency his administration's reluctance to name the Rwandan mass killings of 1994 "genocide" and to intervene accordingly.[1]

In the world of scholarship, comparativists, cultural sociologists, and globalization scholars will want to know why global or nationally distinct definitions of a situation of mass violence come to bear. Especially, why do national distinctions become manifest for a globally recognized problem such as Darfur, in which powerful international actors are engaged? Further, sociolegal scholars and criminologists are eager to learn how nation- and field-specific leanings interact with the potential of legal proceedings to shape visions of the past and to thus prevent future violence. Finally, human rights scholars, as well as activists, ask what enhances—and what impedes—the unfolding of the "justice cascade," the massive increase in individual criminal accountability for grave human rights offenses in the late twentieth and early twenty-first centuries (Sikkink 2011).

In the following chapters I introduce the reader to my discoveries about how global actors, national contexts, and distinct fields interact to create at times conflicting social constructions of the reality of aggression and suffering in Darfur. To do so, I engage different interrelated themes, all central to current scholarship and all implicated in these introductory paragraphs: (1) the criminalization of grave human rights violations; (2) the embeddedness of actors in competing fields of criminal justice, diplomacy, and humanitarian aid; (3) the role media play in communicating messages from these fields to a broad public; (4) tensions and interactions between global and national actors; and (5) consequences for the shape that knowledge about atrocities takes and potential effects on civil society and governmental responses. Throughout, I provide much space to let the actors speak, aiming toward an interpretive understanding of their actions. Combining such understanding with an analysis of the conditions their respective fields impose contributes to an explanation of unfolding responses to the mass violence. A few words on each of the central themes are followed by a brief reminder of what occurred in Darfur and by an exposition of the data and methods I put to work.

JUSTICE CASCADE, FIELDS, AND REPRESENTATIONS BETWEEN THE GLOBAL AND THE NATIONAL

The first theme concerns the long journey from disregard, often denial (Cohen 2001), at times even glorification (Giesen 2004b) of mass violence toward, via cautious steps, its definition as criminal and what political scientist Kathryn Sikkink (2011) has recently called a "justice cascade," a global fight against grave violations of human rights. This journey has been promoted by problem entrepreneurs whom I shall take seriously in this book—together with their challengers. I thus link a prominent line of scholarship in constructivist criminology, including the by now classical scholarship of Turk (1969), Chambliss (1964), and Gusfield (1967) and more recent contributions (e.g., Jenness 2004), to a new line of work on the criminalization of human rights offenses (Keck and Sikkink 1998;

Sikkink 2011; Neier 2012). Activists invest great hopes in these trends, and some scholarship supports their hopes. Yet, to judge the potential of new legal strategies, we have to recognize the actors' location within social fields and the challenges they face from competing fields.

The second theme is thus the embeddedness of actors in distinct social fields. I here initially focus on the fields of criminal law and justice (Hagan 2003), humanitarian aid (Krause 2014; Redfield 2013; Weissman 2011), and diplomacy (Power 2002; Scheffer 2012; K. Smith 2010).[2] As I examine conflicts within and between these fields for the case of Darfur, I use the concept of fields liberally, linking elements of field theory as developed by Pierre Bourdieu (1987, 1988, 1998) and his followers (Benson 1998, 2006, 2013; Hagan and Levi 2005) with notions of strategic action fields proposed by Neil Fligstein and his collaborators (Fligstein 2001; Fligstein and McAdam 2011). Despite important distinctions, both approaches share basic insights. They sensitize us to the fact that fields are made up of real social actors. These actors pursue specific goals such as justice, humanitarianism, and peace while simultaneously seeking to strengthen their own position within their respective fields. They are also carriers of habitus, a set of relatively fixed dispositions that reflect their trajectories and their position within the field. To achieve their distinct goals, actors have to incorporate into their habitus their field's dominant institutional logic, a notion borrowed from Weberian ideas (Weber 1978) as specified in the work of Luhmann (2004). In criminal law, for example, this means a focus on specific individual actors (as opposed to social structures a sociologist might stress), on a binary logic of guilty versus not guilty (avoiding differentiations of social psychologists), and on those types of evidence that are compatible with procedural requirements of the law (not those deemed relevant by a historian).

To complicate things further, fields are often interlinked and their inhabitants draw on diverse sources of habitus. Fields thus interpenetrate each other. One interviewee, for example, the director of an operational center of a major humanitarian aid agency in Europe, should not be inclined toward criminal justice responses. Yet, trained as a lawyer in the United States, he deviated from many of his humanitarian colleagues in this respect. His position in the organizational field, his educational background, and his national upbringing simultaneously contributed to his distinct knowledge and habitus. Biographical trajectory and field demands may thus not always harmonize. Instead, they often produce a tension that creates room for improvisation.

Third, as I explore how competing fields and their definitions of reality interact with civil society, I examine their impact on the journalistic field. Very few members of Western societies ever encounter mass violence in places such as Darfur directly. In contrast to other policy areas, most learn about such events only through media messages. Through them they become subject to distant suffering (Boltanski 1999). To the degree that policy decisions are informed by public perceptions of social issues, media thus become important social forces that affect whether and how governments will respond to mass violence in distant places. Recent Bourdieuian work on journalism (Bourdieu 1998; Benson 1998, 2006, 2014; Benson and Neveu 2005), lines of research that explore the boundaries between the journalistic and the political fields (Mazzoleni and Schulz 1999; Revers 2014; Strömbeck and Esser 2014), and culturally inspired work on journalism (Hannerz 2004; Zelizer 1993) provide inspiration for this analysis. In addition, historical and sociological literature contributes theoretical ideas and empirical information on ways in which crime and genocide narratives created in the judicial field are processed in media reports (Pendas 2006; Jardim 2012; Savelsberg and King 2011).

Fourth, one of the complications of the fields we study is their location in the intersection of the global and the local. A social movement organization may be international, yet be composed of national sections. The International Criminal Court operates at the global level, but its governing body is the Assembly of States, in which those countries that have ratified the Rome Statute are represented. Its lawyers were trained in their home countries. Throughout I shall thus pay close attention to the simultaneous engagement of actors at global and national levels. Should we not expect globally unified representations of an event such as Darfur in which so many international actors are engaged? Globalization theorists such as the World Polity School of John Meyer and his neo-institutionalist followers would suggest exactly that (e.g., Boyle and Meyer 1998; Frank, Hironaka, and Schofer 2000). But others insert a note of caution; some in fact thoroughly disagree. They highlight nation-specific social forces, carrier groups, interests, institutions, and cultural sensitivities, rooted in a country's history, through which global themes, representations, narratives, or norms are filtered (Bendix [1949] 1974; Gorski 2003; Roth 1987; Rueschemeyer 1973; Kalberg 1994, 2014; Savelsberg and King 2005).[3] And, indeed, empirical work shows national particularities in the way Western governments (K. Smith 2010; Power 2002) and NGO actors (Stroup 2012) respond to genocide and mass atrocities. More recently, even work inspired by the World Polity School has examined nation-specific patterns in the promulgation (Halliday and Carruthers 2009) and implementation of law, including human rights law (Boyle 2002, on laws against female genital cutting). Yet other scholars write about cosmopolitanism, especially in the realm of human rights (e.g., Levy and Sznaider 2010). They take the nation level seriously, while insisting that international and global concerns are increasingly incorporated into national ideas, memories, and practices.

Within this complex intersection of overlapping and conflicting fields there emerge cognitive and normative tools and policy responses to situations of mass violence. This book is thus linked to a fifth theme or intellectual tradition: the sociology of knowledge, rooted in classical works of Emile Durkheim and Karl Mannheim. Its tools further contribute to our explorations of how our competing fields, at national and global levels, constitute distinct conditions and interact to produce patterns of collective representations (Durkheim [1912] 2001; P. Smith 2008) that are selectively communicated by news media. As I examine such representations, I pay particular attention to four forms they may take: acknowledgment (Cohen 2001), framing (Goffman 1986; Benford and Snow 2000), arguments about causation, and bridging strategies (Alexander 2004). The last-named form links contemporary events, still diffuse in the public mind, to past ones for which a clear understanding has emerged. Collective representations then constitute a cultural repertoire of tools (Swidler 1986), from which creators of collective memory (Halbwachs 1992; Olick 1999; Osiel 1997; Savelsberg and King 2011) and cultural trauma (Alexander et al. 2004) will eventually be able to draw.

Understanding these patterns is a crucial precondition for making sense of, explaining, and predicting ways in which civil societies and governments respond to mass atrocities and grave violations of human rights. And such responses affect chances of breaking cycles of violence (Minow 1998, 2002) that have repeatedly tortured humanity throughout its history. These responses will determine if, at the global level, a degree of pacification can be achieved that many societies have arrived at in centuries of modern state formation (Elias 1978; Johnson and Monkkonen 1996).

DARFUR: SCHOLARLY DEFINITIONS
OF THE SITUATION

In addition to myriad activist and journalistic accounts, several academic books about the violent conflict in Darfur have been published (e.g., Flint and de Waal 2008; Hagan and Rymond-Richmond 2008; Mamdani 2009a; Prunier 2007). Reading these books reveals a scholarly consensus that massive violence unfolded, that many people lost their lives, and that two to three million Darfuris were displaced during the first decade of the twenty-first century.

Yet reading social scientific accounts of the mass violence in Darfur quickly reveals fundamental differences and tensions as well. I here briefly describe agreements and disagreements for the example of three (sets of) authors who wrote remarkable books on Darfur. All three occupy distinct locations within the academic field, which should affect the knowledge they contribute. John Hagan and Wenona Rymond-Richmond wrote *Darfur and the Crime of Genocide*, published in 2008 by Cambridge University Press. Julie Flint and Alex de Waal updated their *Darfur: A New History of a Long War* in a new edition published in 2008 by Zed Books in association with the International African Institute, the Royal African Society, and the Social Science Research Council. Finally, Mahmood Mamdani wrote *Saviors and Survivors: Darfur, Politics, and the War on Terror*, published in 2009 by Doubleday.

While Julie Flint is a journalist, the other authors are scholars. But all differ in sociologically significant ways. Hagan, a former president of the American Society of Criminology, is a professor of sociology and law at Northwestern University and codirector of the Center of Law and Globalization at the American Bar Foundation. Rymond-Richmond, a former student of Hagan, is on the sociology faculty at the University of Massachusetts at Amherst. De Waal, educated as a social anthropologist, has worked in several prestigious multidisciplinary social science institutions and now teaches at the Fletcher School of International Affairs at Tufts University. One of his book's photographs is of Sheik Hilal Mohamed Abdalla, taken in 1985 by the author himself and attesting to his long-term ethnographic familiarity with the region. The sheik, as those familiar with the history of Darfur know, is the father of Musa Hilal, one of the leading Janjawiid perpetrators. Finally, Mamdani, a political scientist and anthropologist, is a professor at Columbia University. The biographical blurb in his book describes him as "a third-generation East African of Indian descent [who] grew up in Kampala, Uganda, and received his Ph.D. from Harvard in 1974" (Mamdani 2009a:399). Even these brief sketches reveal that our authors occupy distinct places in the field of academia. There they compete for recognition, but they do so beyond the world of scholarship as well. The publication of two of the three books by at least partially commercial presses attests to the latter. So does the engagement of de Waal in policy and consulting positions, for example, as a senior advisor to the African Union High Level Implementation Panel for Sudan, a role in which he served from 2009 to 2011. Not surprisingly, my interviews indicate that de Waal is by far the best known of these authors among journalists, policy makers, and NGO workers.

The position of these scholars in the academic field should affect which ideas they find acceptable or even thinkable, a link Pierre Bourdieu famously documented in his work *Homo Academicus*. Bourdieu (1988) also argues convincingly that not just the position of scholars in the academic field but also the relationship of an academic field to other societal fields affects knowledge. One of Bourdieu's chapter headings cites Kant's reference to the "conflict of the faculties," suggesting that closeness to the government places faculties on the right side of the political spectrum. But closeness to other institutional fields and movements also matters. The field of international criminal law and justice fares prominently in our case. Hagan and Rymond-Richmond are oriented toward it. So does the anti-postcolonialism movement, with which Mamdani is allied. And finally, de Waal is linked to the field of international governmental organizations, especially the African Union. Each of these fields entails specific sets of knowledge, and such knowledge is likely to color the depiction of Darfur by those affiliated with it. I thus suggest that we briefly consider events in Darfur by taking into account the overlaps and tensions between these books, written from distinct locations and covering themes of suffering and victimhood, responsible actors, origins, causes, and frames through which the violence is interpreted and, finally, policy preferences are formed.

All three books agree that great suffering has befallen the people in the "land of the Fur," to use the English translation of Darfur, that western part of Sudan, once a powerful Sultanate, incorporated into Sudan under British colonial rule and divided into three states by the Sudanese government in 1994. Population was estimated at seven million in the early stages of the mass violence in 2004. There is also little disagreement that violence dates back at least to the 1980s; that it initially peaked in the "First Arab-Fur War" of 1987–1989 (Flint and de

Waal 2008:277) and in the 1995–1999 Arab-Masalit conflict; but that the most destructive wave of violence occurred in 2003 and 2004. In this our three authors concur with almost all who have written about Darfur. People have been killed, raped, and displaced, their livelihood destroyed. Yet differences appear when we examine the victim count and the details into which the authors go to depict the suffering in Darfur.

Hagan and Rymond-Richmond (2008) base their account on an analysis of the qualitative and quantitative materials entailed in the Atrocities Documentation Survey (ADS), a massive data collection initiated by the US Department of State under then–secretary of state Colin Powell. The survey was conducted in summer 2004 among more than one thousand Darfuris who had crossed the border into neighboring Chad to seek protection in newly established refugee camps. These authors pay minute attention to the death toll and to the extent of other forms of victimization. They quote generously from qualitative interview materials, sharing with the reader horrendous stories that refugees told about their experience of mass killings, destruction, and rape campaigns: "First vehicles attacked the village. After one hour, planes came and bombed; after this military came on camels and horses and began shooting at random. They cut open the stomachs of pregnant women and split the throats of male fetuses. Bombs from airplanes killed a lot of animals and people. The military took women away. The village was burned and destroyed. They shot at anyone: man, woman, or child" (Hagan and Rymond-Richmond 2008:7–8).[4]

Hagan and his collaborators also seek to establish numerical estimates. Critiquing public health researchers who focus on mortality resulting from malnutrition and disease in displaced-person and refugee camps, they add survey-based estimates of deaths that are directly attributable to the violence. Hagan with Alberto Palloni, a past president of the Population Association of America, estimates a death toll of 350,000 (Hagan and Palloni 2005).[5]

Flint and de Waal (2008) do not engage in the accounting of victimization à la Hagan and Rymond-Richmond. Yet they do cite social movements, such as Save Darfur, and these movements' estimates of a death toll of 400,000 (Flint and de Waal 2008:186). Their text further takes pains to display the horrific violence, at times based on ICC accounts of specific events:

> Starting in August 2003, according to the ICC, Security [Forces] and militias worked hand-in-glove to clear a swath of Wadi Saleh. . . . A fertile area, long coveted by Arabs of Chadian origin, Wadi Saleh was now crowded with tens of thousands of displaced Fur and Masalit. By the end of the year, thirty-two

villages and hamlets along its tributary, Wadi Debarei, had been burned and displaced villagers had converged on the market town of Deleig. Over a period of weeks, army and Janjawiid captured and killed 172 people in the Deleig area. Some had their throats cut and their bodies thrown in the stagnant pool of a seasonal river just south of the town. (Flint and de Waal 2008:129–30)

The authors also describe in some detail the attacks on villages by Antonov planes of the Sudanese Armed Forces (SAF), often followed by Janjawiid raids that completed the destruction and killings and drove away any remaining residents.

Mamdani's account (2009a) of victimization differs substantially. He does not provide analyses of fatalities himself, and he abstains from confronting the reader with detailed descriptions of the brutalities committed on the ground. He also keeps his distance from any attempt to account for the number of victims. Instead he reviews, at times ironically, the "numbers debate" (Mamdani 2009a:25). He displays different and shifting death estimates that range from the tens of thousands up to a half million. He interprets the divergences as expressions of political strategizing by "human rights entrepreneurs" (28), including John Hagan ("most authoritative" [28]); Eric Reeves, an English professor at Smith College and frequent commentator on Darfur ("most prolific" [28]); and Nikolas Kristof from the *New York Times* ("another indefatigable crusader" [29]). While not providing his own estimate, he appears to sympathize with the doubts about high-end estimates expressed in a 2006 study by the US General Accounting Office. If indeed the struggle over numbers is part of a political game, as Mamdani suggests, he certainly is one player in this game.

Just as the tales of victimization and suffering differ between the three (sets of) authors, placed in different locales within the academic space, so does their depiction of responsible actors. Hagan and Rymond-Richmond (2008) see as aggressors the Sudanese government, the SAF, and the Janjawiid, the infamous Arab militias that received massive material and symbolic support from the Sudanese government. These two sociologist-criminologists go further, though. They reconstruct the chain of command, and—based on ADS reports—identify specific individuals as responsible for the mass violence, including those who are now indicted by the ICC. Both Flint and de Waal (2008) and Mamdani (2009a) attribute responsibility differently. To be sure, they never exempt the SAF or the Janjawiid from charges of gross atrocities. In fact, they attribute direct responsibility to some of the same actors identified in Hagan and Rymond-Richmond, such as the former minister Ahmed Harun (Hagan and Rymond-Richmond 2008:123, 133) and Janjawiid leaders Ali Kushayb (130) and Musa Hilal (35ff., 125). Yet the attribution of responsibility by Mamdani and Flint and de Waal is more diffuse. Flint and de Waal (2008) spell out atrocious attacks by rebel forces against Arab groups (135), and they examine the roles that outside actors such as Libya's Gaddafi (47) and Chad's Idriss Déby (27) played in the buildup of violence before it escalated to catastrophic levels in 2003. Mamdani (2009a) also does not deny the agency of the Sudanese state and the militias that drive what he labels "counter-insurgency" (5), but he highlights more clearly the violence committed by insurgents themselves. In fact, he attributes victim status to Arab tribes that are often defined as a crucial source of aggression. To him the rebels were recruited from "the tribes with land who sought to keep out landless or land-poor ["Arab"] tribes fleeing the advancing drought and desert" (4).

These and other differences between the three sets of authors are depicted in table 1. Clearly, distinct identifications of victimization and responsible actors correspond with further differences along a set of analytic dimensions that prove crucial throughout this book: time frames, the attribution of causes, and the framing of the violence. We shall see how representations of the mass violence in Darfur shift along these dimensions depending on the sector in which they were produced and, over time, under the influence of judicial interventions.

Considering the time frames, always crucial in the interpretation of mass violence,[6] Hagan and Rymond-Richmond decidedly focus on recent events and actions. They apply to Darfur an "endogenous conflict theory" that sees ethnic violence as the product of shorter-term dynamics initiated by concrete state actors to whom societal groups responded. Flint and de Waal instead situate the violence in a longer-term history of conflict among the groups populating Darfur. They inform the reader, for example, of troubles that government authorities had with the "camel-herding Abbala Rizeigat" Arabs, back in "the time of the Sultans," and of long-term desertification resulting from droughts and associated struggles for resources they caused already in the 1980s (Flint and de Waal 2008:40).[7] Mamdani (2009a) also reaches far back into history, taking as his point of departure the colonial era, especially the British colonial administration's effort at "retribalizing Darfur" (152ff) and "marginalizing" (163ff) the region. He interprets both strategies as crucial sources of the violence that was to plague the region in subsequent decades and into the present.

TABLE I. ANALYTIC DIMENSIONS OF THE DARFUR CONFLICT AND THEIR USE BY
HOLDERS OF DIFFERENT POSITIONS IN THE ACADEMIC FIELD

	Authors		
Analytic Dimension	Hagan and Rymond-Richmond (2008)	Flint and de Waal (2008)	Mamdani (2009)
Suffering/ victimization	graphic accounts high numbers	graphic accounts high numbers	no depictions ironizing "numbers game"
Responsible actors	GoS,* SAF, Janjawiid, specific individuals	GoS, SAF, Janjawiid, rebels, outside forces (Libya, Chad)	GoS, SAF, Janjawiid, rebels (against impoverished Arab groups)
Origins/time	Short-term, 2003–	Long-term, Drought of 1980s	Long-term, Colonialism
Causes	Ethnopolitical entrepreneurs and processes	Complex historical, cross-national	History of colonialism
Frame	Crime, genocide	War (of total destruction)	Neocolonial, counterinsurgency
Policy conclusions	Criminal justice	Negotiations	Negotiations

*Government of Sudan

Consider, finally, differences the authors apply in their accounts of causes, interpretive frames, and associated policy conclusions. Hagan and Rymond-Richmond (2008) develop a "critical collective framing approach" in which collective action generates a "Sudanese genocidal state as an endogenous system" (163). Crucial in this process are "ethno-political entrepreneurs" who cultivate fear and disrespect, manipulate racial symbols and identities, and develop "crisis scripts" and apply them to conflicts. In this context, demonizing and supremacist ideologies intensify divisions between Arab and black African groups. They stimulate the use of racial epithets that create a sense of collective effervescence (Durkheim) and feed "collective fury." The final outcome is genocidal violence. The frame Hagan and Rymond-Richmond apply to interpret the violence in Darfur is one of crime, specifically genocide.[8] It supports a criminal justice response to the violence in Darfur.

Flint and de Waal (2008) differ decisively from Hagan and Rymond-Richmond's "endogenous" approach. Drawing on their cultural capital, a deep familiarity with the history and ethnography of Darfur, they elaborate on complex historical and cross-national processes that contributed to the events of 2003. Theirs is best characterized as a war frame, specified as "a war of total destruction, 2003–04" (116), to cite the title of one of their chapters. Policy conclusions cautiously point toward peace negotiations: "When the political alignments for a negotiated peace recur—which could be a few months' hence or, more likely, many years into the future—the players, the issues, the context, and the solutions could all be different" (388).

Mamdani (2009a) takes a distinct position regarding causes, frames, and policy conclusions. He argues that the roots of the violence in Darfur lie in the history of colonialism and that reactions to the conflict are to be explained by the postcolonial interests of Northern powers. His focus is on "politics of violence, whose sources include both a state-connected counterinsurgency and an organized insurgency" (145).[9] Mamdani thus applies an insurgency and counterinsurgency frame, which itself is embedded in a neocolonial frame. His policy conclusions are guided by the insight that "anyone wanting to end the spiraling violence would have to bring about power sharing at the state level and resource sharing at the community level, land being the key resource" (146). Neither criminal law nor humanitarian intervention, in his view, can enhance these objectives. A settlement is to be achieved via negotiation.

Three (sets of) authors, each with specific locations in the academic field and in relation to other societal fields, provide—despite overlaps—quite distinct representations of the mass violence in Darfur along the dimensions of victimization and suffering, responsible actors, time frame, causes, interpretive frames, and policy conclusions.

IN SEARCH OF ANSWERS: COLLECTING AND ANALYZING DATA

If even scholarship defines the events of Darfur in conflicting ways, then disagreements across distinct societal fields are to be expected. The questions posed above reemerge with particular urgency: How and why does knowledge about Darfur vary across societal fields and over time? Why do we find affinities, varying not only by societal field but also—overlapping with fields—by country, toward applying the crime frame to Darfur and to calling the atrocities genocide? Why do some actors instead prefer to describe the violence as a case of civil war, insurgency and counterinsurgency, or as a humanitarian emergency? Again, to answer these questions, I conducted systematic, semistructured interviews, supplemented by many conversations and use of an observational method, and a large-scale content analysis of media reports from eight countries. Before addressing the nuts and bolts of my methods of data collection, one methodological clarification is in order.

Beyond "Methodological Nationalism," "Cosmopolitanism," and "Universalism": Toward Empirical Investigation

I collected data at the levels of individual media reports, even statements within reports; international organizations; national institutions such as foreign ministries; newspapers; and national sections of international NGOs (INGOs). By prominently including national institutions as units of data collection, however, I do not subscribe to "methodological nationalism" (Beck and Sznaider 2006). Instead, gathering data at the national level reveals information about the intersection of global, national, and local forces. An interview with the Africa correspondent of a German newspaper provides a telling example:

> In Nairobi [one of the few central bases of most Western Africa correspondents] things are rather informal. There is not a sense of competition. So you sit down with colleagues to learn from others who have just been to an area what things look like out there. There is quite a lively exchange of experiences and information—and that certainly also leads to some kind of opinion formation. . . . Often that is not possible in Africa in any other way. As a single person one cannot . . . charter a plane. . . . The trip to North East Congo included journalists from the US, UK, Switzerland, and Germany. . . . [Also,] there was this foreign correspondents' club. There I met Canadian colleagues, Zimbabwean colleges, etc. (author's translation)

The interview from which this quotation is taken tells us how a German journalist, working for a German paper in a specific locale in an African country, is simultaneously embedded in a global network of correspondents and NGO workers from diverse national contexts. It illustrates one way in which the national and the global are intimately intertwined in the representation of events, including mass violence.

What I find in the world of journalism applies in the political sphere and civil society as well. There, human rights, as a new principle of legitimacy, have come to challenge the notion of national sovereignty and advanced a move toward cosmopolitanism—that is, an incorporation of foreign and distant suffering (Boltanski 1999) into local and national concerns—famously explored by Daniel Levy and Natan Sznaider (2010) and Alejandro Baer (2011). Three forces are at play. One is the weakening capacity of nation-states to shape representations of past and current events; instead, local groups and competing affiliations promote a fragmentation of representations. A second is the growing weight of media and communication institutions as producers of representations: distant events create local resonance and identification through the globalization of media images and communication technologies.[10]

A third force toward the emergence of cosmopolitanism, one that moves to center stage in the following chapters, is the law. Again I agree with Levy and Sznaider (2010) that "recent trials related to human rights abuses are an important locus for the production of cosmopolitan ideals and their criticism" (19). More specifically, the post–Cold War era advanced the cosmopolitanization of human rights regimes through a substantial number of *domestic* human rights trials and the incorporation of international law into *domestic* jurisdictions (internalization of human rights norms by states). Another indication is the creation of the International Criminal Court with its *complementarity* principle, securing states' rights to prosecute human rights perpetrators as long as they are willing and able to do so. Global norms thereby become incorporated into national legal institutions.

I here tackle as an empirical question the debate between proponents of methodological nationalism versus universalism versus cosmopolitanism. Based on quantitative and qualitative data on the case of Darfur, I examine the *degree* to which different types of countries actually incorporate international human rights concerns into their legitimacy basis; the *degree* to which global legal interventions produce narratives to lay the groundwork for collective memory across countries; and the *degree* to which these representations are filtered through a particular judicial logic and colored by political constraints under which law operates, especially international law. While broad statements that sanctify the national, the global, or the cosmopolitan may neatly align with "invisible colleges," I place myself between those positions. Again, through systematic collection of data, I examine *degrees* to which representations of ongoing atrocities are inspired by national forces, universal standards, and cosmopolitan sensitivities.

Why These Eight Western Countries?

Considered in this book are two North American and six European countries: Canada and the United States on the western side of the

Atlantic, and Austria, France, Germany, Ireland, the United Kingdom, and Switzerland on the eastern side. The focus on Western countries, all democracies with capitalist economies, warrants justification. Clearly, perceptions and representations from other parts of the world matter. Representations of Darfur in China, Russia, and Arab and African countries differ substantially from those in the West, and they have affected responses of the international community. And yet Western countries are a research subject in their own right. They are crucial players on the world stage. From a methodological point of view, limiting the argument to countries that are similar in basic respects (democracy, capitalism, and wealth) has a major analytic benefit: it reduces variation and thus allows for a controlled comparison along a set of crucial variables.

The set of countries selected for this study includes three permanent members of the UN Security Council (France, UK, US); large countries such as the United States and Germany and small ones such as Austria, Ireland, and Switzerland; countries with varying identities vis-à-vis mass atrocities and genocide, from that of a liberator (US) to that of a perpetrator nation (Germany); countries with colonial involvement in Sudan (UK) or in neighboring countries such as Chad (France), or a lack thereof; countries tightly woven into alliances (France, Germany) to ones that are relatively neutral (Austria and Switzerland); and finally countries in which one of three languages dominates: French, English, or German. It should not be denied that the researcher's ability to read and speak these languages was a pragmatic consideration that supported this selection.

Sources of Data

Several key sources of data helped in the exploration of representations of Darfur and changes in them over time, especially in relation to judicial interventions: a set of systematic, semistructured interviews with central contributors to those representations; many individual conversations and observations of meetings of key players; a detailed content analysis of news media; and an analysis of documents produced by, among others, foreign ministries and NGOs.

Interviews and Observational Method

Between November 2011 and November 2012 I traveled across North America and Europe to conduct semistructured interviews with Africa correspondents, NGO specialists, and Sudan experts in foreign ministries. I had selected one rights-oriented NGO, Amnesty International, and one humanitarian aid–oriented NGO, Médecins Sans Frontières (MSF, or Doctors Without Borders). I also selected two prominent newspapers, one left-liberal, the other conservative or center-right, from each country. Most of the interviews lasted between sixty and eighty minutes, with a few as short as a half an hour or as long as two hours.[11] I followed a positional sampling strategy as I attempted to include at least one Darfur specialist from each of the five organizations in each of the eight countries (thirty-eight country-organizations). I was able to secure forty-two interviews, covering seven foreign ministries, twelve newspapers, and thirteen national divisions of NGOs. Consent was secured from each interviewee in line with the approval by the Institutional Review Board of the University of Minnesota. The interviews were audio-recorded and transcribed. No interviewee is referred to by name in this book. Specific positions of interviewees are explicated only where an appropriate understanding necessitates doing so. In some cases, a respondent's gender ascription may be changed to further disguise his or her identity. After I had collected these European and North American interviews, Wahutu Siguru, a doctoral advisee and collaborator, traveled to Nairobi, in his native Kenya, and to Johannesburg, South Africa, and, following an identical methodology and guideline, conducted interviews with African journalists who had written about Darfur.

Interviews with NGO specialists and Sudan experts in foreign ministries served to explore features of societal fields that contribute to the formation of knowledge about Darfur and with which journalists interact. Interviews with Africa correspondents who contributed a substantial number of articles to the newspapers we analyzed allowed for triangulation: to examine whether positions expressed in specific media confirm or differ from positions their journalists take in interviews. The degree to which they differ tells us something about the independent impact of the media organization for which a journalist works, including its editorial process. All interviews, finally, served to explore the actors' habitus, shaped by their position in the field and their field's position vis-à-vis other fields. Interviews also tell us about the actors' biographic trajectories, their social and economic backgrounds, and the career through which they arrived at their respective positions—factors that also contribute to shaping their habitus.

The structure of the interviews was closely aligned with my thematic concerns. After inquiring about the interviewees' background (education, relevant socialization experiences, career path, and work context), I asked about perceptions of victimization, actors responsible for the violence, and causes of the conflict; appropriate frames of interpretation, policy goals, and strategies (and potential conflicts between them) and institutions to execute them (with a special emphasis on the pursuit of justice and the ICC); positions of the interviewees' organization and their nation's government; the role of historical experience; and sources of information (see appendix B for interview guidelines).

In addition to the formal interviews, numerous informal conversations with a diverse array of actors provided insights into the representation of Darfur. I visited with conversation partners in their offices, in coffee shops, and in the context of two conferences. They included European scholars specializing in Sudan; Sudanese informants, specifically anthropologists, journalists, and opposition politicians from Sudan; two US foreign policy makers (ambassadors); other journalists; lawyers from the International Criminal Court; the director of a genocide memorial museum; and Darfur activists. The conferences included a January 2011 symposium titled "War Crimes Journalism" at the Vassar Institute in The Hague, and a summer 2012 conference, "Discourses on Darfur," at the Rockefeller Bellagio Center.[12] I conducted two additional formal interviews with a member of the governing board of one of the Darfur rebel movements and with a Sudan expert of the foreign ministry of a ninth country.

Newspaper Articles and Commentaries

A detailed international comparison of the changing representations of Darfur can be gained from a fine-grained analysis of news media reports. Together with a group of graduate students, I conducted a content analysis of 3,387 newspaper articles, editorials, and op-ed pieces from the eight countries—a massive undertaking. Following an intense week of training, six coders spent several months laboring individually while regularly joining in group sessions to assure continued agreement regarding the meaning of coding categories.

There are good reasons for such investment. News media, after all, continuously bring the reality of atrocities and grave human rights violations into the homes of people around the world. In fact, media are usually people's only source of knowledge about ongoing atrocities in distant lands. We may argue, with Bourdieu, that media power is "power to consecrate," to name an event, person, or idea worthy of further consideration (Benson 1998). Media reports affect ways in which societies think about events, especially those in distant lands, too remote for personal observation.

In addition, media are also indicators of collective knowledge repertoires and processes. Scholarship has documented, and my interviews with Africa correspondents confirm, that journalistic reports and commentaries are the outcome of complex collective action among actors within and outside the media field. Media reports thus constitute collective representations—supra-individual ideas, scripts, beliefs, values, or cognitive and normative images—to which Emile Durkheim ([1912] 2001) alerted us long ago in his work on the elementary forms of religious life.

Prominent newspapers are not the only media that communicate news from abroad. In France, for example, beginning in the 1960s and 1970s, the dominant role that *Le Monde* and *Le Figaro*, the most prestigious liberal and conservative newspapers, respectively (and part of our sample), played in the formation of public and elite opinion has been passed on to the television (Bourdieu 1998). The same can be said for these newspapers' equivalents in other countries. Simultaneously, however, the weight of television ensures that what appears prominently on TV will almost always make its way into prestigious newspapers. A newspaper analysis is thus unlikely to miss themes that are prominently displayed on television. The same can be said for electronic communication. My interviews reveal that journalists are very much attuned to the Internet and, in their work, draw on information it provides.

As newspaper analysis is thus generally a useful tool, it is especially advantageous to focus on prestigious papers in the current context.[13] Not only are these papers more likely than others to cover foreign news, but their content is hardly ignored by policy makers. Further, in countries such as the United States, the nationally most prominent papers reach far beyond their own readership. Regional and local newspapers across the country, lacking resources to investigate beyond the local or state levels, frequently reprint articles on foreign policy themes from papers such as the *New York Times*.

I therefore present a comparative and comprehensive exploration of representations of the mass violence in Darfur by examining reporting and commentary in the eight countries' most prestigious daily newspapers with national or supraregional distributions. In what follows, the selection of newspapers, the time periods covered, the sampling and coding strategies, the selection of coders, and issues of intercoder reliability are addressed (see table 2).

TABLE 2.   NUMBER OF MEDIA DOCUMENTS (ARTICLES AND OPINION PIECES)
CODED, BY NEWSPAPER AND COUNTRY

	Number of media documents (and opinion pieces)				
Countries	Conservative	Total	Left-liberal	Total	Country total
Austria	Die Presse	137 (22)	Der Standard	103 (20)	240 (42)
Canada	Toronto Sun	120 (22)	Globe & Mail	213 (36)	333 (58)
France	Le Figaro	162 (19)	Le Monde	341 (31)	503 (50)
Germany	FAZ	326 (34)	SZ	420 (68)	746 (102)
Ireland	Irish Times* 242 (35)				
Switzerland	Neue Zürcher Zeitung* 209 (5)				
United Kingdom	London Times	197 (50)	Guardian	215 (45)	412 (95)
United States	WSJ	171 (43)	NY Times	531 (107)	702 (150)

NOTE: WSJ = Wall Street Journal; FAZ = Frankfurter Allgemeine Zeitung; SZ = Süddeutsche Zeitung
*Not placed in the left-right typology as it is the only paper in this country with substantial foreign news reporting.

1. Selection of newspapers. One conservative-leaning and one center-left–leaning newspaper from each of six of the eight countries was selected for analysis, based on reputation and readership numbers. The exceptions are Ireland and Switzerland, where only one paper regularly covers international news. In total, fourteen papers were selected. Table 2 lists the newspapers and details the total number of articles as well as the subset of opinion pieces coded for each.

2. Time periods. Articles from these papers, published between January 1, 2003 (the beginning of the period of massive violence), and May 30, 2010 (the end of the bulk of our coding work), underwent content analysis. While tensions in the Darfur region developed over several decades, most of the extreme violence occurred during this period. (For an account of the most recent intensifications of violence, see the postscript to this book.) To examine the effect of judicial and quasi-judicial interventions on representations of the violence, I conceptualize the time frame as broken into nine periods. The eight dates below, following the February 2003 rebel attack and the subsequent massive repression by the Sudanese military in conjunction with the Janjawiid, separate these periods:

September 18, 2004: UN Resolution 1564 establishes an International Commission of Inquiry on Darfur.

January 25, 2005: the commission delivers its report to General Secretary Kofi Annan.

March 31, 2005: the UN Security Council (UNSC) refers the Darfur case to the ICC.

February 27, 2007: the ICC prosecutor applies for an arrest warrant against two midlevel actors for crimes against humanity and war crimes.

April 27, 2007: the ICC issues a warrant for the arrest of both actors for war crimes and crimes against humanity (publicized on May 2, 2007).

July 14, 2008: the ICC prosecutor applies for an arrest warrant against Sudanese president Omar al-Bashir for crimes against humanity, war crimes, and genocide.

March 4, 2009: the ICC issues an arrest warrant against President al-Bashir for crimes against humanity and war crimes (to be supplemented, on July 12, 2010, with genocide charges).

May 18, 2009: Bahr Idriss Abu Garda, a rebel leader who had previously been summoned to appear before the ICC under seal, makes his initial appearance before the court.

3. Sampling strategy. Newspaper articles, editorials, and op-ed pieces from each of the fourteen papers were selected using a stratified random sampling strategy. When possible, we utilized the newspaper's online archives of print articles. Online archives were made available by *Der Standard, Die Presse*, the *Süddeutsche Zeitung*, and the *Toronto Sun*. Where online archives of print articles were not available, searches were performed in both LexisNexis and ProQuest Newsstand. The *Wall Street Journal* was obtained from ProQuest Newsstand, as it was not available through LexisNexis; all other papers were accessed through Lexis Nexis.[14] Only for the *Neue Zürcher Zeitung* did we have to rely on the online archive, not knowing whether all articles coded in fact appeared in print. While there is little reason to believe that this difference significantly affects results for the Swiss paper, and while I triangulate these findings via an interview with its most senior correspondent, I cautiously interpret patterns for this paper.

My coding team identified all articles in the fourteen papers written during the period of interest and containing the search term "Darfur."[15] We included all articles and opinion pieces except letters to the editor. We excluded articles that mentioned Darfur but that, upon closer review, did not pertain to the conflict in Darfur. From all relevant documents, we selected every other article for most time periods and every sixth article for two lengthy time periods that passed without judicial intervention. Overall, we analyzed a total sample of 3,387 articles.[16]

4. *Coding Strategy.* Although we coded at the level of the article, we treated each article as a collection of statements. All information, including quotations and paraphrased information, was coded if it spoke to the violence in Darfur. Often, a single article included several viewpoints, and in such cases all were coded. Yet coders did not attribute rare sentences or viewpoints that the author clearly and explicitly rejected.

Content analysis was conducted based on a coding scheme that comprised 179 variables of interest, organized into several major thematic categories (see appendix C). Given the detailed nature of the coding scheme, information on some variables was frequently missing. Yet missing information in this case is relevant in its own right. It tells us what aspects and details of the conflict are underexposed in journalistic depictions. The following themes encompassed the majority of variables:

- *Degrees and types of acknowledgment of victimization and suffering, such as killings, rapes, displacements, or torture.* We coded forms of suffering that were mentioned; numbers of affected Darfuris, where provided; and specific episodes that were displayed in detailed accounts. Such acknowledgment challenges states of denial, as explored by Stanley Cohen (2001).
- *Actors involved.* Here I am interested in the degree to which rebel forces, Janjawiid militias, and government officials are named as actors. The coding scheme further distinguished between references to individuals or collectivities and references to the rank of individuals within the hierarchy of their organizations.
- *Perceived causes.* Causes may point to distant events and conflicts, to the colonial past, to natural events such as the desertification of the Sahel zone and struggles over increasingly scarce resources, or to conscious decisions and strategies—such as the

push toward Islamization, the neglect of the periphery, or the stirring up of racial resentment by central players on the ground and in high government offices.

- *Frames or lenses through which the violence is interpreted.* The coding scheme distinguishes between an insurgency frame, a civil war frame, a humanitarian emergency frame, a crime frame, and an aggressive-state frame that depicts the violence as disproportionately aggressive but not criminal. Frames can be *diagnostic,* identifying and attributing problems; *prognostic,* proposing solutions; or *motivational,* providing a rationale for engagement (Benford and Snow 2000). For example, while a civil war diagnostic frame identifies violence as a civil war, its prognostic equivalent may suggest negotiation as the appropriate response. The motivational frame provides a rationale or goal such as (in the civil war case) the establishment of peace. The coding scheme took account of these distinctions. Yet, one single article could invoke various frames. In fact, articles frequently included statements that fell in line with different frames in discussing violence in Darfur, for example, by characterizing it as both a civil war and a humanitarian emergency. Furthermore, articles at times included a statement that diagnosed the violence in a civil war frame while simultaneously offering a prognosis aligned with the humanitarian emergency frame. Such seeming contradictions typically result from journalists interviewing and citing, in the same article, different actors with distinct positions. In short, articles, with the exception of opinion pieces, are rarely characterized by a single frame.

- *References to past atrocities.* Producers of narratives often make use of bridging strategies. They seek to shed light on a new and yet unknown situation, here Darfur, by linking it to a past event whose meaning is well established. Coders were thus asked to code whether past atrocities were mentioned in association with Darfur. Building on our previous work (Savelsberg and King 2011:60–64), the instrument further asked coders to document the use of different types of bridging: that the violence in Darfur was similar to a past atrocity (mimetic bridging); that the context of the violence was similar to that of past violence (contextual bridging); that this violence will have a similar outcome as a past atrocity (predictive bridging); or that Darfur differs from a past atrocity (bridging challenge).

- *Sources.* When articles included quotations, sources were coded, especially organizational affiliations and, in some instances, names of individual informants.

5. Coders and Intercoder Reliability. Six coders, all PhD students in sociology, history, or political science, were chosen based on their language abilities (English, German, or French) and their familiarity with content analysis and social scientific methodology. Coders received one week of training and met weekly to discuss any questions or issues that arose during coding. In addition, coders coded three of the same articles (from different newspapers and time periods) each week in order to assess intercoder reliability; the principal investigator–author and Hollie Nyseth, lead research assistant, also periodically and randomly reviewed articles to assess each coder's work. Coding was done by hand, and each variable was assigned a quantitative code. Results were compiled into a dataset and analyzed using the stata statistical analysis program.

Intercoder reliability was higher for some variables than for others. It was almost perfect where no interpretive judgment was needed, for example, to determine whether or not killings were mentioned. Identifying frames in an article demanded more interpretive work by coders, and reliability was lower for those variables. Yet even the lowest Cohen's Kappa for variables used in the analyses on which this book is based demonstrated considerable agreement between coders. Intercoder reliability for all items present in this book was high (Cohen's [2001] Kappa ranging from 0.72 to 1.00).[17]

Additional Sources of Data. Several additional data collection efforts supplemented the interview and content analysis work. They include analyses of multiple documents and press releases issued by the International Criminal Court on the situation in Sudan during the period under study; related documents of the foreign ministry websites of the countries included in this study; content analysis of 161 speeches, press releases, and reports from NGOs in the United States; and all press releases on Darfur from foreign ministries of seven of the countries under study.

ROADMAP: DIRECTIONS FOR TRAVELING FROM HERE

Guided by the questions and theoretical tools laid out thus far, and with a wealth of data at hand, I invite the reader to accompany me on a journey through the following chapters. In Part I of the book,

"Justice versus Impunity," chapters 1–3 explore the criminalization of the violence in Darfur in the context of the justice cascade. Chapter 1 focuses on the UN Security Council, the International Commission of Inquiry on Darfur, and—at the core of the justice field—the International Criminal Court. I examine conditions of the justice cascade, their application to the case of Darfur, and associated hopes invested in the cultural potential of judicial intervention. Hopes are confronted with constraints inherent in the institutional logic of criminal law. Chapter 2 examines INGOs dedicated to human rights issues by focusing on Amnesty International. I reconstruct Amnesty's representation of the violence in Darfur, adherence to rights discourses, and professional and national divergences. In chapter 3, I discuss the role of the United States, a country that—despite its resistance against the ICC—embraced a criminalizing discourse vis-à-vis Sudan more than other countries. I pay particular attention to the Save Darfur Campaign, to government positions and US media narratives as they contrast with those in other Western countries, and finally to Amnesty USA in the context of the broader American Darfur movement.

A primary potential challenge to the notion of justice and the justice sector's representation of the mass violence in Darfur arises from the humanitarian aid field. I address this challenge in Part II, entitled "Aid versus Justice." Chapter 4 examines INGOs that have a humanitarian aid focus, specifically Doctors Without Borders (MSF), and the representation of Darfur generated in this field. We shall see that this representation differs distinctly from that which arises from the justice cascade. Chapter 5 investigates the "humanitarian complex" through the case of Ireland, a country with a memory of suffering and a foreign policy oriented toward humanitarian and development aid. Insights from interviews with Irish foreign policy makers and journalists are linked with an analysis of specific patterns of Irish media reporting.

Part III, "Peace versus Justice," engages the diplomatic field, a second potential challenger to the criminalizing narrative. Chapter 6 draws on interviews with Darfur and Sudan specialists in foreign ministries. I challenge depictions of foreign policy makers as actors guided by rational reasoning when they stay clear of genocide rhetoric so as to evade normative commitments to intervene, as suggested by Samantha Power (2002) for the United States and Karen Smith (2010) for Europe. Instead, dedramatizing rhetoric reflects the habitus of diplomats, cultivated in a field in which representatives of the perpetrating state are central players. Chapter 7 shows how the diplomatic field overlaps with national conditions characterized by varying social forces such as Sudanese lobbying, past colonial rule, foreign policy foci on humanitarianism or mediation, social movements, or collective memories. Each of these forces is more or less pronounced in each of the eight countries under analysis. Together they contribute to cross-national variation in the diplomatic field's representation of the mass violence in Darfur. Some countries, such as Switzerland, that invest prominently in mediation efforts to resolve foreign policy crises produce a representation of mass violence in Darfur that approximates the ideal typical diplomatic representation.

In part IV, entitled "Mediating Competing Representations: The Journalistic Field," I investigate the mediation of the justice narrative and its competitors from the humanitarian and diplomatic fields to a broad public in diverse countries. Chapter 8 explores the habitus of Africa correspondents, their career paths and the field in which they are embedded, the genres available to them, and the sources of information on which they depend as they report about Darfur. Chapter 9 traces the patterns of reporting based on the statistical analysis of the Darfur media data set. The chapter focuses especially on journalism's relationship with neighboring fields, including those discussed in the preceding chapters. How do political actors and market forces affect the intensity of reporting about Darfur? How do ICC interventions color the framing of the violence? What are the effects of the diplomatic and humanitarian fields? Chapter 9 also documents that the journalistic field is not homogeneous. Here, too, national distinctions color journalistic representations of the mass violence in Darfur as do a paper's ideological orientation and the gender of journalists.

Finally, chapter 10 summarizes lessons learned throughout the book and explores theoretical insights. How do field conditions shape representations of mass violence? Can those forces that drive the justice cascade successfully redefine responsible actors as criminal perpetrators? Do the humanitarian and diplomatic fields indeed hamper this effort? What is the role of the journalistic field in producing, reinforcing, and mediating to a world audience the competing definitions of mass violence? And how do global and national forces interact in the representation of mass violence? Answers to these questions matter as definitions of the situation become real in their consequences.

The postscript reflects on the most recent developments in Darfur and on international responses, especially among those institutions and fields that are the focus of this book.

Justice versus Impunity

PART ONE

Justice versus Impunity

CHAPTER I

Setting the Stage

The Justice Cascade and Darfur

How do responses to mass violence in Darfur square with theses about a justice cascade in the late twentieth and early twenty-first centuries? At issue is the massive increase in individual criminal accountability in cases of grave human rights violations. We know that the UNSC and the ICC intervened, supported by social movements, INGOs and national governments. These interventions are in line with notions of a justice cascade, its nature, and its conditions. In the following review of the judicial steps taken on Darfur and the conditions supporting them, I am also concerned with the consequences. Fighters for a justice cascade invest great hopes in deterrence through the threat of punishment, but also in the cultural effects of judicial interventions: their contribution to the construction of delegitimizing narratives about mass violence. It is these cultural effects that I am particularly concerned with. Judicial representations are, after all, based on years of investigation, on a vast variety of documents, and on witness testimony. I thus take the hopes of proponents of the justice cascade seriously but confront them with cautionary notes. Even optimists will concede that judicial representations are constrained by the limiting institutional logic through which judicial proceedings filter events on the ground and that they are challenged by competing narratives.

JUSTICE CASCADE AND THE CRIMINALIZATION OF HUMAN RIGHTS VIOLATIONS

Political and military leaders responsible for mass killings and atrocities have, through much of human history and occasionally still today, been celebrated as heroes (Giesen 2004b). We do not have to go back as far as Homer's *Iliad*, but the words of one of its "heroes," the Greek prince Agamemnon of Mycenae, are especially telling. Speaking about the Trojans to his brother Menelaus, he proclaims: "We are not going to leave a single one of them alive, down to the babies in their mothers' wombs—not even they must live. The whole people must be wiped out of existence, and no one be left to think of them and shed a tear" (quoted in Rummel 1994:45). Later, and less unambiguously celebrated, those responsible for mass violence were—and still often are—subject to denial and forgetting (Cohen 2001). Genocidal leaders have believed they can count on such forgetting, as Adolf Hitler's often cited words illustrate: "It was knowingly and wholeheartedly that Genghis Khan sent thousands of women and children to their deaths. History sees in him only the founder of a state. . . . The aim of war is not to reach definite lines, but annihilate the enemy physically. It is by this means that we shall obtain the vital living space that we need. *Who today still speaks of the massacre of the Armenians?*" (quoted in Power 2002:23).

Yet the twentieth century brought remarkable change. Legal scholar Martha Minow (1998) suggests that the century's hallmark was not the horrendous atrocities committed in its course (too many past centuries can compete), but humanity's new inventiveness and efforts toward curbing human rights violations. This is in line with, albeit more broadly conceived than, Kathryn Sikkink's (2011) argument that the late twentieth and early twenty-first centuries are characterized by a "justice cascade," that is, a massive increase in individual criminal accountability for grave human rights violations. Leaders of human rights movements express similar optimism (Neier 2012). Supporting such optimism is a very different but long-standing school of thought on the criminalization of a wide range of human behaviors. Dating back to the almost classic works of scholars such as Bill Chambliss (1964), Joe Gusfield (1967), and Austin Turk (1969), this school has recently shifted its focus from status politics as a driving force toward criminalization to processes of globalization and institutionalization: "Many scholars now . . . suggest that criminalization is best viewed as a process of institutionalization that involves the diffusion of social forms and practices across polities comprising an interstate system" (Jenness 2004:160). What, then, is the character of this institutionalization and diffusion across polities, this justice cascade, and how does Darfur fit into the picture?

Setting the Stage for Darfur: Shape and Conditions of the Justice Cascade

In 2011, political scientist Kathryn Sikkink published her remarkable, albeit much debated, book *Justice Cascade: How Human Rights Prosecutions Are Changing World Politics*. The book, published by a commercial house, was enthusiastically welcomed by some. The Robert F. Kennedy Center for Justice and Human Rights awarded it the 2012 Robert Kennedy Book Award. Sikkink documents in this book how prosecutions against individual human rights perpetrators in domestic, foreign, and international courts increased almost exponentially in recent decades. She counts by country the number of years in which prosecutions were conducted. Values, in the single digits during much of the 1980s, rose to about one hundred by the mid-1990s, to three hundred a decade later, and then approached 450 by 2009 (Sikkink 2011:21).

Domestic justice systems drive this increase, partly because a growing number of countries have adopted international human rights norms. Their willingness is enhanced by the complementarity principle of the Rome Statute: domestic courts have primary jurisdiction as long as they are able and willing to pursue cases (Article 17). As nation-states thus operate "in the shadow" of the ICC, they prosecute cases at times specifically to keep them under their own domestic jurisdiction. Conflicts between the ICC and postrevolution Libya over the extradition of members of the Gaddafi regime are but one illustration. The adoption of the Rome Statute in 1998 and the establishment of the ICC in 2002, on the heels of a series of ad hoc tribunals (for Yugoslavia, Rwanda, Sierra Leone, Cambodia, and East Timor), document the weight of the international level of the justice cascade in its own right. Indeed, international and foreign prosecutions also increased substantially. ICC charges against those responsible for the mass violence in Darfur are the essential example in our context.

What were the sources of this remarkable development? Here, too, Sikkink (2011) provides at least preliminary answers. While not discounting the Nuremberg and Tokyo trials, orchestrated by the victorious powers of World War II, she sets the stage with more challenging cases that did not result from military defeat. Her detailed studies of

Greece (1975), Portugal (1976), Spain (1975–1978), and Argentina (1985) show that regional opportunity structures had developed by the 1970s that favored transitional justice proceedings. Examples of such structures include the creation of the European Court of Human Rights in 1959 and the foundation of Amnesty International in 1961, an organization that played a central role in the Darfur crisis and the details of which I turn to in chapter 2.

Soon after its founding, Amnesty International became actively engaged in Greece. Its activism coincided with a supportive international legal environment, and this situation advanced the launching of trials. The 1975 "Torture Declaration" was prepared concurrently with the Greek torture trials and adopted by the UN General Assembly just a few months after their conclusion. Yet, at this time, trials occurred only after "ruptured" transitions from dictatorship to democracy (Greece, Portugal, Argentina) as opposed to "pacted" transitions (Spain). By the 1990s, however, conditions had changed. Ruptured transitions were no longer a prerequisite for criminal trials against human rights violators, as the cases of Guatemala, Chile, and Uruguay illustrate. The institutionalization of the human rights regime had progressed, and the fear of blowback had diminished in light of experiences from the 1970s.

Initial steps toward human rights prosecutions eventually resulted in a decentralized, interactive system of global accountability that challenged national sovereignty. Sikkink (2011:96–125) identifies two contributors, or "streams," to use her metaphor. The first stream is constituted by international prosecutions, from Nuremberg and Tokyo, to the International Criminal Tribunal for the former Yugoslavia (ICTY) and its Rwanda equivalent (ICTR), to the ICC with its jurisdiction over cases of aggression,[1] war crimes, crimes against humanity, and genocide. The second stream consists of domestic and foreign prosecutions such as those in Greece, Portugal, and Argentina in the mid-1970s and the Pinochet case of 1998–1999. In addition, a "hard law streambed" led from various compacts such as the Genocide Convention (1948), Geneva Convention (1949), Apartheid Convention (1980), and Torture Convention (1987), through the Inter-American Convention on Forced Disappearances (1996), to the Rome Statute (1998).

This spread of human rights initiatives, and their solidification in a system, was not simply the result of contagion. Instead, individuals, associations, transgovernmental networks penetrated by an epistemic community of criminal law experts, and NGOs such as Human Rights Watch (HRW) and Amnesty International achieved the progressive institutionalization of individual criminal liability, that is, *criminalization* and *individualization* of international law. This focus on actors builds on earlier work in which Sikkink, in collaboration with Margaret Keck, examined advocacy in international politics. Their much cited book drew attention to transnational advocacy networks (TANs) and the engagement of TANs in information politics that tie networks together, leverage politics that shame evildoers, and accountability politics that, to hold nations accountable, "trick" them into commitments that they might enter into merely for symbolic and legitimatory reasons. The 1975 Helsinki Accord is only the most famous example (Keck and Sikkink 1998).

A tendency to privilege advocacy as a driving force of criminalization is, not surprisingly, shared by leaders of the human rights movement. Aryeh Neier, former executive director of HRW and later president of the Open Society Institute, confirms that even after the success of early truth commissions, "some in the international human rights movement continued to espouse prosecutions and criminal sanctions against those principally responsible for the most egregious offenses" (Neier 2012:264). Neier describes the role of the Italian organization No Peace Without Justice (NPWJ), but especially of Emma Bonino, an Italian politician and civil liberties campaign veteran, in the establishment of the ICC: "In the period in which the ICC was being established, Bonino was a member of the European Commission, . . . and she took advantage of her post and her contacts with heads of state to ensure the participation of high-level officials from many countries in NPWJ's conferences. . . . The result was that by the time the conference took place in Rome—Bonino's city—many governments were ready to support establishment of the ICC" (Neier 2012:270). Also, on the path to ratification, for which some countries had to go so far as to modify their constitutions, "[l]obbying by a number of nongovernmental organizations—including the Coalition for an International Criminal Court—played an important part" (270). Neier further highlights the role of Amnesty International (Neier 2012:55–56, 188).

Other analysts emphasize the weight of different types of actors in the establishment and spread of human rights norms. Hagan, for example, in his study of the ICTY, focuses on officials within judicial institutions, specifically successive chief prosecutors, each of whom brought a new form of "capital" to bear. All of them combined innovative strategies with established legal practices, from securing international support (Richard Goldstone), to sealed indictments and surprise arrests (Louise Arbour), to Carla del Ponte's charges against former president Slobodan

FIGURE 2. The building housing the International Criminal Court in The Hague.
Photograph © ICC-CPI.

Milošević. Innovative strategies eventually become "doxa," Hagan argues: taken-for-granted legal standards in the emerging international criminal tribunal in The Hague.[2] In contrast, David Scheffer, former US ambassador and right hand of US secretary of state Madeleine Albright, highlights diplomats as crucial contributors to the establishment of international judicial institutions, from the ICTY to the ICC (Scheffer 2012).

No matter the relative weight of each of these types of actors, their interactions contributed to the passing of the Rome Statute in 1998 and the establishment of the ICC. The ICC entered into force in 2002 when sixty countries had ratified the statute. By 2013 the number of ratifying countries had more than doubled, and many—though not all—of those charged have made acquaintance with the imposing court building in The Hague (see figure 2). The continuation of this trajectory is, of course, not yet known and difficult to forecast.

Responding to Darfur in the Context of the Justice Cascade

In 2000, around the time of the formation of the ICC, disturbing events began to unfold in the Darfur region of Sudan. Activists against Sudan's ruling elite had issued *The Black Book: Imbalance of Power and Wealth in Sudan*. Distributed widely, especially in areas surrounding mosques after Friday prayers, the *Black Book* castigated the domination of Sudan by "only one Region (Northern Region) with just over 5% of Sudan's population" (Seekers of Truth and Justice 2003:1). A March 22, 2004, translation, signed by "Translater," informs us that "[a]s of last year (March 2003), some of the activists involved in the preparation of the Book took arms against the government" (Seekers of Truth and Justice 2003:1). Indeed February and March 2003 saw the formation of the Sudan Liberation Army (SLA) and the Justice and Equality Movement (JEM), two organizations that led a violent rebellion against the government of Sudan. Their armed actions were surprisingly effective. In April 2003 rebel groups attacked the Sudanese military's el Fasher air base, destroyed numerous planes of the Sudanese air force, and killed almost one hundred soldiers. The government of Sudan and its military, supported by Janjawiid militias, responded with brute force. A first wave of mass killings unfolded between June and September 2003. Targets included not only armed rebels but primarily civilian villagers, including women, elderly men, and children. A cease-fire held only for a few months, and in December 2003 President al-Bashir vowed to "annihilate" the Darfur rebels. His vow provoked a second wave of mass killings, lasting from December 2003 through April 2004. Massive displacements of the civilian population ensued. Tens of thousands of lives were extinguished as a direct result of the violence, and many more died during the Darfuris' flight from the violence and because of problematic conditions in displaced-person camps in Sudan and refugee camps in neighboring Chad.

Much of the Western world began to take note only after the first peak of killings (summer 2003) had subsided and when the second wave (winter 2003–2004) was under way. The first public pronouncement, a "genocide alert," issued by the United States Holocaust Memorial Museum (USHMM) in January 2004, was followed by a series of op-ed pieces in prominent American print media; a speech before the UN General Assembly by UN Secretary-General Kofi Annan on April 7, 2004, on the occasion of the tenth anniversary of the Rwandan genocide; passage on September 18, 2004 of UNSC Resolution 1564, instituting an International Commission of Inquiry on Darfur; and the UNSC's referral of the case of Darfur to the ICC on March 31, 2005. Parallel to UN interventions, a massive civil society movement evolved. In the United States, the Save Darfur movement gathered almost two hundred liberal and conservative organizations under its umbrella. The US Congress resolved that the violence in Darfur amounted to genocide. Secretary of

State Colin Powell initiated the famous "Atrocities Documentation Survey," a survey of more than one thousand Darfuri refugees in the camps of Eastern Chad. Based on findings from this survey, he declared, at a hearing before the Senate Foreign Relations Committee on September 9, 2004, that genocide was being committed. President George W. Bush followed suit a few weeks later.

Importantly in our context, soon after the UNSC referred the case of Darfur to the ICC on March 31, 2005, the court took action. After almost two years of investigation, on February 27, 2007, the ICC's chief prosecutor, Luis Moreno-Ocampo, applied for an arrest warrant against Ahmad Harun, then Sudan's deputy minister for the interior, responsible for the "Darfur Security Desk," and against Ali Kushayb, a Janjawiid leader. Both were charged with crimes against humanity and war crimes. On April 27, 2007, the court issued a warrant for the arrest of both actors for war crimes and crimes against humanity. It took another year until the prosecutor also applied for an arrest warrant against Sudanese president Omar al-Bashir, charging him with crimes against humanity, war crimes, and genocide (July 14, 2008). The judges did not initially follow this application in its entirety, but on March 4, 2009, they issued a warrant against al-Bashir for crimes against humanity and war crimes (see figure 3). With more than a year's delay and five years after the UNSC referral to the ICC, on July 12, 2010, the court followed up with a warrant against the president of Sudan for the crime of genocide.

The ICC thus places itself at the center of the judicial field and its engagement with the mass violence in Darfur. Its interventions clearly seek to discredit potential denial of atrocities and, certainly, glorification of those responsible for their perpetration. Consider the following statement from the initial charging document against President al-Bashir of March 4, 2009. After spelling out several conditions, the first warrant concludes as follows:

> CONSIDERING that, for the above reasons, there are reasonable grounds to believe, that Omar al Bashir is criminally responsible as an indirect perpetrator, or as an indirect co-perpetrator [footnote], under article 25(3)(a) of the Statute, for (i) intentionally directing attacks at a civilian population as such or against individual civilians not taking direct part in hostilities as a war crime . . . ; (ii) pillage as a war crime . . . ; (iii) murder as a crime against humanity; (iv) extermination as a crime against humanity . . . ; (v) forcible transfer as a crime against humanity . . . ; (vi) torture as a crime against humanity . . . ; rape as a crime against humanity. . . .
>
> CONSIDERING that, under article 58(1) of the Statute, the arrest of Omar Al Bashir appears necessary at this stage to ensure (i) that he will appear

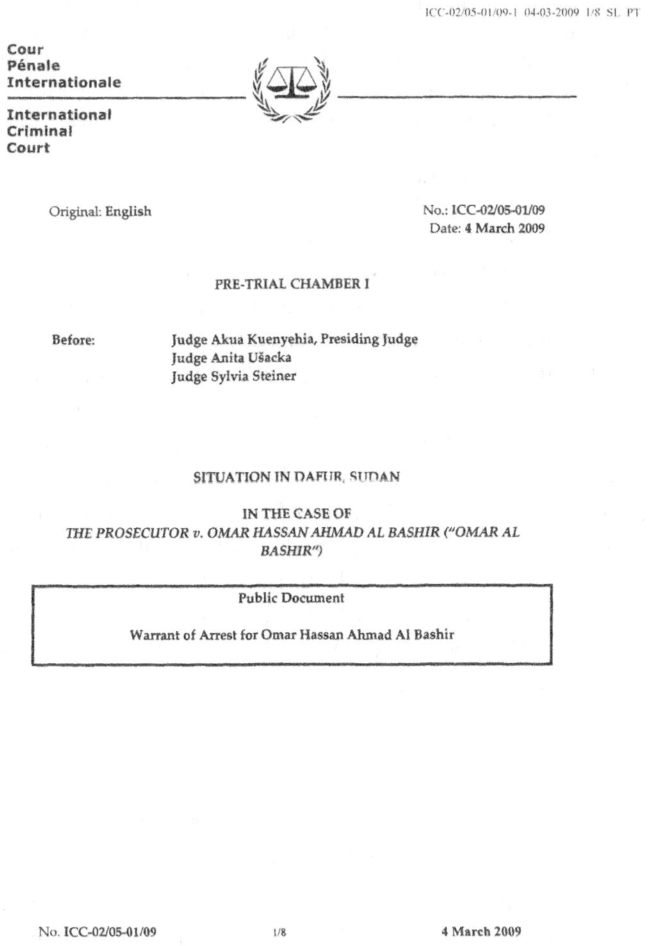

ICC-02/05-01/09-1 04-03-2009 1/8 SL PT

Cour
Pénale
Internationale

International
Criminal
Court

Original: English

No.: ICC-02/05-01/09
Date: **4 March 2009**

PRE-TRIAL CHAMBER I

Before: Judge Akua Kuenyehia, Presiding Judge
            Judge Anita Ušacka
            Judge Sylvia Steiner

SITUATION IN DAFUR, SUDAN

IN THE CASE OF
*THE PROSECUTOR v. OMAR HASSAN AHMAD AL BASHIR ("OMAR AL
BASHIR")*

Public Document

Warrant of Arrest for Omar Hassan Ahmad Al Bashir

No. ICC-02/05-01/09   1/8   4 March 2009

FIGURE 3. Title page of indictment of President Omar al-Bashir.

before the Court; (ii) that he will not obstruct or endanger the ongoing investigation into the crimes for which he is allegedly responsible under the Statute; and (iii) that he will not continue with the commission of the above-mentioned crimes;

FOR THESE REASONS [THE COURT],

HEREBY ISSUES:

A WARRANT OF ARREST FOR OMAR AL BASHIR, a male, who is a national of the State of Sudan, born on 1 January 1944 in Hoshe Bannaga, Shendi

Governorate, in the Sudan, member of the Jaáli tribe of Northern Sudan, President of the Republic of the Sudan since his appointment by the RCC-NS on 16 October 1993 and elected as such successively since 1 April 1996 and whose name is also spelt Omar al-Bashir, Omer Hassan Ahmed El Bashire, Omar al-Bashir, Omar al-Beshir, Omar el-Bashir, Omer Albasheer, Omar Elbashir and Omar Hassan Ahmad el-Béshir.

Done in English, Arabic and French, the English version being authoritative.[3]

Not only did the court issue this warrant, but through its press offices, it also sought to disseminate it to a broad public.[4] My analysis shows that media from across the globe, at least in the sample of countries included in our analysis, responded to the indictment and communicated its message to a world audience: the depiction of President al-Bashir as a criminal perpetrator. The chances that media would present crime frames to display violence increased with several of the court's interventions (see chapter 9; Savelsberg and Nyseth Brehm 2015).

In short, civil society, INGOs, TANs, national governments, the UN, and the ICC acted to criminalize the violence of Darfur and to initiate a legal case. Darfur thus took its rightful place in the context of the justice cascade. The driving forces were the same as those the literature has identified in other cases. But what were the consequences? What expectations were invested in the justice cascade, and how did they materialize in the case of Darfur?

CONSEQUENCES OF THE JUSTICE CASCADE: BETWEEN HOPE AND CAUTIONARY NOTES

Scholars as well as movement actors and practitioners anticipate consequences of the justice cascade with substantial optimism. Darfur provides one case with which to examine the foundation of this optimism. Sikkink (2011) herself draws hope from her Transitional Trial Data Set, an impressive collection of data on a large number of transitional justice situations. Her statistical analyses suggest, cautiously worded, that prosecutions of human rights perpetrators, including high-level actors, while achieving retribution, do not systematically produce counterproductive consequences as some critics have suggested. They may in fact advance later human rights and democracy records, especially in situations where trials are accompanied by truth commissions (Kim and Sikkink 2010).[5] Observations by practitioners support such findings. Neier (2012), for example, notes, "The fact that international humanitarian law has now been enforced through criminal sanctions that the various tribunals have imposed on hundreds of high-ranking military officials, guerilla leaders, civilian officials, and heads of government has contributed immensely to awareness of the rules for the conduct of warfare and for the seriousness with which they must be regarded" (132).

Others challenge such optimism (Goldsmith and Krasner 2003; Snyder and Vinjamuri 2003–2004; Pensky 2008). Most recently, Osiel (2014), while expressing sympathy with the idea of international criminal justice, declares that "international criminal law is unlikely to endure as anything more than an intermittent occasion for staging splashy, eye-catching degradation rituals, feel-good spectacles of good will toward men." He points to the absence of the world's largest powers from among the countries supporting the Rome Statute, power politics in the UNSC (consider Syria in the early 2010s), the risks of coups d'état when nations prosecute past ruling juntas or dictators, partisan case selections in posttransitional justice proceedings, and the risk of "victors' justice."[6] Others highlight the risk that one-sided memories of victimization and a competition for victim status—both potential outcomes of flawed transitional justice—may in fact propel cycles of violence (Barkan 2013).

It is easy to sympathize with both sides of the dispute. Both the criminalization of human rights offenses and the internationalization of criminal human rights law are in their infancy, and it is hard to forecast their future. But we can put theory and empirical work to use and apply to our scholarship Max Weber's advice to those involved in politics: engage in the drilling of hard boards with passion and sound judgment. It is in this spirit that I examine the effect of criminal justice intervention, specifically its cultural effects: the representations of mass violence in the case of Darfur.

From Broad Expectations to the Role of Collective Representations and Memories

The construction of delegitimizing representations of mass violence is one of two potential mechanisms through which criminal proceedings may contribute to improved human rights records. The other mechanism, deterrence, combines a notion of political and military figures as rational actors with an understanding that an increase in the risk of prosecution and punishment from zero to at least modest levels may reduce the inclination to commit future crimes. Support with regard less to the severity than to the likelihood of punishment comes from criminological research (e.g., McCarthy 2002; Matsueda, Kreager, and Huizinga 2006).

But even for deterrence to work, memories of past sanctions must be ingrained in the minds of future cohorts of political and military actors. Past sanctions must become part of the collective memory they share.

The cultural argument may thus be more powerful: a socialization mechanism, not just as a precondition of deterrence but as a force in its own right. Building on a recent line of scholarship, this argument posits that collective memories created by criminal proceedings against human rights offenders potentially delegitimize grave violations, thus reducing the likelihood of their recurrence. Potential violations may no longer even appear on the decision tree of rational actors.

Expectations of criminal law's delegitimizing functions are grounded in classic writings (Mead 1918) and supported by a new line of neo-Durkheimian work in cultural sociology. Here criminal punishment is interpreted as a didactic exercise, a "speech act in which society talks to itself about its moral identity" (P. Smith 2008:16). The potential weight of this mechanism for our theme becomes clear if indeed the IMT in Nuremberg and the Universal Declaration of Human Rights initiated the extension of the Holocaust and psychological identification with its victims, as Jeffrey Alexander (2004a) argues for the memory of the Holocaust. Judicial events such as Nuremberg, the Eichmann trial in Jerusalem, or the Frankfurt Auschwitz Trial produced cultural trauma: members of a world audience were affected by an experience to which they themselves had not been exposed.

Empirical research by historians and sociologists shows that criminal trials have the capacity to color not just narratives of recent events but also the collective memory of a more distant past in the minds of subsequent generations (Savelsberg and King 2011). Once generated, delegitimizing memories—in a positive feedback loop—further promote human rights standards. This notion is consistent with Daniel Levy and Natan Sznaider insight that "[t]he global proliferation of human rights norms is driven by the public and frequently ritualistic attention to memories of their persistent violations" (Levy and Sznaider 2010:4).

Scholarly expectations are in line with hopes of those practitioners who, long before the take-off of the justice cascade, expected much from criminal tribunals against perpetrators of grave human rights crimes. Consider Justice Robert Jackson, the American chief prosecutor at the IMT in Nuremberg, who famously argued: "Unless we write the record of this movement with clarity and precision, we cannot blame the future if in days of peace it finds incredible the accusatory generalities uttered during the war. *We must establish incredible events by credible evidence*" (quoted in Landsman 2005:6–7; my emphasis). President Franklin Delano Roosevelt thought along similar lines. As his confidant Judge Samuel Rosenman noted: "[Roosevelt] was determined that the question of Hitler's guilt—and the guilt of his gangsters—must not be left open to future debate. The whole nauseating matter should be spread out on a permanent record under oath by witnesses and with all the written documents" (in Landsman 2005:6). Here Justice Jackson and President Roosevelt add a history-writing or collective memory function to the common functions of criminal trials, a truly innovative step. While some of the authors cited above might support these practitioners' hopes, others raise doubts.

A Cautionary Note: Institutional Logic, Knowledge Construction, and Representations

Reasons to caution the optimists abound. Critics are right when they argue that power relations often matter more in the international community than legal norms. Suspected perpetrators continue to hold on to power. In the Darfur case, Sudan's President Omar al-Bashir is still in power in 2015, after having been indicted for genocide years ago. They even find signs of appeasement from the international community for a number of reasons. Al-Bashir, for example, initially appeared to hold the key for an agreement that was to end the long and bloody war between the North and the South of Sudan. One of my interviewees, responsible for the Sudan desk in the foreign ministry of a large European country, stated: "The essential key to peace in the region is the inclusion of the regime in Khartoum in the peace process, its liberation from international isolation, combined with respective incentives, which then will have to be kept by the international community" (author's translation). In addition, Western powers saw in al-Bashir an ally in the fight against terrorism (Hagan and Rymond-Richmond 2008:85–93).

Al-Bashir's NCP ally Ahmed Harun, himself indicted by the ICC for war crimes and crimes against humanity, was nominated and elected governor of South Kordofan, a conflicted state along the border of South Sudan. Building on his track record in Darfur, he there appears to be repeating some of the bloody practices against potential allies of South Sudan, no matter the death toll among civilians. While actors such as al-Bashir and Harun may no longer travel freely abroad, and while resulting restrictions may weaken their base in Sudan—despite well-orchestrated demonstrations in support of al-Bashir, in response to his indictment—they have been holding on to power. The ICC prosecutor can only hope to see them as defendants in court on some future day (see the postscript on the most recent developments).

But even if the constraints of power could be broken, the construction of a damning narrative in the global collective conscience faces restraints in its own right. They include divisions within the field of criminal law and justice, conflicts across fields, and tensions arising from the involvement of global versus national or local actors. All of these difficulties are discussed for the case of Darfur in following chapters, but here I first turn to one crucial constraint: limitations imposed on historical narratives by the specific institutional logic of criminal law. I consider the arguments and illustrate them with documents from the pre-legal and legal process on Darfur.

History told by criminal proceedings, and the collective memories they shape, differs from those produced by actors in fields such as scholarship or journalism or by executive commissions.[7] Criminal law, after all, is subject to a particular set of institutional rules. These rules become part of the habitus of practitioners in the field. They function as filters through which legal actors interpret the world: in order to function successfully, actors have to incorporate into their habitus their field's dominant institutional logic. What, then, are the constraints of criminal law?

First, criminal law focuses on individuals. Social scientists, by contrast, would also consider social structure and broad cultural patterns as precursors of mass violence. Second, criminal law—the most violent and intrusive among all types of law—is rightly constrained by specific evidentiary rules, at least under rule-of-law conditions. Evidence that historians or journalists might use would often be inadmissible in a criminal court. Third, criminal law is constrained by particular classifications of actors, offenses, and victimization. It may be blind, for example, to the role played by bystanders whom guardians of moral order would want to implicate. Fourth, criminal law applies a binary logic. Defendants are found guilty or not guilty. Social psychologists would apply more differentiated categories, and philosophers, historians, and even some victims see "gray zones" among perpetrators and victims (Levi 1988; Barkan 2013).

Wise jurists are aware of the limits of criminal law as a place for the reconstruction of history. Such wisdom is reflected in the words of the judges of the Jerusalem court in its 1961 proceedings against Adolf Eichmann, key organizer of the Nazi annihilation machine:

> The Court does not possess the facilities required for investigating general questions. . . . For example, to describe the historical background of the

catastrophe, a great mass of documents and evidence has been submitted to us, collected most painstakingly and certainly out of a genuine desire to delineate as complete a picture as possible. Even so, all the material is but a tiny fraction of the existent sources on the subject. . . . As for questions of principle which are outside the realm of law, no one has made us judges of them and therefore our opinion on them carries no greater weight than that of any other person who has devoted study and thought to these questions. (quoted in Osiel 1997:80–81)[8]

Social theorists and empirical researchers confirm these concerns. In discussing cultural trauma, the collective memory of horrendous events, Alexander (2004b) spells out several preconditions for such trauma to emerge: claims-making by agents; carrier groups of the trauma process; speech acts, in which carrier groups address an audience in a specific situation, seeking to project the trauma claim to the audience; and cultural classifications regarding the nature of the pain, the nature of the victim, the relation of the trauma victim to the wider audience, and the attribution of responsibility. Alexander observes that linguistic action, through which the master narrative of social suffering is created, is mediated by the nature of institutional arenas that contribute to it. Clearly, some claims can be better expressed in legal proceedings than others, which will forever remain, adapting Franz Kafka's famous words, before the law. Some carrier groups have easier access to law (on the privileged position of "repeat players," see Galanter 1974). Further, some classifications of perpetrators, victims, and suffering are more compatible with those of the law than others. In its construction of the past, the kind of truth it speaks, the knowledge it produces, and the collective memory to which it contributes the law is thus always selective.

Empirical research confirms such selectivities of criminal law. *The Limits of the Law* is the subtitle of historian Devin Pendas's famous book *The Frankfurt Auschwitz Trial, 1963–65* (2006). Without losing sight of the political context and extrajudicial forces at work in this trial against twenty-two former functionaries of the most murderous annihilation camp, Pendas takes "law on the books" seriously even while studying "law in action." He is right as the former may, directly or indirectly, affect the "social structure of the case" (Black 1993), providing the strategic frame within which actors apply tactics to advance their goals.

The Frankfurt trial, for example, faced several legal constraints. First, the German government had annulled the occupation (Control Council) law in 1956 with its criminal categories such as "crimes against humanity" and its sentencing guidelines (including the death penalty).

Second, the German Basic Law, while acknowledging the supremacy of international law, prohibited ex post facto prosecutions. "Genocide" could be prosecuted only for future cases. Third, the Frankfurt court thus relied on standard German criminal law, created with crimes in mind that differed radically from those committed in the context of the organized annihilation machinery of Nazi Germany. This law was limited by its strict Kantian focus on subjective intent and its distinction between perpetrator and accomplice (the latter considered a tool rather than an autonomous actor in the execution of the crime). This type of law, Pendas shows, was ill suited for confronting the complex nature and organizational context of the crimes committed at Auschwitz, especially the systematic annihilation of millions. Instead, prosecution was successful in particular cases of especially atrocious actions, such as brutal acts of torture during interrogations, in which malicious intent could be documented and in which defendants could not present themselves as tools of the will of others. We might thus suggest that Pendas had referred, in his subtitle, to the limits of *German* criminal law, were it not for research by scholars such as Michael Marrus (2008), who documents similar limitations for the Nuremberg "Doctors' Trial," conducted by American authorities under occupation law. Here, too, particularly atrocious practices came more to light than did institutionalized ideas of the medical profession or routine practices of physicians that provided the foundation for human "experiments."

Legal constraints thus limited not only the Frankfurt trial's representational but also its juridical functions. They frustrated the pedagogical intent with which Fritz Bauer, prosecutor general of the state of Hessen, had advanced these collective proceedings. Inspired by the 1961 Eichmann trial in Jerusalem, he sought a large, historical trial that would stir the collective conscience, increase awareness, and instill in Germans' collective memory the horrific nature of the Nazi crimes. He partly succeeded, but only within the limits of the law, which directed attention to those lone actors who had engaged in particularly excessive cruelty beyond the directives under which they worked in Auschwitz. While Nazi crimes were thereby put on public and terrifying display, the trial did little harm to the "accomplices" who ran the machinery of mass killing. And it paradoxically helped Germans to distance themselves from the crimes of the Holocaust. Perpetration appeared, in the logic of the Auschwitz trial, either as the outgrowth of sick minds or as executed in the context of the machinery set up by the Nazi leadership, in which ordinary Germans acted without or even against their own will. The German case thus illustrates with particular clarity what Bernhard Giesen (2004b) elsewhere has called the "decoupling" function of criminal law.

In short, criminal law faces limits to its history writing and collective memory–forming missions. These limits result in part from its institutional logic: its focus on the behavior of individuals, consideration of only a limited set of behaviors, the constraints imposed by rules of evidence, and its binary logic and exclusionary intent. Each of these features has consequences for narratives that result from legal procedures, and, through them, for the formation of collective memory. These constraints are visible in pre-legal and legal documents on Darfur. Later chapters examine how this logic of criminal law corresponds with that of news media, with which it shares a focus on individuals, dramatic events, and a tendency to distinguish starkly between good and evil. Consequences for the collective representation of mass violence are substantial.

Constructing the Darfur Narrative through the Lens of Criminal Law and Justice

Initial warnings regarding horrific events unfolding in Darfur were included in a December 2003 confidential memo by Tom Eric Vraalsen, the UN special envoy for humanitarian affairs in Darfur, to Jan Egeland, the UN emergency relief coordinator. Vraalsen reported that "'delivery of humanitarian assistance to populations in need is hampered mostly by *systematically denied access*. While [Khartoum's] authorities claim unimpeded access, they greatly restrict access to the areas under their control, while imposing blanket denial to all rebel-held areas'—that is, areas overwhelmingly populated by the African Fur, Zaghawa, and Massalit peoples" (cited in Reeves 2013; emphasis in original).

Official pronouncements by the United Nations followed initial journalistic efforts in early 2004 by college professor Eric Reeves and *New York Times* op-ed writer Nicholas Kristof. They began with Secretary-General Kofi Annan's April 7, 2004, speech before the UN General Assembly, held on the occasion of the tenth anniversary of the Rwandan genocide. The "action plan" Annan called for demanded:

> swift and decisive action when, despite all our efforts, we learn that genocide is happening, or about to happen. . . . In this connection, let me say here and now that I share the grave concern expressed last week by eight independent experts . . . at the scale of reported human rights abuses and at

the humanitarian crisis unfolding in Darfur, Sudan. Last Friday, the United Nations Emergency Relief Coordinator reported to the Security Council that "a sequence of deliberate actions has been observed that seem aimed at achieving a specific objective: the forcible and long-term displacement of the targeted communities, which may also be termed 'ethnic cleansing.'" His assessment was based on reports from our international staff on the ground in Darfur, who have witnessed first-hand what is happening there, and from my own Special Envoy for Humanitarian Affairs in Sudan, Ambassador Vraalsen, who has visited Darfur. (Annan 2004)

Annan's speech, coinciding with the peak of the second wave of mass violence in Darfur, was followed by now well known UN actions. On September 18, 2004, the UNSC adopted Resolution 1564. This resolution threatened to sanction the Sudanese government should it fail to live up to its obligations on Darfur. It also established the International Commission of Inquiry on Darfur (ICID) to investigate violations of human rights in Darfur and invoked, for the first time in history toward such purpose, the Convention for the Prevention and Punishment of the Crime of Genocide (Genocide Convention). The resolution, sponsored by Germany, Romania, the United Kingdom, and the United States, was adopted by eleven votes in favor, no objections to the resolution, and four abstentions (Algeria, China, Pakistan, and Russia). As nation-states and their governments are the constituent members and thus the crucial actors of the organization, their economic and strategic interests and cultural sensitivities are important determinants of the path the UN follows. I discuss some of the countries cited here in greater detail throughout this book.

Soon after Resolution 1564 passed, in October 2004, Secretary-General Annan appointed commissioners to the ICID, which began its work on October 25, 2004. In line with the resolution, the commission was charged "'to investigate reports of violations of international humanitarian law and human rights law in Darfur by all parties'; 'to determine also whether or not acts of genocide have occurred'; and 'to identify the perpetrators of such violations' 'with a view to ensuring that those responsible are held accountable'" (ICID 2005:9). Clearly, the mandate was framed in the terms of criminal law, specifically international humanitarian and human rights law. The selection of commission members, in terms of their educational backgrounds, careers, and positions, further solidified the placement of the Darfur issue in the field of criminal law and justice. The ICID consisted of five members whose short bios, describing their positions at the time of appointment, appear in its report (ICID 2005:165–166). The commission chair was the late Antonio Cassese from Italy. A renowned law professor, Cassese had published prominently on issues of international human rights law and international criminal law. Previously, he had served as the first president of the ICTY. Mohamed Fayek, from Egypt, is a former minister in his country's government and secretary-general of the Arab Organization for Human Rights, an NGO. Hina Jilani, from Pakistan, had served as a special representative of the UN secretary-general on human rights defenders and as secretary-general of the Human Rights Commission of Pakistan. She was then a member of the District Court and Supreme Court Bar Association in Egypt. Dumisa Ntsebeza, from South Africa, served as a commissioner on the Truth and Reconciliation Commission of his country. He led that commission's Investigatory Unit and was head of its witness protection program. Ntsebeza was an Advocate of the High Court of South Africa and a member of the Cape Bar. Finally, Therese Striggner-Scott from Ghana was a barrister and principal partner with a legal consulting firm in Accra. She served on her country's High Court, as an ambassador to France and Italy, and as a member of the "Goldstone Commission," which had investigated public violence and intimidation in South Africa. In short, the ICID was dominated by members from the Global South with a background in law, especially international human rights law and international criminal law. Three of its five members were from the African continent.

The commission was supported by an investigative team that included forensics experts, military analysts, and investigators with expertise in gender violence. It traveled to Sudan and the three Darfur states, met with the government of Sudan and with government officials at the state and local levels (for a mixed assessment of government cooperativeness, see ICID 2005:15–16), met with military and police, rebel forces and tribal leaders, displaced persons, victims and witnesses, and NGO and UN representatives, and it examined reports issued by governments, intergovernmental organizations, UN bodies, and NGOs (2–3). Many of these actors are identified above as the driving forces behind the justice cascade. Here they provide evidence in the examination of criminal wrongdoing in a specific case.

On January 25, 2005, three months after its constitution, the commission delivered a 176-page single-spaced report to the UN secretary-General (ICID 2005). Ten pages of the text are devoted to "the historical and social background" of the conflict (17–26). There we learn about those social forces we encounter elsewhere in much of the historical and social science literature on Darfur: demographics of Sudan and Darfur;

colonial rule, including the incorporation of the Sultanate of Darfur into Sudan during British rule; fluctuations between military regimes and democratic rule after independence; the 1989 coup by Omar al-Bashir; internal power struggles; the North-South war and the Comprehensive Peace Agreement (CPA); the land tenure system and conflict over land; a history of intermarriage and socioeconomic interconnectedness between tribes, but an intensification of tribal identifications under conditions of conflict; desertification and growing struggles for resources, especially between agriculturalists and nomadic groups; devaluation of traditional law, once a potent tool for settling land disputes; an influx of weapons from neighboring countries; the emergence of the Arab Gathering, an alliance of Arabic tribes, and of the African Belt, composed of members of the Fur in the 1980s; the emergence of the Sudan Liberation Movement/Army (SLM/A) and the Justice and Equality Movement (JEM), the former inspired by the *new Sudan* policy of the South Sudanese SLM/A, the latter by trends in political Islam; militant activities by these groups; the government's shortage of military resources due to the civil war in the South, its resort to exploiting tensions between different tribal groups, and its equipping of mostly Arabic nomadic groups with ideological and material support, thus laying the foundation for the "Janjaweed" militias (named by "a traditional Darfurian term denoting an armed bandit or outlaw on horse or on camel" [ICID 2005:24]); and previous unsuccessful efforts at finding a peaceful solution.

Obviously, ten pages of text allow very little space to discuss each of these many factors. Correspondingly, all of these factors are irrelevant in light of the ICID's mission, cast in terms of criminal law and justice and constituting part of the justice cascade. Indeed, throughout the report, the commission strictly follows the legal logic. It categorizes actors ("1. Government Armed Forces"; "2. Government supported and/ or controlled militias—The Janjaweed"; "3. Rebel movement groups" [ICID 2005:27–39]), spells out the legal rules binding on the government of Sudan and on the rebel groups, identifies categories of international crimes, and associates available and legally relevant evidence with those legal concepts (ICID 2005:40–107). In summarizing its findings, the ICID first speaks to the *actus reus* with regard to "[v]iolations of international human rights law and international humanitarian law:"

> The Commission took as the starting point for its work two irrefutable facts regarding the situation in Darfur. Firstly, according to United Nations estimates there are 1[.]65 million internally displaced persons in Darfur, and more than 200,000 refugees from Darfur in neighbouring Chad.

Secondly, there has been large-scale destruction of villages throughout the three states of Darfur. The Commission conducted independent investigations to establish additional facts and gathered extensive information on multiple incidents of violations affecting villages, towns and other locations across North, South and West Darfur. The conclusions of the Commission are based on the evaluation of the facts gathered or verified through its investigations. (3)

Having thus summarized the facts on the ground—as established by multiple actors, including the UN, its suborganizations, and NGOs, and supplemented by the commission's own investigation—the report proceeds to link this evidence to the legal categories of the Rome Statute, and concludes:

Based on a thorough analysis of the information gathered in the course of its investigations, the Commission established that the Government of the Sudan and the Janjaweed are responsible for serious violations of international human rights and humanitarian law amounting to crimes under international law. In particular, the Commission found that Government forces and militias conducted indiscriminate attacks, including killing of civilians, torture, enforced disappearances, destruction of villages, rape and other forms of sexual violence, pillaging and forced displacement, throughout Darfur. These acts were conducted on a widespread and systematic basis, and therefore may amount to crimes against humanity. The extensive destruction and displacement have resulted in a loss of livelihood and means of survival for countless women, men and children. In addition to the large scale attacks, many people have been arrested and detained, and many have been held incommunicado for prolonged periods and tortured. The vast majority of the victims of all of these violations have been from the Fur, Zaghawa, Massalit, Jebel, Aranga and other so-called "African" tribes. (3)

By identifying the acts of violence as "widespread and systematic," the ICID determines that they amount to crimes against humanity, as defined in the Rome Statute, and thus fall under the jurisdiction of the ICC. The ICID thereby lays the ground for its recommendation to the UNSC that the case be referred to that court.

Simultaneously, mindful that the violence in Darfur may be interpreted differently, the commission seeks to preempt potential challenges:

In their discussions with the Commission, Government of the Sudan officials stated that any attacks carried out by Government armed forces in Darfur were for counter-insurgency purposes and were conducted on the basis of military imperatives. However, it is clear from the Commission's findings that most attacks were deliberately and indiscriminately directed against civilians. Moreover, even if rebels, or persons supporting rebels, were present in some of the villages—which the Commission considers likely in only a very small number of instances—the attackers did not take precautions to enable civilians to leave the villages or otherwise be shielded from attack. Even where rebels may have been present in villages, the impact of the attacks on civilians shows that the use of military force was manifestly disproportionate to any threat posed by the rebels. (3)

The Commission obviously seeks to challenge a counternarrative based on an insurgency and counterinsurgency frame and proposed by the government of Sudan. By not referencing early attacks by the SLA and the JEM against institutions of the Sudanese state, the commission plays down the insurgency part of the history of the unfolding violence. Yet the evidence to challenge the (counter)insurgency frame seems readily at hand: a counterinsurgency would have been directed against militants, whereas, according the commission's evidence, civilians were the targets. Further, should militants or members of rebel groups have hidden among the civilian population, the military would have been obliged to protect civilians in the ensuing fighting.

The commission nevertheless follows its mandate to also assess the involvement of rebel groups: "While the Commission did not find a systematic or a widespread pattern to these violations, it found credible evidence that rebel forces, namely members of the SLA and JEM, also are responsible for serious violations of international human rights and humanitarian law which may amount to war crimes. In particular, these violations include cases of murder of civilians and pillage" (4).

The quotations offered here summarize the commission's work. They reflect a report that spells out a series of behaviors by the Sudanese government and its associates and by rebels that constitute crimes based on norms of international criminal law and on the available, legally relevant evidence.

Finally, while major parts of the report refer to organizational actors such as the government of Sudan, militias, or rebel groups, the ICID eventually follows the logic of criminal law also by attributing responsibility to individuals. It does so in a later section of the report, "Identification of Perpetrators":

Those identified as possibly responsible for the above-mentioned violations consist of individual perpetrators, including officials of the Government of Sudan, members of militia forces, members of rebel groups, and certain foreign army officers acting in their personal capacity. Some Government officials, as well as members of militia forces, have also been named as possibly responsible for joint criminal enterprise to commit international crimes. . . . The Commission also has identified a number of senior

Government officials and military commanders who may be responsible, under the notion of superior (or command) responsibility, for knowingly failing to prevent or repress the perpetration of crimes. Members of rebel groups are named as suspected of participating in a joint criminal enterprise to commit international crimes. (4–5)

Not only does this segment of the report follow the individualizing logic of criminal law, but the commission also employs legal concepts, developed and refined in the history of international criminal law, in order to establish the criminal responsibility of individuals who acted in complex organizational contexts. "Command responsibility" seeks to prevent those from washing their hands of guilt who delegate the dirty work to others, lower in the organizational hierarchy. Further, in an effort to identify individuals as potential criminal perpetrators who acted in the context of complex organizations, the report applies the notion of joint criminal enterprise. This term, which appears twice in the report, developed out of the concept of conspiracy in American criminal law.[9] First developed in the United States in the fight against organized crime, the concept mutated into "criminal organization" in the London Charter of 1943, on which the Nuremberg tribunal was based, and into "joint criminal enterprise" in the ICTY's proceedings (Meierhenrich 2006). In addition to illustrating the application of concepts from international criminal law, this excursus into legal history illustrates how the global is constituted from below, in this case from the law of the United States (see Fourcade and Savelsberg 2006).

One more section from the ICID report merits lengthy quotation as it speaks to legal rules of evidence and as it became the center of some of the fiercest debates in the narratives on Darfur. Consider the following passage on the question "Have acts of genocide occurred?"

The Commission concluded that the Government of the Sudan has not pursued a policy of genocide. Arguably, two elements of genocide might be deduced from the gross violations of human rights perpetrated by Government forces and the militias under their control. These two elements are, first, the *actus reus* consisting of killing, or causing serious bodily or mental harm, or deliberately inflicting conditions of life likely to bring about physical destruction; and, second, on the basis of a subjective standard, the existence of a protected group being targeted by the authors of criminal conduct. However, the crucial element of genocidal intent appears to be missing, at least as far as the central Government authorities are concerned. Generally speaking, the policy of attacking, killing and forcibly displacing members of some tribes does not evince a specific intent to annihilate, in whole or in part, a group distinguished on racial, ethnic, national or religious grounds.

Rather, it would seem that those who planned and organized attacks on villages pursued the intent to drive the victims from their homes, primarily for purposes of counter-insurgency warfare. (4)

It is noteworthy that the commission here applies the notion of counterinsurgency that it rejects elsewhere in the report (see above). More important, the authors are torn when they apply, in this context, the criteria of the Convention for the Prevention and Punishment of the Crime of Genocide (Genocide Convention): "The Commission does recognise that in some instances individuals, including Government officials, may commit acts with genocidal intent. Whether this was the case in Darfur, however, is a determination that only a competent court can make on a case by case basis" (p. 4).

It is at least conceivable that, in the deliberation on the applicability of "genocide," political concerns intruded upon the ICID's strict application of legal logic. Such intrusion is not uncommon when crimes of a highly political nature are concerned. But why does the commission show such caution regarding the symbolically highly loaded notion of genocide when its reference to "a competent court" that alone can make a final (legal) determination applies to statements about war crimes and crimes against humanity as well? The reason likely lies in the kinds of voices I cite above, and to which I return in detail below: statements by foreign policy makers that urged against potential provocations of the government of Sudan and its leadership at a time when diplomats hoped for their cooperation in the North-South peace process and in the referendum over the independence of South Sudan.

The same tension observed here for the ICID later plagued the ICC when the case of Darfur was added to its docket. Based on the ICID report, the UNSC referred the case of Darfur to the ICC on March 31, 2005. And the ICC acted, adding the case of Darfur to Sikkink's "first stream" of the justice cascade—namely, international prosecutions—while simultaneously mobilizing what Sikkink calls the "streambed" of new judicial institutions, here specifically the Rome Statute. The court's first chief prosecutor, Luis Moreno-Ocampo, investigated the case and began his series of prosecutorial decisions against Ahmad Harun, Ali Kushayb, and President Omar al-Bashir, as described above.

In short, the ICC is now placed at the center of the judicial field in response to the mass violence in Darfur. In this case, and generally, the court is exposed to tensions well known from domestic criminal law, conflicts to which I turn next.

Conflicts within International Criminal Law and Justice

As institutions of international criminal law involve different profession-al groups, and as they are exposed to a highly political environment that they often cannot disregard, internal conflict is unavoidable. Within the ICC conflicting reasoning has been detected between lawyers and techno-crats (Meierhenrich 2014; for other legal institutions, see Stryker 1989), reflecting the tension between a formal and a more substantive orienta-tion of law that pervades international even more than domestic criminal law.[10] On the one side of the dividing line is law's formal rationality, oriented toward a system of legal criteria alone. Codifications such as the Rome Statute have indeed laid the groundwork for the pursuit of legal rationales, beginning to revolutionize a world in which foreign affairs were subject to political reasoning alone.[11] Some legal philosophers in fact argue that international criminal justice and human rights law can secure legitimacy in the long run only through strict adherence to formal legal criteria and abstinence from political rationales (Fichtelberg 2005).

Yet the court has to work against strong contenders, as the space granted the law has not been fully conceded among foreign policy mak-ers. The words of one of my interviewees illustrate this lack of accep-tance. This respondent, from the foreign ministry of a major European country, who specialized on issues of the ICC within his ministry's Divi-sion of International Law and represented his country in the Assembly of States, expressed his frustration as follows:

> As to my interlocutors in the [foreign ministry] . . . there were constantly conflicting perceptions. I do remember quite a number of quarrels I had with my colleagues in the political department. . . . And the reason is that we had two different approaches. Their approach was purely political. My approach was both political, but also legal and judicial. And that is extremely difficult to combine at times. Because, if you are only confined to making political as-sessments, then it is difficult to evaluate the work of a court, to accept a court, to accept any independent legal institution. And that is really something new in the international field where people are trained to assess complex issues by political means only. And you can find that very, very tangibly when you talk to United Nations staff, because they have for decades been trained in hav-ing an exclusively political view on issues. Now there is a new factor, a new player on the ground [the ICC], which does not make a political assessment, but which simply applies the law. That is a new phenomenon, and I think for those who have an exclusively political approach, that is difficult to accept.

Actors in foreign policy who fend for the autonomy of interna-tional law obviously face contending forces within their own minis-tries and within in the UN. In addition, the Rome Statute opens the door to substantive, political concerns to intrude into the work of the ICC. The UNSC and its permanent and temporary members—countries that are no strangers to the consideration of geopolitical and economic interests—are authorized to refer cases to the ICC.[12] This intrusion of political rationales is further supported by Article 16 of the Rome Statute, a window built into the edifice of the statute to keep political considerations in plain view: "No investigation or prosecution may be commenced or proceeded with under this Statute for a period of 12 months after the Security Council, in a resolution adopted under Chapter VII of the Charter of the United Nations, has requested the Court to that effect; that request may be renewed by the Council under the same conditions."[13] Decision makers on the court will thus have to be mindful of the UNSC's political reasoning if they hope to maintain control over their cases. The court's vulnerability vis-à-vis political powers is further increased by the fact that many countries have not yet ratified the Rome Statute, including ones—as is well known—as powerful as the United States, the People's Republic of China, and Russia.[14]

Finally, apart from external pressures, substantive outcomes of legal decision making also matter directly to jurists. Max Weber (1978), in his classic on the sociology of law, sees status interests of lawyers as a bulwark against the application of a purely formal rationality. Legal decision makers resent, he argues, being reduced to automatons into which one drops facts and fees and out of which spew decisions (and opinions). Instead, lawyers seek discretion, enabling them to consider ethical maxims or practical concerns of politics, economics, or geopolitics in their legal decisions. The long history of criminal law speaks to this tension between formal and substantive rationality. Historically, the pendulum has swung to alternatingly privilege formal rational or substantive rational models. In international criminal law, substantive considerations have particular weight, as thousands of lives may be at stake if conditions on the ground and practical consequences of legal decisions are disregarded. Applied to the case of Darfur, many foreign policy makers, including several interviewees for this book, expressed concern that charges against President al-Bashir might threaten the North-South agreement and the referendum on the independence of South Sudan. It is hard to imagine that these concerns were not on the minds of decision makers at the ICC.

In short, despite its particular institutional logic, criminal law is no stranger to internal contradictions and conflicts. Conflicts between formal legal criteria and substantive concerns, while dividing legal and political actors, also create ambivalences and internal tensions within the legal field. The ICC and the case of Darfur are no exceptions.

CONCLUSIONS: DARFUR IN THE JUSTICE CASCADE

Responses to the Darfur conflict are part of what Kathryn Sikkink has called the justice cascade: mass violence and grave violations of human rights have led the UNSC, ICID, and ICC to pursue individual criminal accountability. This pursuit is driven by forces that advanced the justice cascade in the first place: international organizations and social movement organizations, specifically INGOs with a human rights focus.

The case of Darfur thus provides insights into the strengths and limits of the justice cascade. Clearly, ICC charges are a victory for those who drive the justice cascade. Yet might this be a Pyrrhic victory? Realist critics who focus on the actual distribution of (hard) power point to the fact that none of the principal actors have thus far been apprehended and that powerful nations in fact have sought to appease the government of Sudan and its leaders in the pursuit of political goals.

But despite such constraints, the judicial process produced representations of the Darfur conflict and its participants, and it has cast them in the frame of criminal violence, even before a case has gone to trial. The publication of the ICID report and the ICC's indictments depicted powerful political actors as criminal perpetrators. This depiction was, as indicated in the introduction, and explored in greater detail below, communicated to a world audience. Supporters of the justice cascade consider this a success.

Simultaneously, however, the production of a judicial narrative of Darfur also illustrates the narrative constraints of criminal law. Analysis of crucial segments of the ICID report shows that the commission was well aware of the social and political conditions of the conflict. Yet such insights are marginalized in a "background" section. They do not color the conclusions and recommendations. In the logic of criminal law, the mass violence is attributed to a very few, albeit powerful, individuals. Other contributors are omitted from the narrative. Structural conditions and the organizational context within which the accused acted are not reflected in the conclusions. Further, while the ICID narrative avoids the simplification of social reality encountered in some social movement narratives, and while the report does acknowledge criminal violence by rebel groups, it divides the world of Darfur neatly into perpetrators and victims. And the commission's and the ICC's goal is justice, and the remedy is punishment, irrespective of concerns about competing actors.

The criminal law narrative obviously contradicts the accounts of historians and political scientists such as Alex de Waal and Mahmood

Mamdani, encountered in the introduction. It is more compatible with the narrative provided by sociologist-criminologists John Hagan and Wenona Rymond-Richmond. Yet, different from this social scientific examination, and despite its reference to "command responsibility" and "joint criminal enterprise," the commission report does not spell out the organizational mechanisms through which violent motivations were mobilized and actors on the ground ideologically and materially equipped for perpetration. The report also does not engage in the fine-grained and statistically sophisticated analysis of data such as that found in the Atrocities Documentation Survey (already available when the ICID did its work). It was this analysis, however, that enabled Hagan and Rymond-Richmond to document the role of racial motives in the atrocities. The statistical patterns they identified suggested to them, in contradistinction to the commission's report, that genocide had been committed.

This critical discussion, while highlighting the limits of criminal law narratives, is not to deny the capacity of criminal investigations, charges, or trials to contribute to the formation of collective representations and memories of mass atrocities. In fact, subsequent chapters—especially chapter 9—demonstrate their representational effectiveness.[15]

In sum, social and political forces that drove the justice cascade also helped move the case of Darfur toward judicial intervention by exactly those institutions that they had helped build in the first place. While no Darfur case has reached the trial stage, court interventions have provided a criminal law and justice frame through which the events of Darfur can be interpreted. Media communicated this frame to a broad public in a diverse array of countries, through a process analyzed in chapters 8 and 9. Criminal law's representation of Darfur thus provides a highly relevant definition of social reality, and the hopes of practitioners such as Justice Jackson and President Roosevelt seem defensible. Yet the limitations of criminal law–inspired accounts, diagnosed in historical and sociological literature, are also at work in the case of Darfur. Law's institutional logic produces a limited representation of mass violence that neglects central elements of social reality.

The court does not act alone, of course, in building a criminal justice representation of the mass violence in Darfur. It is supported, and in fact preceded, by actors at the fringes of the judicial field, human rights INGOs and governments that spearheaded the definition of Darfur's violence as criminal and even as genocidal. Their representations are the foci of chapters 2 and 3.

CHAPTER 2

The Human Rights Field and Amnesty International

International actors, including the ICC, do not work in isolation. Others precede and contribute to their interventions and their rights-based representation of mass violence. Turning to those other contributors, located at the periphery of the legal field, this chapter focuses on civil society actors that advocate for human rights. How do they support a criminal law response to mass violence? How do they represent the events in Darfur? Specifically, what is their contribution to advancing a criminalizing frame for the interpretation of mass violence? I examine Amnesty International as a civil society case study. In my interview with her, the Darfur specialist in Amnesty's International Secretariat at the time of the most intense violence confirmed the centrality of the Darfur issue. She also spoke to her organization's focus on the rights perspective: "We are a human rights organization and we document, we try to document, human rights abuses, human rights violations. And we try to raise awareness, and we try to provide recommendations for all the actors who can have an influence to sort of change the situation."

This chapter begins with an overview of literature that attests to the growing role of INGOs in the prosecution and representation of mass atrocities. Then I present an in-depth discussion of Amnesty International, spelling out organizational goals and strategies and how goals are perceived by Amnesty staff and what representations of Darfur they generate. The analysis shows that the institutional logic of the legal field colors Amnesty actors' narratives about Darfur, the suffering of its people, responsible actors, and appropriate frames. An exclusive focus on features of the human rights field, however, would be misleading. The final section of this chapter shows how, even in an international and highly centralized organization such as Amnesty, national contexts of sections and workers interpenetrate with and at times weaken the logic of the legal field. Conclusions summarize insights gained in this chapter and anticipate chapter 3's discussion of the role of the United States.

CIVIL SOCIETY'S HUMAN RIGHTS GROUPS AND THE ROLE OF AMNESTY INTERNATIONAL

Generally, INGOs have been playing a growing role in the representation of mass violence to a global audience. Their number has grown substantially in recent decades (Khagram, Riker, and Sikkink 2002), and their presence is associated with greater respect for human rights within countries (Hafner-Burton and Tsutsui 2005; Tsutsui and Wotipka 2004). INGOs draft human rights documents, promote human rights, document abuses, conduct research, condemn or praise states and other actors, mobilize public opinion and public action, lobby governments, and provide humanitarian relief. Most specialize, for example, along the lines of human rights protection or humanitarian aid delivery. No matter their specialization, in all of their actions INGOs acknowledge and interpret violence. They frame it in various ways, in line with their central mission, and disseminate their representations of violence to a broader public.

INGOs and other international organizations are often part of larger, nonhierarchical networks called transnational advocacy networks. As explored in chapter 1, TANs are bound together by shared values, a common discourse, and dense exchanges of information and services. Margaret Keck and Kathryn Sikkink (1998), who pioneered the study of TANs, focused on the power of ideas and norms, often called soft power, rather than more traditional forms of power. Information and the ability to frame violence are key to the power that activists, NGOs, social movements, and other members of TANs mobilize in order to draw attention to and increase support for their cause.

On the occasion of violent conflicts, INGOs are among the first actors to respond. My interviews with Africa correspondents from leading European and North American newspapers suggest that journalists often rely on NGOs as one crucial source of information. Journalists who reflect on their response to crises confirm that assessment (see the contributions in Thompson 2007). Such patterns of communication are to be expected given that major NGOs are represented in many parts of Africa, while even the most renowned newspapers typically have only one journalist on the ground, based in places such as Nairobi or Johannesburg, to cover the entire continent. Ways in which NGOs frame events may thus directly influence how violence is reported in news media across the globe, a topic to which I return in detail in chapter 9.

The importance of INGOs in the dissemination of knowledge is highlighted in the scholarly literature. World polity theorists, for example, argue that INGOs reflect the expression of world society and operate as carriers of global models and ideas (Schofer et al. 2012). These scholars suggest that NGOs facilitate the global diffusion of a uniform narrative of events.

Critical theorists who write about INGOs agree with the reputed global character of NGO messages, but they strongly disagree with regard to their content. They insist, instead, that rights-based INGO narratives are colored by neocolonial interests. To them notions of human rights are Western in origin, reflect narratives of linear progress, and disguise interests of the Global North (Kennedy 2004). When NGOs frame human rights abuses and atrocities by using a metaphor of victims, savages, and saviors, Western countries and organizations appear as "saviors" (Mutua 2002). Their stories of human rights abuses suggest clear dichotomies between virtue and evil, while ignoring the nuances and complexities of social situations. In the case of Darfur, scholars such as Mahmood Mamdani (2009b) reproach Western media for conducting a "moralistic discourse whose effect is both to obscure the politics of the violence and position the reader as a virtuous, not just as a concerned, observer" (149). Mamdani has in mind a wide variety of Western actors, from NGOs to writers such as Samantha Power, now US ambassador to the United Nations (see also Mamdani 2009a).

Constructivist traditions similarly embrace the importance of cultural models and norms. However, constructivists point out that NGOs are not just passive conduits of norms and ideas, as some world polity and critical research traditions assume, but rather actors with their own interests and desires to shape behavior (Keck and Sikkink 1998), actors also who operate against the background of nation-states and their institutional environments, in which they originate and where they are headquartered (Stroup 2012). NGOs do not just disseminate global narratives about conflicts; they create, modify, and interpret them, and they do so in line with their missions and foci. In the Darfur case, for example, humanitarian NGOs assess victimization and the role played by the Sudanese government more cautiously than rights-based NGOs, perhaps because they depend on the cooperation of the Sudanese government to deliver their aid (Hagan and Rymond-Richmond 2008).

THE CASE OF AMNESTY INTERNATIONAL

Amnesty International, together with organizations such as Human Rights Watch, the International Crisis Group, and the Enough Project, played a crucial role among INGOs in mobilizing world opinion and government action on behalf of Darfur. Amnesty's central role is not surprising in light of the organization's well-known history and current standing. Founded in 1961 by British lawyer Peter Benenson, Amnesty today is the best-known and largest human rights NGO. London is the seat of its headquarters, the International Secretariat. Here the organization maintains its research office, whose primary mission was, early on, to identify and gather information on individual "prisoners of conscience" and to distribute such knowledge worldwide, a mission that has since been broadened (on Amnesty's history, see Neier 2012:186–203). Amnesty's success was partly based on its strict political impartiality. It took on cases under right- and left-wing abusers alike. It refused to accept government funds, instead relying solely on donations from small private donors and members. Highly qualified researchers, writing reports in its London office, strictly avoided sensationalism. The resulting moral authority contributed to a membership base of 160,000 in 107 countries by the mid-1970, a number that grew further to more than 500,000 in 160 countries after Amnesty was awarded the Nobel Peace Prize in 1977. Over the years, Amnesty expanded its reach beyond representing the interests of individual political prisoners. One central mission became the mobilization of public opinion and enactment of government policies when massive violations of human rights occurred anywhere around the globe. Darfur became one of those cases.

In 2013, for example, on the occasion of the tenth anniversary of the mass killings in Darfur, Amnesty International issued a report to update the public. The following short excerpt highlights the organization's concern both with the massive violation of the local population's human rights and with the impunity of leading political actors:

> As the Darfur conflict marks its 10th anniversary, the human rights situation in the region remains dire. Civilians continue to face attacks by government forces, pro-government militias, and armed opposition groups. In the last

three months alone, 500 people were reportedly killed and roughly 100,000 displaced in attacks against civilians that have involved members of government forces. The government in recent years has continued to carry out indiscriminate aerial bombardment and deliberate attacks against civilians. In addition, security services carry out torture and other ill-treatment against detainees and, alongside the police, use excessive force against peaceful protesters. And impunity reigns. Government officials, including President Bashir and a leader of the "*janjaweed*" pro-government militia Ali Kushayb, indicted by the International Criminal Court on counts of war crimes, crimes against humanity and genocide remain at large and there is little or no accountability for these crimes.[1]

The online publication cited here lists seventeen previous reports Amnesty issued over the past decade on the violence in Darfur. The first alert cited was issued during the second peak of mass killings ("Sudan: Darfur: 'Too Many People Killed for No Reason,'" February 3, 2004).[2] An early example of intense field research, conducted by experienced research staff, appeared five months later under the title "Sudan: Darfur: Rape as a Weapon of War: Sexual Violence and Its Consequences."[3] Following the typical division of labor, a researcher visited the field—specifically, the refugee camps in Chad—to interview affected women, and her colleague in London, in this case the campaigner for Sudan and East Africa, wrote the report. In the words of the latter, one of my interviewees at the International Secretariat: "[The rape study] was done by Annette [Weber], who went to Chad to do this. . . . I worked on the reports that came out of that." Reports and statements cited here illustrate well Amnesty's focus on the safeguarding of human rights. Means are not limited to criminal justice interventions, but they decidedly include them. Behaviors are referred to as crimes. Perpetrators, identified as targets of ICC prosecution, are named, including President Omar al-Bashir. Some of the evidence gathered in Amnesty reports is in fact suited for use by the prosecutor. Images displayed on Amnesty websites support the organization's messages (see figures 4 and 5).

Reports issued by Amnesty's International Secretariat in London are delivered to the national sections. There, country and theme specialists on Amnesty's staff use them to collaborate with volunteer groups on various campaigns in seeking to inform a broad public. They also pressure policy makers to take notice and to act on behalf of human rights. The following statement from an interviewee at Amnesty-Germany in Berlin describes how such work is executed:

I am here responsible for the coordination of our political work, that is, to pass on and present Amnesty demands and recommendations to the federal

FIGURE 4. Darfur village attacked and burned by the Janjawiid. This image appeared on Amnesty International's website.

FIGURE 5. Darfuri refugee women and children in Chad. This image appeared on Amnesty International's website.

administration and the legislature, and also to foreign embassies here in Berlin. A focus on which I really worked intensively is the impunity issue. That is not assigned to the country experts, but it's one of the themes that are coordinated by the secretariat general. These are the areas—impunity, work on the United Nations, the Human Rights Council, those issues thus—where country work coincides with institutional questions. And to decide, when we have a concern regarding Darfur, an arrest warrant against Bashir, for example, do we direct this to the legal department or the country section in the foreign ministry? What resources might have to get involved? Are we going to do this alone or in collaboration with other NGOs? . . . I am responsible for these kinds of strategic questions. (author's translation)

The respondent, trained as a political scientist and responsible for political work at Amnesty-Germany, rushed from the interview we conducted in a fishbowl-like conference room to her office for a telephone conference with members of other NGOs. This conference's purpose was to prepare for a meeting with the Africa representative of the foreign ministry, a previous ambassador to Kenya and until recently head of his ministry's crisis staff. "The upcoming telephone conference," she told me,

serves the coordination among the participating NGO colleagues. When we are ten, to enter into a conversation with the other side and have one hour available to us, we then have to coordinate a bit. Who says what? Who pursues what foci? Where do organizations have common concerns that could be presented by just one participant? [Participating organizations at the upcoming conference included] Medica Mondiale, for which sexual violence against women is a central theme. That is also an important topic for Amnesty, but here we say that this is something that should rather be presented by Medica Mondiale, and where we say that we support their position. Then the humanitarian organizations will participate: World Vision, Oxfam, the Ecumenical Network Central Africa [Ökumenisches Netzwerk Zentralafrika], a very broad spectrum thus, also Human Rights Watch. (author's translation)

Amnesty International is a formal, centralized organization, and its guiding philosophy and crucial case-specific information, passed down from the International Secretariat in London, is taken seriously at the grass roots. One interviewee, a specialist for issues of arms and impunity for Amnesty-France in Paris, sheds light on (and supports) the highly formal and centralized nature of his organization. When asked about those he works with in his daily pursuits, he answered:

In general we depend strongly on Amnesty Londres [French for London]. . . . For example, Amnesty Londres said [to] us all the sections have to work on

Sudan and Darfur and the arrest of Omar al-Bashir, because we have [a] strategic date in [a] couple of months to make pressure on [the] international community. So during six, seven months you have to concentrate . . . and . . . organize the pressure in France to push France in [the] UN Security Council to push Sudan to arrest Omar al-Bashir and render Omar al-Bashir to the ICC. . . . [I]in general I am waiting for the strategy of Amnesty Londres. And with the strategy of Amnesty Londres I organize the work in Amnesty France. And with my volunteer team I say, so you have to write to the ministry, plan meetings; you can organize an event with a movie, for example, to [sensitize] people; you have to write press releases to push France and have interviews with journalists. . . . [W]e have sixty or seventy sections in the world: Asia, Africa, Americas. . . . In each country of the world Amnesty Londres has the capacity to mobilize volunteers to manage . . . a situation. If we have not this coordination, I think it will be very dangerous to work or inappropriate or inadequate. We will not be efficient. . . . And London has the capacity of research. In London you have all the researchers.

When asked about the most important source of information they rely on when seeking to understand a situation like that in Darfur, Amnesty staff and volunteers align closely with the above sentiments. All interviewees first refer to Amnesty's own reports. Most mention other sources only upon being prompted. Again the reply by the respondent of Amnesty-France may serve as an illustration. Asked what sources of information are most important to him when familiarizing himself with a case like Darfur and the indictment against al-Bashir, he answered:

Amnesty information. The [strength] of Amnesty International is the fact [that] we have our own research. . . . If I have information which is not checked by my researcher in London—I have a problem. . . . [S]ometimes when I have a doubt . . . I call or write London to have a discussion, to discuss the reliability, credibility of the information. . . . We are unique in the world in this respect, because our research is reliable. It is serious. In terms of information, it is information from Amnesty thus that is most important to me. (partially translated by author)

Despite its centralization and the clear guiding definition of a human rights–based philosophy, Amnesty International is a living organization, composed of human actors of diverse nationalities, genders, and educational and occupational backgrounds who act in varied national environments. Thus, to learn about Amnesty's involvement in the case of Darfur and about ways in which it narrated the events, I turn in greater detail to a set of ten interviews. Seven interviewees were staffers; the other three, volunteers. Staff respondents were placed at different levels of the organization's hierarchy, ranging from the secretary-general of a national organization to theme or country specialists in national sections.

Four had academic backgrounds in political science and international relations; four in law, including international human rights and criminal law; one volunteer had an engineering background (with the tenth's background unknown). Half had some additional educational degree, from anthropology to advertising. Most respondents had reached their current position via a variety of appointments. Yet none left any doubt about their identification with the pursuit of human rights as the organization's central mission. I conducted nine of the ten interviews in person, and one over the phone. Sites included the International Secretariat in London and national offices (staff) and homes (volunteers) in Paris, Washington, Berlin, Bielefeld, Vienna, and Bern.

Goals as Perceived by Amnesty Actors

Respondents at Amnesty International, like all other interviewees, were asked which goals should have primacy with regard to Sudan. I offered four options, but allowed for alternative suggestions: (1) seeking justice (by means of criminal law); (2) securing the survival of those affected by violence (through aid); (3) establishing peace (through negotiation); and (4) securing the sovereignty and integrity of the Sudanese state. The fourth option has obviously been a principle of international law since the Treaty of Westphalia of 1648, which ended the Thirty Years War and which was negotiated with the hope that principles of nonintervention would secure international peace. Respondents spoke to all of these goals. Some merged the second (survival) and third (peace) to add a fifth: helping those affected through military peacekeeping missions.

Amnesty interviewees did not support all goals equally. In line with expectations, they most strongly backed the achievement of justice or, in other terms, the prevention of impunity. Every respondent subscribed to this goal. Three in fact identified justice as the only objective or declared that other goals (e.g., lasting peace) could be achieved only if justice was served. These three were lawyers, leaving only the fourth lawyer with a more varied portfolio of purposes. Four respondents wanted the pursuit of justice to be combined with the goal of helping the affected population survive. One of these declared that survival was one side-effect of the pursuit of justice. Seven pleaded for peace or peacekeeping as goals in addition to the pursuit of justice; one of these cautioned, however, that the establishment of peace must not occur at the expense of justice. One respondent expected that justice served would lead to peace. And only one saw a dilemma between the goals of achieving peace and justice simultaneously. Securing sovereignty, finally, was supported by only one respondent, a volunteer with an engineering background. In the Amnesty context, international rule on behalf of human rights clearly trumps national sovereignty.

One interviewee, responsible for political communication at her country's section office, spoke clearly to the primacy of the justice goal. When asked about potential conflicts between justice and aid delivery, she responded:

> When we, in the case of Sudan, negotiate with the foreign ministry, jointly with colleagues from other NGOs, then that [the topic of cooperation with the government in Khartoum on humanitarian aid] will pop up. That, however, is not a point of contention within Amnesty, as we simply have a very clear position in favor of prosecution. Amnesty continues to be part of the grand coalition in favor of the ICC, and that can be summarized in the words "no peace without justice." There our position is very clear. Two years ago, on the occasion of the indictment against al-Bashir, we had a rather intense confrontation with Doctors Without Borders, for example, which took a very different position. We also had an exchange, not conducted in public, to communicate our positions to each other. Yes, this is an important point, but not a conflict within Amnesty. (author's translation)

Many interviewee statements could be added to illustrate this position, but I limit myself here to just one more, by an Amnesty-France interviewee. While the German respondent above draws a boundary between Amnesty's rights- versus humanitarian aid–inspired stances, this French respondent speaks to the distinction between a diplomatic position and that of Amnesty:

> Justice is not negotiable. . . . No one has ever proven that the arrest warrant against Omar al-Bashir impeded the peace process. For how many years has the peace process been going on!? For how many years has the government of France organized the conference in Doha, with the different rebel groups, with the government of North Sudan!? For how many years has one discussed!? For how many years!? . . . And the arrest warrant has never kept these negotiations from proceeding, never. That is thus a false problem [faux problème]. And how can one have peace, how reconstruct a country with the victims, if there was no reparation, no truth? That is not possible, not possible. The case of South Africa is emblematic. They had a Truth and Reconciliation Commission. Now, one can critique that commission, one can critique their work and how they went about it, but all Africans recognized that that commission played a central role in the reconciliation between black and white at the end of Apartheid. . . . Today, how do you want to construct peace at the expense of justice and have trust in those who have massacred their population? . . . It is thus that we never juxtapose justice and peace. For us they are intimately related. And one knows that justice

has a deterrent effect. Milošević participated in the Dayton Accords—and that was followed by a process which contributed to his arrest because there was an international tribunal. And the Bosniac forces contributed to his arrest and extradition to the tribunal because the tribunal also had the capacity to dissuade those who had endured the violence from taking violent revenge, but rather to favor the arrest of that person. Justice has a deterrent effect, extremely strong. (author's translation)

Elsewhere in the interview, the same respondent stressed that Amnesty staff are not uninterested in sociological and political conditions of conflict, but that these concerns are subordinate to the rationales of the justice perspective:

> One denounces, and one does not cease to denounce, for example, the death penalty. But one does not tell the Chinese—or China—"adopt a US type regime, for example, adopt a Chinese democracy." No. One simply denounces all they inflict upon their population. Here you go. And I believe that this is one of the strengths of Amnesty, to have that distance to the international political system or to political situations at the national level, such as in Sudan, in order to report nothing but the voice of the victims. . . . A right constitutes obligations. Obligations, responsibilities, pursuit of justice. . . . [Asked if sociological or political causes are thus irrelevant to Amnesty, he adds in English:] Yes. But we are not stupid and we need to understand personally the situation. So maybe we go to a conference to meet specialists on the question, to have a view, a general view of the situation and understand ethnic problems, energy problems, political problems. But it is to facilitate our work; it is not a condition of our work. (partially translated by author)

In short, these statements illustrate that not just official proclamations and declarations by the International Secretariat in London, but also goal setting as articulated by my interviewees from Amnesty from a diverse group of countries, place the organization unmistakably in the justice field, albeit at its periphery. Respondents' identification with Amnesty's institutional logic is especially pronounced where organizational membership coincides with legal training.

Interviews do not reveal if this identification of justice, or the avoidance of impunity, as a goal results from selective recruitment or socialization into the organization's culture. Socialization through organization and communication does seem crucial, though, as indicated by participants' almost unanimous orientation toward the International Secretariat as the best source of information. Be that as it may, membership in Amnesty, for volunteers, but especially for staff, appears to color the habitus of its members, as well as their identification with an institutional logic that corresponds with the pursuit of justice by means of criminal law.

Representations of Darfur by Amnesty Activists

How does this identification with the organizational goal of human rights and justice translate into Amnesty workers' representation of the Darfur conflict? How similar is their narrative to those encountered in legal documents (chapter 1) or to the account of criminologists such as John Hagan and Wenona Rymond-Richmond (introduction)? The narrative or representation of the Darfur conflict, as presented by Amnesty interviewees can best be explored along the dimensions of suffering and victimhood; origins of the conflict, time dimension, and causes; identity of actor-perpetrators; and frames applied. Seven out of ten Amnesty interviewees, representing the International Secretariat in London and five individual countries (United States, France, Germany, Austria, and Switzerland), provided substantive answers to most of the themes covered here.

In response to questions about suffering and victimhood, seven interviewees spoke about victimhood and the suffering of the Darfur population; one additional respondent (Ireland) referred me to related accounts in an Amnesty report. Specifically, six interviewees spoke about killings and death, and one about executions and disappearances. Six addressed rape (including "mass rapes" and "mass rape as an instrument of ethnic cleansing"), and six referred to displacements (including those termed "irreversible"). Torture, looting, destruction, and violations of human rights are also mentioned. Obviously, suffering and victimhood are foremost in the minds of Amnesty interviewees, and they are primarily described in the language of criminal law.

When asked about causes and origins, Amnesty interviewees, while also speaking to long-standing conflicts in the region of Darfur, especially old conflicts between ethnic groups and between pastoralists and farmers, focused on present-day conditions. A major concern was with government policies that "discriminate" and "marginalize." Respondents thereby attributed responsibility to the government of Sudan for creating background conditions that foster conflict. But they went further by also identifying government action as a direct cause of the violence. They spoke to the "politicization of old conflicts" or the "instrumentalization" of tensions in the region by the al-Bashir government and to the government supplying "Arabs" with weapons. Such a focus on the present is in line with the criminological representation of the Darfur conflict by Hagan and Rymond-Richmond. It approximates judicial narratives.

Interviewees were more specific yet. Seven of them named actors whom they deemed responsible for the suffering of the people of Darfur. All but one mentioned the *government of Sudan*; five referred explicitly to al-Bashir, the "Bashir regime," or government actors "up to the Presidential level." Four mentioned the *Janjawiid* or "Arabs, supplied with weapons"; and (only) two see *"rebels"* or "opposition groups" as responsible for the violence.

One interviewee came closest to representing the violence in Darfur in almost ideal-typical terms of criminal law and justice. This is not surprising, as here we encounter a young lawyer, the head of Amnesty-Germany's volunteer group on issues of impunity, a former intern at the ICC's prosecutor's office who had also spent time with the tribunal in East Timor and who was earning her living as a prosecutor in Berlin. She spoke about causes, suffering, and perpetration of crimes in Darfur in these terms:

> I would say it is a conflict that originates in ethnic tensions and that has been instrumentalized by the central government in Khartoum, to document its territorial claims in Darfur. The causes of the conflict lie in the differences between the ethnic groups in Sudan, but also in their ways of life and in a will of those groups living in Darfur to continue to conduct their self-determined lives and to distance themselves from the central government, an attempt that the central government does not necessarily support. The execution of the conflict is yet another question. . . . The government sent out [horse/camel-]riding groups, collaborated with the Janjawiid militias thus, which it instrumentalized, and that helped their country's army, to show their dominance, as it were. In the course of this, hundreds of thousands have been driven from their homes and killed. Rapes were a strong characteristic of this conflict, and it is one of the cruelest conflicts of the past years. . . . And it was planned and purposefully conducted. Different from descriptions by many, it was not simply a clash between ethnic groups that conducted a civil war. That, I would say, it was exactly not. But what precisely occurred, and how it is to be evaluated judicially, there we have to wait for word from the ICC—when one day proceedings will finally be under way. (author's translation)

Not only is this narrative in line with the logic of criminal law and justice, explicating the *actus reus,* naming offenders, and declaring their intent, but it is also partially subservient to the juridical proceedings. The final story can be told, in the mind of this respondent, only once the court has done its work. I found the same deference, the same hesitancy to label the crimes without the court having spoken, in a number of interviews with lawyers, not just at Amnesty.

Finally, inquiring about the appropriate frame through which the Darfur conflict should be interpreted, I again offered interviewees four options: a rebellion or insurrection frame (understanding government action as counterinsurgency); a civil war frame; a humanitarian emergency frame; and a state crime frame. In their responses, only one respondent supported the insurgency frame (engineer-volunteer), one rejected it explicitly (general secretary, lawyer), and three subscribed to it either with hesitation or by stressing that the insurgency by rebel groups was a response to government action. Only one respondent accepted the *civil war frame,* three rejected it explicitly, and one accepted it only under the condition that civil war in Darfur be seen as a consequence of previous criminal state action. Almost all respondents accepted the label of humanitarian catastrophe, though one of these insisted that it should be considered as such only if one recognizes that the crisis resulted from criminal aggression by the state. One respondent hesitated using the label *humanitarian catastrophe* as, in his opinion, it omitted the situation's human-made character (general secretary, lawyer). Yet, in line with the narrative described here along four analytic dimensions, all of the respondents but one wholeheartedly embraced the state crime frame.

In short, interviewees among Amnesty's staff and volunteers were largely in line with the guidance provided by the International Secretariat in London. They were determined that the pursuit of human rights is of the utmost importance, that criminal law and justice should play the central role in response to mass violence, and that impunity must be avoided by all means. Some also insisted that pursuing justice will eventually serve other goals such as the survival of those affected and the establishment of peace. Potential goal conflicts were thus neutralized.

Despite such unanimity, I observed patterns of distinction even within our small sample of interviewees. The lawyer-versus–political scientist distinction appears to carry particular weight, with lawyers defining goals and presenting narratives in ways even more clearly in line with the ideal type of criminal law and justice than those of other Amnesty members, staff, or volunteers. This pattern resembles those identified elsewhere in political administration (Stryker 1989) and within the ICC (Meierhenrich 2014). But I have to pour more water into the wine of a pure criminal justice perspective. Another pattern I observed demands that we modify the notion of a universal and globalized representation of mass violence by an international rights-oriented organization. I refer to national distinctions, to which I turn now.

NATIONAL CONTEXTS OF NGO WORK AND THE CASE
OF AMNESTY

International NGOs are, by definition, border-crossing organizations. Their emergence and influence is in line with theoretical arguments from the world polity, neoinstitutional, and constructivist schools. Yet a specific branch of neo-Weberian work in comparative sociology and recent insights particularly regarding INGOs have stressed the considerable weight of national context in the definition of situations. Most INGOs continue to be headquartered in the countries where they were founded, and they continue to receive a substantial portion of their funding from within these "home" countries. Developing this point through an empirical examination, Sarah Stroup (2012:3) argues convincingly: "While many NGOs are increasingly active in *international* arenas, I find that actual organizational structures and strategies are deeply tied to *national* environments." Her detailed analyses confirm that this pattern applies especially for humanitarian, but also for human rights INGOs. Stroup focuses on regulatory frameworks, political opportunity structures, availability of resources, and social networks as features to which INGOs are exposed and that vary by country. She shows how such contextual conditions color INGOs' professionalization and management, fund-raising, advocacy and research, and issue selection. My point here is that they also color the representation of human rights violations.

The rights-based INGOs that Stroup examines include United Kingdom–based Amnesty International and, by contrast, Human Rights Watch, based in the United States, along with the Fédération Internationale des Ligues des Droits de l'Homme (FIDH), based in France. Compared to the latter two, and owing to donation patterns in the United Kingdom, Amnesty depends more on fund-raising from multiple individual donors. Levels of professionalization also differ. HRW, for example, depends on a high level of professionalization, a functional necessity because of its dependence on large foundation donors. Consequently, HRW also relies more on insider strategies (e.g., links to the US government), compared to a preference for grassroots mobilization within Amnesty and, even stronger, in FIDH. In terms of issue selection, both HRW and Amnesty have been much more reluctant to address social, economic, and cultural rights issues than the French FIDH. Stroup attributes this caution to the American and British constituencies' greater attunement to free market and individual rights principles than their French counterparts exhibit.

But Stroup goes further. Beyond identifying differences across distinct human rights organizations, she also explores distinctions of national sections within INGOs. For Amnesty, for example, despite its high degree of centralization and the concentration of more than a quarter of its $200 million budget in the International Secretariat in London, she finds significant national particularities. Among the eighty national sections, Amnesty-USA depends more than the others on large financial donations of less involved supporters, a funding pattern similar (albeit not as pronounced) to that of HRW. National donation practices thus matter at the level of sections, as well. Further, while research at Amnesty is "in some ways a valuable end in itself," the US section sets somewhat different priorities. As one staffer indicated, "We in the US think in terms of timeliness and impact, but they [the International Secretariat] think in a way that is unhurried, more thorough, and these are cultural differences. . . . To me, it sometimes feels like a group of people in universities in London, developing long, detailed documents" (cited in Stroup 2012:160).

Country-specific opportunity structures that affect organizations and sections within organizations spelled out by Stroup are supplemented by others, including nation-specific carrier groups, historical experiences, and the distinct cultural sensitivities these evoke. Collective memories and cultural trauma—for example, those pertaining to war and mass violence—and associated national identities take country-specific shape (Savelsberg and King 2005, 2011). In addition, civil society is more easily mobilized in some countries such as the United States, with its strong tradition of associational life and prominence of single-issue groups, but slower to move to action in others with more neocorporatist arrangements (Kalberg 2014). Also the organization of news media varies. Market-driven media, as compared to publically funded ones, are more receptive to societal sentiments and prone to sensationalist reporting (Benson 2013), for which the United States provides a good example. In addition, government institutions are more or less open to civil society input. And here too the boundary between civil society and the state is more porous in the United States than in other Western democracies, as a long line of sociological work has shown (Bendix [1949] 1974; Roth 1987; Rueschemeyer 1973; Kalberg 1994, 2014; Savelsberg and King 2005).

Interviewees at Amnesty were clearly sensitive to the state- and society-based contexts within which their sections have to operate, despite their frequent deference to the International Secretariat. They know, for example, that their governments are more receptive if the issue at hand concerns a former colony, especially if the country hosts refugees and expatriate organizations from those former colonies. In the words of a respondent at the International Secretariat in London, an energetic person of French descent (from an overseas French province) who had earned a degree in political science and international relations at Science Po in Paris and in anthropology at the renowned School of Oriental and African Studies (SOAS) at the University of London:

> I think—obviously, because we are based here—you know, we do have more regular access to UK diplomats, but I think I am also maybe more aware of the role that the UK plays on Sudan, on Darfur, because they played a very important role in the North-South peace process, [because] they are the former colonial power, and because of their seat at the Security Council. . . . [Y]ou will hear a lot more talking about Sudan and former British colonies in the UK. And if you are in France you will hear a lot more about Algeria, Morocco, Tunisia, etc., etc. . . . I think it is often because there is a lot of Sudanese refugees in the UK, there is a lot of refugees and migrants from North Africa in France. . . . [W]e have to try to take advantage of all this attention to try to push for our human rights agenda.

Two French Amnesty interviewees strongly confirmed the weight that status as a former colony has for their national government, and they drew conclusions for their strategizing. In the words of one:

> The French section works a lot on African countries, and the old colonies of France—because we know that France has the capacity again to influence these countries, because of the history of France and Africa and these countries. So, yes, we have a particular focus on francophone African countries. . . . [I]n Amnesty-France we have two researchers, who are based on the second floor, and they are specialists on western Africa.

Another country-specific feature Amnesty workers have to be mindful of if they hope to communicate effectively with their governments, is the history and status of the country's neutrality. Asked whether Switzerland's position vis-à-vis the Darfur conflict differs from that of other countries, an Amnesty staffer in Bern argued: "I think it barely does with regard to the evaluation of the Darfur conflict. In terms of practice, I'd say "yes," first because Switzerland almost never, as a matter of principle, participates in UN peacekeeping missions. [JJS: No humanitarian interventions?] No, or if ever, just as an alibi, two, three officers or such" (author's translation).

In addition to being sensitive to their government's position when they launch campaigns, Amnesty respondents appear to be especially attuned to their constituents' sensitivities and motivational forces. A sense of historical obligation, for example, resulting from their country's execution of the Holocaust, resonated from my interviews with German Amnesty staffers and volunteers alike. One volunteer, head of Amnesty-Germany's impunity group, illustrated this historically grounded sense of commitment well. She simultaneously indicated, though, that such commitment may be associated more with a leaning toward humanitarian than toward penal responses to mass atrocities:

> The churches are very much engaged in this respect, partially out of humanitarian concerns, but also with a view toward our own past, and the churches do have substantial influence in Germany—still. This group I would name. And they just have strong roots in the bourgeois [bürgerliche] middle classes. . . . It's more motivated by humanitarianism in Germany. Many people are engaged in humanitarian charities. I would always look at things from a criminal law perspective, but only few do so. Most see this as a humanitarian catastrophe with immense consequences. (author's translation)

This statement suggests that carrier groups and the strong position of churches in Germany's neocorporatist makeup influence the reception of the Darfur issue in that country. Another factor appears to be the institutionalization of the theme of genocide in German school curricula. The same interviewee spoke to the resulting responsiveness of the public to genocide issues by drawing on her own experiences:

> I think many Germans easily understand, as genocide and our history are being taught in school. One is able to draw parallels quickly when one begins to engage with the conflict. I certainly experienced that with Rwanda. I was still young back then, but both Rwanda and Yugoslavia were prominently reported in the news media. . . . That was 1994 and I was fifteen years old, in tenth grade, so this was a topic [in school], also at home, and these two conflicts had a strong influence on me. (author's translation)

Again, historical experiences and their processing into collective memory create public sensitivities that sections of INGOs such as Amnesty have to take seriously in order to act effectively toward their domestic constituents. The foregoing interview segment illustrates further that it matters which organizations and carriers dominate in the processing of history and in its application to current situations of mass violence. Needless to say, the respondent's perception is not based on social science analysis. But what matters here is the perception of an Amnesty member and its potential to color her organization's representation of the Darfur conflict.

Related historical legacies create additional country-specific sensitivities that INGOs have to take seriously if they want to function effectively in a given country. These include devastating experiences with aggressive militarism and their subsequent processing. Interviews with Amnesty staff in both Germany and Austria indicated that such experiences have generated pacifist leanings, especially within those population segments attracted to joining human rights organizations. And such leanings affect the discursive range available to their respective sections. A German Amnesty volunteer, head of the Sudan group, spoke to this point: "In 2006 we had the big issue here at Amnesty when the UN was supposed to receive a stronger mandate. . . . Then we had a major debate, especially here in Germany, because we have many Amnesty members from the peace movement, who rejected that, when the word *intervention* was articulated and *intervention* is always associated with the use of military force in the back of one's mind" (author's translation).

Another domestic force made itself known in my interviews, particularly in my conversation with the secretary-general of Amnesty-Austria: the entanglement of a country's industry in mass violence abroad, and the response that the discovery of such involvement evokes. In the Austrian case it became a motivating factor, in the absence of which the section, small and thus selective by necessity, may not have addressed the Darfur conflict. The story began with an American journalist who found a brand-new Glock pistol, made by the renowned Austrian firearms producer, in the hands of a Darfur rebel. The journalist noted the weapon's serial number, and when Amnesty was informed, it began to question Glock and the Austrian government, "How can that get there?" the secretary-general recounted.

> Darfur is a weapons embargo zone, for both the UN and the EU. There are of course millions of old weapons, hundreds of thousands of old weapons, but a recognizably brand new Glock pistol, for which you can still trace how the embargo was broken . . . That was a very tricky question, initially, and weapons' trade is maddeningly difficult, it's a very untransparent realm, where there is little transparency on the side of states: . . . "Dear Glock company, dear state of Austria, please explain to us how that got there. To whom did you sell this first, how did it move on from there, has it been stolen, sold on the back market?" (author's translation)

Glock responded, irrationally in the judgment of my interviewee, by suing Amnesty as an organization and its secretary-general personally. The criminal court process for defamation before the district court (*Landgericht*) was accompanied by a suit in trade court (*Handelsgericht*) for damages amounting to 200,000–300,000 Euros. The trials, which the company eventually lost, lasted three years and attracted much publicity. "And Glock tried all the time to insist that that is not possible," the secretary-general continued,

> because this pistol was exported to Kuwait and surely did not move on from there. Because they put so much pressure on us, we invested a lot of investigatory energy and were thus able to prove that there is a hunting weapons, that is, a hunting safari, business in Kuwait, with a branch in Sudan, because Sudan is such an attractive hunting ground, and that safari participants were equipped with weapons, and that weapons can also be smuggled along this path. Having been put under such pressure, we thus invested much energy to trace the path and identified one of the, of course, thousands of weapons trade and smuggling routes, where Glock certainly was not the smuggler, but knew full well why that little weapons trader in Kuwait was so interested in such large amounts. There was thus a purely accidental but intensive interest . . . in the human rights situation in Darfur. . . . Research, legal background, . . . also public issue raising, always more under the angle of weapons trade, but also to explain, of course, why this embargo is so important, because the human rights situation in Darfur is so catastrophic. (author's translation)

In short, national sections of INGOs have to be mindful, first, of their domestic government's priorities if they seek to affect government policies and, second, of public sentiments if they hope to mobilize followers and secure donations. While strongly oriented toward the International Secretariat, staff and volunteers at Amnesty's national sections were mindful of specific domestic opportunities and constraints: the government's power position in the international community (e.g., representation on the UNSC); colonial history and the representation of expatriate communities (e.g., the United Kingdom and Sudan); the section's size (number and selectivity of issues addressed); links between local forces, such as industries, and actors in the conflict zone (e.g., the Austrian Glock story); collective memories and a resulting sense of obligation (e.g., memories of the Holocaust and militarism in Germany and Austria); and dominant carrier groups (e.g., churches and humanitarian aid organizations in Germany). Amnesty-USA faces yet a different set of conditions, to which I turn shortly.

CONCLUSIONS

The core of the justice field, especially the ICC, does not fend for itself in the pursuit of criminal justice. Establishing a criminalizing frame through which to interpret the mass violence in Darfur is propelled by a variety of global and national forces in support of the justice cascade (Sikkink 2011). Prominent among global actors are INGOs (Keck and Sikkink 1998). My in-depth analysis of Amnesty International concerning the case of Darfur illustrates this organization's fight to end impunity. Its narrative resembles that of actors in the criminal law and justice field. While Amnesty members also highlight goals such as the establishment of peace and the survival of victims, interviews show how activists rationalize away potential conflicts between the latter goals and the pursuit of justice. They insist that justice, once achieved, will help reach other goals, or even that other goals cannot be reached if justice is not served. Such relative unanimity among my interviewees, despite distinct national backgrounds, supports the recent scholarly focus on globalizing forces in the formation of norms and scripts and their potential effect on local and national practices, for example in research by the World Polity School (e.g., Meyer, Ramirez, and Soysal 1992; Frank, Hironaka, and Schofer 2000; Schofer and Fourcade-Gourinchas 2002).

Yet caution is warranted. Unanimity is only relative. The case of Amnesty shows that—despite its hierarchical organization—conditions within which national sections operate also matter. This finding is in line with recent literature about national contexts of INGO work (Stroup 2012), as well as a long tradition of neo-Weberian scholarship that focuses on nation-specific carrier groups and institutional arrangements (Bendix [1949] 1974; Gorski 2003; Roth 1987; Rueschemeyer 1973; Kalberg 1994, 2014; Savelsberg and King 2005). It is, finally, congruent with recent scholarship that shows how the spread of global norms is filtered through cultural specifics at the local level and through a country's power position within the international community (Boyle 2002; Halliday and Carruthers 2010). Interviews make clear that Amnesty workers within national sections are aware of their government's traditions, interests, and policy foci when they seek to influence government policies. They are also mindful of nation-specific cultural sensitivities and business interests (as in the Austrian Glock case) when they mobilize volunteers and the public and raise funds. Such mindfulness in fact is a precondition for effective work at the local and national levels, even among international NGOs.

My interview with an American Amnesty activist about her organization's functioning in the context of the Save Darfur campaign especially illustrates how Amnesty volunteers, despite the organization's centralized organization, adapt to national environments through organizational and linguistic strategies. This adaptability may be considered a strength or a weakness. In the case of Amnesty it certainly did not weaken the INGO's unifying message as represented in official outlets such as Amnesty-USA websites. These observations should in any case direct our attention to ways in which national sections of INGOs are embedded in and interact with other civil society and government actors in specific national contexts. The United States provides an excellent example in the context of the justice field, as it eventually became a strong supporter of a rights-oriented criminal justice response to the violence in Darfur, despite its objections to the ICC. How did this seeming paradox become possible? The following chapter seeks to provide an answer.

CHAPTER 3

American Mobilization and the Justice Cascade

In addition to civil society groups, and often tightly interwoven with them, state actors contributed to raising awareness of the mass violence in Darfur and contributed to its representation as human rights crimes. One interviewee from a large European country had worked for his foreign ministry's human rights division and represented his country on the ICC's Assembly of States during the period when the UN Security Council referred the Darfur situation to the court. A lawyer by training, he strongly stressed the primacy of human rights concerns ahead of other goals: "You need to give them justice, and once they have the feel that justice, more or less, is taken care of, then I think you can create within such a society a willingness to overcome postconflict and enter a new phase of peace building."

This chapter, on state actors and their linkages to civil society in the human rights field, highlights the case of the United States—among the countries considered here, the most pronounced supporter of a criminalizing response and a strong proponent of the application of the genocide label. After a brief review of the US Save Darfur campaign, a massive mobilization of civil society organizations, I look at American media representations (outliers in international comparison) and discuss government responses. Those responses show how a state–civil society amalgam emerged and made itself unmistakably heard with its intense pursuit of criminalizing definitions of the violence in Darfur.

The American story is particularly interesting as the United States has never ratified the Rome Statute and generally keeps a critical distance from the ICC. William Schabas (2004) in fact writes about "United States hostility to the International Criminal Court" (see also Deitelhoff 2009). Specifically with regard to Darfur, the United States initially displayed considerable resistance against a referral of the Darfur situation to the ICC. Yet, in a surprising and quite radical turn, it eventually embraced a criminalizing strategy and abstained from the UNSC vote on Resolution 1593, thereby allowing the case of Darfur to be referred to the ICC. According to the Security Council minutes:

> ANNE WOODS PATTERSON (United States) said her country strongly supported bringing to justice those responsible for the crimes and atrocities that had occurred in Darfur and ending the climate of impunity there. Violators of international humanitarian law and human rights law must be held accountable. Justice must be served in Darfur. By adopting today's resolution, the international community had established an accountability mechanism for the perpetrators of crimes and atrocities in Darfur. The resolution would refer the situation in Darfur to the International Criminal Court (ICC) for investigation and prosecution. While the United States believed that a better mechanism would have been a hybrid tribunal in Africa, it was important that the international community spoke with one voice in order to help promote effective accountability.[1]

I ask why the US government eventually aligned with a strong civil society movement, despite its refusal to ratify the Rome Statute. In the end, civil society, the federal government, and media alike were international outliers in their determination to articulate the story of Darfur as one of criminal—in fact, genocidal—violence. A closer look at representations that emerged from these American discourses sheds additional light on the nation-specific conditions that color representations of mass atrocities. They include the peculiarities of US civil society, the organization of government in the United States, and its media market. Based on interviews and media data, we shall also see, as we did in chapter 2, that the institutional logic of law still colors representations of mass violence at the periphery of the legal field, albeit in a weakened form compared to that applied at the center. Toward the end of this chapter, in a brief excursus, I examine how the US section of an international rights–based NGO, again Amnesty International, maneuvers within a highly mobilized civil society environment, dominated by Save Darfur, with which it disagreed on a number of positions. What organizational and linguistic strategies did it use to act effectively in this context?

THE SAVE DARFUR MOVEMENT IN THE UNITED STATES

The United States Holocaust Memorial Museum took the lead in the American civil society movement when, in January 2004, it issued a genocide alert on the situation in Darfur. The first, widely publicized media pronouncements articulating the plight of the people of Darfur for a broad public soon followed. Eric Reeves, an English professor at Smith College and one of the leading individual problem entrepreneurs on Darfur, had his famous, trendsetting op-ed published in the *Washington Post* on February 24, 2004, following rejections of previous submissions. One month later, on March 24, the *New York Times* followed with an op-ed by Nicholas Kristof, the first in a series of his contributions on Darfur. A wave of other opinion pieces followed. Deborah Murphy (2007), in counting editorial responses to Darfur by select (prominent) US media in 2004, identifies twelve in April, eight in May, nine in June, sixteen in July, fifteen in August, and nineteen in September.

Following the USHMM's January 2004 genocide alert, the first op-ed pieces, and UN secretary-general Kofi Annan's April 2004 speech on the occasion of the tenth anniversary of the Rwandan genocide, a massive wave of civil society activism unfolded in the United States. It partly preceded, but also accompanied and followed, formal interventions by the UN and the ICC. Most noteworthy, the period between June 2004 and July 2005 witnessed the founding of the Save Darfur Coalition, which eventually brought together almost two hundred organizational members under its umbrella. Prominent among the great variety of groups were Christian evangelical groups, including Christian Solidarity International (CSI), that represented an important constituent bloc for then-president George W. Bush. These conservative groups and churches formed a rare coalition with liberal organizations such as the American Jewish World Service (AJWS); various specialized organizations, including the USHMM and Africa Action, a Washington, DC–based NGO; and mainstream human rights organizations such as Amnesty-USA.

Preceding and advancing the constitution of the Save Darfur coalition, the USHMM organized a July 2004 conference at the City University of New York. There Holocaust survivor and Nobel Peace Prize laureate Eli Wiesel delivered a forceful speech in which he linked the violence in Darfur to the Rwandan genocide. The wave of activism was further spurred by the release of the film *Hotel Rwanda* in September 2004,

FIGURE 6. Save Darfur demonstration in Washington, DC.

which by depicting the Rwandan genocide in Hollywood fashion, helped explicate it for a broad public. About one year after the second peak of the violence in Darfur, in April 2005, Harvard's John F. Kennedy School of Public Policy hosted a largely student-led event on divestment from Sudan. One year later some fifty thousand people gathered on the National Mall in Washington, DC, for an impressive demonstration under the title "Save Darfur: Rally to Stop Genocide." Speakers included Barack Obama, Elie Wiesel, Nancy Pelosi, and celebrities such as George Clooney. Speakers and demonstrators demanded a UN peacekeeping force, better humanitarian access to refugees, adhesion to existing treaties and cease-fire agreements, and a commitment to a lasting peace agreement in the Abuja peace talks. Importantly, they also called for justice to be delivered (see figures 6 and 7). Along the way, activists sought to exert direct influence on the political process, as when Save Darfur leaders met with Deputy Secretary of State Robert Zoellick and organized a "National Call-in Day" on Darfur. And civil society organizations found strong resonance, and reinforcement, in the way American media covered Darfur.

FIGURE 7. Save Darfur demonstration in Washington, DC.

DARFUR IN US MEDIA

The *New York Times* and the *Wall Street Journal* are among America's most prestigious print media; both are mainstream, though the former occupies the left-liberal and the latter the conservative end of the political spectrum. Neither the presidential administration nor Congress would be ignorant of positions taken by these papers. While a more detailed analysis of media is presented in chapters 8 and 9, I here highlight patterns that speak to the special role that US media played, in comparison to media elsewhere in the world, to generate a criminalizing account of the situation in Darfur. Numerous articles and commentaries appeared between 2003 and 2010 in both the *New York Times* and the *Wall Street Journal*. They acknowledged the suffering in Darfur, contributed to framing the violence, and built bridges to past mass atrocities (for details on analytic strategies see the introduction).

Acknowledgment

American media are more likely than those in the other seven countries in the comparison group to acknowledge most forms of victimization.

This applies to all media documents, somewhat to news articles or reports, and decidedly to opinion pieces.[2] Consider the reporting of killings (analyzed separately from natural deaths), of rapes, and of displacements in Darfur. Figure 8 (A–C) shows that the likelihood that American media reports informed readers of killings and, especially, rapes was substantially higher than that for media reports from outside the United States. The same applies, even more strongly, to opinion pieces. Only for displacements do we find only minor differences, partially even a reversal of the pattern observed for the other types of victimization. This should not be surprising as addressing displacements is more in line with a humanitarian emergency and aid frame, as I show in detail in chapter 5.[3]

Framing

Framing, more than acknowledgment, is an interpretive endeavor. Where we find substantial variation in terms of acknowledgment of victimization and suffering, we might expect a wider range in the framing of violence. As in the interviews I conducted, the coding scheme for the analysis of media reports asked about different frames, the presence or absence of which in the articles were to be noted. Frames included rebellion or insurgency, humanitarian emergency, civil war, and criminal violence. Here I report only on the last-named frame as I am concerned with the criminalizing discourse on Darfur.

Figure 9.A shows that US media used the crime frame more often than those of other countries. Yet the difference is remarkable only for opinion pieces. There, where normative and value-based statements are expected, almost 60 percent of editorialists in all papers used the crime frame, whereas about three-quarters of opinion pieces in American media did so. The difference becomes more pronounced for the use of the genocide frame (figure 9.B). While US news reports cited the genocide frame more frequently, the difference more than doubled for opinion pieces.[4]

Bridging

In addition to frame selection, another way of making sense of news events that we otherwise cannot yet interpret is the strategy of bridging. Journalists cite past occurrences on which interpretive clarity has been reached and use them to shed light on current-day events. In the context

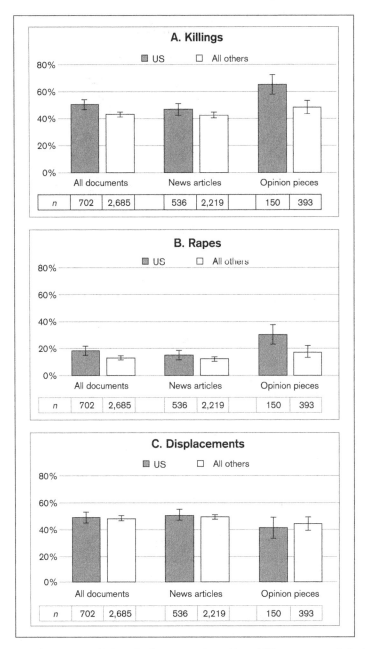

FIGURE 8. Percentage of US media documents that address killings, rapes, and displacements, compared to all other media documents.

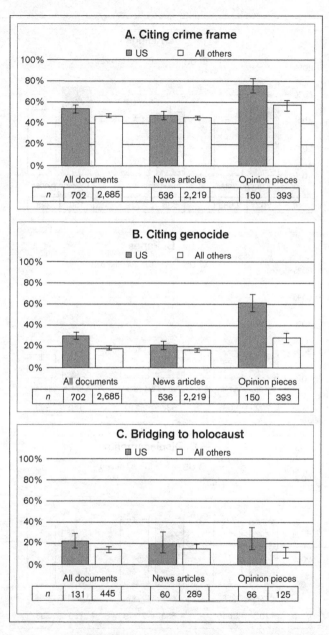

FIGURE 9. Percentage of US media documents citing the crime frame, using the genocide label, and bridging to the Holocaust, compared to all other media documents.

of genocide, the most powerful reference is to the Holocaust. Figure 9.C shows the percentage of news articles that built analogical bridges from the Holocaust to the violence in Darfur. The introduction offers an especially powerful example from the op-ed pieces of renowned *New York Times* journalist Nicholas Kristof, who used terms such as *Lebensraum* and *final solution*. The numbers presented here show that the likelihood that journalists would cite or make such comparisons was more than one-third higher in American news reports than in those from other countries and more than twice as high in opinion pieces.[5] Here we see a strong affinity between frames chosen by American movements focused on Darfur and representations in American media. This linkage between civil society movements and media representations is likely to be enhanced by the relative competitiveness of the US media market (Benson 2013). Under such conditions media organizations keep their eyes on and ears attuned to sentiments of those publics they target as customers. Irrespective of such causal issues, however, data show that American civil society and media were major promoters within the international community of criminalizing the violence in Darfur.

UNITED STATES GOVERNMENT

Given the strength of the Save Darfur movement in the United States, and the substantial support social movements received from media reporting, the US government found itself in a peculiar position within the international community. On the one hand, it had declined to ratify the Rome Statute and in fact fought the creation of the ICC; to this extent, its position to enhance criminal justice intervention against Darfuri actors was weakened. On the other hand, the United States tends to embrace criminalizing frames, domestically and in cases of foreign atrocities, and it was under massive civil society pressure to do so. How did it respond?

Different branches of the US government were certainly receptive to the Darfur-focused movement, which included groups in American society ranging from very conservative to very liberal. The movement was predominantly white, but included passionate involvement of African Americans who identified with those seen as victims of the violence: black Africans. It was thus no surprise when, on June 24, 2004, Representative Donald Payne, Democrat and leading member of the Congressional Black Caucus, joined forces with conservative Republican senator Sam Brownback to introduce a resolution into their respective chambers of Congress. Barely a month later, on July 22, 2004, the House and Senate simultaneously passed a resolution declaring that genocide was occurring in Darfur. In the meantime, on June 30, 2004, Secretary of State Colin Powell returned to Washington from Khartoum, declaring the he did not have the information needed to decide whether the violence constituted genocide. Simultaneously, however, he commissioned a survey to be conducted among Darfuri refugees in camps in Chad, just beyond the border of Sudan and Darfur, to gather appropriate information. A basic analysis of this "Atrocities Documentation Survey," with 1,136 respondents, helped change Powell's position. In a famous hearing before the Senate Foreign Relations Committee, on September 9, 2004, he declared that responses to the survey indicated:

> first, a consistent and widespread pattern of atrocities: killings, rapes, burning of villages committed by Jingaweit [*sic*] and government forces against non-Arab villagers; second, three-fourths of those interviewed reported that the Sudanese military forces were involved in the attacks; third, villages often experienced multiple attacks over a prolonged period before they were destroyed by burning, shelling or bombing, making it impossible for the villagers to return to their villages. This was a coordinated effort, not just random violence. When we reviewed the evidence, . . . I concluded that genocide has been committed in Darfur and that the Government of Sudan and the Jingaweit bear responsibility. . . . We believe the evidence corroborates the specific intent of the perpetrators to destroy 'a group in whole and in part,' the words of the [Genocide] Convention.[6]

A few weeks after Secretary Powell's testimony, President Bush himself declared, in a speech to the UN General Assembly, that genocide was part of the pattern of violence in Darfur.

The US government's rhetoric both followed and promoted the American movement that pushed for intervention in Darfur, for labeling the violence genocide, and for criminal prosecution of those responsible. It thus became a player in the field that placed Darfur in the justice cascade. Again, this is remarkable given the US stance regarding the Rome Statute, on which the ICC is based, the very court to which the UNSC referred the Darfur case. The United States allowed the referral to go forward, despite its objections to the ICC, by abstaining from the vote (together with Algeria, Brazil, and China). Actions of the US government were considerably more cautious, however, than its rhetoric. They included, at the UN, sponsorship of the resolution that created the Commission of Inquiry; support, on August 31, 2006, for a new UN peacekeeping force for Darfur; and—domestically—President Bush's signing into law the Sudan Accountability and Divestment Act on December 31, 2007. This law authorizes local and state governments to divest from Sudan, and excludes companies from federal contracts that operate in Sudan's military, minerals, and oil sectors.[7]

Among the countries I examined, the society-government amalgam in the United States turns out, in cross-national comparison, to have been the strongest force for promoting a crime-focused representation of the Darfur conflict. Specifically, the American narrative privileged the most dramatic depiction of the violence, and its characterization as genocidal, much more than civil societies or governments did in other countries. Three questions arise. Why this forceful amalgam in the case of the United States? Why such as strong movement specifically concerning Darfur? And why did strong representation not translate, in this case, into similarly forceful government action? While I return to country-specific patterns of foreign policy and diplomacy in detail in chapter 7, a brief paragraph on each of these questions is in order here.

First, reasons for the close correspondence between civil society and government rhetoric lie in the nature of American institutions. The boundary between state and society is particularly porous in the United States (Bendix [1949] 1974; Gorski 2003; Roth 1987; Rueschemeyer 1973; Kalberg 2014; Savelsberg and King 2005). Candidates for legislative office are selected via popular vote in primary elections; the head of the executive branch is elected in a general election; and even many officeholders in the judiciary branch are elected. As a consequence, wherever strong mobilization occurs among civil society groups, especially among constituents of the current administration, the administration and the Congress are likely to be attentive to their demands. And exactly this situation occurred in the case in Darfur. Also the role of media (as a branch of civil society) in the United States is exceptional. Journalism scholarship applies the term *media-politics complex* to the US, alluding to especially close ties between media and politics; these scholars stress that "the experiences of other countries have been significantly different from the experience of the United States" (Mazzoleni and Schulz 1999:258). In addition, news media are driven more strongly by competitive pressures in the US than elsewhere (Benson 2013). Consequently, they seek alignment with market forces and target groups. A strong civil society movement, encompassing several sectors of society and including a diverse ideological spectrum, is thus likely to leave its traces in media reporting—and especially media commentary—and government actors better listen up or pay a political price.

Second, the strong American mobilization specifically in the Darfur case is remarkable. Such a response can never be taken for granted when genocide or other mass atrocities occur (Power 2002). In this particular case, however, it resulted from a combination of forces. First among them was the strong representation issuing from specific carrier groups, the crucial contributors to national patterns of knowledge formation to which Max Weber (2009) and Karl Mannheim (1952) alert us in their classic works (see also Kalberg 1994). In the American Darfur mobilization, influential carrier groups included, first, conservative evangelical Christians, a highly mobilized and well-represented constituency for President Bush. Evangelicals had been most active in missionary work in the southern part of Sudan (today South Sudan) when they learned about mass violence in Darfur. When the violence was initially misrepresented as perpetrated by Arabs against Christians, these religious groups spoke up, and the Bush administration listened. Second, once the specter of genocide was raised, Jewish groups became engaged in the cause of Darfur. The USHMM and the AJWS played crucial roles. Further, once victims of the conflict were identified as black, African Americans and the Congressional Black Caucus mobilized. Finally, as public representations now depicted "Arabs" or "Muslims" as perpetrators, it was easy for broad segments of post–September 11 American society having anti-Arab or anti-Muslim sentiments to sympathize with the message of the Save Darfur movement. Such mobilization of carrier groups on behalf of Darfur interacted with particular cultural features of US society: a preference for black-and-white depictions of conflicts and an associated punitive orientation toward perpetrators (Whitman 2005), a savior identity in world affairs (Savelsberg and King 2011), and a dominant progressive narrative (Alexander 2004a). Thus, the availability of mobilized, well-organized carrier groups and a conglomerate of cultural features (explored in previous scholarship) help explain the amalgam of forceful state-society representations of mass violence in the case of Darfur as we observed it for the United States.

Third, there were multiple reasons why the US government, despite intense American rhetoric, did not more aggressively pursue the case of Darfur in its actions. These factors include, first, the growing skepticism toward military engagement abroad that began to grow among the American public after the costly and much debated interventions in Afghanistan and especially Iraq. Government actors were also concerned with the country's increasingly thin-stretched military capacities. In addition, the US government sought cooperation from the Sudanese government in its fight against al Qaida terrorism. To secure such cooperation, it was even willing to temporarily downgrade its rhetoric and lower its estimates of the death toll in Darfur as Hagan and Rymond-Richmond (2008) show. The American administration had also been a strong force in the Comprehensive Peace Agreement between North and South Sudan, and many diplomats likely saw cooperation on the part of the al-Bashir regime as a necessary condition for its implementation. Finally, social movements can at times be easily pacified by symbolic government actions, such as those the US administration and Congress delivered.

EXCURSUS: AMNESTY AND SAVE DARFUR—STRATEGIES OF GLOBAL ACTORS IN NATIONAL CONTEXTS

Within the massive Save Darfur movement, Amnesty-USA had to find its place without disconnecting from the principles of the international organization, its many other national sections, and its headquarters in London. My interview with an American Amnesty activist, volunteer, and coordinator of the US Darfur campaign, revealed organizational and linguistic strategies that helped the national section navigate between its international obligations and its domestic environment:

> Amnesty International wanted a Darfur coordinator. . . . I volunteered to do this, but I recognized that there was a lot more with this than report to the group what Amnesty was doing and have them sign letters. I saw what the interests were of the group members. Somebody was very interested in violence against women, so I connected that [Darfur] to violence against women in armed conflict. . . . I created a yearlong panel series on violence against women in armed conflicts. . . . And it was very successful. I got funding from Amnesty. This was all as a volunteer.

In addition to strategies to broaden the campaign and bring it in line with diverse strains of American civil society engagement, Amnesty activists had to manage divergences between Save Darfur and Amnesty-USA strategies. One example is Save Darfur's demands for divestment, a method Amnesty did not support. One interviewee described organizational strategies to circumvent such conflict: "I saw an opportunity to marry two strains of activism, to keep Amnesty current and to bring people into the fold that wanted to work with Amnesty but couldn't because they supported divestment and Amnesty didn't. So I created an economic activism campaign, centered on the oil industry. So that way, people who wanted to do Amnesty, and who were interested in divestment . . . could do stock- and stakeholder engagement. It gave them a way to try to impact the oil industry."

Such organizational inventiveness, a skilled effort to maneuver between American activism and international, centralized Amnesty, is supplemented by linguistic strategies. Again, a conflict had to be resolved, in this case conflict over language. The Save Darfur movement insisted on calling the violence in Darfur genocide, a position Amnesty rejected. In the words of the volunteer interviewee: "I had to work with a lot of people who thought we should . . . call it a genocide. I spoke to a lot of groups, gave a lot of talks. And I would always say, whether you call it genocide or crimes against humanity, we know there were mass atrocities, and that the government is targeting its own civilians. And whatever we want to call it, the response is the same."

Working in the context of the larger US movement, Amnesty activists thus became organizationally and linguistically innovative. This allowed them to operate effectively in the United States—another illustration of the fact that national conditions matter even within INGOs, and an observation in support of Stroup's (2012) findings about the weight of national contexts in INGO work.[8] But these adaptive strategies also show that contradictions between international and national positions can be managed. It also matters, of course, that Amnesty-USA is Amnesty's largest national section. Activists are aware of the fact that Amnesty-USA's size provides them with strength within the larger organization despite the formal leadership of the International Secretariat. "Well, the US section is the largest," one respondent said. "I was in Amsterdam for a meeting of different sections that were working on Sudan. And I was learning that European sections were coming to the US website and using our materials. . . . The reason I bring this up is that the US section was driving more of the Darfur campaign. We wanted more. We wanted to be doing more. We wanted to push the envelope. [JJS: "More than the International Secretariat?"] Yeah. Yeah." This comment is significant as it illustrates how activists within a national section do not just have to engage in organizational and linguistic maneuvers between contending forces in their home country, vis-à-vis the discipline demanded by their international headquarters. To bridge the gap, they may actually seek to pull the INGO over to their national campaign strategy, at least when representing a powerful country such as the United States. And yet the effect of such strategies is limited. National sections continue to be bound by the organization's agenda as defined, in the case of Amnesty, by the International Secretariat.

Interested in the effects this tug-of-war between national movements and INGOs has on the representation of Darfur, I worked with two students at the University of Minnesota, Meghan Zacher and Hollie Nyseth

Brehm, to analyze the websites of Save Darfur and Amnesty-USA.[9] Methodological and substantive details of this study are reported elsewhere (Zacher, Nyseth Brehm, and Savelsberg 2014; see also note 4);[10] a summary of findings suffices here. Our analysis of websites shows that representations of the Darfur conflict, as part of a broad-based American civil society campaign, did differ between Amnesty-USA and Save Darfur. Amnesty's website engaged in a more detailed depiction of different types of victimization. The pages displayed rapes much more frequently than Save Darfur and, somewhat more often, killings and the destruction of livelihood through looting, burning villages and crops, and poisoning water sources. Amnesty webpages also referred more often to categories of international criminal law, depicting the violence as a violation of international humanitarian law and human rights. Save Darfur web entries, on the other hand, used simpler and more dramatic vocabulary. Instead of specifying types of crimes, they more often simply referred to what had occurred as "criminal violence" (85% compared to Amnesty's 31%). Most important, while Amnesty-USA web entries almost completely avoid reference to genocide, in line with the international organization's policy, Save Darfur sites—in line with the central message of the campaign—insist on calling the violence just that: genocide (more than 70% of all Save Darfur entries).

In one respect, however, Amnesty-USA (in line with the International Secretariat's policy) and Save Darfur agree. Both urge interventions by the ICC. Even if such support is explicated somewhat more frequently on Save Darfur sites (35%), it certainly appears prominently on Amnesty-USA sites as well (25%). On February 1, 2005, after the delivery of the Commission of Inquiry report to the UN Security Council, executive director of Amnesty-USA Dr. William F. Schulz was quoted as saying: "Given the scale and sheer horror of the human rights abuses in Darfur, anything less than immediate action on the report's findings would be a travesty for the people of Darfur. The International Criminal Court should be given jurisdiction to prosecute war crimes and crimes against humanity that have taken place in Sudan."[11] In the United States such a demand is backed by Save Darfur, the movement within which Amnesty-USA was one among almost two hundred constituent organizations. For instance, in an article written on April 27, 2007, the day on which an arrest warrant was issued against Ahmed Harun and Ali Kushayb, two leading perpetrators in Darfur, Save Darfur's executive director stated, "We welcome the ICC's continued efforts to ensure accountability for the genocide in Darfur. This important step by the court sends yet another message to the government

FIGURE 10. Naomi Natale's artistic rendering of genocidal violence, mounted by the One Million Bones project in Washington, DC, June 2013. This photo appeared on Save Darfur's website.

of Sudan that the international community will bring to justice those responsible for these horrendous crimes."[12] Clear statements were accompanied by massive demonstrations and demands for justice. They also spurred artistic depictions, which appeared on the websites of movement organizations (see figure 10).

In short, while interview statements illustrate how activists of national sections of INGOs (here Amnesty-USA) seek to build organizational and linguistic bridges to domestic political movements (Save Darfur in our case), public representations of massive violence as displayed on websites of the national section remain distinct from national contexts and in line with the INGO's central policies. With regard to the perceived necessity of ICC interventions, however, both organizations agree: they strongly advocate criminal justice intervention by the International Criminal Court against those responsible for the mass violence in Darfur. In their general assessment of the situation—as a campaign of criminal, indeed genocidal, violence or as war crimes and crimes against humanity respectively—and in the conclusions drawn for judicial intervention, NGOs in the United States aligned closely with other segments of American civil society, as our media analysis documented. And they shaped the rhetoric of the US government.

CONCLUSIONS REGARDING THE PERIPHERY OF THE JUSTICE FIELD

Clearly, in the United States, civil society and government stood out in international comparison as both sought to advance a criminalizing frame for Darfur and a definition of the violence as genocide. This does not mean, as we have seen, that rhetoric necessarily translates into action. Obviously the Clinton administration was mistaken when it refused to identify the 1994 violence in Rwanda as genocide, fearing that such a label would necessarily prompt military intervention. The George W. Bush administration proved this assumption wrong in the case of Darfur. It spoke loudly about genocide but refused to intervene decisively. Further, despite the rather forceful mobilization and rhetoric in the Darfur case, the world cannot always rely on the United States and American civil society when mass atrocities are being committed. As discussed above, the American response to Darfur was characterized by a particular constellation of societal and cultural conditions. It contrasts with the silence shown in many other cases, such as the long-lasting lack of public and governmental attention to the long and painful history of the Democratic Republic of Congo with its fractured lines of conflict. More extreme are cases, such as those in Guatemala, in which American civil society long failed to react to massive human rights violations and genocidal violence abroad despite the US government's own contributions to their execution.

Despite noting gaps between rhetoric and practice, and even instances of massive cynicism, this chapter shares one essential finding with the preceding ones. It shows how the entire justice field, both core and periphery, including international judicial institutions, rights-oriented INGOs, civil society movements, and supportive governments, contributes to a representation of the mass violence of Darfur that deviates radically from those of comparable situations in past centuries and millennia. The emerging narrative depicts those responsible for mass violence as criminal perpetrators and their actions as crimes. This narrative has moved us far from eras in which leaders of violent campaigns were celebrated as heroes (Giesen 2004b). In addition, this new narrative and its construction across national boundaries opens the eyes of the public to the suffering of victims. It supports Jenness's (2004:160) contention that criminalization processes in late modernity reflect an "institutionalization that involves the diffusion of social forms and practices across polities comprising an interstate system." In Darfur and in other cases like it, global actors, here especially the UNSC and the ICC, play a central role in this diffusion process.

Finally, the justice narrative has at least the potential of ingraining in the global collective conscience the notion of mass violence as evil, through a process described in recent work on collective memory (Bass 2000; Osiel 1997; Levy and Sznaider 2010) and its classical predecessors (Durkheim [1912] 2001; Halbwachs 1992). That representations of mass violence adapt to national context may be considered a disadvantage by some; others may regard it as advantageous, as global movements always concretize in local contexts, succeeding only if they adjust to local conditions. The story of Amnesty International in the US context is a case in point. An earlier word of caution bears repeating, though. By creating criminalizing narratives, the justice field buys into the limits imposed by the institutional logic of the criminal law. The resulting account, neglecting structural conditions and historical roots, may be too limited a foundation for long-term policies that can prevent mass violence and genocide. Then again, the criminal justice field is not the only representational force. Its narrative faces other, conflicting ones, narratives to which I now turn.

PART TWO

Aid versus Justice

The Humanitarian Field

CHAPTER 4

The Humanitarian Aid Field and Doctors Without Borders

The human rights field is not alone when it takes positions on mass violence. Other, often more powerful actors have vested interests in situations and places in which such violence occurs. Among them are national governments with geostrategic ambitions and corporations seeking profit. Since 2013, the blockade by at least one permanent member of the UN Security Council against decisive intervention in the Assad regime's horrendous violence in Syria has provided a particularly striking, but not at all uncommon, example. Accordingly, narratives generated by governments and corporations frequently clash with human rights representations. At other times, these actors may use human rights rhetoric to disguise their pursuit of altogether different agendas.

In this and the following chapter I focus on just one potential competitor the human rights field has to contend with in its struggle for binding representations of mass violence: humanitarian aid. This field has grown immensely in recent decades as budgets for humanitarian relief, at US$2.1 billion in 1990 rose to US$12.9 billion in 2012 (Krause 2014:3). I ask what representations this field contributes to the world's understanding of Darfur, and how those representations relate to actions and representations proposed by the human rights sector. In Darfur, aid-oriented NGOs such as CARE (Cooperative for Assistance and Relief Everywhere) and Oxfam (Oxford Committee for Famine Relief) were well represented. In the perhaps hyperbolic words of one interviewee, staff of a humanitarian aid INGO, Darfur is the story of the "largest-scale humanitarian intervention that the world has ever seen. . . . There were like ten thousand aid workers, like a thousand international aid workers, which is unheard of—in the Sudanese context, at least."

In this chapter I provide an in-depth analysis of the role of one particular aid-oriented INGO, Médecins Sans Frontières (MSF, or Doctors Without Borders), in the representation of Darfur. In the following chapter, I examine the role of one country that shows great affinities with the humanitarian narrative. Just as the United States took that place in the context of the human rights narrative, Ireland played a comparable role with regard to humanitarian aid-colored representations.[1]

Humanitarian aid INGOs share all the features discussed regarding NGOs in chapter 2. They too are part of a global civil society, members of the transnational activist networks (TAN) that Keck and Sikkink (1998) discussed in their pathbreaking work, and contributors to global scripts, in the terms of the World Polity School (e.g., Meyer, Ramirez, and Soysal 1992; Frank, Hironaka, and Schofer 2000). And their contributions reflect organizational interests, to which the constructivist tradition alerts us, just as they operate within national contexts, the impact of which Stroup (2012) spells out.

Yet, despite such commonalities with rights INGOs, humanitarian aid organizations occupy a distinct field. This field is engaged in a project in which agencies provide relief for a market where donors are the consumers and the beneficiaries become "part of a commodity" (Krause 2014:4). Simultaneously, the humanitarian field is exposed to a body of international law that rules humanitarian action and for which the Geneva Convention is but one example. The field is further governed by a set of nonlegal norms, among which impartiality toward the conflicting parties and commitment to the delivery of aid to civilians stand out. In terms of social actors, this field includes a range of humanitarian organizations that coordinate the distribution of aid—and that do not typically interact with human rights NGOs. The social field of humanitarian NGOs almost always includes government actors from the very countries in which mass violence unfolds. These governments, their rulers, and front-line agents may in fact be accused by human rights NGOs for grave human rights violations and charged by international courts with human rights crimes. In the words of one of my interviewees who spoke about his work in Sudan: "I then was head of missions . . . in Sudan, based in Khartoum, which means more of the overall management of the humanitarian projects—and their representation, negotiation with the government and other actors. . . . You negotiate with representatives of the government in order to secure the delivery of services, to have permission to have international staff in Darfur, and for the particular services as well."

In light of such particularities of the aid-oriented NGO field, and in line with Pierre Bourdieu's arguments about the impact of the structure of fields on the knowledge of its participant actors, we should expect representations of mass violence to differ markedly between humanitarian aid and human rights INGOs. In particular, we should expect different definitions of the situation in Darfur, distinct narratives of the mass violence. We should also expect conflicts over appropriate representations within the world of INGOs and within the TANs in which they are embedded.

Conflicts are likely aggravated by the distinct professional and occupational groups that dominate in human rights versus humanitarian aid fields. The dominant position of lawyers in the former and of physicians and other aid workers in the latter will almost certainly intensify divergent perspectives.[2] This expectation is supported by John Hagan, Heather Schoenfeld, and Alberto Palloni (2006) in their work on mortality estimates in Darfur. They find massive differences in estimated mortality rates between public health researchers on the one hand and scholars representing a criminological perspective on the other. Estimates by the latter are substantially higher, as they are not limited to deaths from problematic health conditions in refugee and displaced-person camps, but decidedly incorporate the number of deaths that directly result from violent acts in towns, villages, and the countryside. More generally, actors in the aid field are reluctant to use the crime frame and instead apply a language of "complex humanitarian emergencies." This assessment by Hagan, Schoenfeld, and Palloni is supported by patterns Alex de Waal (1997) identified in his description—for Africa—of a complex of humanitarian NGOs and relief agencies that often engage in a consequential "strategic embrace" with the very states that commit human rights crimes.

The following sections first provide a brief overview of the history and organization of MSF, an aid-oriented NGO, but one that distinguishes itself somewhat from other aid organizations by including in its mission the duty to bear witness. Both its commonality with other aid NGOs and its distinctiveness are reflected in the organization's goals, the tensions within MSF, and especially, conflicts between MSF and other organizations. And both commonalities and distinctiveness color the particular types of representations that emerge, the depiction of which constitutes the core of this chapter. I finally offer a brief comparison of representations by MSF-USA with those by two rights-oriented American NGOs, thus controlling for national context. Addressing the weight of national contexts more generally leads in chapter 5 to an analysis of Ireland, the most decidedly aid-oriented country among the eight countries under investigation.

THE CASE OF MSF: PRINCIPLES, ENGAGEMENT IN DARFUR, AND REPRESENTATIONS

In 1971 a group of French physicians responded to the long-standing policy of the International Committee of the Red Cross (ICRC) not to publicize government abuses of civilian populations in order to secure access to the field and to allow for the delivery of aid. Providing aid had, after all, been the ICRC's primary purpose for a century, and with its policies the Red Cross paid its dues to a field in which violent regimes always had to be accounted for. In this the ICRC, up to the present, resembles most closely the ideal type of aid-oriented NGO. The price to be paid for such neutrality became painfully clear on several occasions. One low point in the ICRC's history was its 1944 visit and "inspection" of the Nazi concentration camp of Terezin in today's Czech Republic, then in German-occupied Czechoslovakia. Instead of investigating the concentration camp system as a whole and publically displaying the inhumanity of the Nazi system, the ICRC allowed itself to be instrumentalized by the SS for legitimatory purposes. The ICRC visit at Terezin provided the Nazis with the opportunity to stage a model ghetto, carefully prepared for the occasion with clean facilities, cultural events, and cheering crowds at soccer matches. After World War II, the Red Cross stuck to its definition of neutrality by insisting on the delivery of medical and aid services to suffering populations, even if that meant keeping quiet about the horrors governments imposed on peoples under their rule.[3]

It was during the murderous 1967–1970 civil war in Biafra in southeastern Nigeria that resistance against the dominant policy of silence emerged from within the ICRC. A small group of young French physicians, clinicians, and nurses, many of them leftist activists of the 1960s, had signed up to conduct medical work in this war-torn region of Nigeria. Resenting the ICRC's restrictions on publicizing atrocities and its insistence on maintaining neutrality, they joined together with journalists to work toward an alternative form of organizing and engaging in aid delivery. According to MSF's self-presentation of its origins:

> [Max] Recamier and [Bernard] Kouchner [members of the French group of physicians in Biafra] believed the world needed to know about the events they were witnessing: civilians being murdered and starved by blockading forces. They openly criticized the Nigerian government and the Red Cross for their seemingly complicit behavior. In the following three years, other doctors began to speak up. These doctors, or "Biafrans," as they were known, began to lay the foundations for a new and questioning form of humanitarianism that would ignore political or religious boundaries and prioritize the welfare of those suffering.[4]

Consequently, in December 1971 this group of physicians founded a new organization, Médecins Sans Frontières. MSF initially consisted of a rather loosely organized group of some three hundred volunteers, doctors, nurses, and other staff who were willing to simultaneously risk their lives in dangerous settings in order to provide medical help and bear witness to the horrors they observed. In subsequent years the organization became increasingly professionalized, especially after a formal decision to do so in 1979.[5] For twelve years after this fateful decision, MSF continued to grow under the presidency of Rony Brauman. According to its 2014 website, since 1980 it has opened "offices in 28 countries and employs more than 30,000 people across the world. Since its founding, MSF has treated over a hundred million patients—with 8.3 million outpatient consultations carried out in 2012 alone."[6] In 1999 the organization was awarded the Nobel Peace Prize. Clearly, MSF had grown to become one of the world's most prominent humanitarian aid NGOs.

Internationalization accompanied formalization and professionalization. MSF grew beyond its country of origin to mutate into an INGO. Returning MSF volunteers began opening chapters in their home countries, specifically in Belgium, Holland, Spain, and Switzerland. While these (operational) sections today run programs around the globe, sections in many other countries engage in the recruitment of volunteers and in fund-raising.[7] An international secretariat, MSF International, links these sections and coordinates their activity. And, while each section enjoys a substantial degree of autonomy, Stroup (2012), in her study on borders among activists, nevertheless finds that the entire organization is shaped by organizational principles that reflect its origins. Like other French NGOs, MSF is almost entirely funded by private donations (about half from France). It maintains a *relatively* low degree of professionalization, despite the changes of the 1980s and following decades, compared to other humanitarian NGOs such as CARE or Oxfam. Volunteers provide much of the work in section offices and in the field alike. And MSF displays a preference for outsider advocacy (movement protest strategies), rather than direct communication with government officials. The national origin of the founding organization thus continues to matter after its mutation into an INGO.

Guiding Principles, Goals, and Conflicts

Members of all MSF sections subscribe to the organization's guiding principles, enunciated on its website:

> Médecins Sans Frontières provides assistance to populations in distress, to victims of natural or man-made disasters and to victims of armed conflict. They do so irrespective of race, religion, creed or political convictions. Médecins Sans Frontières observes neutrality and impartiality in the name of universal medical ethics and the right to humanitarian assistance and claims full and unhindered freedom in the exercise of its functions. Members undertake to respect their professional code of ethics and to maintain complete independence from all political, economic, or religious powers.[8]

Clearly, the delivery of aid is the primary mission of MSF. Yet the organization distinguishes itself from other aid NGOs as its neutrality does not require silence. James Orbinsky, then president of the MSF International Council, expressed the difference in his 1999 speech accepting the Nobel Peace Prize on the organization's behalf: "Silence has long been confused with neutrality, and has been presented as a necessary condition for humanitarian action. From its beginning, MSF was created in opposition to this assumption. . . . We are not sure that words can always save lives, but we know that silence can certainly kill." The French word for the program of bearing witness is *témoignage*. This form of witnessing is closely linked with humanitarian work in the field.

And this is the distinguishing feature of MSF among aid-oriented INGOs: the simultaneous pursuit of the goals of delivering aid and bearing witness. Such simultaneity, not surprisingly, generates conflict within the organization, and in the course of its history the pendulum has swung several times between the aid pole and the witnessing pole. In addition, conflict has plagued MSF over the purposes that bearing witness should serve. Should it encourage or legitimize "humanitarian intervention" by military means for the protection of civilian populations, criminal prosecution of perpetrators of violence, or something altogether different?

Fabrice Weissman (2011) of MSF-France provides a minute insider's view of these tensions between and shifts in MSF's positions. A brief journey through this tormented history sets the stage for a detailed analysis of MSF's place vis-à-vis the Darfur conflict.

By the late 1970s, MSF, not quite a decade old, had fully committed itself to speaking out. MSF's director announced in 1978 that staff would be "reporting human rights violations and unacceptable events they witnessed to the bureau. . . . The bureau will then make an executive decision on whether to inform the public, in cases in which MSF was the sole witness" (cited in Weissman 2011:178). In 1979 and 1980 MSF leadership organized and actively participated in demonstrations at the Thai-Cambodian border against inhumane policies of the pro-Vietnamese Cambodian government. The demonstrators sought to publically display the Cambodian government's opposition to the independent distribution of food and aid in its country. In the 1980s, in a broader shift toward taking political positions, MSF leaders (especially the French section) demanded a redoubling of efforts among liberal democracies against human rights abuses in Communist countries. Elsewhere MSF spoke out when it witnessed humanitarian aid contributing to criminal governmental violence and found food distribution centers becoming traps for help seekers. Ethiopia during the great famine of 1985 was a case in point when the government distributed help exclusively to those willing to be resettled, thereby isolating rebels in the north of the country. MSF was expelled from the country following this campaign of *témoignage*.

The 1990s saw the need for aid shift from refugee camps to conflict zones. Large-scale projects that required the consent of several belligerents became more common generally and in the work of MSF specifically. Somalia and Liberia are examples, while countries such as Iraq, Myanmar, and Sudan were generally opposed to interventions by western NGOs. As the UN, in this new context, increasingly authorized the use of military force to secure aid operations, MSF critiqued the international community's limiting the use of such forces to humanitarian purposes. The terms *band aids* for victims and *humanitarian alibi* were first uttered in 1991 in response to "Operation Provide Comfort" in Iraq, where an international military intervention by US and French forces provided several dozen NGOs, including MSF, an opportunity to participate in the repatriation and aid programs for displaced Shiite and Kurdish populations. Later, in the Bosnian civil war, MSF conducted surveys among war refugees and eventually joined "neo-conservatives and liberal internationalists" to demand "that western governments conduct war against oppressive regimes rather than protect relief operations" (Weissman 2011:186).

But the world in which MSF functioned changed, especially in the years after the Rwandan genocide. The number of international military interventions grew, including those in Kosovo, East Timor, and Sierra Leone, followed by US attacks in Afghanistan in 2001 and Iraq in 2003. UN forces became the second largest army operating in foreign countries. UN secretary-general Kofi Annan was among many who strongly supported both a new doctrine of intervention ("responsibility to protect," or R2P) and new international institutions of criminal justice, especially the ICC. This altered environment created new concerns within MSF. The organization declared neutrality as its guiding principle in situations in which international forces were involved, and it challenged the notion of "humanitarian war." MSF was now concerned that its contributions to "exposing war crimes and misappropriations or obstruction of humanitarian assistance . . . may have been encouraging the use of international military or legal measures against the perpetrators" (Weissman 2011:192). Specifically with regard to international criminal justice interventions, important factions within MSF feared that ICC policies would convince perpetrators of war crimes, humanitarian crimes, and genocide to remove humanitarian organizations from areas of violent conflict—"especially since the [ICC] prosecutor and the NGOs supporting his actions called explicitly for humanitarian organizations to provide information to help him determine the appropriateness of launching an investigation and prepare the cases. And coupled with this controversy was a fierce debate on the political virtues of the international criminal justice system" (Weissman 2011:192). A conflict between MSF, primarily a humanitarian aid INGO despite its mission of bearing witness, and the human rights and judicial fields was thus programmed, and it was to play itself out in the context of Darfur by affecting MSF's representations of the mass violence.

Aid Delivery and Témoignage in Darfur: Between Principles and Pragmatism

Early in 2004, at the peak of the second major wave of mass atrocities, MSF had only a dozen workers on the ground in Darfur, providing basic assistance to some sixty-five thousand people. This was not even 1 percent of the population the UN estimated to be in great need of help at that point. MSF thus decided to speak out in order to increase international awareness of the suffering. The organization added its voice to a growing wave of international pressure exerted on the government of Sudan by NGOs, the UN, and various other governments. Specifically, MSF-France became engaged, producing a retrospective mortality survey in the internally displaced person (IDP) camps. The authors concluded that several thousand people, or 4 to 5 percent of the original population of attacked villages, had been killed during massacres. MSF thus became the first INGO to challenge the government of Sudan's insistence that no massacres had been committed.

The joint pressure on the Sudan government by a multitude of organizations was in fact followed by a substantial decline in violence by the summer of 2004. By the winter of 2004 some 13,000 humanitarian workers, 900 of them international, were deployed by INGOs and UN agencies. Out of these, some 200 MSF expatriate volunteers served about 600,000 people in twenty-five projects. These efforts yielded substantial success. By early 2005 the mortality and malnutrition rate in the IDP camps was below the emergency threshold (Weissman 2011:193).

Despite this success inner tension within MSF continued. On the one hand, MSF rejected the notion that genocide had occurred. MSF-France president Jean-Hervé Bradol even used the words "propagandistic distortions" (quoted in Weissman 2011:195). On the other hand, other sections, especially MSF-Holland, were not opposed to dramatizing the situation. Its operations director declared his dissatisfaction with the aid-only approach, and Nicholas Kristof, picking up on his critique, castigated the aid-only approach in the *New York Times* as an "aid effort [that] is sustaining victims so they can be killed with full stomachs" (quoted in Weissman 2011:195). In March 2005, the Dutch section published a report that documented some five hundred cases of rape committed in the context of "ethnic cleansing" campaigns and that demanded an end to impunity. This report preceded by just a few weeks the UNSC's decision to refer the case of Darfur to the ICC. But MSF had a price to pay, especially after the report was cited by Kofi Annan before the UN General Assembly. In the words of one interlocutor: "This report ["Crushing Burden of Rape"] probably would not have attracted any attention had Kofi Annan not quoted from it on World Women's Day, March 9, 2005, . . . in a speech before the General Assembly. Through that the report immediately found widespread attention. Our head of mission and deputy head of mission were arrested shortly thereafter and interrogated by the Sudanese authorities. They were then locked up for several days because of this report" (author's translation).

The price to be paid by MSF was to increase in 2009 when the French and Dutch sections were expelled from Sudan just after President al-Bashir was indicted by the ICC. The government of Sudan accused them of breaking the principle of neutrality and collaborating with the ICC and in fact providing it with evidence. Later the Swiss section withdrew from Darfur.

Fabrice Weissman summarizes MSF's compromise position and the lessons drawn from the Darfur experience:

> Afraid of being seen as a stake-holder in legal or military processes, and thus compromise its access to conflict zones, it [MSF] tends to let other international actors speak for it, hoping to distinguish itself as the language police by tracking down misuses of humanitarian semantics. . . . If it wants to offer impartial, effective aid, MSF must distance itself equally from the liberal imperialism of the societies of its origins and the despotism of many of the countries where it intervenes. Experience has shown that it can only succeed with the support of political and diplomatic coalitions of convenience, rallied through an engagement in the public space, without which humanitarianism is only a passive instrument in the service of power (Weissman 2011:196–197).

Clearly, MSF takes a particular position in the humanitarian field. Different from organizations such as CARE, it insists on independence from states and avoids what Bourdieu would call, in the tradition of Durkheimian sociology, pollution of its very principles. It also keeps a distance from religious fields, unlike the Irish aid organizations discussed in the following chapter. Its *témoignage* principle helps it maintain independence from host countries such as Sudan, but it moves the organization closer to nonstate political actors, potentially exposing it to "movement pollution" (Krause 2014:112–113). Conflicts between *témoignage* and functional pressures of aid delivery result in internal struggles and occasional shifts in emphasis. Cultural anthropologist Peter Redfield (2013), after extensive field research with MSF, indeed finds "an internal culture of reflection, debate and critique" (36; see also Bortolotti 2010). MSF's position as a player in the humanitarian aid field and its particularities within that field should be reflected in the minds of its actors when they speak about Darfur, and it should color their narratives of the violence. I expect greater caution than among human rights NGOs, but more outspokenness than found in narratives of other aid NGOs.

VIEWS FROM THE FIELD: INTERVIEWS AND DATA

How, then, are the statements of purpose cited above and the conflicts between *témoignage* and delivering aid reflected in the minds of MSF workers? What strategies do they find useful in dealing with them? Finally, what representations of the Darfur conflict grow out of this field? How do they reflect the habitus of those who occupy it?

During my travels across Europe and North America I conducted interviews with eight MSF staff members in five countries, supplementing the statistical analysis of the MSF-USA website and those of other American NGOs. I approached the different sections and inquired about staff with particular expertise on Darfur. In some cases I contacted specific individuals who had been recommended by staff in other sections. A noticeable caution among MSF workers was associated with a relatively high rejection rate in response to requests for interviews, higher, for example, than among Amnesty activists. Several who declined interview requests referenced the sensitive situation in Darfur.[9] This is not surprising given the history of arrests and kidnappings of MSF workers in Sudan, the expulsion and withdrawal of three of MSF's five operational sections, and the continuing work of two sections in the field of Darfur.

Those who did agree to be interviewed were of diverse professional background: two staff with medical degrees and one with some medical training; one lawyer who specializes in international law, with degrees also in philosophy and development; one activist who had abandoned legal training and switched to political science with a focus on African studies; one political scientist with a degree in history; one staff member with journalism training; and one with an engineering degree and some training in management and journalism. The interviewees' positions within MSF also differed. Most respondents had experienced a variety of placements in the course of their MSF careers: a former long-term president of his section, now a researcher and consultant; an MSF project coordinator, previously a field coordinator in Khartoum; one project manager in an operational center; a previous head of mission in Sudan, now a project supervisor; one general director of a national section; one program manager; one head of personnel affairs in his section; and one manager for medical and humanitarian communication who had previously served as a press officer. All but two had experienced deployments in Sudan. In terms of national affiliation, three interviewees were located in the Paris office, one in Geneva, one each in London and Vienna, and two in the US office in New York City. In three cases the interviewee's nationality differed from that of the section for which she or he worked.

GOALS AND GOAL CONFLICTS AS EXPERIENCED AT THE FRONT LINES

Not surprisingly, all MSF respondents, when asked about four potentially competing goals to be pursued in Darfur (i.e., aid, justice, peace, state sovereignty), highlighted—or at least included—the delivery of aid or humanitarian assistance; or they used some other wording to describe this central mission of an aid-oriented NGO. One interviewee urged "modesty": "Our priorities were clearly to be able to provide, to respond to those needs, to do so in a relevant, evidently independent way, with the goal of alleviating some of the suffering." Another respondent also focused on alleviating suffering but stressed that this goal may be reached through aid delivery and also through bearing witness: "For me the goal would be first and foremost to help the largest part of the population to survive the war. This means humanitarian assistance, but this also means pressure on the government not to unleash its army or its militias as it did in 2003 and 2004." To this respondent the missions to exert pressure by bearing witness and to secure survival did not appear contradictory. Pressure on governments, for example, by publicizing atrocities, may in fact be a precondition for the delivery of aid. Another interviewee who acknowledged the tension between diverse goals argued that securing survival may be a precondition for justice at some later point:

> As a humanitarian organization we are not pacifists. And we sort of take for granted that wars will erupt. But that people should not pay with their lives. Civilians and non-combatants should not pay with their lives when there is a breakdown in the political process that leads to war. So we try to maximize our operational space to see how much aid we can deliver to people, to restore them to their capacity for choice. And then it is their choice what they want to do in terms of pursuing justice.

Simultaneously, the notion of conflict between the delivery of aid and *international* criminal justice is deeply ingrained in the minds of my interviewees. The eviction of two MSF sections from Darfur, following the issuing of the 2009 arrest warrant against President al-Bashir and the arrest and interrogations of two MSF leaders in Sudan after the release of the 2005 rape report, in all likelihood contributed to this sense of antagonism. One project manager, a learned physician, described the conflict as follows:

> In March 2009, with the ICC decision, I think it had a big impact on the conflict and on many issues. You know of course that it resulted in the expulsion of many NGOs immediately from Darfur. And not only that, but it really was the beginning or at least the visible beginning of the attempt by the Sudanese government of domesticating the Darfur crisis—a deliberate strategic policy to reclaim ownership over Darfur, [to] try to remove international influence in Darfur. It was the straw that broke the camel's back. . . . I think for many years the Khartoum government has been troubled by international influence on what they see as their affairs. I have talked with ministers, with the Sudanese ambassador to the US; . . . they said very clearly these things. Another word they use is "Sudanization," the Sudanization of humanitarian aid. . . . That's a term that people in the government in Khartoum use, "Sudanization of aid." It's coming from Bashir. . . . It's not just expulsion from the country; it's also the restriction of work in Darfur. . . . One of our MSF teams was kidnapped, early—I think it was two weeks after the ICC decision.

MSF workers who highlight the conflict between MSF and the ICC also tend to cast more general doubt on the ICC. I encountered this (conscious or unconscious) strategy of rationalizing the MSF position toward the ICC in several interviews. One respondent, for example, spoke to the uneven risk countries run of seeing their leaders indicted by the ICC. He pointed to the many nation-states, including some of the most powerful, that have not ratified the Rome Statute and concluded: "It is not an even playing field to begin with. I understand completely: a lot of people would disagree with me. But it's not just my opinion. In MSF there is an article that you can get online by Fabrice Weissman on the ICC; it is called 'grounds for divorce,' between MSF and ICC."

Indeed, the general skepticism of some MSF actors against the ICC is articulated on the MSF website, and its message appears to resonate with many in the organization. Another interviewee became more concrete while expressing similar skepticism:

> As a citizen I am skeptical that it [ICC] is just going to be a tool that the wealthy, powerful countries use to bludgeon whatever enemy they determine of that day. I mean I won't believe in the ICC until Henry Kissinger is in the dock. I mean if you are going to talk about a breach of international conventions and war crimes etc., I mean, Henry Kissinger should be at the top of anyone's list. Or John Yoo, for example; I mean, how do you write a torture memo like that?

In addition to casting doubts on the equal treatment of different countries before the ICC, one other MSF interviewee challenged the notion of justice in the international realm in principle: "I have a problem with international justice due to the fact that I think justice, I mean judicial justice, so to speak, is not a proper way to judge mass crimes. . . . Of course, justice, I mean a trial, can bring more knowledge. It is obvious. But factual knowledge is not the overall understanding of a criminal or a violent process that is going on. . . . I think it is misleading, it is a misleading device." This respondent supplemented his general critique of international criminal justice with that of particular personnel, especially the ICC chief prosecutor at the time, Luis Moreno-Ocampo. He also stressed, though, that his critique reflected his personal philosophy (albeit one influential within MSF), and that MSF, for good reason, had no official position on the ICC.

Despite such broad skepticism, MSF actors on the ground contribute through their practice to the potential for criminal justice intervention, and they may be mindful of that contribution. The interviewee cited above as having intense skepticism concerning the ICC's equal treatment of different countries spoke about strategies for providing proof for future criminal justice proceedings:

> I don't think it is a binary opposition [between aid and justice] personally. . . . You know, victims of sexual violence are able to receive a [medical] certificate, in case they want to bring some judicial proceedings against the perpetrators of that sexual violence. They have used that. . . . [In Congo] the judiciary had just started to function in a kind of independent fashion. And lo and behold, . . . like fifty women in this same rural Congo village came and testified against the police officers that had raped them.

Another respondent, who had listed aid delivery as the organization's primary aim, nevertheless offered an additional strategy—linking the delivery of medical assistance to measures that may contribute to others' responses in the pursuit of peace or justice. It is worth quoting at length from his discussion:

> One is always on the safe side if one does not repeat things others have told, but testifies directly. If I have someone, and there were such cases, where shooting wounds run parallel to the body's axis, . . . [and the patients say,] "I was shot at from a helicopter," then there is a clear link. We cannot say in our communications, . . . "These people were shot at from a helicopter." Then one would be at risk of abandoning the principle of neutrality. But if one says one has treated so many people with gunshots along their bodies' axes, then everyone with some knowledge of such conflicts can conclude:

"They've been shot at from above." And who has helicopters in this area? Then one can establish a link. (author's translation)

The same interviewee told a similar story about discreet ways in which medical aid work can interact, and divide labor, with human rights organizations:

> We want to save lives and ameliorate suffering. . . . It would be ideal, then, if Human Rights Watch or similar organizations were to take over this political mandate by documenting these things. And we have done that, for example, in 2008 in Abyei . . . [when] we had many gunshot wounds in the backs, because they all had to flee. These stories, for example, I told [to] Human Rights Watch representatives. They came to me and inquired about this. Among them was a former MSF worker, and then I said: "Will this report be linked to my name or to MSF?" And she told me that she knew full well that that would be quite disadvantageous for us here and for our project, for the people. She just needed two or three independent confirmations, and then she could report about it. (author's translation)

This example of a division of labor between humanitarian aid and human rights organizations illustrates well that it is problematic to think of aid delivery on the one hand and justice seeking on the other as a zero-sum conflict, even though the respondent was concerned about the potential detriment to MSF programs in the region of bearing witness. This same interviewee expressed strong personal support for the ICC, unlike some of the statements cited above. He even attested to potential positive impact of ICC work on humanitarian workers on the ground: "If there is not justice, when will it end? I personally see the international court as something important. Because I also noticed in Darfur that . . . people are afraid of it" (author's translation). This same respondent also distinguished between himself and his convictions as an individual and citizen, on the one hand, and the organization for which he works, on the other:

> Somewhere we are also individuals. And, of course, I also try to act within our principles and our charter, as I do act accordingly. When I talk, as head of mission or project leader, with a journalist from [name of local paper], or when you interview me, or when I speak with a representative of the Sudanese authorities, of course. But should I be asked to testify as a citizen, then it is my duty to provide truthful answers. . . . I have to follow the laws. If it is international law, then I have to obey international law, and that also applies to me as a citizen of my country. (author's translation)

These statements provide two insights. First, besides principled personal opposition to the ICC, some MSF staff and sections support judicial intervention generally and in particular welcome, in open or subtle ways, international criminal justice intervention. Second, they also find ways of bearing witness that, through cautious wording, contribute to the message of human rights NGOs and judicial interventions.

One other MSF interviewee expressed support for legal intervention generally. It is not by chance that this respondent is a US citizen (albeit working for a European section) who was trained in international law at a prestigious American university. Remember that among Amnesty International interviewees those with law degrees showed much more unambiguous support for the ICC. Remember also that the United States was immersed in movements that favored the full range of criminal justice interventions, including genocide charges against Omar al-Bashir. The director-general of a national section, this interviewee is not without influence, and a close look at his position is in order. He first unambiguously confessed to the mandate of *témoignage*: "You provide pills, blankets, food, medical treatment. But that is essentially a Band-Aid. And underneath is something else going on and causing it. Children don't naturally have scrap-metal wounds. You try to change the situation by exposing it, confronting perpetrators with their actions. . . . We see rising levels of malnutrition and we go and confront WFP [the World Food Program] with that. That is the basic idea behind bearing witness." And not just UN agencies should be supplied with information about suffering, according to this interviewee, but also journalists: "If people are coming in and they are starving and . . . they tell you the rains did not come, that is one thing. If they tell you the soldiers have been stealing it—that is another. And very often it is the latter. . . . There was a steady flow of MSF press releases, like from other organizations. And that is part of the attempt behind that. It is not promotion of ourselves; it is to try to expose the situation."

This lawyer interviewee indeed went further. His support for bearing witness extended to open support for legal intervention, albeit broadly understood and explicitly including the model of the South African Truth and Reconciliation Commission (for which another MSF interviewee also expressed great sympathy). He also spoke about peace as a potential consequence of the pursuit of justice: "No justice, no peace." While he cited the situation of Charles Taylor and his refusal to bargain in light of the risk of arrest, he said: "I take the side of the victims at some point. That is not an excuse for not pursuing something like justice."

Yet even this American-trained lawyer expressed concerns about potential backlash. Decisions to go public with information about grave human rights abuses should—in his mind too—depend on the circumstances. He refers to the example of "Burma, where we've got lots to say and we just don't, because 90 percent of the HIV-AIDS patients receiving anti-retroviral therapy in Burma get it from us. . . . We can't afford to be tossed out of that country. There are no other actors to take our place. In Darfur, you know, it is quite apparent that there are other actors." And, beyond this particular situation and despite his relatively open attitude toward justice responses, in the end this MSF interviewee, too, identified with the principle of aid delivery and showed skepticism toward the ICC:

> We don't publicize with the goal or objective of attaining justice. But many would, and then use the same facts and figures to do that. And that is a problem now for the aid agencies. It is a problem in fact and it is a problem in perception. If governments or bad actors anywhere perceive you as an agent or [as] anyway related to the pursuit of justice, that creates a barrier, an obstacle to access to populations. And whereas MSF has always pointed its finger at people too, they haven't pointed their finger at individuals. They have pointed their finger at, you know, a government's health care system. . . . It is a lot less threatening than an individual believing that you are going to point a finger at him or her directly with evidence for criminal prosecution. . . . We have had a real discussion in the organization about our relationship to the ICC. In 1999, when accepting the Nobel Peace Prize, we called for the ratification [of the ICC], and we've since backed away quite considerably from it. . . . Bashir is able to justify the expulsion on the ground that these agencies cooperated with the ICC investigation. They are not there to do humanitarian work. They are there to spy on us. Ocampo doesn't help by saying things like "We used data from humanitarian aid agencies to do this." . . . We really needed to distance ourselves.

While the goals of delivering aid and securing the affected population's survival and its relationship with the principle of justice dominated the responses of my MSF interviewees, several interlocutors also recognized peace as an important goal. One interviewee, however, perceived a conflict between the pursuit of peace and aid delivery. He referred to the situation in Liberia, where MSF sought to bring relief goods into an area controlled by Charles Taylor, at the same time that the UN sought to build a blockade around Taylor's National Patriotic Front: "There was a real clash between peacemaking, peace enforcing, which was a priority of the United Nations, and providing relief—to the point that, in fact, UN-chartered, or at least UN-sponsored, jet fighters, attacked relief convoys." The same respondent, a person with particular prestige in the organization, was also the lone MSF respondent who

FIGURE 11. This image from MSF's website shows displaced Darfuris and their "housing."

saw merit in the principle of national sovereignty: "Well, securing the Sudanese state is, I think, an issue as well. Although I am a doctor without borders, I do believe that states and borders matter. . . . Borders are something that protects a given people, a given society, from imperial strikes."

In short, MSF is an organization dedicated to the delivery of humanitarian, especially medical, aid. It differs from other aid NGOs in that it also engages in *témoignage*, in bearing witness. Both missions are reflected in our analysis of websites and in my interviews. They are also on display in images I found on MSF websites (see figures 11 and 12). But the weight of *témoignage* has fluctuated over time, and it is more pronounced in some sections than in others. Some respondents perceived bearing witness to be in conflict with the primary goal of securing survival. On the ground, however, some sections or staff had discovered "under the radar" methods of collecting and distributing information on grave violations of human rights so that affected victims or human rights NGOs could use it.

In general there is no doubt that MSF is, despite several modifications, a humanitarian aid organization, embedded in a field with specific

FIGURE 12. Darfuri women and children at an MSF medical service site, in a photo from MSF's website.

norms and surrounded by a particular set of actors that includes representatives of the perpetrating state, with whom aid NGOs have to collaborate to get their assistance to the affected people. How, then, does this position in the field of humanitarian aid affect MSF workers' narratives about the Darfur conflict?

REPRESENTATIONS OF DARFUR

Two sources of evidence speak to the ways in which MSF defined the situation in Darfur during the first decade of the twenty-first century. The first is a comparative analysis of documents, press releases, reports from the field, interview transcripts, and position statements, published on websites of the American section of MSF and their Amnesty International and Save Darfur equivalents (for methodological details, see chapter 2 and Zacher, Nyseth Brehm, and Savelsberg 2014). The second source of data consists of my interviews with MSF staff and volunteers. Interview responses take us backstage and provide insights that go into greater depth and are at least partly freed from constraints of official representations. They come closer to reflecting the genuine mindset of humanitarian aid actors, most of whom have actually experienced the violence and its consequences on the ground in Darfur and interacted with agents of the Sudanese state. Not to be mistaken for public pronouncements, they do feed into the conflicted discourses within the organization, and they shine through as communication that, while not formally sanctified, still reaches beyond the organization's boundaries, as we shall see. I organize the MSF representation of Darfur along the same set of dimensions used in the analysis of three academic books (Hagan and Rymond-Richmond 2008; Mamdani 2009a; Flint and de Waal 2008) and of the human rights field: suffering and victimhood; causes and origins of the conflict; actors; and framing.

Interview accounts of suffering and victimhood show substantial overlap with those we encountered in the human rights field. Several interviewees spoke about deaths and enhanced mortality (even mass murder), rape, destroyed villages, lost homes and livelihood, displacement, injuries (specifically scrap-metal wounds), and (in one case) psychological trauma. Our quantitative analysis of the American NGO sections' websites, however, shows noteworthy differences regarding the frequency with which different sorts of suffering are publicized. Compared to Amnesty, MSF Web documents refer to killings and rapes less frequently, but to displacement and destruction of livelihood somewhat more often and to disease and shortages dramatically more frequently. We thus find highlighted, in publicized documents, exactly those types of suffering that call for intervention by humanitarian aid organizations.

Suffering may result from many different causes; and different causal explanations attribute different meanings to suffering. To what degree do MSF actors interpret it as a result of human action, specifically criminal action? Even more precisely, do they refer to criminal actions as constituting human rights crimes, war crimes, crimes against humanity, or genocide? Remarkably, the content analysis of websites shows almost no statements that refer to even one of the types of crimes for which the ICC has jurisdiction. We did, however, find references to behaviors commonly understood as criminal, including murder and rape (Zacher, Nyseth Brehm, and Savelsberg 2014). These are actually mentioned slightly more frequently on the MSF-USA site than on Amnesty-USA's site. Yet, beyond referring to specific crimes, rarely does the MSF site explicitly categorize the violence as criminal violence, and—again—it strictly avoids reference to those types of crime that would fall within the jurisdiction of the ICC. In interviews, too, I find great caution with regard to the use of such terms. As one respondent explained:

> In practice, what they [Global South actors] see now in the Western world
> is [how] . . . these sorts of statements that a government has committed

violence against its people are so instrumental and are [so] politicized that you just end up looking like a Western actor beating up on [a Global South government]—you know, the double standard–based Western discourse that uses human rights, in some ways, to subordinate the developing world. And you get caught up in the discourse to some extent. So, you know, they believe we really need to distance ourselves from it. And it is very hard, then, to say: "Well but actually the government is committing violence against people."

While humanitarian aid websites and interviewees thus speak freely about the suffering of the people of Darfur, the cautionary note about the use of crime labels is reflected in MSF interviewees' stress of those causes and frames that apply to the conflict but do not invoke the volition of specific actors. The statistical analysis also shows that MSF web documents rarely name offenders. They differ from both Amnesty and Save Darfur particularly in their hesitancy to refer to the Sudanese state as a criminal perpetrator (Zacher, Nyseth Brehm, and Savelsberg 2014:42). To be sure, MSF interviewees are not uncritical of the Sudanese state. Instead, almost all stressed the center-periphery conflict and the neglect of the periphery by the government in Khartoum as central causes of the conflict. This charge is much in line with the grievances, documented in the famous *Black Book* (Seekers of Truth and Justice 2004), that played a crucial role in the foundation of the Darfur rebel organizations. One MSF respondent actually cited the *Black Book* when speaking to the center-periphery conflict in Sudan. But interviewees also emphasized that the current government of Sudan inherited this center-periphery tension from old times, reaching back to the colonial period. "Taking over from the colonial period in the early 1950s," one respondent reflected, "it is a very centralized government where power is held by a very small group of people. There was never really an established modernized, modern country. . . . All the peripheries feel that they are neglected by their government in terms of resources, in terms of representation mainly."

In addition to the neglect of the periphery by the center as the basic source of the Darfur conflict, half of MSF respondents also highlighted a series of secondary conditions for which the government of Sudan is not responsible, among them desertification—the extension of the Sahara Desert southward and the resulting intensified competition for natural resources between herder-nomads and agriculturalists, a competition that breeds violence in combination with other external factors. One interviewee described the situation:

You have issues of local conflict dating back decades if not centuries. . . . More or less it is the nomadic population, competing for grass, for water access, with the agricultural group. And this has been the case, tensions and conflicts, traditionally for longer than it is probably written in history. And that desertification, . . . the change of the climate within Darfur has been a factor—plus increasing population pressures—means there has been more competition for land and water, more tensions. The introduction of weapons in Darfur meant that these local conflicts have become more serious, more complicated, and very difficult to resolve with the traditional peacemaking mechanisms. . . . You know what happened with the flow of small arms in Darfur, [which is] . . . one of the factors as well. . . . So you have . . . layers of conflict. You have local conflict and then the national-level conflict of the Darfur rebels versus Khartoum. Then you have a regionalization of the conflict as well—Chad, Sudan, Libya. . . . Darfur was and still is a regional conflict, or at least complicated by regional issues. . . . It's a complicated picture, but if you go back to what I said in the beginning: you wouldn't have this type of conflict or the scale of conflict or the disaster you saw in Darfur if there wasn't this problem between the periphery and the center.

While the government of Sudan does appear, in statements such as these, as a contributor to the very background conditions underlying the violence of Darfur, it is also presented as the heir of imperfect state formation that reaches back to colonial days. Further, in the twelve hours of interview material with MSF staff, the government is rarely depicted as contributing to the foreground conditions of criminal violence. Instead, respondents pointed to a series of other complicating factors. One interviewee spoke about the mobilization of Janjawiid militias. While he argued that the government used promises of money and land to lure them into supporting the military, he also stressed that the Janjawiid violence eventually developed an autodynamic and became independent of the government. In this description the government no longer appears as a perpetrator, but as the sorcerer's apprentice who lost control of a process he had initiated: "I think that they [the Janjawiid] just became uncontrollable, that they developed an independent dynamic, that the militias split up into ever smaller groups with distinct interests. The whole process could, in the end, no longer be controlled by the government" (author's translation). Another respondent similarly described a process that ended with "much more localized, fractured violence between all communities." He compared the use of the Janjawiid to a "Pandora's box" that the government had opened but was not able to close again. The American-trained lawyer who among the MSF respondents showed the greatest openness toward justice-focused responses argued similarly. On the one hand, he used categories of international criminal law ("there were crimes against humanity and there were war crimes committed"). On the other hand, he challenged the narratives we typically encounter in the human rights field, especially depictions of a clear divide between one group as good and the other as an evil force. Instead this MSF interviewee, like others, stressed patterns of fractionalization and pointed to problematic side-effects of good-versus-evil narratives: "The simplifications that some social movement actors have engaged in are in part a reinforcement of things that the government of Sudan has done, as it has contributed to creating, it seems to me, those clear ethnic boundaries."

Other interviewees attributed responsibility more squarely to the government of Sudan. Simultaneously, however, they provided explanations, albeit not necessarily justifications, for the actions of the Janjawiid. One respondent questioned the common image of the Janjawiid as a cruel and disorganized horde of killers:

> I spoke with a sheik in Kerenik, who told me everything, how that [the violence] unfolded . . . that one was flown to Khartoum, lavishly treated and lured into the [government's] agenda. He really told me: "I allowed them to put me to use, more or less, but what was the effect? I lost almost half of my men here, and now I have to take care of their families. The money never arrived. The promises were not kept. We were simply instrumentalized. And now one sees that the abyss is deep." And then he chose his words carefully and said: "Really we do have the same grandmother." (author's translation)

Another respondent similarly spoke to the oppressive conditions of those groups from which militias were recruited. He referred to the government's use of a "counterinsurgency campaign, relying on . . . the poor, the poorest against the poor, on mobilized marginal populations of Darfur to fight local insurgencies." The same interviewee simultaneously attributed greater responsibility to rebel groups than is common among human rights activists. And he combined this attribution of agency to rebel groups with a reference to what he considered a problematic approach to the North-South conflict in Sudan and the role played by international diplomacy: "The North-South process has been a trigger. . . . By only taking into consideration the South, it gives the message [that] the only way for all peripheries to be considered was to take up arms and to deal with it in their own terms." Again, the agency of rebel groups as violent actors is underscored, this time as actors who drew inspiration from the North-South negotiations.

Such narratives concerning causes of the conflict complicate, and compete with, the common human rights account of the violence in Darfur. To be sure, MSF respondents in oral communication highlight the same actors as crucial contributors to the violence as we find referred to in human rights accounts. References to the "government of Sudan," "political leadership," "Bashir," "the president," the "business and military apparatus," the "army," and the "security apparatus" are frequent throughout the interviews. Also "Arab militias" or "militias equipped by the army" are named. But the role of these actors appears in a different light than it does in human rights narratives. Also, website statements typically avoid reference to any perpetrators, especially the government of Sudan, as responsible for the violence.

One interviewee's reference to "bystanders," the majority of Sudanese who live their lives as though mass killings never took place, sheds an interesting light on the larger domestic context within which NGOs and the Sudanese government operate:

> [Nyala in South Darfur] was basically a place where middle-class Sudanese would go for their weekend away from Khartoum, from the big city. And it used to be dotted with all of these cute little B-and-B hotels. . . . You would not know there was a crisis unless you actually went to the camps. Nyala itself is a bustling city of hundreds of thousands of people. It was really bizarre. A similar dynamic is in Khartoum. . . . I was reading the press all the time, reading the newspapers, talking to the relatively educated elite, local reporters, etc.: very little indication that there was a war going on. For me that spoke to the disconnect between the *populus* and the actions of the government.

A look at framing strategies sheds further light on the interpretation of the events in Darfur by MSF respondents. In my interviews, I again offered four options: a rebellion or insurrection frame (understanding government action as counterinsurgency); a civil war frame; a humanitarian emergency frame; and a state crime frame. Whereas only one Amnesty interviewee clearly supported the insurgency frame, almost all MSF interviewees found this an acceptable interpretation of the violence. Only one rejected it outright, and another expressed skepticism. The civil war frame was more strongly favored by MSF respondents than by their Amnesty counterparts. Astonishingly, though, while almost all Amnesty respondents found the humanitarian catastrophe frame acceptable (much in line with expectations), half of the MSF interviewees expressed caution. For example: "It is the term which I don't like, because it does not say much. I prefer to describe facts. I prefer to say massacres, famine. . . . *Humanitarian catastrophe* is a label which does not tell us very much, except that people are suffering." Another MSF interviewee, like the previously quoted speaker, also from MSF-France, argued similarly:

Humanitarian disaster is a tag I never use, because I don't know what it means. . . . Is a massacre a humanitarian disaster? Is an earthquake a humanitarian disaster? Is Fukushima a humanitarian disaster? Is Iraq a humanitarian disaster? What is a humanitarian disaster? . . . It is a catchphrase that I never use because it is so vague. . . . I think it is misleading. . . . It is a very recent formulation. As far as I know, that concept or the syntax of the humanitarian crisis was used for the first time in the June '94 resolution of the Security Council, the genocide in Rwanda [resolution]. And the idea was that the word *genocide* shouldn't be used. So, in order to turn the problem around, they decided that it was a humanitarian crisis. . . . It was instrumental to the decision of the White House not to use the G-word. So the G-word was a humanitarian crisis. It was a lie.

Not surprisingly, though, MSF interviewees did not find the state crime frame appropriate for an interpretation of the violence in Darfur. In fact, while all Amnesty respondents wholeheartedly embraced this frame, I found great skepticism among MSF staff. Only two respondents were somewhat supportive, but even one of these stressed that this was his personal opinion: "That is always what we are asked to avoid as employees of Doctors Without Borders: to position ourselves and to say this is state crime or this is genocide. We talk about a humanitarian catastrophe [but see interview statements above]. Where that comes from and what its causes are, on that we may have our personal opinions, but those will not be released to the public. I personally can say about that [definition as crime]: 'yes'" (author's translation).

One other interviewee rejected the notion of state crime and drew a distinction:

I think it is a state that uses violence, commits crimes, but . . . what state doesn't? And I think the Sudanese state has committed more of them, but I don't think it is a useful way of understanding the state. I think it is certainly a way of understanding certain actors in the state. . . . Partly because the state is fairly enormous here. The ministry of health isn't criminal. The ministry of agriculture isn't criminal. [When challenged with the fact that the Nazi state, too, included government agencies not directly involved in the commission of crimes, he responded:] I don't think here [in Sudan] the strategic objectives were criminal. I believe the methods and tactics they used were quite criminal.

One MSF respondent did not reject the notion that crimes were committed, but he insisted that the state crime frame does not adequately capture the events in Darfur: "It is much more than state crimes. . . . It is a rebellion. It is a political movement. It carries a social and political dynamic. . . . All this belongs to the concept of rebellion, civil war, political movement." What is at stake here is a perceived contrast between a criminalizing frame and an interpretation of the conflict as political.

Another MSF interviewee rejected the state crime frame outright. Much in line with the foregoing statement, he deferred to lawyers' and courts' decisions about the criminal nature of the violence. To my question whether he would also "negotiate with the devil" to get humanitarian aid on the ground, he replied:

> What is the devil? Good and bad—we don't necessarily see the world in that way. As a person coming from a different background you have your personal opinions on those sorts of things. But as an organization we don't, and that is something we defend very strongly. On Iraq, I did a round of meetings with the State Department, with the Pentagon, . . . and I challenged them with that. I said, "Do you have a problem with us having communication and links with terrorist organizations, Al Qaida, insurgent groups in Iraq, and so forth?" . . . We need it [communication], because to be present in an area you need acceptance by the groups.

The foregoing statement brings us full circle to the notion of the humanitarian aid field and the ways in which this field structures knowledge and basic categories of thought. To be sure, things are not clear-cut, especially for a humanitarian aid NGO such as MSF with its dedication to bearing witness. MSF actors surely do not downplay the suffering of the Darfuri population. To the contrary, they produce—through medical examination and published records and reports—evidence of such suffering, evidence that may later be put to use in criminal court proceedings and that is feared by representatives of the Sudanese state. Interviewees also named all the actors involved in the violence. Their narrative does not differ substantially, in this respect, from that of human rights campaigns.

Yet the representation assembled from my interviews with MSF staff and our content analysis of the MSF-USA website suggests that the identification of causes and the framing of the violence differ substantially between human rights and humanitarian aid organizations and their agents. Again, responses from the latter interviewees emphasize natural conditions more strongly than do human rights narratives. And, while they surely hold militia groups responsible for atrocities, MSF respondents also interpret them as victims of resource shortage, neglect, and the Sudanese state's false promises. Rebel groups instead are considered in a somewhat more critical light than is common in the context of human rights campaigns.

Both human rights and humanitarian actors blame the state, but the attribution is much more indirect among MSF personnel. The latter see the state more as a contributor to long-standing background factors, as opposed to highlighting contemporary state strategies as foreground factors and direct causes of violence. Further, they break the state up into components, only some of which bear responsibility. Finally, the crime frame is generally not regarded as satisfactory, and judgments on criminal responsibility are left to lawyers and the courts. This is in line with our comparative quantitative analysis of framing strategies used by the American section of MSF. Here too the explicit crime frame is rarely used, the state is almost never referred to as a perpetrator, and support for international prosecution is missing altogether (Zacher, Nyseth Brehm, and Savelsberg 2014:42). In short, MSF—a prominent example of an INGO in the humanitarian aid field, in which the Sudanese state is a crucial player—is an important producer of representations of the Darfur conflict and contributes significantly to the definition of the situation. Its representation differs substantially from the one we encountered in our examination of the center and the periphery of the human rights field.

COMMUNICATING REPRESENTATIONS

Representations of mass violence that grow out of humanitarian aid–oriented NGOs matter, not least because they can contribute to shaping public opinion and to challenging human rights narratives in the public sphere. This applies to official pronouncements and NGO reports as well as to opinion formation among NGO staff and volunteers. My interviews with journalists indicate that NGOs are crucial sources of information, a theme to which I return in greater detail below. Interviews with MSF staff confirm this notion. Specifically, they spell out at least four pathways by which humanitarian NGO narratives may reach those who report about the conflict to broad audiences across the globe.

First, not surprisingly, communication is used strategically by MSF sections of different countries. One interviewee, a "manager of medical and humanitarian communications," described these efforts: "We want to make sure it [public communication] is in line with our medical and operational priorities. . . . We really want our public events to have a strategic element; that means targeting better audiences, whether they are medical or academic or diplomatic or NGO communities."

Second, diffusion of MSF representations also occurs in the field. A "crisis communications manager" who was serving MSF in Khartoum in the summer of 2004 described the issuing of a press release entitled "No Relief in Sight."[10] The release was based on a retrospective mortality survey and accompanied by an epidemiological report. It was ready for posting at the exact time when UN secretary-general Kofi Annan und US secretary of state Colin Powell came to Khartoum. "I was in West Darfur, and there was a big scramble to get me back to Khartoum because there was going to be the entire press corps, following Colin Powell. And I remember coming into the press room, just walking from one person to the other and handing out our press release, the 'No Relief in Sight.' And I believe it was quoted a lot in those initial stories." Chapter 9 offers a detailed analysis of the actual effects of this particular initiative on media reporting.

Third, communication with journalists arises within opportunity structures in the field. Speaking about Nicholas Kristof of the *New York Times,* one interviewee reported: "He visited with a lot of MSF teams in Darfur and we helped arrange that. We helped arrange briefings for him in the early days." Also, "Christiane Amanpour [of CNN] stayed in our compound because there was nowhere else to stay. So she threw down her sleeping bag inside of our compound and during the day would go out and do reports." These partially accidental contacts in the field are nevertheless structured.

Fourth, spontaneous encounters are supplemented by planned interactions with the media. One respondent reported that MSF held editorial board meetings on the subject of Darfur with the *New York Times,* first in 2004 and again in 2006 or 2008.

Cautionary notes are in order, though. First, while humanitarian NGOs obviously have several channels of communication to the media (and to actors from other sectors in public life), as illustrated here for MSF, their capability to impress on journalists the humanitarian aid definition of the situation is limited. I have already cited Kristof and the *New York Times* with their embrace of the genocide frame for Darfur, as well as Kristof's generous use of Holocaust analogies to shed light on the situation in Darfur. Humanitarian aid NGOs may thus feed information to journalists, but the media put this information to use according to their own rules. The degree to, and the ways through, which NGO representations translate into media reports warrants further empirical examination, which I offer in later chapters.

Second, if we encounter nation-specific discourses even in a rather centralized rights-oriented NGO such as Amnesty, a more decentralized humanitarian NGO will have to face inner conflict in its attempt to define a situation. Competing representations may thus reach the public, as should be obvious in the account provided thus far.

Finally and crucially, however, even as humanitarian aid INGOs such as MSF release information about the suffering of the local population in conflict zones, they will always be mindful of the government as an essential actor in the field in which they have to operate. In the words of one interviewee: "We try to be transparent. We provide the government with our press releases, or at least inform them that we are going to communicate publically on an issue."[11] Such considerateness should not come as a surprise given the organization's dependency on permits and cooperation by the state. As we have seen, this policy of restraint does not keep the aid NGO from displaying the suffering, but suggests causal interpretations and a frame that advances interpretations of violence of a very different nature from those emanating from the human rights field.

CONCLUSIONS

The humanitarian aid field and the INGOs within it, here examined for the case of MSF, obviously take a different shape from the human rights field. The government of the aid-receiving country is a major player in the aid field. In our case this is the government of Sudan, leading representatives of which have been charged with the gravest of crimes by the ICC. INGOs have to deal directly with the government of the receiving country—even MSF with its insistence on independence from governments at home and abroad.

In line with our expectations about the relationship between the characteristics of fields on the one hand and the knowledge repertoires generated by them on the other, we also see that the representation of the Darfur conflict takes distinctive shape in the humanitarian aid world. To be sure, this is not a world in which suffering is denied. To the contrary, the population's pain and deprivation in areas of conflict is not just acknowledged but also documented, at times dramatized, and communicated to a world audience, in both words and images. Those aspects of the suffering, however, that can be addressed by humanitarian aid programs are the ones most likely to being highlighted. That observation would apply to displacements and to deprivations in IDP or refugee camps more than to the mass killings by military and militia or rebel groups. Starker than this difference are those of representations of actors and the framing of the violence. Generally, aid narratives treat the government of Sudan with greater caution. Long-term policies that contributed to laying the groundwork for the current violence, especially the neglect of the country's periphery, are most certainly highlighted, while short-term actions that more directly caused the violence are more commonly downplayed. Respondents typically attribute causal primacy for the outbreak of violence to the rebel groups—even if government responses are termed disproportionate and escalating. In line with such caution, actors in the aid field are reluctant to choose the state crime frame. Most stress instead the supremacy of the humanitarian catastrophe frame. Responses to questions about the insurgency and civil war frame are ambiguous. Actors in the humanitarian aid field are especially reluctant to apply the term *genocide* to the conflict, a label that so much dominated the criminal justice–oriented discourse, particularly in the United States.

Clearly, what we diagnose as an elective affinity between the humanitarian aid field and the representation of the violence by aid actors involves causal ties. Depending on the cooperation of the Sudanese state in the granting of visas and permits to travel and deliver aid, humanitarian actors apply caution with regard to the government of Sudan.

Why, then, do we not find in the aid field a pure ideal-typical depiction of a humanitarian catastrophe? Note that MSF, the aid INGO selected for this in-depth study, is also dedicated to bearing witness. In that sense I made a conservative choice when seeking to demonstrate the emergence of an aid-oriented representation. Other aid INGOs should display a narrative even closer to an ideal type of humanitarian representation. In addition, fields are never pure. They overlap, or interpenetrate, with other fields, as when lawyers are being recruited into leading positions within the humanitarian aid field, especially lawyers socialized in a country with a strong criminal justice tradition such as the United States. Remember that even within the human rights field, lawyers embraced the logic of the justice cascade more unambiguously than members of other professions.

The empirical analysis also speaks to the ability of international institutions to create a global representation of mass violence, a theme that relates to debates between the World Polity School, with its focus on global scripts, versus its challengers that highlight national contexts and organization-specific constructions of knowledge. In support of the World Polity School we witnessed the emergence of a global understanding of the conflict in Darfur within the humanitarian aid field. Yet, just as we observed national specifics in sections of INGOs in the human rights field, the humanitarian aid INGO examined here, less centralized in its organizations, shows even greater discrepancies across national sections.

Finally, linking insights from this chapter with observations from the preceding ones, we see competition between two distinct scripts—those emerging from the human rights field and others generated by the humanitarian aid field. Clearly, we observe an intense competition over the representation of the Darfur conflict across fields. At times, however, this competition gives way to a division of labor, whereby a humanitarian organization produces evidence of suffering that may be used by human rights organizations to draw conclusions regarding criminal responsibility for the suffering. The competition between the two fields should thus not be misunderstood as a zero-sum conflict.

In addition to humanitarian INGOs, states may also focus on humanitarian aid delivery, often in close interaction with NGOs. Ireland is a fascinating case in point. I address this example in the following chapter, where I call the close networks of humanitarian NGOs, government institutions, and other actors a "humanitarian complex" and examine the effects of this complex on the representation of mass violence in Darfur.

CHAPTER 5

The Humanitarian Complex and Challenges to the Justice Cascade

The Case of Ireland

Aid organizations such as Médecins Sans Frontières are not the only entities devoted to the delivery of humanitarian aid. Countries and their governments may also focus on humanitarian aid policies, often in the context of development programs. Such governments may find themselves in a position similar to that of aid NGOs': they too have to take account of the government of the receiving country. In addition, donor governments often have strong organizational ties with domestic aid-oriented NGOs that may have deep roots in and a strong cultural resonance with the local population. Important for our purposes here, such constellations should affect how a donor country defines the situation in the receiving country, including the potential involvement of the receiving country's government in mass violence. Ireland, more than the other countries in our sample, approximates the ideal type of a humanitarian and development aid–oriented country. Among the eight countries included in this study, Ireland's aid budget is by far the highest as a percentage of the country's gross national income.[1] While Ireland is embedded in international organizations, especially the EU and the UN, and in important ways aligned with their policies, we should see the government's position in the aid field reflected in Irish representations of the mass violence in Darfur.

My description of Ireland is informed by two sources of data. The first is a content analysis of 242 articles, including 35 opinion pieces, published in the *Irish Times,* the dominant Irish paper on issues of foreign affairs. I supplemented this set of quantitative data by correspondence with this paper's foreign correspondent and by an interview with a prominent Irish journalist of RTÉ, Ireland's public radio and television station who had reported from Darfur on several occasions.[2]

The second source of data is a set of interviews I conducted in Ireland's Department of Foreign Affairs (DFA). One respondent represented Irish Aid, the humanitarian and development aid branch of the foreign ministry.[3] An energetic woman profoundly dedicated to her mission, she had entered the foreign service some fifteen years earlier after earning a degree in political science. She had worked on Northern Ireland issues, served as her government's humanitarian contact point to the UN in Geneva, and begun working on aid issues in the Dublin headquarters in 2004. She had visited Darfur in April 2005.

Two interview partners were located in the DFA's Political Division. The first, the head of the Africa desk, had had a long and distinguished career with the DFA. He had worked on EU external relations and served in the UN permanent mission in New York, among other assignments. He had degrees in English literature and economics and a master's in international public policy from a renowned private American university on the East Coast. The second interviewee, also from the Political Division, had been assigned to the Irish embassies of both Vienna and Tokyo and had been involved in the Northern Ireland talks. At the time of the interview, he was responsible for coordinating Ireland's role in the Common Foreign and Security Policy (CFSP) of the European Union, with a special focus on Sudan and the Horn of Africa. His PhD thesis had focused on the history of Irish foreign policy.

IRISH FOREIGN POLICY AND HUMANITARIAN AND DEVELOPMENT AID

Irish foreign policy makers express a pronounced orientation toward humanitarian and development aid. Not surprisingly, the respondent from Irish Aid articulated this stance most clearly. She reported that the Irish development and humanitarian aid program has a long history, dating back to religious missionaries "who would have gone to Africa and Asia in the nineteenth century." She also highlighted the "outward looking" nature of Ireland resulting from its emigration history. Despite Ireland's small size, such "strong roots" provide Irish policy makers with "confidence of a lot of history behind the program." Speaking of the current day and of Sudan in particular, she said:

A lot of our focus on Sudan was humanitarian. It doesn't matter that you are a small donor when you have a humanitarian focus. You can play quite a large policy role or you can have quite a large profile if you are an honest broker—because we are neutral. . . . There would still be about two thousand missionaries whom we fund for their development work. There would also be NGOs whose roots would have been in the Catholic missions—Trócaire, for example; it means "mercy." And they would be one of the big three Irish NGOs, and they would come from a Catholic ethos background.

In addition to Trócaire, described on its website as "the official development agency of the Catholic Church in Ireland,"[4] the interviewee referred to two other major Irish NGOs, Concern Worldwide[5] and GOAL.[6] Both are characterized as more secular, but, according to my interviewee, "GOAL would have done a lot of work over the years, again with the missionaries."[7]

In line with this focus on aid policy, the interviewee's response to my question about priorities in foreign policy goals is not surprising. Again, I offered four options: securing the survival of the affected, establishing peace, serving justice, and securing state sovereignty. While she saw these goals as lying on a "spectrum," she insisted on the "humanitarian goal essentially as the first intervention. . . . If you assist people who are suffering, . . . that's your sticking plaster."

This position may not be surprising coming from a representative of the aid branch of the foreign ministry. Yet the aid mission was also mentioned frequently in my interview with the two officials from the Political Division. While seeing the four as a cluster of goals that would be reached successively, one respondent viewed the survival of the affected as an "immediate imperative for us, coming from the development and humanitarian perspective. But we recognize that you have to perceive that in tandem with securing peace and you cannot have peace in the absence of justice." I return to the specific understanding of justice in greater detail below. Suffice it to say here that members of the Political Division, too, perceive the humanitarian goal as an immediate imperative.

The weight of the aid mission was further highlighted when I raised the issue of the peculiar status of Ireland's foreign policy. While both of the Political Division representatives hastened to stress the Irish alignment in foreign affairs with positions taken by the European Union, they also insisted that they "would bring to discussions on Darfur a particular humanitarian focus. . . . It would always be something we would raise, both the humanitarian needs of the population and the importance of maintaining humanitarian space for aid delivery. . . . That is because we have a particularly developed [humanitarian] policy compared to some other EU member states."

COLLECTIVE MEMORY: CULTURAL SUPPORT FOR AID POLICY

Policy makers are mindful of the cultural traditions and historical experiences in which current Irish foreign policy is rooted. We have shown elsewhere elective affinities between collective memories and current-day policies, legislation, and implementation of laws (Savelsberg and King 2005, 2007). There we spelled out distinct mechanisms through which even a causal relationship may be established that leads from memories to legal forms. These mechanisms include analogical references to the past, historical consciousness that invites receptivity to commemorations of past events (King 2005; Olick and Levy 1997), and carrier groups that transport notions of the past while simultaneously speaking to contemporary issues (Weber 1978; Kalberg 1994, 2014). This argument builds on earlier work that recognizes how symbolic depictions of the past provide a cognitive and moral framework that can impel current policy. Symbols, after all, stand for larger ideas. They "evoke an attitude, a set of impressions, or a pattern of events associated . . . with the symbol" (Edelman 1985:6; see also Geertz 1973).

Ireland seems a prime example of the memory-policy link. Certainly an elective affinity can be found between Irish memories and the humanitarian orientation of Irish foreign policy. All interviewees are mindful of this affinity; indeed some believe in a causal relationship. In a first step, interviewees from the Political Division of the DFA highlighted relevant historical experiences that have been processed and incorporated into the collective memory. An extended segment of the interview, as it unfolded between the interviewer (JJS) and the two interviewees, A and B, is revealing:

A: I could hand you our aid report; it always recounts the missionaries that were first in Africa.

B: And missionaries in Africa experienced a famine in Ireland in the nineteenth century, and the population collapsed.

A: We identify with this kind of hardship strongly in Ireland.

JJS: Do you think this is just rhetoric, or is there a real base?

A: No, I think it can be quite visceral at times.

JJS: We see all over the city memorials for the famine.

B: Yep.

A: Exactly. I think the people have a memory of themselves as one that went through and died of the famine. . . . Many have relatives in the US etc. who are there as a consequence of the kind of deprivation that occurred in and after the famine. So it is quite a real historical memory in Ireland. It certainly would be a reason, amongst others, that you would support the development program.

B: Yep.

A: And even in our very severe economic straits—

B: Yeah. I was going to say that.

A: it has survived reasonably intact.

B: Local, not general, calls for cuts.

A: You will get—I mean, this is democracy—people who say the first thing we should be cutting is aid to others in dire straits. But it actually does not resonate very well.

B: It has strong popular support.

One of the interviewees concluded that the humanitarian aid focus of Irish foreign policy is not simply a choice made by a small group of officials, but that it finds support in Irish popular understanding of African conflicts: "It is firstly the humanitarian aspect, the extent to which people are actually being forced into dire poverty or facing death or insecurity." Not only do such statements express the belief of policy makers in the Irish public's memories and the resulting popular support for aid policy, but the very dynamic of this exchange also indicates the interviewees' own identification with Irish collective memory and their sense that such memory motivates and legitimizes policies oriented toward humanitarian and developmental aid.

The same Irish collective memory was highlighted by my interviewee from Irish Aid, who sees the Irish humanitarian emphasis as supported by "the vulnerability that we trace back to our famine in the mid-nineteenth century, not specific to Sudan, I suppose, but any situation where food security is threatened, any situation where even the manifestation around the humanitarian crisis is around access to food and famine."

FIGURE 13. The Famine Memorial in Dublin, Ireland.

A second, and related, aspect of Irish collective memory that respondents linked to foreign policy preferences is the nation's memory of British rule over Ireland, a point raised by the respondents in the Political Division: "Many Irish people would say we were the subject of colonization. . . . This is an important aspect of Irish identity to this day. . . . It would be very present in their [the Irish people's] sense of who they are." Accordingly, in one respondent's view, the Irish public strongly supported the decolonization movement of the 1950s and 1960s. The Irish public and policy makers also understood, in light of their country's history, that decolonization can be effective only if accompanied by economic development. Development, in fact, was seen as a prerequisite for peace and security.

While interviewees conceded that Ireland is not alone in its view that peace and security have to be coupled with aid programs, they insisted that this emphasis is especially strong in Irish foreign policy. It was in this spirit, they argued, that the foreign ministry established the aid and development program in the early 1970s as part of the Department of Foreign Affairs. "That has stayed as part of the way we have approached foreign policy in the last thirty years or so," one respondent said. "So it is intrinsic to our foreign policy approach."

STRUCTURAL SUPPORT FOR MEMORIES AND POLICIES: THE HUMANITARIAN COMPLEX

Policy practices, guiding ideas, and associated collective memories co-exist in symbiosis with a field of supporting social and organizational relationships. Actors in this field include the government of Ireland, here specifically the DFA; the major Irish aid NGOs, in part associated with the Irish Catholic Church; Ireland's national news media, especially RTÉ; and the government of Sudan. In addition, the government of Ireland is embedded in a network of international relations, including relations with international organizations, especially the EU, the UN and its aid organizations, and the African Union (AU). I call this network of relationships the *humanitarian complex* and I now briefly sketch its structure as revealed in my interviews.

The first and perhaps central component of this network is a triangle consisting of the government of Ireland, Irish NGOs—partly in conjunction with the Irish Catholic Church—and the government of Sudan. The interviewee from Irish Aid spoke about NGOs whose roots are in the Catholic missions. As cited above, she highlighted Trócaire as the leading example, but she also points at Concern Worldwide and GOAL, the other two major Irish aid NGOs. While both are secular, GOAL also has a long tradition of working in close collaboration with Catholic missionaries. All three major Irish NGOs execute aid programs supported by the Irish DFA.

The tie between NGOs and the Irish government is further strengthened by regular consultations. One interviewee spoke about conferences: "We would generally bring in all of our Irish NGOs, our minister, and talk through a lot of the issues with them. . . . It works very, very well, and I think Darfur was probably one of the initial testing grounds for that type of approach." While this interviewee recognized the NGOs' interest in independence from the government, she insisted that they accept substantial ties nevertheless. An interviewee in the Political Division, when asked about sources of information about Darfur, replied: "Often we will hear, through an Irish NGO, the views of the Anglican bishops or the Catholic Church in Sudan."

The government-NGO tie intensifies whenever the Irish government helps NGOs gain access to regions of need. Regarding Darfur, the Irish Aid interviewee explained: "They [NGOs] might also have discovered that we can be of some assistance. . . . In Darfur the issue was often around access, visas, and bureaucratic problems with the government [of Sudan]. And we managed to solve a few of those problems over the years." This ability to smooth the path for aid organizations depends of course on the relationship between the governments of the donating and receiving countries. The link between these countries thus constitutes the second tie in the initial triadic relationship within the humanitarian aid complex. It is strengthened, but also constrained, by Ireland's focus on humanitarian aid. The Irish Aid interviewee explains how a humanitarian focus, in combination with an "honest broker role" and a sense of "neutrality," substantially strengthens her country's policy role vis-à-vis countries such as Sudan. In addition, government actors see reason for treading cautiously in light of Irish NGOs' engagement in the conflict zone. Speaking about the much more restrained wording the Irish government used in its critique of Sudan, especially as compared to US rhetoric, the RTÉ journalist stated that the Irish government "was also tempered by the fact that there were so many Irish people down on the ground, working away, and a sense that organizations like GOAL were achieving a lot. So that wild political rhetoric might be one thing. But if you are looking after 180,000 people and you are looking after sixteen hospitals and medical centers around Khartoum, then you are doing something important." He adds that, while Ireland cooperated with the EU to pursue peace and justice, the Irish foreign minister's visits to Sudan were "more about providing support on the ground to the aid agencies, to enable them to afford as much help to the people who are in the difficulty. That would have been the focus. . . . You know, postindictment [of al-Bashir], GOAL, for example, was the only aid agency that was allowed to stay in North Darfur. Why was that? Because it had been there for thirty years and because it had not been seen as being overtly political."

The humanitarian aid complex, the structural context in which ideas and policy programs are developed and memories regenerated, also includes Irish media, as indicated by the foregoing statement from a RTÉ journalist who had reported from Darfur. This interviewee highlights links between RTÉ on the one hand and Irish NGOs and the Irish government on the other:

Our team covered incidences in southern Sudan and the difficulties there, and Darfur had been off our radar. There was a report from a man called Walt Kilroy who was a former correspondent with RTÉ, who worked for an Irish aid agency called Trócaire. . . . He did a broadcast back to say "What's happening here is incredible." And that was one of the first sort of ringing the bell in the Irish context. . . . And then, by 2004, the Irish government was beginning to make sense of it, primarily because we had agencies like GOAL. . . . It had a base in North Darfur. And then we had another organization called Concern Worldwide, and it had a base in [Darfur]. So there was a junior government minister, Tom Kitt, and he decided to go out and see what was going on. We had been trying to secure visas from the Sudanese government, but they were not in a position to give any guarantees of getting a filming license to travel to Darfur. So we jumped in the plane with the minister. That would have been in May 2004. And we flew into Khartoum, spent a couple of nights there, got an update from Mike McDonagh, who was of the UNOCHA [UN Office for the Coordination of Humanitarian Affairs], and then we traveled to [several places throughout Darfur, including Al-Jenina, Nyala, Fashir, and the GOAL center in North Darfur]. So we were sending reports back for radio and television. . . . For him [Minister Tom Kitt] there was an awful lot of Irish aid agency involvement; there was a lot of Irish aid agency staff; there was a lot of Irish aid agency money. And I think it was probably . . . a combination of the minister's interest and NGOs wanting to have the political influence that goes with having the minister come in and sitting down with people and saying, "This is very important and can you afford protection to our people."

Pieces of information gained from interviews with the journalist and with DFA policy makers thus reinforce each other. They equally reveal network ties between the government of Ireland, Irish NGOs, Irish media, and the government of Sudan.

I should make clear, Irish foreign policy is not oriented toward the humanitarian aid field alone. Ireland is also firmly embedded in a network of international organizations. One central tie is with the European Union, and Irish foreign policy makers insist that their policies are aligned with EU policies. But EU institutions also allow Irish policy makers to focus on their chief concerns. Interviewees spoke of their engagement in the European Commission's aid-related institutions. They pointed, for example, to a formal humanitarian aid working group that met every four weeks. Instituted only after the height of the Darfur conflict, it was, however, preceded by regular information meetings that also addressed issues of aid to Darfur during the peak of the conflict. In this institutional context, EU special representative Rosalind Marsden was a regular addressee of Irish pleas that the EU keep its eyes on the suffering in Darfur.

Ireland's involvement in humanitarian aid issues also colors the ties it has with UN suborganizations. Respondents referred to Mike McDonagh, an Irish citizen working for the UN Office for the Coordination of Humanitarian Affairs (UNOCHA), specifically for the office in Sudan, who was appointed its head in 2007. McDonagh had moved into this position after working for Concern Worldwide, the Irish NGO cited above, for thirty years. In addition to linking the Irish NGO tradition with UN work on Darfur, he also provided information for Irish journalists. The RTÉ interviewee characterized him as someone with "a wide experience of disaster conflict and the impact it has on people involved. So, he was a core [source of information]."

Irish foreign policy, finally, also maintains a mission to the African Union in Addis Ababa, as does the EU, and foreign policy interviewees in Dublin recognized and paid tribute to the AU's increasing weight on the African continent.

In short, even a brief look at the field of Irish foreign relations reveals a network of actors that clusters around humanitarian and development aid and that includes members of the Political and Aid Divisions of the Department of Foreign Affairs, major Irish NGOs, the Catholic Church (with which one of these NGOs is closely affiliated), and Ireland's public media. By necessity, members of this network who are responsible for organizing aid need to maintain working relationships with the government of Sudan or at least with some of its agencies. Just like aid NGOs, these actors depend on that government for visas, access to the region, and permits to operate in different regions of Sudan, including Darfur. And again, while Ireland is incorporated into various international organizations whose members bring diverse policy foci to the table, and while Ireland cannot be reduced to an aid perspective, its structural position, cultural orientation, and policy practices most closely approximate the ideal type of an aid-oriented country. Irish foreign policy is enabled and constrained by the institutional logic of the aid field, and the habitus of its actors reflects their identification with the aid mission.

In short, I found an elective affinity between Ireland's policy orientation toward humanitarian and development aid; the collective memories that nourish that orientation and that are reproduced by it; and the structure of the Irish foreign policy field. This ensemble of social, cultural, and political forces is likely to color Ireland's collective representation of the Darfur conflict, to which I now turn.

IRISH REPRESENTATIONS OF DARFUR

One of the interviewees in the Irish foreign ministry expressed a perspective that resembles Bourdieuian ideas about the knowledge-generating force of fields: "Perhaps it is an unusual situation that much of our engagement in Africa is a development engagement. And that is a prism we see many African issues through." To portray the Irish representation of the Darfur conflict, I again organize findings along the same set of dimensions used in the analysis of US news articles in chapter 3: suffering and victimhood; causes and origins of the conflict; actors; and framing. Here I draw on my interviews with Irish foreign policy makers and on the systematic content analysis of reporting on Darfur in the *Irish Times,* part of our Darfur media data set from eight countries. These data allow a comparative analysis of the particularities of Irish media reporting.

Suffering and Victimhood

As in the depictions of suffering encountered in documents and among interviewees from the aid NGO Doctors Without Borders, Ireland's orientation toward humanitarianism in no way diminishes the acknowledgment of suffering. The Irish Aid interviewee cited the "one and a half million" people who were deprived of "basic human needs" such as "shelter, clean water, protection, food." Despite her aversion to a deeper discussion of the causes of the conflict, she did add that this deprivation occurred in a context in which "insecurity was also overlaid on top of the deprivation of basic needs. . . . People were also living in an atmosphere of uncertainty and violence." Yet she contrasted her organization's efforts to "report dispassionately" with the "sensationalized" nature of media coverage. And, again, while she referred to Janjawiid "attacks on IDP camps and . . . attacks, if I recall correctly, in the first instance on villages," she is reluctant to go into greater depth: "My focus was [more] on alleviating the suffering than necessarily on needing an entirely complete analysis of the perpetrators. Identifying the victim was certainly important; identifying who was suffering was very important, and targeting the needs of the population. In a complex emergency like that a lot of my focus would have been on that rather than saying the rights or wrongs of the situation."

When asked about the number of victims, she cited the numbers typically published by the UN (200,000 dead). She added, though: "I've never seen any UN official report to say that all deaths were from attacks by either side. They were deaths because people were deprived of basic needs and services." This focus on the causes of death associated with deprivation in IDP camps aligns with her humanitarian perspective.

Also, when commenting on the rape of women, she highlighted those incidents in which women left IDP camps to gather firewood, and she stressed the need for protection of these humanitarian aid settings. My questions regarding the degree and types of suffering, when directed at the interviewees from the Political Division, yielded little additional information.

Unlike the DFA interviewees, the RTÉ respondent spoke more directly to the violence in Darfur. While he insisted that journalists must report each actor's view of the situation, including the Sudan government's, he added that journalistic investigation would provide evidence that allowed the viewer or listener to form an independent judgment on the events:

> In 2004 we were able to go to some of the villages that had been burnt down. . . . We were able to get people's firsthand accounts of how they spoke first about the bombings that happened from the air. Bombings from the air happen only one way—that is, through government support. And after that, men on horseback or camels or trucks came through. . . . They rounded up the men, raped the women. People were herded out. Everyone who was deemed to have been a problem was killed, and the place was erased to the ground.

This journalistic account demonstrates that media involvement in the network of the humanitarian aid field does not eliminate journalistic independence. The sentiment we encounter in this statement is certainly not cast in diplomatic or humanitarian caution. This interview finding is confirmed by our quantitative analysis. News reporting in Ireland generally did not downplay the suffering of the victims of Darfur. Figure 14.A shows that the *Irish Times* addressed killings in Darfur at about the same rate as the major newspapers in seven other Western countries. Rapes were reported even more frequently than elsewhere (figure 14.B). Putting this observation in perspective, I should add that rape was reported in the English-speaking countries at about double the rate in the French- and German-speaking ones. The overrepresentation of rape reports is actually less pronounced for Ireland than it is for the average reports of the United Kingdom, the United States, or Canada. Finally, and importantly, displacements were reported more often in the *Irish Times*, especially in opinion pieces, than in papers from the other seven countries (Figure 14.C).[8] This is in line with the attention that humanitarian aid organizations directed at the very people who sought refuge in IDP or refugee camps.

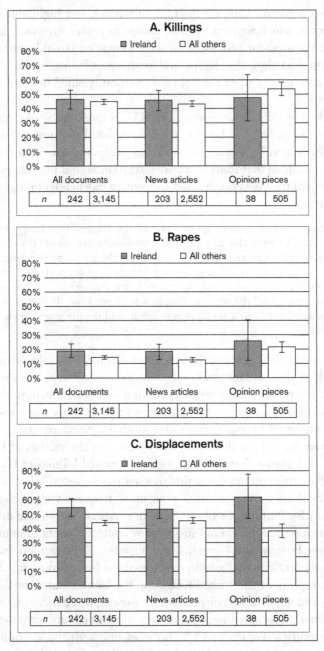

FIGURE 14. Percentage of Irish media documents that address killings, rapes, and displacements, compared to all other media documents.

Causes, Actors, and Frames

While Irish representations acknowledge the suffering in Darfur, the narrative related by the interviewee from Irish Aid already indicated some caution about implicating the Sudanese state as a perpetrator of violence. Differences between the aid policy depiction and the human rights representation become starker when we consider accounts about causes, responsible actors, and the framing of the violence.

One of the Political Division interviewees, when asked about the origins of the conflict and responsible actors, first spoke to the neglect of Sudan's periphery by its center. His colleague confirmed the center-periphery conflict and also commented on the destabilizing role of surrounding countries such as Chad, the rebel groups (JEM), and the Janjawiid, "supported by the Sudanese government." That latter comment notwithstanding, the interviewer implicated Khartoum less directly than the human rights narrative did: "At the earlier stages it was a highly complex conflict in which a variety of forces—be they supported from Khartoum, be they semi-resident in Chad, be they part of the Darfuri community itself—all were struggling to gain an advantage, keep territory, and undermine others. And within that there was no space for protecting citizens." When asked about responsible actors, the interviewees in the Political Division uttered neither names nor positions. Regarding the government of Sudan, one reasoned that it "arrived at a point where it has effectively either ungoverned or misgoverned spaces in its own country." The same respondent did, however, commend the ICC for having "done a good job in identifying those who carried out and supported certain atrocities." As in other instances of diplomatic speech, wherein institutions or individuals refuse to name names, referring to court decisions appears to be one acceptable way of indirectly hinting at responsible actors.

The Irish Aid interviewee responded with similar caution to my questions about causes and responsible actors. She referred to tribal conflict, "land degradation issues and climate issues that occurred over a fairly long period of time." Taking a shorter-term perspective, she said that the "SLA [Sudan Liberation Army, a rebel group] basically lost patience and . . . they felt that their side was being pushed around in terms of access to resources, and—at the rebel level—they decided that they were going to take up arms. You will see in anything you read about Darfur that the violence certainly emanated initially from the rebel side, but that it was the scale of the reaction by Khartoum that exacerbated the whole situation." While the respondent did not deny the escalating role of government actions, she focused on the rebels and their violent actions against the government as the initiators of the conflict. This line of argument is consistent with humanitarian programs' need to maintain constructive relationships with the government of the receiving country.

Even the RTÉ journalist, who had used rather blunt words when asked about the victimization of the local population, expressed more caution in his responses to questions about the causes of the conflict and responsible actors. He too referred to "increasing desertification," issues between "farmers and nomadic people," the center-periphery conflict in Sudan, Chadian destabilization, and the inspiration rebels received from the apparent success of the southern rebellion in achieving an independent state. He supplemented such cautious speech, however, by pointing to the Janjawiid, who either worked "hand in glove with the government" or were "a response to armed actions by the SLA." But, then again, he insisted that "the situation is so much more complex and the conflict lines are so much less clearly drawn than it is sometimes presented." He spoke of the "splintering of the armed opposition groups in Darfur," mixed in with "banditry." Talk about complexity is likely to reduce responsibility assigned leading state actors, and this interviewee made that point explicit in one additional statement: "You are either of the view that the president controls absolutely everything and if he wanted it [snaps fingers], it would happen right then. Or you are of the view that this is an area of disintegration, and that would be more my view."

When asked about appropriate ways to frame the conflict, all respondents emphasized humanitarian catastrophe. Least surprisingly, the Irish Aid interviewee found the humanitarian perspective a "point of view that's the most relevant. It's an impact lens rather than a causality lens." Also the interviewees in the Political Division and the journalist interviewee accepted this frame unambiguously. I received more mixed responses, on the other hand, when inquiring about the insurrection and civil war frames.

Responses to my inquiry about the appropriateness of applying a state crime frame to the violence in Darfur are of special interest, as I contrast the humanitarian with the human rights narrative. The interviewee from Irish Aid provided a somewhat meandering answer worth quoting:

> I'm not a lawyer, and that has always troubled me a bit in terms of the likes of the ICC and how one attributes responsibility. I often feel people are very quick to judge a situation and draw conclusions. . . . There certainly seemed

to be plenty of anecdotal evidence, the likes of the media reportage around those burned villages. It could be said that there was a level of evidence of state involvement. . . . I suppose I prefer my focus to come across as being that my predominant interest in the situation was on the humanitarian portfolio and that, as a result, I am doing 99 percent of my work without needing to attribute responsibility. . . . It certainly did not escape my attention that it was not a clear-cut situation, because nothing in Sudan is. It is a very complex, opaque construct.

This response leads us from a reference to lawyers and the ICC as concerned with identifying responsible actors, to a cautious accusation of the Sudanese state, and finally back again to an insistence that identifying responsible actors is outside the jurisdiction of the Irish DFA, especially Irish Aid. Respondents in the Political Division are more openly critical of the Sudanese state, but they, too, express caution about the crime frame:

Clearly Sudan is not a failed or failing state, but for large parts of its territory it's at best a negligent state. . . . But, you know, criminal—some of the acts of the Sudanese government one could classify as criminal in terms of the use of violence against the population. But before it was criminal, it was negligent. But negligent is almost too benign because I think it's active negligence. . . . There is certainly a degradation of all facilities and rights and organization of the state that citizens would have some right to expect. And that, then, leads to the degree of not policing, allowing impunity, for example. At that point the law has virtually no meaning. It becomes a matter of interchange between tribes, and so that is what was allowed to develop, even going beyond "allowed to develop," it was participated in by the Khartoum government.

This statement betrays much uncertainty as it refers to the Sudanese state alternatingly as a negligent state, an actively negligent state, and a state that engages in some acts that could be considered criminal.

Only the RTÉ journalist unambiguously embraced the state crime frame: "Absolutely. You cannot bomb villages and send troops through, or at least be aware of that happening, and not take steps to prevent that from happening." He simultaneously rejects the notion of genocide: "In my reporting I never gave an opinion. . . . I wouldn't feel legally savvy enough. . . . That really is a matter for the courts."

Our quantitative data, based on content analysis of reports about the Darfur conflict published in the *Irish Times*, reflects the sentiments that prevailed in the interviews. While the acknowledgement of suffering and victimization of the Darfuri population does not lag in Irish interviews and media reports, media messages are more cautious about citing the crime frame. To be sure, as Figure 15.A shows, media reports do not shy away from referring to the violence as criminal. Yet they do so more cautiously than media from the seven other countries under examination. As in previous analyses, differences are more pronounced in opinion pieces than in news articles. The same pattern applies to media reports referring to the violence as a case of genocide (see figure 15.B).[9] This again is not surprising, as genocide is generally treated with particular caution among those who seek not to dramatize the violence in Darfur.[10]

Skepticism about Criminal Justice

Irish reluctance to apply a state crime frame to the violence in Darfur suggests that support for a legal response, especially a criminal justice response, will be weak, at best. Given the experience with MSF interviewees, we should expect caution to be especially pronounced in interview statements by the respondent from Irish Aid. And, indeed, her responses do reflect considerable reservations about criminal proceedings in Irish foreign policy. While she did express some openness toward transitional justice in the broader sense of the term, she was skeptical about any role for criminal courts in the Darfur conflict:

> I don't think Sudan would be alone if an impunity road was chosen. . . . I am not even sure you characterize it exclusively as impunity, do you? You've got your truth commissions, you got your amnesties. There are different positions taken by countries coming out of conflict. In the north of Ireland there is consensus on whether a truth and reconciliation commission is the right approach. There was effectively an amnesty in 1998, I think, for prisoners, for people who were already in prison for terrorist offenses. So that's not impunity per se. . . . You've seen lots of very interesting transitional justice processes in Africa, the likes of the *gacaca* in Rwanda, and you've had your truth and reconciliation commissions. And Sudan is so huge; it's not a monolith, it's not a homogeneous context. . . . [A pure criminal justice approach] would be a strong component if you can bring absolutely everybody who is responsible for anything to justice. But in the context where it is not quite so clear and where you look at how development is to be allowed to take place, I think you need a certain amount of creativity in terms of how you respond to peoples' justifiable need for some redress. But if the quality of their lives is not going to improve because you have made the issue two-sided again, . . . there is no likelihood that development gains will happen, because the situation is so polarized. It defeats the purpose of redress.

Respondents in the Political Division were more open to legal responses, but they too expressed some degree of doubt and prefer a

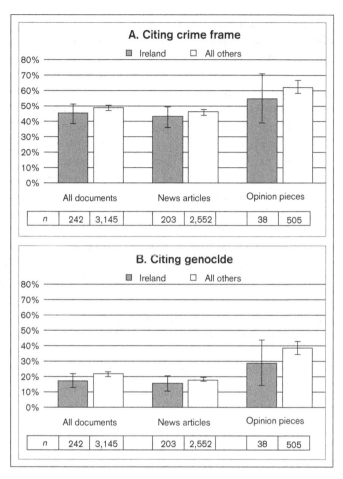

FIGURE 15. Percentage of Irish media documents citing the crime frame and using the genocide label, compared to all other media documents.

cautious approach. After having stated that development depends on peace and that there cannot be secure peace without justice, one interviewee continued: "The pursuit of justice in South Africa is a good example here. Justice needs to be part of the peace process and not allowed to become used as an obstacle to participation." His colleague added that "the isolated pursuit of justice is possible, but it is likely to have considerable limitations in its effect if it is not accompanied by other aspects." To be sure, the criminal justice process, especially ICC interventions, were not seen in an entirely negative light. Both interviewees in the Political Division agreed that ICC prosecution might push President al-Bashir into a more conciliatory approach, that he may "recognize that a more responsive and a more responsible policy in relation to the South may mitigate the way he may be handled in the future or, who knows, he may hope it gets him off the hook entirely."

The skepticism we encounter here toward a criminal justice response to Darfur is in line with the tension observed throughout this chapter between an aid approach and penal strategies. In addition, the Irish interviews reveal traces of collective memory that nourish such skepticism. This more recent memory to which my interviewees referred concerns the Northern Ireland conflict and the above lengthy statement of the Irish Aid interviewee speaks to that. Not accidentally, she had previously worked on Northern Ireland issues in the foreign ministry. She remembered that the situation was dealt with as a "terrorist situation" and that one "could have taken a very strong approach, which was done up until 1994. . . . And eventually everybody came to the conclusion that . . . neither side would win." This memory of the Northern Ireland conflict is not free-floating, and it is not fully explained with a reference to carrier groups. Instead it is institutionalized within the political administration. Interview respondents in the DFA told me about a unit within the Political Division, set up with the goal of drawing lessons from the Northern Ireland experience and applying such lessons to conflicts globally. I encountered confidence that such lessons will become a major part of DFA humanitarian and development aid programming.

CONCLUSIONS: THE HUMANITARIAN COMPLEX AND
ITS REPRESENTATIONS OF MASS VIOLENCE

This study of Ireland, a country with a strong humanitarian aid orientation, confirms and adds to insights from the previous chapter on humanitarian NGOs. For aid-oriented government actors, as for humanitarian aid organizations, the government of the receiving country is a major player in attempts to deliver assistance to suffering populations. This is also true when leaders of that government are charged with grave crimes by the ICC or any other court. In fact, the situation for countries with aid-oriented foreign policies is more complex than that for INGOs. In the case of Ireland, the government itself is tied into a field I have termed a humanitarian aid complex. It involves major NGOs, partly affiliated with the Catholic Church; the governments of the donating and receiving countries; and even media organizations of the donating country.

And, as in the case of MSF, the representation of the mass violence in Darfur takes a particular shape, quite distinct from that of the human rights field. Again, there is no denial of suffering. In the humanitarian complex, too, the pain and deprivation of the population in areas of conflict are documented and communicated to a world audience. Yet here, as in the case of INGOs, those aspects of suffering are stressed that can be addressed by humanitarian aid programs. The depiction of displacements and the deprivation suffered in IDP or refugee camps trumps that of mass killings by the military and their affiliated militias. And again, critique of the government of Sudan is more muted than that encountered in the human rights field. In line with such caution, the humanitarian emergency frame is privileged over the state crime frame.

The elective affinity identified between the humanitarian aid field and the specific representation of the violence by aid actors clearly involves causal ties. As they depend on the cooperation of the Sudanese state to grant visas and permits to travel and deliver aid, humanitarian actors exercise caution with regard to the government of Sudan. This argument is further strengthened when actors in this field include religious organizations such as the Catholic Church in Ireland. Amnesty interviewees in Germany likewise indicated that the public understanding of the Darfur conflict was inspired by the country's major churches and was oriented more toward a humanitarian catastrophe than toward a criminal accountability model.

The Irish case of the humanitarian complex, like that of MSF, thus approximates an ideal-typical depiction of a humanitarian catastrophe in the aid field. But the lesson is broader. Elsewhere, using advanced statistical analysis, we confirmed that the patterns identified for Ireland apply across countries with varying foci on humanitarianism (Savelsberg and Nyseth Brehm 2015). In other words, the more a country is invested in humanitarian aid, the more likely will its media subscribe to a narrative dominated by humanitarian concerns. Note further that Ireland only approximates a humanitarian ideal type. Even here, the country's aid-oriented focus is partly neutralized by its membership in international organizations that represent a wider range of policy preferences. Global and international scripts, too, matter to Irish policy makers, in line with the World Polity School. Yet the stress, common in historicizing branches of neo-Weberianism, on national carrier groups and cultural sensitivities finds especially strong support in the case of Ireland.

How, then, are humanitarian representations communicated to global society? Before turning to this question, part III examines another field whose representation of mass violence may conflict with that generated in the context of the justice cascade: diplomacy and foreign policy and their the construction of narratives about the Darfur conflict.

PART THREE

Peace versus Justice

The Diplomatic Field

CHAPTER 6

Diplomatic Representations of Mass Violence

"If you want to make peace in Darfur through negotiations, you have to deal with the Sudanese government and you have to deal with the people who hold the power in the Sudanese government, and that includes Omar al-Bashir. If you want to achieve justice through the International Criminal Court, well, then you should stigmatize someone who is indicted. You shouldn't talk to Omar al-Bashir. Right?"

One of my interviewees from the world of foreign policy and diplomacy thus succinctly addressed a key difference between the justice field and that of foreign policy, where diplomacy is a central tool. Actors in the latter seek to include players in the field, no matter their responsibility for immense suffering; actors in the former seek to exclude certain players. Foreign policy is not identical with diplomacy, of course. Threats of military intervention and the potential of economic sanctions, positive and negative, are among its tools. And so are hints at judicial consequences for human rights offenses. Diplomats may use such threats (and rewards) as they engage with leaders and agents of foreign governments. But engage with them they do, and they thus depend on maintaining network ties—diplomatic capital. Diplomacy differs from the justice field in another essential way: it is oriented toward substantive outcomes, in stark contrast to the procedural orientation of criminal proceedings. What are the consequences of these differences for representations of the Darfur conflict in the diplomatic field?

Previous scholarship has identified the cautious rhetoric of governments regarding the term *genocide*. Samantha Power (2002), now the US ambassador to the United Nations, argued in her Pulitzer Prize–winning book, *A Problem from Hell: America and the Age of Genocide*, in the case of the United States: "The U.S. Government not only abstains from sending its troops, but it takes very few steps along a continuum of intervention to deter genocide. U.S. officials . . . render the bloodshed two-sided and inevitable, not genocidal. . . . They avoid use of the term 'genocide'" (xviii). Political scientist Karen Smith (2010) identifies similar patterns for France, Germany, and the United Kingdom, for post–World War II history generally and for these countries' specific responses to mass violence in Bosnia, Rwanda, Kosovo, and Darfur: "[Q]uite a few European governments were hostile to the Genocide Convention, and some took decades to ratify it. Furthermore, European governments are not keen on using the term to describe atrocities" (2).

Power (2002) and K. Smith (2010) do not just describe but also seek to explain the cautious rhetoric of governments. Their argument is based on the assumption that rational foreign policy actors seek to avoid pressure toward intervention, possibly by military means, given that such intervention is almost always unpopular among their countries' populations.[1] This explanation is meaningful but seems incomplete. My data suggest that it needs to be complemented by a theory that takes seriously conditions in the diplomatic field and the habitus it generates. The government of the perpetrating country is a player in that field, and diplomats depend on active cooperation by its agents to pursue their negotiations toward substantive outcomes. It is this field condition that prompts their caution about using exclusionary rhetoric, a hallmark of the institutional logic of criminal law, as well as their caution against the use of direct language, even when rational thought about the political consequences of interventions has not been activated. In short, governments are reluctant to use strong means, especially military intervention, in cases of genocide or mass atrocities in distant lands. This reluctance is reinforced by the inclination of actors in the diplomatic field to capitalize on past social ties in international relations, a disposition that has become part of the habitus of diplomats. Avoiding strong language and strategies that would force a breakdown of communication appears natural to them.

Just as field theory helps explain differences and competition between narratives about mass violence generated in the criminal justice versus humanitarian aid fields, it suggests that we should expect yet another distinctive representation in the field of diplomacy with its unique constellation of actors. My interviews with diplomats and the documents I gathered from foreign ministries show, not surprisingly, that many participants in the foreign policy and diplomacy fields, just like their counterparts in the humanitarian aid field, are cautious to hostile in their views regarding the notion of individual criminal liability for grave human rights violations. They resent the heart of the justice cascade. In fact, their accounts often challenge the idea that responsibility can be attributed to specific individuals or that doing so, even where possible, would be "helpful."[2]

While the display of a common denominator, or master narrative, in diplomatic accounts of the Darfur conflict is in line with field theory, I nevertheless expect foreign policy and its narratives to vary in cross-national comparison—a topic I address in the following chapter. In addition to a common denominator and cross-national variation in responses to Darfur, I further anticipate variation within countries. Foreign policy makers differ in terms of educational background, career paths within the foreign service, and especially the specific organizational units within departments of foreign affairs in which they formulate their positions on mass atrocities. While my interviewees paid at least lip service to the mission of the International Criminal Court, only some clearly identified with its mission. Others—even within the same country—displayed skepticism, in principle or in practice.

This chapter begins with a brief overview of relevant data. I then show how the field of diplomacy presents itself in the case of Darfur. What goals do diplomats identify with? Which actors matter in this pursuit? What sources of information do diplomats draw from? How does their habitus correspond with the field, and what traces from diachronically (education) and synchronically (nation, organizational unit) overlapping fields do we find? Next, I sketch, based on my interviews, a diplomatic narrative of the Darfur conflict. As in previous chapters, I consider causes of the conflict, central actors who bear responsibility for the violence, victimization, and suffering, as well as the frame deemed appropriate for an interpretation of the violence. I indeed identify a diplomatic master narrative, approximating an ideal type, a narrative that starkly contrasts with criminal justice representations of the same event.

INTERVIEWS, FOREIGN MINISTRY WEBSITES, AND THE MEDIA DATA SET

I conducted a total of twelve semistructured interviews with thirteen Darfur experts in foreign ministries, each lasting between one and two hours and yielding some five hundred pages of transcript. Interviewees included actors from all six European countries considered throughout this study—Austria, France, Germany, Ireland, the United Kingdom, and Switzerland, as well as a seventh, the Netherlands. A small conference on representations of the Darfur conflict held at the Rockefeller Bellagio Center included US diplomats from the Bill Clinton and George W. Bush administrations and provided opportunities for formal and informal communication on the issues addressed in my questionnaire. These American diplomats and two European interviewees also supplied me with publications they had authored on the Darfur conflict.

Diplomat interviewees were all engaged in work on Sudan generally, Darfur specifically, issues of international law and the ICC, or some combination of these. Eight were placed in their ministry's political divisions, where treaties are negotiated, arbitration is organized, and communication is cultivated with other governments, including hostile ones. Two worked in legal divisions, with responsibilities for international justice institutions, and one in her ministry's development and humanitarian aid division. Two respondents were at the periphery of the field, in research institutions with consulting and support functions for their respective foreign ministries.

Interviewees had various educational backgrounds. Five held law degrees (two with specializations in international law, one in combination with political science); four held degrees in political science; and one, a degree in international public policy (supplemented by economics and English literature degrees). While law and political science thus dominated, there were exceptions: one respondent had earned his PhD with a thesis on the history of his country's foreign policy; another held degrees in history and geography with a focus on Africa; and yet another had a background in natural science. Not surprisingly, two of the respondents with law degrees were placed in legal divisions of their foreign ministries. In line with insights from earlier chapters we should expect the lawyers in legal divisions of foreign ministries to produce a Darfur narrative that most clearly deviates from the ideal-typical representation of the diplomacy field, one that may well show an affinity with the justice narrative.

Many interviewees, even among the younger cohorts, had substantial foreign experience. Three had done part of their studies abroad, and two of these had earned advanced degrees at foreign universities (both in the United States). Eight had spent substantial portions of their foreign service careers abroad. Some had visited Sudan, including Darfur, and three had worked for extensive periods in their countries' missions in Khartoum. There they had regularly interacted with representatives of the Sudanese state. Within the world of diplomacy, these three actors are structurally closest to that part of the diplomatic field that encompasses the Sudanese state. Their account of the conflict should most evidently be in line with the diplomatic master narrative on Darfur and most distinct from the criminal justice narrative.

Supplementing the interview data is a content analysis of websites of the foreign ministries, specifically foreign ministry press releases found thereon for seven of our eight countries.[3] I also draw on findings from the Darfur media data set to compare diplomatic sentiments across countries with patterns from the societies in which they are embedded.

THE FIELD OF DIPLOMACY AND THE HABITUS OF ITS ACTORS

Interacting with the Sudanese State

When I conducted my interviews, between December 2010 and July 2011, two major diplomatic efforts were under way. The first was the implementation of the Comprehensive Peace Agreement (CPA) of 2005, intended to settle the devastating Second Sudanese Civil War between the country's North and South, with its estimated two million dead. The second was the most recent major attempt to bring peace to Darfur: the Doha peace negotiations, following the ill-fated Abuja Peace Agreement of 2006. These Doha negotiations were finalized in the spring of 2011, after two and a half years of diplomatic labor. Both processes loomed large in the minds of the diplomats I interviewed, and colored their reading of the conflict.

The CPA is also known as the Naivasha Agreement, named after the Kenyan town where most of its components were negotiated between 2002 and 2004 and where the final comprehensive agreement was signed on January 9, 2005. The contracting parties were the government of Sudan and the Sudan People's Liberation Movement (SPLM). The process was advanced by the Intergovernmental Authority for Development (IGAD), a trading group of East African countries, and the IGAD Partners, a consortium of donors that included three of the countries considered in this analysis (i.e., the Netherlands, United Kingdom, and United States). The CPA resulted in the formation of the shaky Government of National Unity for Sudan after 2005 and in the withdrawal of northern Sudanese troops from South Sudan in January 2008. As part of the CPA, a referendum was held in January 2011 in which the population of southern Sudan almost unanimously voted to separate from the North. We know today that the establishment of the new country, enthusiastically celebrated by the South Sudanese population at the time, but accompanied by cautious commentary from political analysts and informed journalists, resulted in a state at risk of failing and in a new, brutal civil war between military factions organized around fiefs, partly on the basis of ethnicity (with the Nuer and Dinka as the dominant groups), within the South. Since late 2013, the death toll has climbed with frightening speed. Yet in 2011 the implementation of the CPA appeared as a major triumph of diplomacy. After all, a long and bloody civil war had been settled by diplomatic means. The question on the minds of many interviewees was whether the government of Sudan would cooperate until the very end and whether it would indeed allow independence to take place and would permit control over massive oil fields to shift to its new neighbor. Simultaneously, would the Sudan government continue the Doha peace process on Darfur, then approaching a conclusion? Or would Khartoum at the last moment destroy the fruit of hard diplomatic labor that was expected to replace a legacy of mass violence with enduring peace?

A diplomat from the political division of the foreign ministry of a large European country who had previously spent years in his country's embassy in Khartoum spoke about diplomatic efforts focused on Sudan. His words illustrate well a diplomatic strategy vis-à-vis the CPA process and the role attributed to the government of Sudan: "Our first priority is securing the Comprehensive Peace Agreement and to accompany it all the way through [to] its, ideally complete, implementation. That is especially, right now, that the referendum on the independence of South Sudan will be held, and then the, in all likelihood, subsequent independence of South Sudan [will take effect] in July 2011. That is the first pillar" (author's translation).

The interviewee then addressed the risk of South Sudan becoming a "pre-failed state," an outcome "the international community cannot afford." Contributing to a functioning infrastructure in South Sudan was thus considered the second component of his country's policy. The third pillar linked the CPA to the Doha negotiations on Darfur: "Of course there will be no peace in the region if the Darfur problem does not get resolved. That means we have to accompany the Doha peace process and promote it in a way that it will result, over [the] short or long [term], in a sustainable peace solution for Darfur, and that then also the UNAMID mission of the United Nations will become a success" (author's translation).

This interviewee, himself head of an interdepartmental task force on Darfur, reported with pride that units within his ministry had come to an agreement regarding their Sudan policy: the most important pursuit vis-à-vis Sudan for 2010–2011 would be to help the peace negotiations in Doha succeed, *with all parties to the conflict included.*

The final pillar of this country's policy consequently addresses the role of the Sudan government in this process:

> And the fourth pillar is the inclusion of northern Sudan into this peace solution and, of course, the stabilization of this region. Because, upon close inspection of the last five years of the implementation of the CPA and the Darfur War, there was always one evildoer, and this evildoer has then, for pure survival reasons or simply in opposition to international pressure against him, torpedoed all peace solutions—or could torpedo all peace solutions. He has done it, too, in the past. The proper key to a peace in the region is thus the inclusion of the regime in Khartoum in the peace solution and its liberation from international isolation, in combination with appropriate incentives to which the international community will then have to stick. (author's translation)

This explanation illustrates well the premium placed on diplomatic efforts and on the inclusion of the government of Sudan in the process of settling the conflict, not just between Sudan and South Sudan but also within Darfur. The same interviewee insisted that appropriate methods include bracketing the ICC charges against al-Bashir (*"gar nicht darüber reden"*) and providing the government with incentives, though with an undertone of potential sanctions should the incentives not work (*"wir können auch anders"*). This interview segment illustrates that the government of Sudan plays an even more powerful role in the field of diplomacy than it does in the field of humanitarian aid. At issue in diplomacy is active cooperation and compromising at the country's leadership level; in humanitarianism, the issue is toleration (and possibly cooperation) at lower levels of state administration, and in exchange for resources provided and services delivered by NGOs and international agencies.

The statements cited above are characteristic of sentiments I encountered in the world of diplomacy generally. One interviewee from another large European country expressed similar hopes and caution regarding the government of Sudan: "There was obviously a lot of work being put in, internationally, into the North-South agreement. . . . After twenty years, two million people killed, there was such desire to bring that to a conclusion and get the CPA signed that people said: 'Look at Darfur, it is terrible, but we can't rock the boat, we can't jeopardize the CPA negotiations.'" Again, the argument goes, the government of Sudan must be kept in the game, treated with respect, even offered incentives, so as to capitalize on the diplomatic investments of previous years. One interviewee spoke with pride about his (relatively small) country's status as a formal witness of the CPA and its chairing of one of three working groups of the Assessment and Evaluation Commission, the international body set up to observe the implementation of the CPA.

Diplomats also report many less visible activities. One of the small European countries with substantial expertise in the banking sector, for example, advised the government of Sudan on issues of debt relief should the North have to shoulder, as a consequence of the CPA, the debt of the entire country. The same country provided the South with expertise on writing a federal constitution for a multiethnic country, a feature both provider and recipient shared. This country had hosted numerous delegations from Sudan, including ministers, legislators, and financiers from the North and South, for seminars on constitution building, currency, and finance.

Within the world of diplomacy, clear rationales seem to drive most diplomatic efforts. Yet actors in the diplomatic field also identify strongly with their role. In fact, their habitus is shaped by their position in the diplomatic field. They have internalized the field's doxa, its matter-of-course assumptions. Diplomats intuitively know what political science research confirms: that as mediators they can succeed only if they strongly relate to the issue at stake, take a moderate position, and abstain from bias toward any one side in the conflict (Kydd 2006).[4] One interviewee, from a smaller European country with a special reputation for its expertise in mediation, reported on his ministry's chief negotiators:

> We had two mediators in the Darfur conflict, both with substantial experience and expert knowledge in the areas of mediation, conflict analysis, constitutional law, peace and conflict research, regional analysis [on] Sudan and [the] Horn of Africa. . . . They were able to play a significant role in the course of the peace processes, one in Abuja; the other spent over three years in Khartoum and was especially involved in the Doha negotiations in support of chief mediator Jibril Basole. Both experts also work as coaches and university instructors. They thus connect theory and praxis in many ways. [Commenting on demanding travel schedules and the resulting hardship for

FIGURE 16. Ambassador Tomas Ulicny, head of the EU delegation to Sudan, and Dr. Hassan El Turabi, head of the Popular Congress Party, engage in peace negotiations, Khartoum, February 3, 2015.

personal and family life:] People who devoted their hearts and souls to these processes [*mit Herzblut in diesen Prozessen waren*], who probably developed a sense: "I can make a difference; I can motivate these people so that they will finally agree to peace." (author's translation)

In short, diplomats engaged in negotiation and consulting activities in a field in which the government of Sudan and its agents played a key role. Their efforts, with which interviewees strongly identified, are directed at the achievement of peace. Some invested heavily in these efforts, at the price of enduring demanding travel schedules and frequent and long-term absences from home and family, reflecting a strong identification with their mission.

Hierarchies of Goals—And the Status of Justice among Them

Settling conflict and establishing peace is obviously a central foreign policy goal in the context of Darfur policies. But how does this goal relate to the others I inquired about in my interviews: the integrity of the sovereign state, the survival of affected populations, and—of special interest here—the pursuit of justice? How do diplomats rank these goals relative to each other? Where do they perceive conflicts between them? Do they see ways of resolving potential contradictions?

Segments from an interview I conducted with a diplomat from one of the large European countries, quoted above, strongly reflect diplomatic reasoning. They highlight as the primary goal replacing war and violent conflict with peace by means of diplomatic negotiations. The goal of justice ought to be bracketed and, if pursued at all, used as a bargaining chip. Four of the diplomats I interviewed—all from the political divisions of their ministries—clearly followed this line of reasoning. Especially telling are the words of one respondent from the sub-Sahara unit of the foreign ministry of a smaller European country, a diplomat with years of experience in his country's mission in Khartoum. Arguing for the primacy of the peace mission, he also commented on the role of justice and the ICC in relation to that primary goal:

> First, we should come to some kind of peace agreement. And then you should work on reconciliation and transitional justice. . . . The underlying problem is not the question of cooperation with the ICC, but is the culture of impunity which prevails until now in Sudan. . . . I think one should put emphasis on strengthening the national legal system in Sudan. The ICC has a very limited role or mandate, and it has not the capacity to investigate all cases of crimes that have been committed in Darfur. So you need to come to strengthening the legal system. I think the African Union panel on Darfur . . . made recommendations on the issue of peace, reconciliation and justice for Darfur. Without going into a competition with the ICC, they managed to keep these on two separate tracks. And I think these recommendations were welcomed by the Sudanese government. And I personally would put more emphasis on trying to convince the Sudanese to implement all of these recommendations instead of repeating every time that they should cooperate with the ICC, because it doesn't bring anyone any further. [Colleagues in the fragile-states unit] agree, and also the colleagues at the embassy in Khartoum, since they are working on a daily basis on the peace process. . . . You cannot expect to have an international trial against the president who is at the same moment an important player in the peace process.

This interviewee called his own position "pragmatic." While he insisted that the ICC indictments complicated the peace process, he conceded that they "could also pressure in a positive way." Instead of opposing the goal of justice, he wanted it pursued later and by means other than the ICC. He thus tempered his general skepticism toward the ICC with a call for developing the justice system in Sudan and a plea to put an end to the "culture of impunity."

Other interviewees from political divisions also had reservations about the ICC, even if they do not reject transitional justice per se. One suggested that justice should not be pursued "right away," and that there are various alternatives to the ICC. Another expressed principled support for the ICC as an institution, acknowledging its potential for a long-term civilizing effect, but insisted that it should be placed on a back burner in the Darfur case. A somewhat different argument was presented by a diplomat who believed that justice is a precondition of peace, but who called—in vague terms—for a different kind of justice than what the ICC has to offer. Some interviewees articulated general skepticism about the ICC; others objected to the way then–chief prosecutor Luis Moreno-Ocampo handled the proceedings. Moreno-Ocampo of course had achieved substantial fame earlier in his career when he courageously prosecuted members of the military junta in his native Argentina. Yet, in the Darfur case, critics challenged Moreno-Ocampo's decisions to specifically charge President al-Bashir and to include the crime of genocide in the indictment. One respondent referred to the prosecutor's "bulldog style" as possibly helpful in the Argentinean cases, but detrimental in the complicated international world in which the new and fragile institution of the ICC is embedded. For this world, and also in the prosecutor's office, he and other diplomats argued, a more *diplomatic* approach was warranted.

Perceptions of conflict between peace and justice were most pronounced in political divisions and among diplomats with substantial experience in foreign missions. Indeed, those at the core of the diplomatic field are most dedicated to the goal of peace and most skeptical toward the pursuit of justice. Skepticism is further intensified among diplomats who had intense exposure to that part of the diplomatic field in which the government of Sudan was a key participant; for example, through work in their respective country's embassy in Khartoum.

The primacy of the peace mission, however, is not uniform in the world of diplomacy. Chapter 5 discusses Irish diplomats who—in line with their country's foreign policy emphasis on development and humanitarian aid—declared the survival of the affected population to be their first priority, placing peace second and expressing considerable skepticism for the justice mission. Such prioritizing was not surprising in Dublin's aid division, but it was at least echoed in the Political Division as well. The Irish case thus illustrates how both national context and the humanitarianism field affect priorities and strategies in the diplomatic field. Those who emphasize aid share with those who prioritize peace skepticism concerning the goal of justice—or at least concerning the primacy of justice and its pursuit by the ICC in a conflict's early stages.

Another branch in the foreign policy field, however, decisively supports the goal of justice and the ICC. Even Irish diplomats alerted me to the strong emphasis on the justice mission in their ministry's human rights division. Interviewees in political divisions elsewhere also stressed that their own focus on the peace mission was not necessarily shared by their colleagues in law divisions. One of them expected his human rights colleagues, as well as his minister, to take an approach more "legalistic" than his own.

Such expectations are confirmed in my interviews with two foreign ministry employees, both lawyers by training, who served in law divisions. Both insisted that the path to peace presupposes the realization of justice. One foreign ministry employee in a small country was placed in a unit on international criminal law where issues relating to Nazi-era compensation claims also fell under his jurisdiction. The other interviewee had served, until shortly before the interview, as head of an office that handled ICC issues within a division of international law. In that role he also represented his ministry on the ICC's Assembly of States. He is from the same country as the coordinator of a Sudan task force and long-term employee of his country's embassy in Khartoum whom we encountered near the beginning of this chapter. Recall that that interviewee focused most strongly on the goal of peace by means of diplomacy. In line with my expectations regarding the weight of organizational placement within the diplomatic field, the position taken by his colleague in the international law division differs markedly:

> There is a tendency from a political perspective to say, well, in certain circumstances we should have peace prevail over justice. Which means, we should . . . postpone a judicial prosecution or any legal proceeding against somebody, because we need that guy to have peace. And my lesson is: that is not true. Because what you consider as peace . . . would not be a sustainable peace, because when I look at hundreds of thousands of victims and I accept that the injustice done against them is not taken into account, that their stories remain untold, then I cannot see how a traumatized postconflict society like this can really make sustainable peace. It is simply not possible. You need to go through that process. You need to give them justice. And once they have the feel that justice, more or less, is done or taken care of, then I think you can create within such a society a willingness to overcome postconflict and enter a new phase of peace building. . . . And the political point I am making is: you don't have to do all the political work yourself, you politicians. Rely on certain aspects that can be dealt with through justice. And simply take the fruits of it. And they can be helpful for the course of your political endeavors and efforts. And that can move things forward. And you can really make a difference.

This interviewee strongly supports prosecution in the ICC, "at least for those who bear the greatest responsibility." But he also speaks about the International Center for Transitional Justice in New York and about alternative transitional justice mechanisms such as truth commissions and "local law" for actors such as those in low levels of the military hierarchy or "a child soldier" who "may be considered a victim himself." He cites "civil society people" who "really work at the grassroots level in Africa" and who "are reporting that things start to change . . . that people at this [high] level start to realize, look, I mean, there is somebody out there who ultimately could go after me. . . . We cannot accept impunity because we need something to prevent future atrocities."

I also inquired about the goals of ensuring survival and preserving the integrity of the state of Sudan. Responses show that these goals appeared much less prominently in the diplomatic field. The intensity of the goal of ensuring survival of the affected exhibited in the Irish Department of Foreign Affairs remains unique. One interviewee explicitly stated that "survival is not enough." Finally, most respondents supported division of Sudan and had given up on the notion of national integrity.

In short, the tension between the goals of peace and justice dominated responses from interviewees in foreign ministries. These goals were not necessarily seen as mutually exclusive, but the diplomatic field produces a set of clear priorities that strongly challenges the logic of the justice cascade. An unambiguous preference for peace over justice applies at least to those actors in the field who are associated with political divisions and engaged in day-to-day diplomatic work.

Sources of Information

In addition to the Sudan government's weight in the diplomatic field and the goals of its practitioners, sources of information should also influence how diplomats perceive the Darfur conflict. I thus asked interviewees what sources they consult to gain an appropriate understanding of the situation in Darfur. I did not ask them to rank their responses, but those mentioned first and spontaneously appeared especially important. All but one respondent mentioned between four and nine sources.

Several diplomats referred to their country's embassies ($n = 6$)—and those who did, did so spontaneously—as one of their first three options. In the words of one interviewee: "The first source is the embassy report, which is steered by our interests [*dann also entsprechend sogar gesteuert wird*]. So they receive concrete questions and are asked to answer them" (author's translation). Many diplomats pointed to international organizations, specifically the UN ($n = 9$; plus UNAMID [3]), the EU (5), and the AU (2). While formal reports of IOs are often considered too neutral to be valuable, personal and professional contacts within these organizations are highly valued.

Note that one-third of the sources (25 out of 70–80) cited were diplomatic. And they were among the first that interviewees mentioned spontaneously when asked. The diplomatic world is thus in part a self-referential system that produces the information it consumes. Yet this judgment would oversimplify reality if taken too far. The other two-thirds of sources include NGOs (9), especially humanitarian NGOs on the ground in Sudan; think tanks and academics (7), even though follow-ups yielded few book titles or names of academics, with the exception of Alex de Waal (see the introduction); media, including Sudanese opposition media such as the *Sudan Tribune* and Radio Dabanga (6); and communication with Sudanese people, locally on the occasion of visits to Sudan, in the diaspora, or virtually over the Internet (5). Finally, and importantly here, only one respondent referred to court evidence. This is the same lawyer-interviewee who had served as a member of the ICC's Assembly of States and whom I cited as making a strong plea for justice.

In short, the world of diplomacy draws much of its information from national and international organizations, primarily diplomatic ones, but from other sources as well, including NGOs, media, think tanks, and Sudanese informants.

REPRESENTATIONS OF DARFUR IN THE DIPLOMATIC FIELD

What representation of Darfur is then generated in a field where the government of Sudan has substantial weight, where peacemaking trumps other goals, and where information from governments and international organizations is dominant? How do diplomats interpret the causes of the conflict? Whom do they identify as responsible actors? What kinds of suffering do they acknowledge? And what do diplomats perceive to be the appropriate frame through which to interpret the violence in Sudan?

Causes of Conflict

Ten interviewees from foreign ministries spoke explicitly about the causes of the mass violence in Darfur. Two referred me to writings, specifically texts by Alex de Waal and by a mediator from the respondent's own ministry. Out of more than thirty arguments articulated in the relevant interview segments, those dominate that deflected responsibility from actors who were charged by the ICC. Instead, diplomats mentioned most frequently factors associated with natural or structural-political conditions. First is the process of desertification, the drought that is moving the Sahara ever further into the Sahel, and the resulting resource scarcity—an argument also common among environmentalism branches of the UN (see Smith and Howe 2015: ch. 8). Diplomats often combine this argument with references to intergroup conflicts caused by these natural conditions, specifically conflicts between "tribes," "ethnic groups," or "nomads" and "pastoralists." Also the center-periphery conflict shows prominently as a long-term feature of the Sudanese state that eventually provoked rebellion. This argument dominates, not surprisingly, among actors with a political science education. As discussed above regarding the human rights and humanitarian fields, educational socialization colors representations in the diplomacy field. It affects habitus and doxa, taken-for-granted assumptions about reality. Diplomats further point at neighboring countries or at rebels from southern Sudan who supplied Darfur rebels with weapons to destabilize Sudan and its government.

Rarely did the aforementioned causes appear in isolation, of course. Interviewees linked them together, and their cognitive maps entail intricate causal relationships between diverse factors. Statements by the Sudan expert in the foreign ministry of a large European country illustrate such a map:

> There are three main reasons why I think the crisis started. The first one is . . . that the Sahara Desert was going south, so all the nomadic tribes had to go further south. There was a bigger competition for water and for wells. . . . So the old system of interaction between agriculture and nomads . . . was challenged by that. You started to have local fighting between the different tribes. But that's what started in the mid-eighties and went on for quite a long time without becoming the big Darfur crisis we have seen. What triggered the conflict really were the two other main reasons. The first one, being a political reason, is not really specific for Darfur. It is the marginalization of all the peripheries in Sudan, compared to the center in Khartoum. Darfur used to be a kingdom before being integrated into Sudan. There is a strong memory of that in the mind of the Darfuri people. And after independence they were quite marginalized. They were completely marginalized if you look at the universities, hospitals, schools. . . . And they were voicing their concerns and what they wanted, but purely politically. And that is where the third part comes in. When the Darfur crisis started, North and South were

discussing, were starting negotiations, and at that time the mediator said: Well, if you want to negotiate, we will take only the people who have guns around the table. . . . So, these Darfuri people who had more or less the same concerns as the southerners realized that . . . the only solution they had to show that they existed was to take up arms and to start a rebellion.

Through such cognitive maps, the central causal factors mentioned by diplomat interviewees—namely, desertification, intergroup and center-periphery conflict, and (as some diplomats argue elsewhere in the interviews) conflicts with southern Sudan, Libya, and Chad—interacted in the minds of diplomats. In at least three interviews the basic logic of the narrative, the stringing together of causal factors, was almost identical with that quoted above.

Implied in many arguments, and at times stated explicitly, is the long-term nature of the violence in Darfur. One respondent actually saw this violence as an element of the natural history of state formation: "The wars that Sudan now conducts, for example, Europeans conducted in the sixteenth and seventeenth centuries: wars of nation building [*der nationalen Identitätsfindung*], wars to settle or eliminate religious differences, ethnic wars" (author's translation). Diplomatic positions thus starkly contrast with Hagan and Rymond-Richmond's criminological "endogenous conflict theory" (2008), which explains the violence as the product of shorter-term dynamics initiated by concrete state actors to whom societal groups responded. The diplomatic explanations are congenial instead with positions taken by Alex de Waal. This homology may help explain why de Waal is the main academic reference point when diplomats refer to scholarship as a source of information.

But the focus on long-term causes does not mean that diplomat interviewees fully neglect the agency of the Sudanese state. One respondent told how the government of Sudan "armed the one side, the nomadic tribes in Darfur, to put down the rebellion." Another insisted that the violence "certainly emanated initially from the rebel side," but, he continued, "it was the scale of the reaction by Khartoum that exacerbated the entire situation." Yet another interviewee reported that the patterns in Darfur were typical strategies of the Sudanese government: "It happened in the South before; it happened in Blue Nile and Southern Kordofan as well. They consider their army isn't strong enough to fight against the rebellion, so they use proxies to support the army, and what they did learn was to use Arab tribes, tribes that consider themselves as Arab, which is mainly nomadic tribes, telling them: 'Well, we'll give you weapons. You fight against those other tribes . . . and you take whatever you want.'"

While references to the Sudanese state are thus not absent when diplomats discuss causes of the violence, they appear less prominently than do ecological and structural forces. In addition, diplomats tend to avoid naming specific actors. They certainly remain more general than position holders in the criminal justice system or in human rights–based NGOs. But would they maintain their reluctance if asked not generally about causes, but specifically about responsible actors?

Asking about Actors

Ten interviewees from the world of diplomacy commented on actors with potential responsibility for the mass violence in Darfur. While they mostly spoke about the government of Sudan, the Janjawiid, and rebel organizations as collective actors, some referred occasionally to President al-Bashir and Ahmed Harun as individuals. Respondents certainly never expressed doubt that the government of Sudan bore responsibility. But, not accidentally, a respondent, educated as a lawyer and from the law division of a large European country's foreign ministry, argued most clearly:

> It is obvious to me that the most serious crimes have been committed. It is obvious to me that government institutions, in one way or the other, have to be held responsible. They share certainly some responsibility with regard to those crimes. And I will also say that if things like that remain without a judicial response, then . . . [perpetrators] get the message you can do all those things and . . . nothing happens. This is impunity. Impunity prevails. And I think the ICC is about the message to say impunity is over.

Yet even this interviewee also adds, somewhat diluting the previous point:

> There is too much focus on the perpetrators. We should much more focus on the victims, and in doing so, I think we get much closer to what actually needs to be done to remedy the situation. But, apparently when you operate in a media-dominated environment, it is of course sexier to have some kind of rogue guy sitting on the bench before the court than possibly having embarrassing interviews with faceless victims.

Other diplomats also spoke to the responsibility of the government of Sudan. "It was a series of the gravest offenses against human rights," one said, "for which—as we know today—the government was responsible" (author's translation). Focusing on the violence committed by the Janjawiid, another respondent added: "Obviously, in terms of responsibility, you also do have to look at the government." A colleague confirmed: "I am convinced that the northern government was involved in the violence perpetrated by those groups who initiated it" (author's translation). Yet another diplomat insisted: "The government in Khartoum has a lot of experience in using proxies, in the South as well, . . . in using tribes or groups of people." While the responsibility of the government of Sudan was thus highlighted, most respondents avoided casting it explicitly in terms of criminal liability. Some interpreted the government's responsibility explicitly as political responsibility: "I think it remains not an ICC matter, but it remains an issue to be brought to the account of the Khartoum government, for having arrived at a point where it has effectively either ungoverned or misgoverned spaces in its own country. . . . It is a political charge against the Khartoum government as much as a charge in relation to direct accountability."

In short, respondents almost unanimously held the government of Sudan accountable for the violence. Some specified organizational units such as the military and the Popular Defense Forces. But diplomats simultaneously urged against focusing on the perpetrators and on criminal responsibility alone, but attending instead to the victims and broadly conceived political responsibility. They rarely named specific government actors. When mentioning al-Bashir directly, interviewees combined such mention with partly exculpating statements. One interviewee reported on conversations he had had with President al-Bashir, describing him as a man "who realizes today that he was fooled in many things . . . by his own people" (author's translation). Another respondent supported this sentiment: "In how far Bashir was informed about everything, I cannot really tell you." The interviewee then drew parallels with North Korea's Kim Il Sung: "He [Kim] was so cut off from the world that he just did not have any direct experience any more. . . . I think in the case of Bashir that he must have understood what kinds of decisions he supported and consented to. But I do not dare to say if he really knew about the real scale, but I personally have to say truthfully: I doubt it. I have met him three times thus far; I cannot easily be misled in these things" (author's translation).

Diplomats also occasionally named Ahmed Harun, until 2009 the Sudanese minister for humanitarian affairs, as a responsible, albeit instrumentalized, actor. One respondent considered Harun "one of the main tools used by the government to put in place these policies of proxy militias, recruiting the militias and using the local population, fueling the conflict, to make sure the army was not too much involved. [JJS: And used by whom?] Well, that is the big question as well"—a question, though, for which the respondent did not provide an answer.

In addition to the government, broadly conceived, and two specific government actors, the Janjawiid appear prominently in the interviews as responsible actors. But this attribution too was relativized in numerous ways. One respondent referred to Janjawiid militias as accomplices ("*Erfüllungsgehilfen*"). In the eyes of another diplomat they were "being armed by the government, paid for by the government." A third interviewee went into greater detail, deciphering the conditions of the nomadic groups from which the militias were recruited. His narrative challenges notions of the Janjawiid common in the criminal justice field:

> I don't like the term *Janjawiid* very much, because it suggests a sort of ultimate evil, and it's not very helpful in terms of gaining a differentiated understanding of the conflict. . . . So, on the surface of things—and this is very much how the conflict has been portrayed—you have Arabs, so the Arab-based Sudanese government and Arab tribes forming these militias, being the perpetrators. And you have non-Arabs being the victims. . . . Now, if you take a step back, . . . you can reverse the image because, as it stands, the Arabs, the nomad Arabs in Darfur, are in many ways the most marginalized group in Darfur. Because they are nomads, they don't have any homeland, and as the desert is advancing, they lose their livelihoods. They are camel breeders, and you can't have camels in the desert. Right. So they lost their livelihoods. They have no lands to go to. . . . They lost their identity as well, which was very much tied to camels, camel trade, and took [up] arms very much in an attempt to defend themselves. Right. So you could look at them as victims as well.

Simultaneously, the same respondent attributed greater responsibility to rebels than we typically encounter in social movements such as Save Darfur or in the criminal justice or human rights NGO narrative, even with some charges having been filed against lower-ranking rebels:

> If you look at the history of the conflict, the rebellion comes from non-Arab tribes. They started this whole thing. And rebels are called rebels because they hold guns and they kill people. Right. So they are perpetrators as well. And so, while the distinction between victims and perpetrators appears obvious in Darfur, I would suggest that it actually isn't, and it is much more complicated. And by even using the labels *victims* and *perpetrators*, we conflate things, and we contribute to an understanding of this conflict which really isn't very helpful if you want to resolve it.

Another interviewee also cast the rebels in a highly problematic light: "That the JEM is primarily interested in justice and equality, that I do not quite believe. No, those are criminals [*Verbrecher*]. . . . One of them plays a central role. He sits in Paris and always says 'no.' So he does not really want a solution and impedes the Doha talks" (author's translation).

In short, when explicitly asked about actors with responsibility for the mass violence in Darfur, diplomats do not shy away from attributing responsibility to the government of Sudan. Yet they tend to frame it as broad political responsibility. They name individuals only rarely and—when they do—tend to cast doubt on their criminal liability. Several interviewees attribute responsibility to the Janjawiid, but they too relativize. Some respondents divert responsibility away from the militias and toward rebel groups, thus countering the dominant narrative of pro–criminal justice actors such as the Save Darfur movement and the ICC itself. Clearly, the responsibility narratives of diplomats reflect the strong role of the Sudanese state in the field in which diplomats act and the substantive, outcome-oriented goals of diplomatic work.

Suffering

Nine diplomats responded to my inquiry about the Darfuri population's victimization and suffering, but only four specified forms of suffering. One respondent from a small European country spoke about people "forced to leave their homes and villages, and their villages have been burned down; their number is estimated at two million." An interviewee from another small country referred to "all these displacements, . . . in many different directions; there have been refugee camps" (author's translation). A diplomat from a large European country addressed suffering in the context of the relative success of international interventions: "I think [UNAMID] has had an effect; the fighting and the displacement is less than it was at the height of it in 2005, but it is still ongoing. And the government is still bombing civilians. The rebels are still fighting." Only two diplomats elaborated on the suffering in greater detail. One, the interviewee from Irish Aid within Ireland's Department of Foreign Affairs, described compassionately the displacement of (her numbers) 1.5 million people; lack of shelter, water, food, and protection; the deaths of 200,000; and systematic rape campaigns. At the same time, however, she cautioned that "if you look at the media coverage of those years, it was quite sensationalized." The other respondent who detailed the suffering and victimization in Darfur was a diplomat from a large European nation's foreign ministry, a specialist with responsibility for Sudan:

> The interesting thing in Darfur is that most of the people who died didn't die from bullet wounds. . . . They lead them to camps so that they could control them easily. And whenever people were getting outside, you could see the women getting raped and all of that. . . . They were fighting a psychological war against the local population, using terror against this population. So I think that is . . . one of the things people suffer the most from. After the very first . . . period of military operations, that didn't last very long—it lasted one year, a bit more than a year—but once everyone was in camps or refugees outside in Chad, the way that the army and these Popular Defense Forces, the Janjawiid who were fighting against the rebels, was to try to use terror against the population, so that they would denounce and try to build a gap between the population and the rebels. Death was another form of suffering, what happened inside the camps because of unsanitary conditions and so on, and rape as a systematic strategy of spreading terror.

While diplomats spoke sparingly about suffering, several interviewees explicitly challenged the victimization numbers that appear often in human rights discourses. One interviewee from the legal division of his foreign ministry deferred to the Africa Department because, from a legal perspective, the precise number of victims was irrelevant. He elaborated that a trial always focuses on just the few cases for which evidence is strong. Another respondent found it "very hard to have access to objective information, very hard to say something about those figures." A diplomat from a large European country explicitly critiqued numerical estimates. This interviewee attributed the prominence of certain numbers in public discourses to media reports, but their origins to NGOs: "[Mass media] publish the first numbers. . . . The high commissioner for refugees or such, he does not count himself; he lets others count and says: 'Care, Oxfam, Deutsche Welthungerhilfe, Red Cross, how many do you have, roughly?' And those, in the middle of a crisis, completely overworked, their hands full, look around; 'well this must be 150,000 now, plus-minus.' And that is how these numbers are constructed. And that then solidifies" (author's translation).[5]

Another senior diplomat from a small European country—a long-term advisor on international affairs to a leading head of state who, during his lifetime, had enjoyed extraordinary respect in much of the Global South—expressed the same skepticism. Indeed he developed the critique further, claiming that NGOs have a vested interest in exaggerating numbers: "The NGOs have a completely understandable interest rather to dramatize because that also improves their financial basis, so to speak. They can secure financial donations much more easily with a dramatizing report than without it" (author's translation). The same interviewee was highly critical of some countries—especially the United States—that, in his perception, advanced dramatizing accounts. "The former foreign minister of Congo," he said, "who then became special envoy for Darfur to the AU and the UN, who one day declared, 'Well, really, the issue of Darfur is now taken care of, things have largely settled down,' he subsequently lost his job. The UN then said: 'Who do you think was behind that?' Well, the Americans who said: 'We do not have use for someone like that at the current moment'" (author's translation).

This interviewee attributed "exaggerations" to national conditions and political interests, somewhat in line with social scientific arguments. Specifically for the US government, he referred to the activation of civil society and the government's responsiveness. He highlighted Christian fundamentalist groups with a strong presence in South Sudan and oil interests: "For the Americans . . . such things then become issues of domestic politics. When you have a Brad Pitt and a George Clooney appear before a large audience, . . . then people look on and they ask: 'Why does our government not do anything?' . . . That all matters in the question of opinion formation. Truth, published opinion, perceived opinion in the public—these are all different things" (author's translation).

The same diplomat attributed similar tendencies to exaggerate victimization in Darfur to the French government. But there, he believed, the motivation differs:

> In France, I know, for example, that the francophone African countries all have an enormous influence on domestic politics. They are all present in Paris. They have their French representative [in the National Assembly] with whom they are friends. An African president picks up the phone and calls the French president, and if he does not reach him right away, then he gets at least to talk to the general secretary, and that is all taken very seriously. . . . In the case of Sudan, France also supported a dramatization, exactly because they perceived Sudan as a potential aggressor against [francophone] Chad. They portrayed Sudan in a completely negative light, and in that question they did not differ that much from the Americans. (author's translation)

In short, actors in the diplomatic field who interact with representatives of the Sudanese state, whose primary aim it is to achieve peace by means of negotiation, and whose explanations of the conditions of the conflict tend to deflect responsibility away from specific individuals, including those indicted by the ICC, simultaneously shy away from questions that probe the suffering and victimization of the population. They instead tend to challenge and cast doubt on narratives generated and diffused by human rights NGOs and criminal justice institutions. Given the intensity of diplomatic concerns about replacing mass violence with peace, it is hard to attribute such patterns to a lack of empathy with those who are suffering. But it appears as though the regular and intense articulation of victimization narratives comes more easily to those who work in the human rights and criminal justice fields, areas in which the Sudanese state and its representatives are not critical actors.

Framing Mass Violence

What frames do actors in the diplomatic field consider appropriate for the interpretation of the mass violence in Darfur? Here too I asked interviewees to comment on the applicability of four frames: humanitarian emergency, civil war, insurgency and counterinsurgency, and state crime. Almost all respondents found the humanitarian emergency frame appropriate. The Irish Aid respondent in fact identified this frame as "particularly relevant." Other responses to my inquiry about the term included "Exactly, yeah"; and "That it is for certain." One interviewee saw a humanitarian emergency as having occurred in the past, but no longer existing in the present: "2004–2005, possibly into the second half of 2006; . . . and then this turned into a case of reconstruction and return" (author's translation). Only one respondent from the diplomatic field expressed doubts, arguing that the humanitarian emergency frame "doesn't really tell you anything about the nature of a crisis. Crises, and especially when they result in armed conflict, are always political."

Most respondents also agreed that a rebellion or insurrection frame is appropriate for an interpretation of the violence, though some limited such framing to the early phases of the conflict. "That fits somehow," one interviewee said. "I mean, in the end it is a lot about marginalized people who stand up for their rights." Four respondents disagreed with the insurrection frame. One argued that the term *protest* is more appropriate, as *rebellion* implied separatist intent, which, he argued, did not apply to Darfur. Diplomats almost unanimously rejected the civil war frame, even though one interviewee referred to the violence as similar to civil war (*"bürgerkriegsähnlich"*). More typical was a statement that rejected the notion of civil war: "It is not a civil war, because Darfur never explained that it sought independence."

Finally, and astonishingly in light of their causal analysis and assessment of victimization, most diplomats considered the state crime frame appropriate, but they expressed some kind of reservation. "The state has a clear responsibility," one respondent told me. "They didn't act upon the crimes that have been committed. . . . There is no justice being done. I think it is obvious that the state is involved in these crimes or at least has responsibility." This and another respondent considered the (in)actions of the Sudanese state as crimes more of negligence than of its own aggression. Others pointed out that crimes were committed on both sides of the conflict. An interviewee from a small European country deemed the term *state crime* appropriate, but insisted that such understanding was not shared by African actors: "State crime? Yes, for us unambiguously, but for the Africans not quite so clearly." Earlier in the interview he argued: "One regards this in Sudan as normal intervention" (author's translation), and he referred to growing African skepticism about the ICC. At least one respondent appeared to have developed sympathies with the AU position. He expressed a clear preference for a "traditional" justice response as opposed to international criminal justice intervention.

In addition to such cautious applications of the state crime frame, I also encountered staunch opposition. One actor from the diplomatic field, trained as a political scientist with a focus on international relations, explicitly challenged the state crime frame, pleading instead for a political-structural mode of understanding the conflict:

> I don't find it [the state crime label] a helpful lens, because if you look at the history of Sudan, since independence in '56, you have different regimes, right? You have democratically elected regimes, you have military regimes, and in the last twenty-two years an Islamist regime, right? They function very differently, have different constituencies that they draw on, different political strategies to secure their rule. Yet mass atrocities happened in all of these regimes. So there is something, I think, systemic that the way in which the Sudanese state functions produces mass violence in certain ways. And by focusing on a few individuals—and since the ICC indictment, a lot of people in the West have focused on the role of President Bashir—and to see the conflict in Darfur in a way as an outcome of the criminal energy of Omar al-Bashir and his acolytes is not actually accurate in terms of understanding why the conflict emerged in the first place, and why the Sudanese government has been engaging in these kinds of atrocities.

Quantitative patterns from an analysis of 210 foreign ministry press releases, by definition written to reach a broad public, show a somewhat greater balance (see note 2). Yet, while references to the frames of conflict and war (25.7%) and humanitarian emergency (28.6%) are privileged only somewhat over the crime frame (20.5%), the patterns for preferred solutions fall in line with responses cited throughout this chapter. Fifty-one percent of press releases suggest diplomatic solutions. Humanitarian aid (35%) and peacekeeping operations (39%) also appear prominently, while legal solutions (10%) and especially military intervention (1.4%) lag far behind.[6]

In short, interviewees from the world of diplomacy display patterns of thought, partly consistent with quantitative findings emerging from an analysis of foreign ministry press releases that cautiously embrace the frame of humanitarian emergency to cast light on the situation in Darfur. They apply the insurgency and counterinsurgency frame at least to the early stages of the conflict. They are skeptical about the civil war frame, and they cast substantial doubt on the applicability of the state crime frame. This is consistent with the tendency of the diplomatic field to attribute the violence to ecological catastrophe, resulting intergroup conflicts, or to structural features of the Sudanese state. It is similarly in synch with reluctance to point at specific responsible actors, especially individuals.

CONCLUSIONS: THE DIPLOMATIC FIELD AND HABITUS—AND WORDS OF CAUTION

The diplomatic field displays specific features that differ from those of the judicial and humanitarian fields. The diplomatic field prominently includes Sudanese state actors. While this field shares this factor with the humanitarian field, diplomacy depends on the active participation of—often high-ranking—Sudanese government actors, whereas humanitarian aid more often relies on mere toleration on the part of lower-level and specialized government administrations. Despite this distinction, the humanitarian and diplomatic fields differ from the judicial field not just in their engagement with actors from the offending government but also in that they are less oriented toward procedure than toward substantive outcomes, with a focus on survival in the former and peace in the latter. Actors in the diplomatic field, just like those in the justice and humanitarian fields, strongly identify with their mission. They have internalized their field's institutional logic and its doxa. All of this is in line with field theory, as are the respective representations of the Darfur conflict in these fields.

Indeed, diplomats used cautious language in interviews when describing the conflict. Causes of conflict that diplomats highlighted privileged ecological conditions; structural features of the Sudanese state, often historically rooted; and neighboring African interests and conflicts. While they did mention the Sudanese state as a responsible actor, they mostly avoided pointing at specific individuals as responsible for the violence. When they named individuals, especially President al-Bashir, they tended to provide exculpating considerations. Most were more sparing in their accounts of victimization and suffering than their counterparts in the justice and humanitarian fields. Finally, diplomats used substantial caution regarding the applicability of the state crime frame. They were especially reluctant to using the term *genocide.*

The latter finding is consistent with Samantha Power's (2002) assessment of US foreign policy and with Karen Smith's (2010) analysis of three European countries. Yet, while Power and Smith explain such caution by pointing to the reluctance of rational actors to incur obligations associated with the use of the term *genocide,* I argue that features of the diplomatic field and the notion of habitus must be built into an effective explanation. Achieving the substantive goals of diplomacy warrants an inclusionary strategy toward actors of the regime that the justice system seeks to exclude by way of prosecution. It urges distance from dramatizing discourses and from narratives that depict social reality through the lens of the justice system.

In short, a diplomatic master narrative, or in other words, an ideal type of diplomatic representation, focuses on long-term and structural causes of conflicts. It avoids naming responsible actors. It shies away from dramatic depictions of victimization. And it rejects the state crime frame, especially the notion of genocide. It is diametrically opposed to Hagan and Rymond-Richmond's (2008) criminological "endogenous conflict theory," which explains the violence as the product of short-term dynamics in which concrete state actors play a central role.

Real types, of course, differ from ideal types. This applies to representations of the Darfur conflict. Even the variation within my relatively small sample of interviews, supported by statistical patterns from foreign ministry press releases, suggests differentiation along lines of organization and educational background. Diplomatic actors with legal training are somewhat more inclined to deviate from the diplomatic master narrative than those with a political science background, which is consistent with my findings for lawyers in human rights organization and the humanitarian field. This tendency is amplified for

FIGURE 17. Signing of the treaty that emerged from the Doha peace negotiations, July 14, 2011.

lawyer-diplomats who work in legal divisions and, even more so, in human rights units within their foreign ministries. The latter diplomats' representation of Darfur actually approximates the justice narrative. Fields, like systems, are thus scholarly constructions. In reality they overlap with other fields, diachronically (through educational socialization) and synchronically (through organizational differentiation)—here within the diplomatic field.

But one more factor needs to be accounted for. The diplomatic field is affected by national contexts. Each nation provides for particular forces that shape its diplomats' habitus and strategic actions. It is such cross-national differences and the social forces that shape them to which I now turn.

CHAPTER 7

The Diplomatic Field in National Contexts

Deviations from the Master Narrative

Comparative studies that address representations of mass violence within the diplomatic field are virtually nonexistent. That is regrettable as comparative analysis promises to shed light on the conditions under which diplomats acknowledge atrocities and, more specifically, distance themselves from the criminal justice narrative more or less decisively.

Political scientist Karen Smith (2010) is a rare exception as she has documented variation for European countries' responses to genocides. Smith, while agreeing with Power's (2002) charge of an overly cautious rhetoric in cases of genocide, identifies noteworthy differences between countries, in particular France, Germany, and the United Kingdom. To be sure, the diplomatic field shows commonalities across countries. Also, Western governments are linked by their countries' bilateral and multilateral ties and treaties. But diplomats nevertheless act under distinct national conditions, including their country's size (as well as weight and visibility in international politics), specific types of resources and expertise, and degree of activation of civil society, as well as the responsiveness of the nation's political institutions to civil society; the presence of expatriate groups, often associated with a country's colonial history; domestic carrier groups; and—especially relevant for responses to mass atrocities—country-specific collective memories of past human rights crimes. In addition to such cultural factors, countries also vary by economic and geopolitical concerns. The latter are especially pronounced, in the Darfur case, for countries such as China, with its massive investments in Sudan, especially in the construction, agriculture and oil sectors.¹ Such immediate interests in Sudan are more limited in the countries under study here, providing for relatively little variation. In addition, all of the countries examined are Western-style democracies. The methodological advantage of this similarity is that it allows for the detection of otherwise hidden social, political, and cultural forces.²

In other words, the national context should matter, as it overlaps with the sectoral field of diplomacy. My earlier discussion of US and Irish particularities in representations of Darfur provided initial indications (chapters 3 and 5). In this chapter I revisit these and examine other countries to generate additional insights. Besides particular domestic conditions, countries also have varying ties to the international community, differing degrees of neutrality, memberships in various international organizations, and ratification of diverse treaties and conventions. The following analysis pays attention to these factors as well.

In what follows, I spell out differences between representations of the Darfur conflict in the countries under study and indicate conditions that potentially lead to such differences. I show that foreign policy makers in different countries deviate more or less from the ideal-typical or master narrative of diplomatic representations identified in chapter 6. A word of caution is warranted, though. As I highlight specific conditions in my discussion of these countries, I never suggest that we reduce the foreign policy of these countries to the features highlighted. That would neither be appropriate given my only limited survey of the national foreign policy fields nor justified in light of the varying narratives I encountered within countries, especially in light of the organizational position of interviewees within their foreign ministries. Nor do I suggest that conditions explored for one country are absent in others.

I first briefly remind the reader of insights gained in previous chapters regarding the representations of Darfur in Ireland and the United States. I then address Switzerland to illustrate a model of diplomatic representation that comes closest to the ideal type depicted above. I subsequently examine the United Kingdom and France as countries that stand out as former colonial powers of Sudan and its neighbor Chad, respectively, with all the historical consequences that colonialism implies. Austria then serves as an illustration for the Sudanese state's lobbying efforts that might have left traces in Austria's representation of Darfur. Finally, I discuss Germany to illustrate how the "cultural trauma of perpetrators" (Giesen 2004a) affects responses to current events, including Darfur.

THE UNITED STATES: MOBILIZATION OF CIVIL SOCIETY AND CRIMINALIZING DEVIATIONS FROM THE MASTER NARRATIVE

The massive mobilization of American civil society, addressed in chapter 3, took organizational shape in the Save Darfur campaign, an umbrella under which almost two hundred organizations assembled, religious and secular, conservative and liberal. Some of these organizations represented carrier groups—African Americans and Jews, as well as evangelical Christians, the latter a crucial constituent of the George W. Bush administration. This civil society movement advanced an interventionist and criminalizing position on the Darfur conflict. "Genocide" became its rallying cry, and the US Holocaust Memorial Museum played a central role in the mobilization. As our look at US media showed, news reports and editorials used the criminalizing frame and applied the term *genocide* significantly more often than media in other countries (see also Murphy 2007). This homology is not surprising given the competitive nature of the US media market.

It is also not surprising—given the porous nature of US political institutions, with primary elections and popular election of executive branch leaders—that the Bush administration applied the term *genocide* to the violence in Darfur more than any other government did. Diplomats of both the former Clinton and Bush administrations articulated support for this categorization and for the pursuit of criminal justice responses, both in conference discussions and in their writings (e.g., Williamson 2009a, 2009b). The American representation of Darfur thus leans further away from the diplomatic master narrative and toward a criminalizing and genocide discourse than do the representations of any other country under study.

Samantha Power's diagnosis of American reluctance to refer to mass violence as genocide thus does and does not apply to the case of Darfur: "It is in the realm of domestic politics that the battle to stop genocide is lost. American political leaders interpret society-wide silence as an indicator of public indifference. They reason that they will incur no cost if the United States remains uninvolved but will face steep risks if they engage" (Power 2002:xviii). Power's argument regarding the alignment of policy toward public opinion is confirmed for Darfur. But in the Darfur case it works in the other direction because—contra Power's thesis—civil society became highly mobilized and produced a strong rhetorical response from the US government. It is also true, however, that social movements can be easily satisfied by government rhetoric. Government actions such as the 2007 Sudan Accountability and Divestment Act fell far behind the force of the verbal campaign.

IRELAND: MERCY, AID, AND COLLECTIVE MEMORY

Irish foreign policy is "aligned" (i.e., in line with that of international partners), as my interviewees in Dublin stressed. The country has indeed ratified all essential international conventions pertaining to human rights. Yet, as discussed in chapter 3, Irish foreign policy also has distinct characteristics that affect Irish representations of Darfur. It is strongly oriented toward humanitarian and development aid. It closely cooperates with aid NGOs, some of which are allied with the Irish Catholic Church. Trócaire (the name meaning "mercy") is the most prominent. Ireland is thus closely tied to the humanitarian aid field and, like aid NGOs, depends on interactions with the Sudanese state. Representations of Darfur I encountered are consequently cautious, in line with the diplomatic master narrative. Also, our quantitative analysis of foreign ministry press releases shows the Irish foreign ministry's strong preference for the humanitarian emergency frame and for humanitarian aid solutions. Positions of the Irish state are supported by civil society, as our statistics on media reporting indicate (chapter 5). Karen Smith's analysis confirms this pattern. Her review of Irish DFA files showed little civil society input, for example, during Ireland's political debates over the country's accession to the Genocide Convention (K. Smith 2010:54).

There is good reason to believe that the Irish focus on aid programs is deeply rooted in the country's collective memories of famine and extreme poverty. The resulting caution regarding criminal justice responses is further grounded in the cultural processing of the Northern Ireland conflict and partly institutionalized in a working group in the Department of Foreign Affairs. It seems as though foreign policy makers have developed an appreciation for the benefits of amnesty and a critical stance toward penal discourses.

SWITZERLAND: NEUTRALITY, ARBITRATION, AND THE IMPERATIVE OF A DIPLOMATIC NARRATIVE

Like Ireland, Switzerland is aligned with the basic principles of its partners in the international community. It has ratified central human rights conventions as well as the Rome Statute. Yet, as in Ireland, I encountered a cautious rhetoric regarding Darfur. Interview statements cited above are well reflected in an essay by political scientist David Lanz (2009) of Swiss-Peace, a policy institute affiliated with the Swiss government. Presenting peace and justice as competing notions, Lanz spells out what he considers highly problematic consequences of the ICC decision to indict President al-Bashir: the eviction of thirteen INGOs from Sudan; the elimination of three Sudanese NGOs; sympathies al-Bashir won from actors in Africa and the Arab world who interpreted the ICC indictment as an expression of neocolonialism; difficulties for countries such as Switzerland that support the ICC but simultaneously maintain strong diplomatic ties with Khartoum; the risks to the North-South peace process; and challenges to a peace treaty for Darfur. Lanz speaks favorably of the option provided in Article 16 of the Rome Statute, by which the UNSC can suspend prosecutions.

Why do we encounter a representation of Darfur that is as cautious as its Irish counterpart? While Switzerland too has a well-developed program of developmental and humanitarian aid, the status of this program in national policy and the national consciousness is far less developed than in Ireland. Switzerland's caution is in fact rooted in a different condition. The following statement from one Swiss interviewee offers a promising lead:

There are several normative constraints and structural constraints for Swiss foreign policy. It's a small country in the middle of Europe and these are the obvious ones. But another characteristic of Swiss foreign policy is structural neutrality. I mean, it is a very, very, very strongly rooted identity of Switzerland as a neutral country—although neutrality arguably in a globalized world does not really make any sense, neither legally nor morally nor politically speaking. But still, if you do surveys, you have 90 to 95 percent of the Swiss public who say, "Yes. We are neutral. We were always neutral. We will always be neutral and our foreign policy should be neutral. . . . So there is very little that Switzerland can do in terms of an activist foreign policy. If you look at Scandinavian countries, all the different projects that they were able to take on, there is very little of that that Switzerland can do. Notably, participation in any military involvement in foreign countries is an absolute no-go area. But at the same time, you have political elites . . . who are aware of the fact that the world is connected and that there is a need for small states like Switzerland. And they, they want to be more active. So they have to find more activities that fit within the structural characteristics of Swiss foreign policy, that don't contradict them, that don't produce backlash in terms of domestic politics. Right? And so one of these things is mediation. It's perfectly in line with Switzerland's identity as a neutral country. . . . And it is also something that is fashionable in terms of world politics. It generates a certain prestigious sort of reputation.

Indeed, Switzerland did actively engage in bilateral and multilateral diplomacy with the Sudan. Swiss foreign policy experts Simon Mason and David Lanz (2009) provide numerous examples: Josef Bucher, Switzerland's representative in Libya and Kenya during much of the 1990s and special envoy for conflict solutions (2001–2005), built strong ties with representatives of the government of Sudan and of the SPLM; after 2000 the Department of Foreign Affairs supported a project entitled "Councils of Traditional Leaders" for leaders in southern Sudan and in the Nuba Mountains; Swiss diplomats participated in negotiations that resulted in a 2000 armistice in the same region; Swiss mediation experts participated in the negotiations that led to the CPA; and Switzerland contributed to monitoring missions following the CPA. These examples already represent an impressive record for a small country (see also Baechler 2011).

Research on Swiss foreign policy reveals motivations that, in the absence of immediate interests, drive such engagement. Indeed, statements from interviews with twenty-five policy makers are in line with the above interview excerpt. Respondents highlighted the Swiss government's desire to contribute to the advancement of peace and the support for suffering populations; to strengthen international legitimacy and Switzerland's reputation as a small country with a strong value orientation; to advance collaboration with international partners beyond the realms of economics and finance; and, domestically, to strengthen the population's image of their country as globally engaged on behalf of human rights, justice, and peace (Mason and Lanz 2009:65–66).

In short, both Ireland and Switzerland are small countries that operate in fields in which the government of Sudan plays a prominent role. The desire to advance humanitarian aid in the Irish case and to advance diplomacy in the Swiss case suggests similar caution vis-à-vis the Sudanese government, a caution that entails distance from dramatizing, criminal justice narratives. I found this caution reflected in representations of the mass violence in Darfur in both countries. Where the United States greatly deviates from the diplomatic master narrative, policy makers in Ireland and Switzerland adhere to it rather closely.

AUSTRIA: FRIEND OF THE ARAB WORLD—AND SUDANESE LOBBYING

Austria is a third small country where narratives about Darfur maintain cautious distance from the criminal justice discourse. To be sure,

Austrian interviewees from the field of diplomacy attested to their country's strong support for the ICC and their alignment with EU positions. One respondent, placed in the legal division of Vienna's foreign ministry and responsible for international criminal law as well as for Nazi-era compensation issues, stressed that Austria has special obligations toward the pursuit of human rights crimes, also in light of the country's involvement in the Nazi empire and the decades of delays in facing that legacy. Yet a prominent long-term Austrian diplomat raised, like one of his Swiss colleagues, the option of activating Article 16 of the Rome Statute and thereby temporarily suspending proceedings against President al-Bashir, albeit under specific conditions. Two Austrian interviewees who had met with al-Bashir also characterized him in ways that challenge the portrayal of the Sudanese president as the demonic leader of a mass-murderous regime.

What might be the root of such cautious distance from criminal justice narratives regarding Darfur—despite assurances of EU alignment? Austria's identity is tied neither to aid programs, as in the Irish case, nor to the surprising intensity of arbitration initiatives we encounter in Switzerland. Nevertheless, interviewees portrayed conditions in which Austrian foreign policy is made that likely contribute to the cautionary narrative.

First, the country is small and is no threatening heavyweight in foreign relations. Second, it emerged from the post–World War II conflicts as a Western democracy, but one with neutrality status. Third, it is perceived by countries in the Global South as relatively friendly toward Southern interests, a reputation considered a legacy of Bruno Kreisky, Austria's long-term socialist foreign minister (1959–1966) and chancellor (1970–1983). Fourth, diplomats present Austria as having historically positive ties to Middle Eastern countries, the Arab world generally, and Sudan specifically. Finally, while interviewees described its foreign policy as not well developed, one Austrian respondent characterized its foreign policy elite as focused on economic interests.

This constellation of features may help explain a recent concerted lobbying effort on behalf of the government of Sudan. In October 2007, a Sudanese consul to Vienna invited one of my Austrian interviewees to visit Sudan. After a series of negotiations, the Sudanese authorities extended their invitation to a group of Austrians consisting of a former defense minister, a high-ranking military officer of the Austrian Defense Academy, the heads of a conservative- and a liberal-oriented foreign policy think tank, a leading foreign correspondent for one of the two most prominent Austrian newspapers, and the president of the Austrian-Sudanese Society, Paul Slatin.³ As the interviewee reported:

> That was an invitation from the Khartoum government, the entire government that is. We conducted conversations. . . . I myself have now been down there for the fourth time and we always had talks with representatives of the South and the North, including with Bashir. We were twice in Darfur, in Nyala, in El Fasher and, as I said, the last time just fourteen days ago. We repeatedly had, especially during the first three journeys we undertook, our own dates, where we met private individuals, business people, journalists, human rights activists, etc., whom we asked to meet in our hotels. Last time we also received a briefing from the UNAMID in El Fasher . . . and talked with Doctors Without Borders. . . . That has pretty much changed my view of the conflict, I'd have to say. (author's translation)

Building on this report, the respondent critiqued what he considered the dominant view of the conflict, which, he argues, was framed by the United States and American celebrities such as George Clooney, motivated by national interests, and adopted by Europeans. Another interviewee, a senior foreign policy maker now retired but still special envoy for Africa, voiced skepticism about the same visits: "All these activities were quite obviously rather much steered by the [Sudanese] government. They paid for it, the travel and also the stay there. They also organized all the interviews there" (author's translation). This interviewee, not part of the visiting group, pointed specifically to the Sudanese secret service's role in manipulating the tour. He contrasted the delegation's experience with his own independent travel to Sudan and his meetings not only with opposition figures but also with President al-Bashir. His own conclusions regarding al-Bashir nevertheless also contrast with those of the common criminal justice discourse:

> We also talked about this affair [the ICC charges] . . . very politely, with friendly words, but still. He of course started with "Well, you have to understand how all of this started," and that he himself is a general and he knows he is the first who wants today that the violence ends. "It's of no benefit to anyone," and he favors peace, that he is the man who can really guarantee the peace. . . . Well, in part there is some truth to that. Everyone can see that those who really are responsible are hiding behind Bashir. . . . He understands only today that he was tricked in several respects. Not by us, but by his own people. . . . Of course I also talked to him about Chad a lot. I told him that we want him to finally make peace with Chad. He then told me that he is always ready to send a delegation. What I did not know, or nobody knew, was that this was already decided, and ten days later a Sudanese delegation visited Chad. (author's translation)

In short, Austria, a small country with a history of neutrality and relatively close ties to the Arab world, including Sudan, has been lobbied by the Sudanese government. Chances are that the information to which Austrian visitors to Sudan were exposed was to some degree vetted by the government. Noteworthy too is that the Sudanese efforts began in 2008, a full year before Austria took a seat on the UN Security Council for a two-year term. At least one other Austrian diplomat traveled independently and met with leading Sudanese actors, including President al-Bashir. He too returned with a skeptical view of the human rights campaign and criminal justice portrayal of the actions of Omar al-Bashir. I do not argue that these contacts necessarily affected Austrian foreign policy. Yet they likely influenced the representations of the Darfur conflict emanating from the Austrian foreign policy field.

FRANCE AND THE UNITED KINGDOM: "AS IF [WE] WERE THE FORMER COLONIAL RULER"

"One thing that really struck me when I first joined the foreign office, especially working on a lot of different African conflicts, was the fact that it almost seemed to be divided up quite as simply as if you were the former colonial ruler. It is your lead. It is your responsibility. So France took on, you know, it leads on Côte d'Ivoire. We lead on Sudan. America leads on Liberia."

The interviewee in the UK's Foreign and Commonwealth Office (FCO) adds to this statement with regard to Sudan "that there is a certain feeling of responsibility . . . for how it was formed, the lines on the map, forcing the North and the South together perhaps." She supplemented earlier statements by NGO interviewees who pointed to the special role of expatriate communities in advancing foreign policy motivations by highlighting the role of the "the press and foreign countries [that] say, 'You created this mess; you drew the lines; you forced communities together that shouldn't be together; . . . you need to help fix this.'"

This interviewee did not rescind, but rather modified, her statement in subsequent responses to questions about the special role of UK foreign policy toward the Darfur conflict. She pointed to British collaboration with others, for example, the leadership role of the "troika" of the United Kingdom, the United States, and Norway ("often seen as very impartial") in the negotiations leading to the CPA (to settle the North-South conflict). Such collaboration was partly welcomed as the United

Kingdom did not want "to direct what happens, because that would be seen as being colonial again." And yet the historical legacy of the colonial power "does require us to speak out first." Contrasting the action on Sudan with the military intervention in Sierra Leone, she said, "It comes back to the sort of pure diplomacy."

It is not possible, based on the interview data, to establish a causal link between such a "pure diplomacy" stance and UK diplomats' representation of the Darfur conflict. But field theory again suggests that we expect a cautious narrative, distinct from the criminal justice account. Not surprisingly, it was this interviewee who had noticed cautious advice in diplomacy circles not to rock the boat because of Darfur when the North-South agreement was at stake. And while she did attribute responsibility for the Darfur violence to the government of Sudan, and while she agreed with the framing of the violence as "state crime," she avoided naming specific individual actors. She would like to see justice delayed, and she rejected the notion of genocide.

The rejection of genocide rhetoric is in line with UK foreign policy makers' official assessment (K. Smith 2010). Specifically for the Darfur case, this position was encouraged early in 2004 by Africa experts such as Suliman Baldo, James Morton, and—again—Alex de Waal before the UK House of Commons International Development Committee. Supported by columnists such as Jonathan Steele of the *Guardian,* it is reflected in numerous statements of leading policy makers. Foreign Secretary Jack Straw, for example, stated in September 2004: "Some people call it genocide, some people call it ethnic cleansing, some people call it civil war, some people call if none of the above. Whatever it is, it's a desperate situation which requires the attention of the world" (quoted in K. Smith 2010:228).

Karen Smith attributes some responsibility for such caution to the report of the International Commission of Inquiry, discussed above (chapter 1). That report had decided against the application of the genocide label, a decision that legitimized avoidance of the term and associated obligations. The "risk" of incurring obligations increased after September 2005, when the UN formulated the "Responsibility to Protect" doctrine. British hesitance, however, did not prevent the United Kingdom from joining forces with France, the only other permanent member of the UNSC that has ratified the Rome Statute, in taking a decisive stance in favor of referring the Darfur case to the ICC. Apart from this step toward prosecution, the United Kingdom limited itself to supporting humanitarian aid and diplomatic efforts in the Doha peace talks.

Just as the United Kingdom is the former colonial overlord of Sudan, so is France the former colonial power over neighboring Chad—and of numerous other West African and Sahel-zone countries. The interviewee in the French Ministry of Foreign Affairs confirmed that such history matters. He pointed to special expertise concentrated in the former colonial power, using the focus on Africa in his own university studies as an example. He stressed that 60 percent of French foreign aid flows to Africa. And he emphasized the role that the memory of colonialism plays, if not in the general population (an attempt to make the Darfur crisis central to the 2004 presidential election campaign did not succeed), then among the foreign policy elite. Associated with such memory is French foreign policy makers' belief in their special influence, "given the history we have in Africa, given the relations we have with Chad or just, you know, the neighboring countries." He portrayed France's position concerning the Darfur conflict as a reflection of "the risk of spillover on Chad"—supplementing concerns with the humanitarian crisis. Simultaneously the French interviewee sketched a shift toward a more "continental" vision on Africa and thus a direct interest in events in Sudan.

Despite his less pronounced diplomatic involvement in Sudan, my interviewee in the French MFA also displayed the habitus of a diplomat and provided the expected narrative of Darfur. While he subscribed to the state crime frame as appropriate for the interpretation of the Darfur conflict, and while he staunchly rejected the application of Article 16 of the Rome Statutes (i.e., suspension of ICC proceedings), his words were nevertheless guarded. His causal explanation of the conflict focused first on desertification, second on the center-periphery conflict, and third on the CPA and the encouragement Darfur rebels might have drawn from it (note that France did not play a central role in these negotiations). And, while he characterized Ahmed Harun, indicted by the ICC, as "one of the main tools used by the government," he responded to the question "Used by whom?" with an answer that avoided uttering the name of Harun's co-indictee Omar al-Bashir. He replied: "Well, that is the big question."

The French Foreign Ministry interviewee, finally, rejected the genocide label, in line with the official position taken consistently by French government ministers (K. Smith 2010:229). Yet, again, together with the United Kingdom, France is the only permanent member of the UNSC that has ratified the Rome Statute and promoted a referral of the Darfur case to the ICC. Earlier, the French government distinguished itself when it lobbied strongly for a reference to Darfur in UNSC Resolution 1547 of June 11, 2004. Karen Smith (2010) reports: "According to one account, France's position went from 'we don't want to do this' to 'we can't let this go on,' because it feared the conflict would spread to Chad" (214).

In short, the cases of the United Kingdom, former colonial power of Sudan, and of France, former colonial power of Sudan's neighbor Chad, confirm the workings of the diplomatic field. Interview statements and official pronouncements are guarded. The name of the president of Sudan is rarely uttered as a co-responsible actor. Causal analysis attributes much of the violence to natural and political-structural conditions. Interviewees avoid applying the term *genocide*. But we also see that diplomacy and criminal justice are not mutually exclusive; their relationship does not constitute a zero-sum conflict. In fact, criminal justice interventions were based on diplomatic work. The UNSC referral to the ICC was strongly supported by both France and the United Kingdom. In fact, this referral may have the benefits, from a diplomatic perspective, that it defers the use of exclusionary language to the court and that deferral of further intervention by national governments is legitimized with the case in the court's hands. Finally, the cases of two former colonial powers show again that a country's history overlaps with the basic features of the diplomatic field. This intersectionality gives the field particular shape and colors the rhetoric and actions of its players.

GERMANY: CULTURAL TRAUMA OF PERPETRATORS—AND CONSEQUENCES

The memory of the Holocaust in Germany is deeply ingrained, especially among the political elite. Giesen (2004a) has written about the cultural trauma of perpetrators in discussing German memories of the Holocaust, and Savelsberg and King (2005, 2011) show how not only national memorial days and memorial sites but also legal codes and positions taken by law enforcers with regard to hate-motivated crimes refer frequently to the Judeocide committed by Nazi Germany. This places Germany, including its foreign policy, in a peculiar, albeit ambivalent, position when mass atrocities occur.

On the one hand, we might expect a particularly aggressive stance and a clear representation of mass violence as criminal, indeed genocidal. Several statements by German NGO workers cited above attest to this sense of a pronounced German responsibility in cases of genocidal violence. The diplomats I interviewed similarly claimed a special sense of obligation. A respondent from the political division of the foreign ministry spoke about a general obligation deriving from the Holocaust. The interviewee from the foreign ministry's legal division spoke most emphatically to this German obligation, for the case of Darfur specifically and for international criminal law generally. He also argued that Germany's foreign policy practice is consistent with such rhetoric, citing as an example the fact that Germany is the second largest contributor to the ICC among the state parties to the Rome Statute. In line with this respondent's observations, comparative research finds not only that Germany uses a comparatively wide definition of genocide that includes episodes of ethnic cleansing (K. Smith 2010:22), but also that German courts pursued cases of Bosnian war crimes especially aggressively (135–36).

Specifically with regard to Darfur, Germany, a nonpermanent member of the UN Security Council in 2002–2004, pushed early for the council to address the mass violence, even though France and the United Kingdom still hesitated (K. Smith 2010).[4] Government ministers used strong rhetoric, exceptional by European standards. In July 2004 Heidemarie Wieczorek-Zeul, the minister for overseas development, called Darfur a "genocide in slow motion." Christa Nickels, chair of the legislature's (Bundestag's) Human Rights Committee called the mass violence something that "equals genocide" and Peter Struck, Germany's minister of defense, argued in September 2004: "For me there is no doubt that we Germans also carry a responsibility for this continent [Africa]. We cannot simply look on when a part of the continent is experiencing genocide" (cited in K. Smith 2010:226). Similarly, opposition politicians such as Gerhart Baum of the libertarian Free Democratic Party, former UN special rapporteur for human rights in Sudan, referred to the massacres as genocide as early as April 2004, a position that enhanced the receptivity of German media to the Darfur theme, as we shall see in chapter 9.

On the other hand, complications inherent in the "cultural trauma of perpetrators" abound. As we have seen, German NGO respondents pointed to the strong representation of pacifists, especially in German sections of human rights organizations. They too base their pacifism on the memory of Nazi Germany, a position that confounds any consideration of military humanitarian intervention. Another NGO respondent spoke to the strong role that the churches still play in German society and the engagement of many mainstream actors in religious humanitarian organizations. Their orientation too is fueled by the history of war and human suffering, yet their humanitarian mission conflicts with a human rights agenda and criminal justice responses to mass violence. This tension is in line with earlier observations from the humanitarian field (see chapters 4 and 5).

Throughout my research I encountered hesitations and complications, some of which are in fact associated with the cultural trauma of the perpetrator. One German Africa correspondent initially rejected the notion that his nationality affected his reporting about mass atrocities and genocide. He then reconsidered, confessing his reluctance to subsume the Holocaust and the violence in Darfur under the same category of genocide. Indeed, our newspaper analysis shows that German media apply the genocide label less frequently to the Darfur conflict than media in all other countries. While the difference is small for news reports (17% versus 19%), it is substantial in opinion pieces (24% versus 34%). The director of one of the major Holocaust memorial sites, a rabbi and son of an Auschwitz survivor, when asked why German memorial sites do not add an alert mission to their commemorative function, as the US Holocaust Memorial Museum does, answered (and I paraphrase): The Americans can do that. If we did this as Germans, we would be accused of relativizing the Holocaust. Journalists' apparent cognitive impediment to linking current mass atrocities to the Holocaust is thus supplemented by a normative hurdle expressed by the director of the Holocaust memorial site.

Finally, our analysis of German newspapers shows only rare uses of analogical bridging between the Holocaust and the Darfur violence. One German media piece in fact poses a bridging challenge. On May 10, 2005, the *Süddeutsche Zeitung* (p. 16) published a review of books by Romeo Dallaire and Robert Stockhammer, entitled *The Ranking of Atrocities*. Alex Rühle, the reviewer, refers to Stockhammer's quotation of works by respected historians: "'Compared to the German death camps during the Holocaust, the daily killing rate in Rwanda was five times higher.' 'At that rate Hitler would have completed the Holocaust in less than nine months, not six years.' . . . The central paradox of such sentences, Stockhammer argues, is that 'here something is compared with that which is synonymous with the incomparable.'" In short, the trauma of perpetrators poses impediments against the use of the genocide label and against analogical bridging that interprets the violence in Darfur in the light of the Holocaust.

Cautionary notes from civil society are reflected in the diplomatic field, modifying the somewhat decisive rhetoric cited above. Germany's foreign minister, Joschka Fischer, of the Green Party, outspoken about the genocidal nature of violence in Kosovo just a few years earlier, was more guarded in the case of Darfur, which he referred to in September 2004 as "a humanitarian catastrophe with genocidal potential" (quoted in K. Smith 2010:225). Also Kerstin Müller, minister of state in the Foreign Ministry, used the terms "humanitarian crisis" and "ethnic expulsions" rather than *genocide*. Still, an interviewee in the Political Division of the Foreign Ministry referred to these two politicians as "rather fundamentalist" and strict observers of the "letter of the law." Social Democrat Walter Steinmeier, Fischer's successor as foreign minister, barely addressed the Darfur issue, partly because of his preoccupation with the situation in Afghanistan, according to an interviewee's assessment confirmed by K. Smith (2010:232).[5]

Caution at the leadership level of the Foreign Ministry is reflected in the words of the interviewee from the ministry's Political Division. He stressed that Germany's "general obligation" based on Holocaust history must not lead to "inflexibility" and "dogmatism." Yet his position seems marred by resignation. While generally advocating diplomatic means, this interviewee acknowledged challenges to diplomatic negotiations in the Darfur case, at least in the short run: "That, however, one can only do when the public dust of excitement has practically settled. Because this diplomatic solution necessitates negotiations with the criminal [*Verbrecher*], with the murderer—necessitates a, let's call it 'value free,' interest-guided approach to the problem, which one—when the images from CNN about the dead in the streets are still fresh—cannot do at all. That's impossible" (author's translation).

Further, hesitation about diplomatic engagement pales in comparison to the rejection of military options. Generally, not just in the Darfur case, the same interviewee rejected the notion of German military intervention, even when the risk of genocide looms or when genocide is already under way: "Germany does not have the foreign policy tools [*auswärtigen Machtmittel*] to intervene—like the Americans do—both militarily and with humanitarian means, . . . We can do logistics, at best, as a member, a useful member of international community operations, that is. But that Germany would take the lead [*eine Verantwortung führen würde*] and would be the 'driver' to prevent some genocide in some part of the world—no, no, that not, because we cannot do that, because we do not even have the military means" (author's translation).

In short, the German Foreign Ministry showed hesitation to intervene in the case of Darfur, and was most reluctant to do so by military means. But even diplomatic means are considered only with great caution. Finally, legal responses, as well, find mixed assessments in the German diplomatic field. In the words of my interviewee from the human rights department of the Legal Division, a strong proponent for ICC intervention:

> As to my interlocutors in the *Auswärtige Amt* [Foreign Ministry], I think it is fair to say that there were constantly conflicting perceptions. And I do remember quite a number of quarrels I had with my colleagues in the political department. . . . And the reason is that we had two different approaches. Their approach was purely political. My approach was both political, but also legal and judicial. And that is extremely difficult to combine at times, because if you are only confined to making political assessments, then it is difficult to evaluate the work of a court, to accept a court, to accept any independent legal institution, and that is really something new in the international field, where people are trained to assess complex issues by political means only.

In conclusion, the German case shows how the cultural trauma of Holocaust perpetrators that afflicts German society and politics enhances at least rhetorical responses, in society and in the German diplomatic field, to cases of mass violence and genocide. But the cultural trauma also imposes constraints. The word *genocide* is applied with greater hesitation, and analogical bridging from the Shoah to contemporary mass atrocities is considered problematic.

I note, though, that the impediments appear more pronounced in deliberations about Darfur than in debates about other genocide cases and mass atrocities. In the Darfur case, the difference K. Smith finds between Germany's typically more forceful rhetoric and the greater caution in the United Kingdom and France is substantially diminished. One potential explanation is the latter two countries' colonial legacies in Sudan and Chad. In comparison to the United States, the responses of the United Kingdom, France, and Germany alike are substantially subdued. The much more ambivalent mobilization of civil society in Europe and the foreign policy sector's lack of receptivity likely explain this difference. Then again, the diplomatic field is not homogenous. Actors in the Legal Division of Germany's Foreign Ministry, especially those trained as lawyers, strongly advocate for criminal justice interventions by the ICC—even if they simultaneously express commitment and voice caution regarding links between the Holocaust and Darfur. In the words of one interviewee:

> I think it is justified to be very, very sensitive and very careful and very restrictive in making those comparisons. However, I mean, since we have that particular burden of history on our shoulders, I think it should be an incentive for us to inquire into cases of genocide. It does not always necessarily imply a comparison to the Holocaust. . . . Genocide is dramatic and horrible in itself. I think we have all reason to maintain that we as Germans have a particular responsibility to make sure that any holocaust [sic] or any genocide or any crime against humanity is not reproduced.

CONCLUSIONS: NATIONAL CONTEXTS INTERSECTING WITH THE DIPLOMATIC FIELD, AND MODIFIED REPRESENTATIONS

Clearly, fields—or national divisions within fields—are affected by national contexts. Previous scholarship has found that human rights discourses, as well as legislation and implementation of laws, differ across countries even in light of global scripts (Boyle 2002). Halliday and Carruthers (2010) show that the adaptation of global scripts depends on a country's position in the international balance of power and on its cultural distance from the global center. This analysis of the diplomatic field shows, as did those of the justice and humanitarian fields, that structural and cultural variation within the world of Western countries also matters.

Several cultural and structural conditions affected the degree to which diplomats from different countries stuck to or deviated from the diplomatic master narrative. Strong mobilization of civil society in combination with a porous state contributes to dramatizing narratives even in the diplomatic field, as the case of the United States illustrates. Frequent and intense interaction with the Sudanese state, especially in the absence of strong civil society mobilization, results in a narrative that sticks closely to the diplomatic ideal type. Such interactions may be fostered by lobbying efforts on the part of Sudan, especially toward a country with long-standing ties with Sudan and the Arab world, as illustrated by the Austrian case. Close interactions may also stem from a country's special expertise, for example, in arbitration and the resulting involvement in diplomatic efforts. Such expertise in the case of

Switzerland is privileged by the country's neutrality status. Finally, special interactions can result from a country's dedication to humanitarian aid efforts, which may themselves be rooted in its collective memory of suffering, as the example of Ireland shows.

Also, a nation's status as a former colonial power matters. Specific regional expertise, the presence of expatriate groups, a sense of obligation—self-perceived or imposed by media and third countries—may contribute to intense diplomatic involvement, as was the case for the United Kingdom. Again, such involvement pushes the narrative on Darfur closer to the diplomatic ideal type. France, affiliated with its former colony Chad, also moved cautiously, but appeared more willing to deviate from the diplomatic master narrative than the United Kingdom.

Germany exemplifies the complex effects of the cultural trauma of the perpetrator of the Holocaust. German narratives display a clear sense of obligation in the face of mass violence. Yet the memory of the Shoah imposes constraints on use of the term *genocide* and the building of analogical bridges between the Holocaust and later mass atrocities. The German case also illustrates the variability of memorial normativity (Savelsberg 2016). Norms embedded in identical memories vary by carrier group. Whereas actors such as the foreign ministry interviewee from the human rights unit may find penal norms supported by the cultural trauma of the Shoah, religiously inspired groups may draw humanitarian lessons from the trauma of perpetrators that advance, much in line with findings in chapters 4 and 5, a cautious rhetoric about the offending country. The latter perspective seems to leave traces in foreign ministry press releases in which the humanitarian frame dominates.

Throughout, national carrier groups, their memories, and the normative implications of memories matter, from African Americans, Jews, and evangelical Christians in the United States to humanitarians in Ireland, foreign policy elites in France, and religion- and church-based middle classes in Germany. This finding suggests modifying Levy and Sznaider's (2010) argument about a shift from communicative memories, based on group-specific carriers, to cultural memories, reproduced through media and communicative institutions. National carriers still matter.

In short, the context of the diplomatic field produces a unique representation of Darfur, one that differs from and competes with representations generated in the humanitarian field and, especially, the justice field. Proponents of the "justice cascade" (Sikkink 2011) thus have to contend with the diplomatic field. At the same time, real narratives deviate more or less from the ideal-typical diplomatic representation. The field of diplomacy intersects in complex patterns with diachronic experiences such as educational socialization and synchronic contexts such as organizational placement and national environment. Implications for communicating competing representations to the public sphere are at the center of the following chapters.

PART FOUR

Mediating Competing Representations

The Journalistic Field

Rules of the Journalistic Game, Autonomy, and the Habitus of Africa Correspondents

In my interview with an Africa correspondent of a prominent Western newspaper, the respondent said of his paper's editor-in-chief that he "thought one does not need a great political analyst for Africa, but someone who travels to countries and is capable of writing reports."

This editor's viewpoint certainly does not tell the full story of journalistic work on Africa. Yet it does reflect an important aspect of contemporary journalism: the relative marginality of Africa in the consciousness of Western media. What are the implications of this marginal place for the communication of information about mass violence in an African region such as Darfur to a broad segment of Western societies? What does this relative marginality mean for the chances that criminal justice, humanitarian, and diplomatic actors have to get their at times competing messages across to the world public? Any satisfying attempt to answer these questions requires that we explore the nature of the journalistic field—its autonomy, its relationship to other fields, the habitus of Africa correspondents, and of course the observed patterns of reporting that emerge in this context.

I address these tasks in two chapters. In the current chapter I examine the nature of the journalistic field, the relative autonomy of the segment of this field under consideration here, and the habitus of Africa correspondents who reported about Darfur. The following chapter lays out the relationship between the journalistic field and others, including the judicial, humanitarian, and diplomatic fields, and it analyzes the actual trends and patterns of reporting on Darfur.

For purposes of the current chapter I draw primarily on my interviews with twelve journalists from seven Western countries who reported on Darfur, and on supporting ethnographic notes from a conference of war correspondents and from the Bellagio conference on representations of Darfur, where correspondents engaged with actors from different fields. As I do in previous chapters for the spheres of criminal justice and human rights, humanitarianism, and diplomacy, in this chapter I use field theory, which Pierre Bourdieu (1998) and his followers have explicitly and successfully applied to journalism (e.g., Benson 1998, 2006). I supplement the Bourdieuian approach with insights from more recent work on boundaries between the journalistic and political fields (Mazzoleni and Schulz 1999; Revers 2014; Strömbeck and Esser 2014), from work on journalism that draws on cultural approaches (Dayan and Katz 1992; Hannerz 2004; Zelizer 1993), and from recent writings on the journalism of mass violence in Africa (Allen and Seaton 1999; McNulty 1999; Thompson 2007). In keeping with my comparative approach, I also add to insights from still-rare internationally comparative studies of journalistic work (e.g., Benson 1998, 2013).

THE JOURNALISTIC FIELD, MASS VIOLENCE, AND DARFUR

Bourdieu, in his little book *Television and Journalism* (1998), sought to "show how the journalistic field produces and imposes on the public a very particular vision of the political field. This vision is grounded in the very structure of the journalistic field and in the interests of journalists as they are produced by their field" (2). The picture Bourdieu paints is not pretty. He reveals media preferences for celebrities over profound knowledge, polemics over reason, political tactics over substance, and a predisposition to overstatement, all of which, he argues, fosters a "cynical view" (Bourdieu 1998:5) of politics on the part of the receiving public, a view simultaneously "dehistoricized and dehistoricizing, fragmented and fragmenting" (7). Bourdieu speaks specifically to media depictions of mass violence:

> Zaire today, Bosnia yesterday, the Congo tomorrow. Stripped of any political necessity, this string of events can at best arouse a vague humanitarian interest. Coming one after the other and outside any historical perspective, the unconnected tragedies seem to differ little from natural disasters. . . . As

for the victims, they're not presented in any more political a light than those of a train derailment or any other accident. . . . . Journalism shows us a world full of ethnic wars, racist hatred, violence and crime—a world full of incomprehensible and unsettling dangers from which we must withdraw for our own protection. (7–8)

Admittedly, Bourdieu directs his scathing critique primarily at television, but he also targets the broader journalistic field. Subsequent critiques of the mediatization of politics have supported Bourdieu's notion that such journalism affects political views and even political practice (e.g., Strömbeck and Esser 2014). But is Bourdieu's depiction of journalism confirmed by our data on Darfur? The media reports on which my empirical evidence is based are, after all, not collected from television but from the most sophisticated newspapers in the respective countries.[1]

Still, several features of the journalistic field apply irrespective of media type, and I am interested in their shape and in consequences they hold for the representation of mass violence. These features include, prominently, the relative autonomy of the field, in which actors follow specific rules of the game (and are guided by institutional logics); the particular habitus of journalists; the journalistic field's relationships with other fields, as shaped by power relations, available communication channels, and (in)compatibilities of language and logics applied in these fields; and the media field's globalization in interaction with persisting national traits. The following sections and chapter 9 address each of these features of journalism in turn and show, based on diverse types of data, how they apply to the case of journalism focused on Darfur.

AUTONOMY AND THE RULES OF THE GAME

Bourdieu (1998) characterizes journalism as "a microcosm with its own laws, defined both by its position in the world at large and by the attractions and repulsions to which it is subject from other such microcosms" (39). He depicts these microcosms as fields, relatively independent or "autonomous," by which he means that they follow their own laws or institutional logics.[2] Adherence to a specific set of rules is not unique to journalism, of course. Modern society is generally differentiated into semiautonomous fields such as politics, the economy, science, and religion, each governed by its own rules of the game, each demanding acceptance of those rules by actors who seek to participate (Benson 1998).

My examination of the fields of criminal law and justice, humanitarianism, and diplomacy in the preceding chapters illustrates how field-specific rules do not just govern the actions but even color the worldviews of participants and their knowledge or perception of Darfur.

Thus, like other fields, journalism is not determined by external criteria. As its agents follow journalism's own rules, its depiction of the world cannot be read, for example, as a reflection of economic interests—even if pursuit of such interests is indeed of vital interest to the operation (and survival) of a newspaper. The portrayal of events instead reflects the rules of journalism. Bourdieu (1998) illustrates these rules for television journalism: there has to be conflict, involving "good guys and bad guys," but exchanges have to be "clothed by the model of formal, intellectual language" (35). By creating excitement in viewers, such confrontation commands their attention (and thus high ratings), while the media gain legitimacy by following the rules of democratic procedure. Further, irrespective of the specific medium, journalists confront space limitations and intense time pressure. These constraints, too, demand adherence to particular genres (Bourdieu 1998:28). Applied to our case of mass violence, journalists may be inclined to simplify stories and to portray the contending sides in a conflict in overly streamlined ways—as representatives of reified primordial ethnic or racial groups, for example. Such oversimplification is a central target for critique in the literature on African civil wars (e.g., Allen and Seaton 1999; McNulty 1999), including works written by Africa correspondents themselves (Crilly 2010; Thompson 2007). Foreign correspondents face further challenges in that they cannot easily resort to strategies used by domestic reporters—for example, by focusing on "actions and statements of those claiming to represent the nation . . . [in order to] help impose unity on what is otherwise a congeries of individuals and groups acting inside a set of geographic and political boundaries" (Gans 2005:297). The task for international journalists is certainly more complex. Which authorities will they rely on to achieve this unity?

Writing specifically on mass violence, historian Devin Pendas (2006) examines the application and consequences of journalistic rules in the context of the Frankfurt Auschwitz trial of the early 1960s. Focusing on elite newspapers, as I do, he finds that here too the hectic pace of events colors journalistic work. One day's report rarely makes reference to the previous day's. Yesterday's information will be disregarded in subsequent reporting, when new events will have occurred. In other words, journalistic reporting is episodic. Shifting uses of the crime frame in the Darfur case confirmed this pattern: journalists may have frequently cited this frame after court interventions, but then neglected it in subsequent periods in which court action moved from the front to the back of the stage (see analysis in chapter 9).

Another journalistic rule is that of objectivity.[3] Facts are supposed to speak for themselves, and interpretation is to be provided only sparingly. Consumers of media-generated information have grown to appreciate and, in fact, demand this feature of journalism. Yet the case of the Frankfurt Auschwitz trial shows problematic consequences. Application of the objectivity rule meant that the logic of the criminal court was directly transmitted to the reader. As the trial was conducted under German criminal law, with its focus on individual intent, the trial (and subsequent media reports) highlighted those cases in which malicious intent was in full display, especially the instances of atrocities and torture. The reports, reflecting the trial proceedings, paid less attention, however, to the bureaucratized mass-murder machine of the gas chambers (e.g., transport, selection at the ramp, gassing, administration), where the "banality of evil" came to full display. Pendas (2006) summarizes the court and media's approach to the trial:

> What might be termed the characterological style in objective newspaper reporting thus entailed both a concern with personality and a tendency to reduce it to monadic types. And in this, a strong homology existed with the judicial emphasis on the subjective dispositions of defendants and the assumption of a causal nexus between motivation and action. The court's tendency to privilege atrocity over genocide, the juridical requirement for excessive brutality, the reduction of mass killing to a form of aiding and abetting rather than murder—all of these were reproduced in the characterology of the daily press. The "why" of the murder, as a matter of personal character, became the predominant theme, and the historical event of genocide was reduced to the psychodrama of the courtroom suspense thriller. (262)

My work with Ryan King (2011) found that media reporting about the My Lai massacre, committed by Charlie Company, a unit of the 20th US Infantry, during the Vietnam War, was similarly constrained by the logic of the courts-martial in which the case was tried. Instead of basing estimates of the number of people killed on a report by the army's Peers Commission or on a Pulitzer Prize–winning book by renowned journalist Seymour Hersh, media reports in subsequent years (as well as history textbooks) were more likely to cite those numbers for which the defendants were charged. Further, instead of attributing responsibility to a diversity of actors, including the military hierarchy, in line with the assessment of the Peers Commission, news reports focused on the responsibility of Lieutenant William Calley, the single person convicted and sentenced in the trial (Savelsberg and King 2011:34–52).

In short, strictures such as the objectivity rule are not just guarantors of relative autonomy but also constraining forces. In situations where journalists lack autonomy, the constraints of journalistic rules are replaced by others that govern neighboring fields such as the economy or the world of politics.[4] Media in authoritarian systems that practice censorship are an extreme example. In capitalist systems, some media obviously place more emphasis on economic forms of capital (such as circulation, advertising revenues, and audience ratings) than on cultural capital (such as literary skill or awards such as the Pulitzer Prize). The former media are closer to what Bourdieu calls the heteronomous pole, where criteria external to the field dominate, while the latter approximate the autonomous pole, ruled by criteria unique to the journalistic field (Benson 2006:190). Given the prestige of the newspapers under study here, the journalism we encounter is closer to the autonomous pole. It differs decisively from TV, especially privately owned or market-driven TV, and from tabloid journalism. This distinction is in line with the composition of its readership, as Benson (2006) observes: "At elite newspapers such as the *New York Times* and the *Washington Post* (data for the *Wall Street Journal* are not publically available, but one can presume the results would at least be equivalent), readers are twice as likely, or more, than the average American adult to have a college degree, to earn more than $75,000 per year, and to hold managerial positions" (191). Very similar readership patterns can be assumed for all newspapers included in this analysis.[5]

And yet, despite the closeness of the journalists in this study to the autonomous pole, all interviewees were mindful of declining subscription rates and growing economic pressures on their papers. The dramatic situation is well captured in one respondent's account of the history of his paper's representation in Africa: "The office in Johannesburg existed throughout. But then, with the big newspaper crisis, which started in 2002 and really hit in 2004, Johannesburg was closed down. Then Abidjan was the last remaining office. I was responsible for the entire continent as of 2004, and that comes with a lot of travel. [JJS: And today too you are the only Africa correspondent?] Yes, I am the only one, yes" (author's translation).

Assigning no more than one correspondent on the ground to the entire African continent was a practice common to almost all the newspapers I examined. The *New York Times* is a major exception. One of the Paris-based newspapers in fact no longer has journalists stationed in Africa.[6] One of the interviewees attributed this omission to the fact that Africa is a "niche subject." Another journalist told me that it takes "extraordinary" events for Africa reports to get on the front page. Whatever the causes may be, massive journalistic underrepresentation—intensified by economic constraints that increasingly weigh on newspapers—restricts reporting from the African continent. Economic pressure is yet more intensely felt by independent journalists. One correspondent, now a freelancer after years working for one of the newspapers under study, wrote in a personal communication in the summer of 2014: "I'd love to travel to Darfur again, but the media interest is so low that I would have to expect a major financial loss. I am now a freelancer [*unabhängig*], and I have to make sure to make a profit. That is not even always easy in Syria" (author's translation). He had just delivered a prime-time TV news magazine report from the latter country.

In short, the media under study are relatively close to the autonomous pole of the journalistic field. Their work is driven by the rules of journalism more than by external forces. Yet even these journalists are subject to external pressures, including economic ones.

THE HABITUS OF AFRICA CORRESPONDENTS

Field theory draws attention to the actors who inhabit a field and the habitus that guides their actions. Journalists, like all actors in social fields, are carriers of such a habitus, defined earlier (following Bourdieu) as a set of relatively fixed dispositions that reflect actors' trajectories and their position within the field (see also Emirbayer and Johnson 2008). Bourdieu liked to refer to jazz musicians or basketball players for an illustration. Both follow rules, but they would be incapable of playing their music or game successfully were they not skilled improvisers. The same should apply to journalists in their line of work. Accordingly, Bourdieu speaks of "cognitive, perceptual and evaluative structures" with which journalists must deal. He attributes these to a "common social background and training (or lack thereof)" (Bourdieu 1998:36). It thus seems necessary to understand the habitus of our Africa correspondents if we hope to make sense of how journalists report about Darfur. What is their demographic and educational background? How did they enter journalistic careers? How were they selected for their work in Africa? What is their position vis-à-vis the papers they work for? And finally, how do their life and career trajectories and positions shape "durable dispositions"? In short, what kind of habitus emerges and how does it color their reporting about mass violence?

Trajectories

A few demographic characteristics of the twelve interviewees are illustrative. All but one of the journalists had grown up in the Global North. The one exception is a native South African. Another correspondent is a second-generation immigrant from Sri Lanka. The likely significance of his background is suggested by his comment that "it possibly increases my sympathy [for Darfur rebels], because the Sri Lanka conflict is a conflict that was with rebel actors against the center. It possibly strengthened my sympathy for a group that was seeking to extract concessions from the political center, and a group that had felt itself discriminated against."

All but two interviewees, and all who had reported from the ground in Darfur or Chad or both, were males. One of the two female journalists reported from the United Nations in New York; the other, a specialist on international relations, from her country's capital city, a seat to many international organizations. Among the male journalists, only one had written about Darfur from his home base as his paper's foreign affairs columnist. All others had worked from their posts in Africa. Most interviewees wrote for newspapers in their country of origin. The exceptions were a Belgian working for a German paper, a German employee of an Austrian paper, the South African who wrote for a British paper, and a freelancer with British-Irish roots who reported primarily for British, American, and Irish papers.

The journalists I interviewed were generally of middle-class background. Several had at least one parent who had been a journalist. All had some kind of academic education. Only one had attended journalism school, while others held university degrees in fields as varied as political science, English literature, German studies, economics, history, philosophy, and genetics.

Speaking about their paths to journalistic careers, interviewees revealed some of their dispositions. A British correspondent told me: "My father was a journalist. So, I guess, it was always in my blood even though I tried to do other things. . . . I enjoyed writing. So it was the obvious thing to do." A senior British journalist and former foreign editor reported a similar background: "Both my parents were journalists. . . .

If I was going to fulfill my ambitions to see the world, then I needed to get someone to pay for that. And, because my own talent was the ability to write well, it just seems that journalism was an obvious outlet for me." Several interviewees had made journalistic forays before entering into their professional careers. An Austrian journalist of German descent, for example, had written for newspapers during her high school (*Gymnasium*) years. She then studied political science in Berlin and Paris (with a focus on Africa), before she moved to Vienna for personal reasons and entered her professional career there. Similarly, one interviewee who tried to enter journalism right out of high school realized that "[i]t was not quite easy for a nineteen-year old without an academic degree. I understood quickly then that I had to do university studies. I did that [Islamic studies and political science] parallel to my travels to Afghanistan and later to Angola and other crisis regions in Africa. That's really how I earned my living. And that also predestined me for the Africa post with the [newspaper name]" (author's translation).

One last example must suffice: "Journalist was always my dream of a profession [*Traumberuf*]. I have to say I got there via detours. I worked for many years as a truck driver to finance my studies. But I never lost sight of my goal to become a journalist" (author's translation).

In short, all interviewees evidenced a relatively high level of education and a joy of writing, some showed a sense of adventurism and desire to travel, and all demonstrated a profound dedication to the journalism profession. Such a habitus should work toward a relatively high level of journalistic autonomy, a strong desire to stick to journalistic rules and to avoid giving in to heteronomous pressures.

But more questions must be asked. For example, how prepared were our journalists for their assignment to Africa? How were they selected for work on that continent? Answers to such questions further advance our understanding of these Africa correspondents' habitus. One French journalist moved from the national to the international section. He was young ("twenty-four or twenty-five years old"), but he told me about others who had started working on Africa at even a younger age: "New reporters start with Africa, usually. . . . It is kind of traditional. Maybe because it takes a lot of time in Africa, and young people normally have no kids, no wives, no lifeline." A British journalist also moved to Africa shortly after beginning his career. One of his first posts was in Nairobi, where he arrived in 2003, the year in which mass violence began to unfold in Darfur and the year before he visited Sudan for the first time to report about Darfur. Other respondents had some previous experience,

FIGURE 18. Journalist Rob Crilly in the field in Darfur.

but no Africa-specific training. "I've been a journalist for ten, eleven years," one said. "I have been working in the UK and did a number of trips during that time to Africa to work. So I decided it was quite an adventure, and it was the sort of journalism I wanted to do. There was no burning ambition to be a human rights journalist or war correspondent or anything like that. It was really for a bit of adventure. And that is what took me to Nairobi as a freelancer." Similarly, the South African correspondent for British newspapers had previous journalistic experience. Yet, while he benefited from having acquired knowledge of Africa previously, he too had no training to be a foreign correspondent for the African continent. Biographical knowledge, though, gained through life experiences, can be a strong motivator, as the following example of a journalist for a German paper shows. He too did not have formal training regarding Africa when he took over as an Africa correspondent. He had started as a young man, working on local news for a major city's newspaper. "Then," he told me,

> a national paper opened a position for someone for Africa, specifically francophone Africa. That was at a time when the paper was still doing financially quite well. We were able to afford that. And I applied for the position and I was selected. Francophone, because at the time there was no continuous reporting from this part of Africa. I then opened up the office in Abidjan. And yes, I have been traveling on the continent for ten years now. Why Africa for me? That has family reasons. I am Belgian, as you know. My entire family on the paternal side tried their luck in the Congo at some point. . . . Congo was a topic at our dinner table. I also spent much time there because my godfather lived his entire life down there. Yes, that's the source of my affinity for the continent. (author's translation)

Indeed, this journalist's affinity proved to be enduring. When I interviewed him in 2011, he had already dedicated ten years of journalistic work to Africa. He had experienced exceptional challenges, including days of captivity in the hands of child soldiers. His reports continue, at the time of this writing, to be among the most informative and analytic ones in the international press. This interviewee's long-term dedication to Africa, however, is exceptional. Several of the other Africa correspondents expressed a desire to move on after having covered Africa for an extended period. The following example is instructive:

> No, I did this for seven years, and it was an extremely intensive time, also with great experiences. I made fantastic journeys there and met great people; my daughter was born there; I got married there, but to a German woman. So I really had the entire spectrum of feelings. I was so exhausted in 2006, however, that I first had to take a half-year off from work. . . . I was at acute risk of death, three times, mostly in Congo and I also had a severe accident in Nairobi etc. So it wears on your psyche and also on your body, so that I was finally totally exhausted. I then wanted nothing to do with Africa any more, initially. . . . See, we lived for five years in Nairobi, and then for two years in Cape Town. We left Nairobi because the security situation was so catastrophic and one felt the psychological impact. When I was in Congo, I was shot at there for hours, together with colleagues, and when we could then escape to the airport and fly out, then we were relieved, having put this behind us again, because that is not my primary task, being a war reporter, but it happens at times; then I sat in the airplane and thought to myself, "When I now return to Nairobi, then I am not certain that my wife is doing well, that my daughter is doing well, and if they may not have been attacked." This permanent state of alarm, it does not serve one well in the long run. (author's translation)

A look at journalists' entry into their careers as Africa correspondents thus sheds further light on their habitus. Many are young, in the

FIGURE 19. Journalist Rob Crilly after interview with SLA commander Ibrahim Abdullah al "Hello" and a rebel in En Siro, North Darfur.

earliest stages of their careers.[7] Most have biographical knowledge about Africa at best (the quotation at the beginning of this chapter speaks to this theme). Many consider Africa an episode in their career path, not a long-term commitment. We may assume that these features have an effect on journalistic autonomy opposite to that of features found above such as high level of education, developed writing skill, and dedication to journalism. They are likely to create dependencies and to weaken journalistic autonomy.

Position in the Field

In addition to their trajectories, the dispositions of Africa correspondents are also shaped by the journalistic environments in which they work. These reporters operate at great geographic remove from their employers. Meetings between editors and foreign correspondents in the latter's home countries are rare. Foreign editors to whom they report provide them with relative discretion. Reporting from Africa is nonetheless expensive. Much travel is involved, and staying in capital cities where journalists wait for visas and travel permits requires considerable resources. Most interviewees told me that projects need to be approved by the foreign editor before they can be started. Only one correspondent reported a substantially greater degree of freedom. Referring to himself as "the last Mohican," he did not need to apply to his foreign editor whenever he wanted to take trips. He decided independently which topics and events to report on. Also, his paper had provided him

FIGURE 20. Journalist Thomas Scheen interviewing rebels in Darfur.

with a five-year contract up front so he could build up the repertoire of knowledge and local ties crucial to good journalistic work. It was this journalist who had spent the longest time reporting from Africa. But, again, this model is more the exception than the rule.

Given the geographic distance from their papers' headquarters, many Africa correspondents depend all the more on contacts with colleagues in the field, especially if they are the only correspondents for their papers on the continent. Such contacts are made easier by the fact that most American and European Africa correspondents are based in only a few places, such as Nairobi and Johannesburg. They are further eased by the pressure to join together for major investigatory journeys, as the following recollection of a British interviewee illustrates: "I suppose in Nairobi there is a sort of quite wide ex-patriot community, which is the European ex-patriot community. And the European journalist community, um, within that group, you would often first be alerted to a story by some discussion within that group. . . . So Darfur, in fact, it was a conversation at a party very early on. It was someone saying I think this is important." Such local information sharing sometimes leads to joint explorations into crisis regions. In the words of another journalist: "When I actually went to go to Darfur, I traveled with . . . journalists from another newspaper or with a photographer who was very experienced. . . . So often you would share a kind of expertise or you would share information, and you sort of worked together to build up a picture."

Collaborative ventures can be extensive, as the account of a German correspondent about his work on the Congo demonstrates:

> In January of 2000 I again traveled with colleagues—the entire world press was part of it, the *New York Times, Washington Post, Time Magazine,* etc.—into Northeast Congo, into the so-called Ituri District. Because a pretty courageous helper for the Christoffel Mission for the Blind had brought a video, on a VHS cassette, on which the massacre was to be seen, burning villages and mass graves etc. This was a very peripheral region that was normally hard to get to. There also were no flights into that place. . . . We then chartered a small plane and traveled there and moved about in the Ituri District for a week. . . . We really all reported prominently about it. I wrote a whole page in the [name of paper]. *Der Spiegel* [German weekly magazine] had several pages on it. The British and American media also reported about it in great detail. (author's translation)

Collaboration in the context of field trips requires embeddedness in journalistic networks in everyday life. One correspondent described those networks:

> Life in Nairobi has a kind of family atmosphere, and there is also no journalistic competition to speak of, and one sits down with colleagues and discusses certain themes and also wants to learn from someone who has just been in a region what things look like out there. So there is a lively exchange of experiences and information. That eventually also leads to some kind of opinion formation. [Collaboration at times also leads to coordination:] Yes, at times one even coordinates when what will be published. To give you just one example, if I travel with a colleague from the [name of weekly magazine] jointly into the Congo and we help each other, then I would destroy his [magazine] article if my article appeared on Thursday in [name of daily]. Then he'll be kicked out on Friday [the day the weekly magazine is published]. . . . Because we share a lot and help each other, I can then tell my paper, "Publish this next Monday." (author's translation)

Such reports fall in line with scholarship that identifies journalists as favoring "horizontal over vertical management, and collegial over hierarchical authority" (Zelizer 1993:221). In addition to many contacts in informal settings, there are also formal institutions in which journalistic exchange unfolds: "There is this foreign correspondent club," one interviewee explained. "There I was always happy to meet colleagues from Kenya or Zimbabwe, because otherwise the Brits are oriented toward other Brits, Americans to Americans, Germans to Germans. That can get a bit boring in the long run" (translation, JJS).

The foregoing comment thus confirms the notion of relatively dense social and professional networks among Western Africa correspondents, networks to which African journalists are primarily linked through formal institutions such as the aforementioned club.[8] The statement further confirms and at once relativizes the international quality of the occupational lives of Western journalists in Africa. To encapsulate the local nature of these networks and the simultaneously international composition of their participants, I suggest the term "clustered local cosmopolitan media networks." The networks are local and international, and thus cosmopolitan, a feature of foreign journalism famously highlighted by Ulf Hannerz (2004:82). At the same time, the term acknowledges national clusters within these networks. All the above comments and depictions at once confirm and give a specific meaning to Bourdieu's assessment of the global nature of media operations: "The position of the national media field within the global media field would have to be taken into account" (Bourdieu 1998:41).

The two journalistic interviewees who reported from international centers in the West also provide lively accounts of collaboration with colleagues across nations. In the words of the French correspondent who reported from the UN headquarters during the height of the Darfur conflict: "At the UN you have some kind of, I call that the security council for journalists. . . . If you want to know what actually the Russians are thinking, you will find a Russian journalists who is going to tell you." And a French journalist who covered the African continent from Paris reported: "Because I am based in Paris, I don't have a lot of journalists calling me, except my friends calling me and saying, 'Hey, are you doing this place?' We are going to travel together or share some of the cost." This interviewee highlights collaboration with *Radio France Internationale,* which employs a substantial number of Africa correspondents.

Media do not just feed on media via journalistic networks. In line with Bourdieu's observation, "a daily review of the press is an essential tool" (1998:24) for our journalists. Yet the motivation behind reading other media is not primarily the desire to avoid being beaten by them—as Bourdieu suggests—but the need to use them as essential information-gathering tools in a world in which one journalist has to cover an entire continent for his paper. Not all of the other news media are considered equal, though, as potential sources of information. One interviewee used the category of "*Leitmedien*" (literally, "guiding media") and referred to the BBC and the *NYT* as examples. Indeed, correspondents mentioned these two as sources most frequently. Other media sources cited by my interviewees include CNN, the *Guardian, Radio France Internationale,* and *Le Monde.* Some interviewees referred to broader categories (e.g., news media, radio), to press agencies (e.g., Reuters, DPA), or to local newspapers and journalists.

In short, journalists are discursively aware of each other and they collectively construct images of the world, including images of mass violence. They thus constitute an "interpretive community" where "narratives and storytelling" (Zelizer 1993:221) reign supreme, a community that in this branch of journalism is simultaneously locally and internationally organized and oriented—a cosmopolitan interpretive community.

CONCLUSIONS

Data gleaned from interviews with Africa correspondents who reported on Darfur seem to confirm Bourdieu's central thesis: journalists are directed by their field's rules of the game. These rules secure the field's relative autonomy, but they also constrain its participants. Autonomy of course is not absolute. In capitalist systems, media markets affect what is reported and how, even if the degree varies to which diverse types of media emphasize economic as opposed to cultural types of capital. The media analyzed in this book are relatively close to the autonomous pole of the journalistic field. As a consequence, those criteria dominate that are specific to journalism. And yet, even prestigious newspapers examined here experience economic pressures. And journalists are aware of them and perceive them as constraints. Such constraints increase correspondents' dependency on some external sources of information (supplementing independent journalistic investigation) and on the community of (mostly Western) journalists within the field. A dispute erupted at the Bellagio conference pitting critics among activists and scholars against journalists. While the former group challenged journalistic reliance on UN and UNAMID sources in a report by Jeffrey Gettleman of the *New York Times* on Darfuris returning from camps into the villages, the latter defended the practice as unavoidable and legitimate. Economic constraints may at times certainly prevent the execution of some investigatory projects and increase reliance on organizations that pursue their own material or legitimatory interests. Again, journalistic autonomy is relative.

The habitus of Africa correspondents, those relatively stable dispositions that color their understanding of the world and their reporting about situations of mass violence such as that in Darfur, is shaped by their specific position in this semiautonomous field and by the trajectories that brought them to their current positions. Most interviewees showed a high degree of identification with journalistic work, an appreciation of the writing process, a high level of education in diverse fields (albeit a lack of education about Africa), some degree of adventurism, a relative degree of independence from their editors (but mindfulness of resource shortages that may stall promising projects), and a substantial degree of dependency on other sources of information, including IO and INGO reports, as well as other news sources, especially guiding media ("*Leitmedien*") and networks of colleagues in the field. In fact, most interviewees clearly speak to what I term clustered local cosmopolitan media networks—cosmopolitan despite the weight of national clusters. This mix of features obviously entails elements that enhance and others that weaken journalistic autonomy, the correspondents' orientation toward journalistic rules of the game.

Given this habitus of our Africa correspondents and the semiautonomy of the segment of the journalistic field in which they work, how do other fields make themselves noticed in journalistic production? What input do they provide that is processed by our Africa correspondents according to the rules of the journalistic game? The following chapter examines interactions between the journalistic field and external forces and shows how these interactions color the patterns and trends of reporting about Darfur.

CHAPTER 9

Patterns of Reporting

Fields, Countries, Ideology, and Gender

Varying degrees of influence come into full view when we examine the relationship between, on the one hand, the human rights, humanitarian aid, and diplomacy fields, with their conflicting representations of the Darfur conflict, and patterns of media reporting, on the other. The link between the judicial or human rights field and media suggests a seeming paradox. Asked about the ICC as a potential source of information, one German Africa-correspondent answered: "Not at all, and I find this really quite regrettable." A French journalist, speaking about his relationship to the ICC told me that "[t]heir time is not our time." Yet, as we shall see, the impact of the judicial field, specifically ICC interventions, on media representations of mass violence is quite remarkable. That impact certainly appears more pronounced than the traces the humanitarian and diplomatic fields leave in journalistic reporting.

In this chapter I describe and seek to explain actual patterns of media representation of Darfur. I speak to ways in which Africa correspondents, acting in the journalism field, with the habitus described in the previous chapter, improvise as they apply the rules of the journalistic game in practice. I explore how they adapt to external pressures and to the constraints they face. I primarily draw on the Darfur media data set, based on the content analysis of 3,387 articles described in the introduction. These data tell us when newspapers began reporting about Darfur and how the number of reports, the depiction of suffering, and the framing of violence changed over time. They also gauge the effect of interventions by actors from surrounding social fields. I show that outside pressures to which the journalistic field is exposed are substantial. They include media markets; economic dependency on advertisers and subscribers (who have become scarcer and thus more valuable in the early twenty-first century); agendas of political actors who impede journalism (in the targeted country or area) and who validate journalistic attention to issues (in the home country); and information dependency on societal sectors that include the judicial, humanitarian, and diplomatic fields. Finally, patterns reveal similarities and differences across countries. Interviews with Africa correspondents help make sense of these patterns. The chapter's conclusions address central Bourdieuian arguments regarding the position of journalism in fields of power, specifically journalism's relationship to neighboring fields, forces that must be considered if we want to make sense of variations in reporting about mass violence in Darfur or elsewhere (Bourdieu 1998; Benson 1998, 2006). The conclusions further add new information to past scholarship about boundaries between political and journalistic fields and debates about the mediatization of politics (Mazzoleni and Schulz 1999; Revers 2014; Strömbeck and Esser 2014). They enrich insights from research and journalistic self-reflections on the reporting about mass violence in Africa (Allen and Seaton 1999; Crilly 2010; McNulty 1999; Mody 2010; Ray 2009; Thompson 2011). And they contribute new, internationally comparative findings to those gained through a small body of previous comparative scholarship (e.g., Benson 1998, 2013).

INTENSITY OF REPORTING: THE JOURNALISTIC VIS-À-VIS THE POLITICAL FIELD AND MEDIA MARKETS

How much attention did media pay to the mass violence in Darfur, and how did the intensity of reporting change over time? Figure 21 depicts how the number of media reports from each country changed from year to year during the conflict. The numbers in this figure reflect the entire population of articles about Darfur that my research team identified in the fourteen newspapers and from which the sample of 3,387 articles was drawn for detailed analysis. It is instructive to follow these lines year by year.

Note first that shifts in the intensity of reporting developed in almost perfect unison. Within the same year a peak in the number of articles in one country is mirrored in those of the other countries. The massive volume of reporting in 2004 and 2007 stands out for all countries.

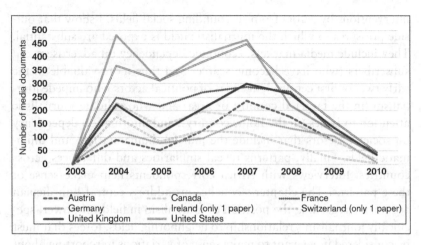

FIGURE 21. Number of articles on Darfur appearing in fourteen Northern newspapers, by country over time.

Second, though, the intensity of reporting differs considerably across countries. The lines for Germany and the United States by far exceed those of the other countries. For the United States this is consistent with the massive civil society movement around the Darfur issue, paralleled by the particularly outspoken engagement of government actors. For Germany the higher level of reporting corresponds with that country's articulation of special historical responsibility. It is also consistent with the generally greater engagement with genocide in German political discourse, as diagnosed by K. Smith (2010) in her comparative analysis of large European countries. In our analysis, frequency of reporting in US and German newspapers is followed—in most years and with considerable distance—by papers in the UK and France, the former colonial powers in Sudan and neighboring Chad, respectively. Note that Ireland and Switzerland are represented by only one newspaper. If we account for the fact that only one paper was analyzed, the Irish intensity of reporting also stands out, in line with the substantial humanitarian engagement in Darfur of Irish aid NGOs and the Irish government (see chapter 5).[1]

Beyond the overall volume of reporting, the cycles of media reports about Darfur across specific time periods pose urgent puzzles. I here spell them out and seek explanations. Virtually no reports appeared in 2003 Yet the first wave of massive killings and displacements unfolded between April and September of that year before it subsided following a temporary cease-fire. This journalistic silence, paralleling disregard or denial in other fields, is of course not the first case in which media have responded late to mass violence on the African continent.[2]

The second massive wave of killings took place between December 2003 and April 2004, when a second cease-fire took effect. At this point media did begin to take notice, and later in 2004, the intensity of reporting actually reached high levels.[3] This new wave of violence differed little from the first and thus might have been accompanied by similar media apathy. But this time the violence went along with highly visible civil society and political responses. As early as December 2003, UN secretary-general Kofi Annan's special envoy Tom Eric Vraalsen reported that the government of Sudan was denying humanitarian access to Darfur. In January 2004, the USHMM issued a "genocide alert" for Darfur. In February, the *Washington Post* published an op-ed piece by scholar-activist Eric Reeves on the violence in Darfur, and one month later the *New York Times* followed with an op-ed by Nicholas Kristof.[4] These pioneers, interestingly, did not include correspondents who were actually working in the field in Africa. Only one month after the second, much noted op-ed, Kofi Annan delivered his famous speech before the UN General Assembly on the tenth anniversary of the Rwandan genocide. By late summer 2004, in the United States the George W. Bush administration began using the term *genocide,* and in September 2004 the UN Security Council charged the International Commission of Inquiry on Darfur to report on the violence. I spell this and other events of 2004 out in greater detail in chapter 1.

Some journalist interviewees addressed factors that motivated their first reporting about Darfur in early 2004. Their statements reveal that the political field generally and the United Nations specifically, as well as human rights NGOs, played a central role in sparking initial journalistic engagement. A distinguished Africa correspondent recalled: "When first messages about a new war in Sudan appeared in 2003, I initially did not take that so seriously. But when the commemorative events unfolded on the tenth anniversary of the Rwandan genocide [April 2004] and Kofi Annan and others said, 'We will no longer tolerate this,' then I also decided to take this conflict seriously and I traveled there" (author's translation).

Another journalist told about his work on the North-South conflict in Sudan and the relief he and his colleagues had felt when the Comprehensive Peace Agreement (CPA) was signed in 2005. Having worked on the North-South conflict in the preceding years, his attention was thus attuned to Sudanese issues. Yet it took an unusual series of events for him to begin his field trips and reporting from Darfur and Chad. Tracing the takeoff of reporting in this journalist's paper is instructive: "We then regularly received messages from human rights organizations informing us of massacres and displacements in West Sudan. We could not really make sense of that, as we are not Sudan specialists. They initially even reported that this was a conflict between Christians and Muslims etc.—until we received detailed studies from Human Rights Watch and Global Witness that described this as a war of expulsion [*Vertreibungskrieg*]" (author's translation).

The pattern of his and his paper's publications about Darfur unfolded during the first half-year of reporting as follows:

- 10/28/2003: AP report based on USAID information (107 words)
- 11/14/2003: overview article by colleague of interviewee based on UN sources (361 words)
- 12/22/2003: article by interviewee on the North-South agreement mentioning Darfur (340 words)
- 1/28/2004: article by interviewee on violence and settlement efforts, partly based on press agency reports (381 words)
- 2/10/2004: article by interviewee on violence and Darfur refugee crisis in Chad, based on UN and Chadian government sources (261 words)
- 3/20/2004: Evangelischer Pressedienst (EPD) agency report on single attack (83 words)
- 3/23/2004: article by interviewee on violence and government of Sudan's denial, based on UN sources (345 words)
- 4/7/2004: article by colleague of interviewee on the aftermath of the Rwandan genocide, including a paragraph on Darfur, citing UN sources and HRW (1,077 words)
- 4/10/2004: Deutsche Presse-Agentur (DPA) report on truce (71 words)

None of these articles appeared in the paper's most visible places, but this soon changed when, on April 23, 2004, the Darfur conflict actually advanced to the paper's front page. It featured an article by the interviewee entitled "Alarming Report of the United Nations: Mass Murder and Atrocities in Sudan" (*Alarmierender Bericht der Vereinten Nationen: Massenmorde und Gräueltaten im Sudan*) (593 words). The article was accompanied by an opinion piece on page 4 (225 words) and an "external report" on page 2 (963 words), the latter written by a former minister of justice who was then a UN special rapporteur on human rights in Sudan. The lead article referred to a not-yet-published report by the UN high commissioner for human rights: "The report charges the Government of Sudan and a closely allied militia with war crimes. There is said to be a 'domination of terror' [*Herrschaft des Terrors*] in the crisis region of Darfur, with ethnically motivated mass murders, rapes and evictions. The regime in Khartoum thus far refuses to allow the UN any access to the region" (author's translation).

The author-interviewee explained:

> And we had the report. And then we were the first newspaper in all of Europe, I believe, that wrote about the Darfur conflict in a lead article on page 1. That found much resonance, also, in other media. This report was then also given to other newspapers, of course. . . . That developed its own dynamic, also because then I traveled with the colleagues [from other papers] to Chad, for example, to tour the border areas and visit refugee camps, gaining an understanding of the situation there. (author's translation)

Communication between the paper's foreign editor and a high-ranking politician with access to a repressed UN report had opened the path for this front-page reporting. My interviewee received permission to travel to Chad to investigate, and his contributions (and those of others) soon appeared in rapid succession: May 27 (article and editorial), May 28 (article by a colleague), May 29 (DPA), June 1 (by colleague and DPA report), June 3, June 5 (by colleague), June 14 (article and editorial), and June 19 (by colleague). Such intensification of reporting was not unique to this paper, but part of what became a flood of journalistic interest in Darfur. This flood crested at the peak of reporting in 2004 as depicted in figure 21. This story of one paper's entry into reporting about Darfur illustrates how communication between a paper's leadership and a high-ranking and respected politician helped bring Darfur to the front page and assure the paper's correspondent a travel permit into the crisis region. There is every reason to believe that this paper's story is representative of others.

The 2004 peak of reporting was followed by a modest but nonetheless noticeable drop in 2005 in all eight countries. This decline, however, did not reflect a lack of events to report on. The ICID issued its report in January. In May the UNSC referred the case to the ICC. Meanwhile in the United States the Save Darfur coalition began to gather steam. The violence continued in Darfur, albeit at a level well below the peaks of mid-2003 and early 2004. Yet neither did the killings cease, nor did the suffering of the surviving population diminish. An epidemiological study finds: "The number of internally displaced persons remained constant, but the number of affected residents tripled; the increase in humanitarian aid was similar to the increase in total number of people affected, resulting in a constant ratio of 40 humanitarian aid workers to 100,000 people affected" (Degomme and Guha-Sapir 2010:296).

After 2005, reporting increased again, reaching a second peak in 2006 in six of the eight countries. It started to drop off in only two countries after 2005. What may have motivated this intensification in reporting about Darfur? Might events on the ground in the crisis region have ignited renewed interest? Again, public health researchers who reported on the state of the Darfuri population inform us that, between the middle of 2006 and late 2007, "because of insecurity, the number of internally displaced people increased by about 40% (from 1,717,092 to 2,387,594); concomitantly, and partly as a result of reduced funding, the number of humanitarian aid workers decreased from 14,751 to 12,112 by July, 2007 (i.e., 29 aid workers for every 100,000 people affected)" (Degomme and Guha-Sapir 2010:296). Insecurity intensified, especially when in May 2006 the DPA was signed but failed to bring peace, and this setback was followed by a new offensive by the Sudanese military in August 2006. Although events on the ground did not initially spark media attention, this time they were accompanied by political and civil society actions, especially in the United States.

There, in October 2006, President Bush signed into law the Darfur Peace and Accountability Act (House Resolution 3127/Senate Bill 1462). The act confirmed the administration's position that the violence in Darfur constituted genocide. It also instructed the government to assist the ICC in its pursuit of the responsible actors—despite the United States' continued refusal to ratify the Rome Statute. This signing into law was preceded by a massive Save Darfur demonstration in Washington in April 2006 (see chapter 3). While these domestic US events may have contributed to an increasing volume of American media reports, it is unlikely that they had an equal impact in raising the number of media reports in the other countries. Instead, global action is more likely to have intensified attention across countries. Such action included the February 2007 application for and the April issuing of an arrest warrant against Ahmed Harun and Ali Kushayb at the ICC, and passage in July 2007 of UNSC Resolution 1769, authorizing the establishment of UNAMID, the UN-AU hybrid peacekeeping mission for Darfur.

Figure 21 shows further that the second peak in the intensity of reporting, registered in 2007, was followed by a massive and steady decline in
each of the subsequent three years. By 2010, the number of reports was
barely above the minimal level of 2003 reporting. This decline occurred
despite continued suffering in Darfur. The public health study cited
above reports that from October 2007 through December 2008, the
beginning of the steep decline in reporting, the "number of internally
displaced people" continued to increase (Degomme and Guha-Sapir
2010:296). Apparently even international responses could not prevent
the decline. Among these responses were the ICC's unprecedented and
much debated steps in 2008 and 2009. On July 14, 2008, the Office of
the Prosecutor applied for an arrest warrant against Omar al-Bashir,
the sitting president of Sudan. The application was based on charges of
war crimes, crimes against humanity, and genocide. On March 4, 2009,
the court issued the arrest warrant for war crimes and crimes against
humanity. Following this decision one Abu Garda, a lower-level rebel
leader made a first appearance before the ICC, on May 18, 2009, and
in 2010—beyond our observation period—the court issued the arrest
warrant against al-Bashir for charges of genocide.[5] In short, the suffering on the ground and ICC actions were substantial. And yet, reporting
declined precipitously.

Interviews suggest several potential explanations for the decline in
reporting. Respondents point at constraints imposed on journalism by
both the economic and political fields. One crucial part of journalism's
political environment, an issue throughout the Darfur conflict but in-
tensifying over time, was the government in Sudan. A German Africa
correspondent spoke about difficulties in obtaining visas for Sudan from
his seat in Nairobi. A British journalist reported that during his May–
June 2004 visit to Sudan he waited "much of the month" in Khartoum
before receiving travel permits to Darfur. The same journalist decided
later in the year to travel to Chad to avoid the political-bureaucratic
hurdles set up by the government of Sudan. Another British journalist
similarly reported having been stuck in (expensive) Khartoum for "a
couple" of weeks before receiving a permit to travel to Darfur. Rob
Crilly (2010), a British Africa correspondent who reported extensively
from Sudan, including Darfur, provides a lively illustration:

> It felt good to be in Khartoum at last. For a year I had potted back and forth to
> the Sudanese embassy in Nairobi enquiring as politely as I could whether my
> visa was ready for collection. . . . But arriving in Khartoum was just the start
> of the journey to Darfur. Each foreigner has to first register with the Police

Department of Aliens. . . . After the Department of Aliens came the Department of Foreign Correspondents and Journalists. . . . Now came the tricky part of obtaining permission to work as a journalist—filling in the "Purpose of Visit" section on my application for a press permit for Darfur. . . . But how to phrase "reporting on genocide" in a way that would be acceptable to the very regime responsible? (7–9)

Needless to say, none of these bureaucratic hurdles was easy to surmount. And, once journalists succeeded in accessing the field, their mobility was further inhibited.[6] These challenges to journalistic work, imposed by the government of Sudan and its bureaucrats, prevailed throughout the reporting period. After 2007 Khartoum imposed even further restrictive policies on foreign journalists, thus likely contributing to the massive decline in reporting. In the words of a Swiss interviewee: "Today Khartoum barely allows any journalists to go there" (*Heute lässt Khartoum ja kaum noch Journalisten dahin*).

Gaining direct access to the field, a challenge in reporting on any conflict, was not the only impediment that worsened. Common sources of information also dried up. Some aid agencies, including three sections of MSF, were evicted, especially after the indictment of al-Bashir, as noted in chapter 4. In addition, aid agencies became ever more cautious in light of the risk of being denied access to the populations in need. After all, evictions were partly based on claims by the government of Sudan that aid agencies had abandoned their commitment to neutrality norms and were supplying the ICC with information on which charges could be based.[7]

Denial of access by the government of Sudan and the drying up of sources of information are obviously weighty factors in any attempt to explain the drop-off in reporting about Darfur after 2007. But they are to be supplemented by forces associated with the journalistic market for information.[8] These market forces are best captured in an interview with a German Africa correspondent who discussed stalemates in the decision-making bodies of the international community:

This Darfur conflict, however, quite decisively disappeared from public view, because—I believe—there emerged an absolute stalemate. [In the UNSC t]he Americans could thus scream, the Europeans could scream, and the Chinese said "no" and the Russians too. Then you realize that there is simply no way forward, and the only thing that still caused attention was that they issued this international arrest warrant against Bashir. But that is totally personalized and focused on one single person. What's going on in Darfur these days is barely being registered, neither by the public nor by journalists, because it is redundant in the end, because it has been happening for years. (author's translation)

It is not surprising that dramatic events are especially appealing in the media market. It was thus unfavorable for journalistic attention that after 2007 the situation on the ground in Darfur showed no major change and that the international community was partially deadlocked. Demands by consumers of news media obviously matter, especially among market-driven media, and this pattern is not unique to reporting about violent conflicts.[9]

In short, the trend line of reporting about Darfur in prominent Western newspapers reflects the impact of market and political forces on the journalistic field. On the one hand, initial journalistic attention and a massive increase in reporting about Darfur proved to be inspired by the political field. Western politicians and the UN played an important role, while actors from the human rights field provided additional support. This causal path does not always apply, of course. Sometimes journalists report from crisis regions for extended periods without being alerted by political actors—and without finding any resonance in the political sphere. The second wave of violence in Darfur coincided with the symbolically laden tenth anniversary of the Rwandan genocide. In addition, the United States experienced a massive civil society mobilization after several American carrier groups, especially evangelical Christians, Jews, and African Americans, identified with victims of the violence and sparked a mobilization that provoked relatively forceful rhetoric among political leaders. On the other hand, the always present restraints that the government of Sudan imposed on journalists intensified with the growing international responses to the conflict. In addition, the flow of information from aid agencies dried up in response to pressure from the authorities in Khartoum. These observations speak to recent scholarship on the mediatization of politics. Yes, the logic of the media field may at times influence political actors, organizations, and institutions (Strömbeck and Esser 2014), but cautionary notes highlighting reverse effects of the political field on journalism are also supported (Mazzoleni and Schulz 1999). Such caution is all the more valid whenever authoritarian regimes are involved.

Finally, political pressures coincided with economic forces within the media market. The cycle of news reporting, with its focus on the new and dramatic, enhanced the decline in media attention about the ongoing suffering in Darfur. The decline would likely have been even more abrupt had the ICC not intervened. Judicial interventions helped keep the media's attention on the conflict, though not at the high level of earlier stages. But how specifically did juridical forces act on the journalistic field? If they could not prevent the decline of attention, could they affect the substance of reporting? What were their opportunities and constraints? What cultural receptivity did they encounter?

THE JOURNALISTIC FIELD, THE JUDICIAL FIELD, AND THE LEGAL COLORING OF REPORTS

The journalism and judicial fields, both semiautonomous, are reciprocally related. Not only do they affect each other—through regulation in one direction, for example, and through issue selection and editorial support in the other—but they may even interpenetrate. Remi Lenoir's (1994) Bourdieuian analysis, for example, diagnoses intrusions of journalism into the legal field similar to those Bourdieu described by which media logic shapes the political field. Lenoir refers to the well-known case of "tough" judges who use mass media to advance their reputation and, by doing so, change power relations within the judicial field. Juridical criteria subsequently lose ground in legal decision making to populist sentiments and media concerns, and the judicial field thereby loses relative autonomy. Arguments about the mediatization of politics (Strömbeck and Esser 2014) may thus also apply to the judiciary. In reverse, the judicial field may strengthen its position vis-à-vis other fields, including that of journalism. Michael Kearny, at a 2011 Vassar Institute conference on war journalism held in The Hague, showed how war reporting is increasingly permeated by the language of human rights and international law, often at the expense of political analysis. This trajectory from political to legal categories proceeds by means of diverse mechanisms, among them NGO informants who, in Kearny's words, "hijack the language of law" or seek to "mainstream the language of human rights."[10] Kearny's argument is reflected in the sentiments of several interviewees. Diplomats and NGO specialists with a political science background charged that legal language endangers a political understanding of mass violence. Relatedly, Pendas's (2006) analysis of the Frankfurt Auschwitz trial, cited in greater detail in chapter 8, shows how rules of the journalistic game, especially the objectivity rule, contribute to a literal transmission of courtroom events through media reporting to a broad public. As a result, historical truth is overshadowed by judicial truth. Trials, and media reporting on them, focus attention on individuals, their criminal intent, and atrocities. The bureaucratic nature of the murder machine and its political context are almost lost from sight (see also Marrus 2008; Savelsberg and King 2011).

Both interviews and patterns revealed by the Darfur media data set speak to the relationship between journalism and the judicial field. The data provide a more mixed portrait than that suggested by opposing strands in the literature on media and law. In line with the statements quoted at the beginning of this chapter, Africa correspondents generally reported a substantial disconnect from the court. A German interviewee from Nairobi told me that he had never been to The Hague. Similarly, a British respondent claimed not to have received any information directly from the ICC. He learned only about special events such as indictments—and only from sources other than the ICC. An Irish journalist confessed that he knew about the ICC and its actions primarily as a newspaper reader. Yet another interviewee told me that information he received about big events at the ICC was based on wire reports. He added that it was always easy to slip a sentence about a wanted war criminal into an article. Other journalists, by contrast, did report interactions with the court. Yet they experienced conditions in the judicial field not compatible with their journalistic habitus. The journalist quoted at the beginning of this chapter as denying that the ICC was in any way an information source for him continued:

> I had occasional contacts with investigators for the ICC, but that was in the context of the Congo, East Congo, and the DFLR [Forces Démocratiques de Libération du Rwanda], those Rwandan militias, and how they acquire funding. These people wanted information from me. I am a journalist. I told them, "One hand washes the other. You can get something from me, give me something of yours, and then we can talk reasonably in whatever way that can be published at all without endangering your work." I never heard from them again. But it would be interesting to learn how often the term *International Criminal Court* is now being used in media reporting. Very often. At the same time we know that those who report about it know nothing about this criminal court, because this court shuts itself off. That is a pity. (author's translation)

This statement illustrates how not just geographic distance between Africa correspondents and the ICC, but also a different habitus and contrasting rules of the game impede communication. The journalist's tit-for-tat practice does not work in interactions with those bound by judicial rules. Another interviewee, an Africa correspondent who works out of the capital city of his European country, noted additional communicative hurdles: "I've been there [ICC in The Hague] once. And it was useless, in fact. . . . Their time is not our time. It is not the same. . . . It is years." The journalist here contrasted the slow progress of judicial proceedings with the fast pace of journalistic work. Journalists also need to explain to domestic readers the institutional particularities of an international court. "We have the problem," the same correspondent pointed out, "that the judicial system used in The Hague is not the French one. So we have to explain to people how it works." This journalist observed that usual translation issues with turning "legalese" into everyday language gain urgency when international courts are the issue: "It is a big part of our job as a journalist, not understanding something and trying to find someone who can explain. . . . I've got a friend who is working for Human Rights Watch. She is focused on just this, on the ICC." This statement illustrates not only an impediment faced by journalists who wish to report about the international court but also a mechanism through which human rights activists may affect media reporting: as translators of international human rights law for use by journalists. This observation adds a significant component to the importance that Africa correspondents in the field attribute to INGOs as informers.

In short, Africa correspondents have little interaction with the ICC, and the interaction they do have is marred by problems. But they are not the only contributors to journalistic work about Darfur. A German Africa correspondent referred me to a colleague who worked from his paper's headquarters and, while not an Africa specialist, did visit the courts. Similarly, a US journalist mentioned her paper's specialist for institutions such as the ICC, who occasionally supplied her with relevant information. One interviewee who covered international organizations from her European capital city spoke about an upcoming trip to The Hague. Finally, a British correspondent reported, and his foreign editor confirmed, that the paper would send someone to The Hague "for the big day." And such "big days" indeed find many journalists gathered in the ICC's pressroom (see figure 22).

Given these conditions of reporting and the ambivalent role of the ICC in its relation to journalists, how do judicial interventions affect media representations of Darfur? Our data demonstrate that several intervention points—but not all—are intensely reflected in journalistic reporting. Figure 23, for example, displays the percentage of articles about Darfur per time period that cited the crime frame in combination with three competing frames. The graph shows that increases in use of the crime frame followed the release of the ICID report, the ICC prosecutor's application for a Darfur-related arrest warrant (against Harun and Kushayb), the application for an arrest warrant against al-Bashir

FIGURE 22. Press conference in the press room of the International Criminal Court, The Hague.

(the rather high level persisting after its issue), and finally a first court appearance of an accused. The crime frame lost ground during the periods marked by UNSC Resolution 1564 (establishing the ICID) and the UNSC's referral of the Darfur situation to the ICC. We shall see below that the latter action was followed by a major diplomatic event (signing of the Abuja Peace Treaty), the leadup to and aftereffect of which appear to have overwhelmed uses of the crime frame. Reporters favored instead the use of the civil war frame during this period, as the respective lines in figure 23 indicate. Another drop in the use of the crime frame, this time surprising and unexplained, occurred after the ICC issued the first major arrest warrants (against Harun and Kushayb). In the following I first focus on the crime frame and afterward return to the alternative and potentially competing frames.

References to particular types of violence and crime, specifically killing and rape, peaked, albeit in less pronounced ways, at the same stages at which the crime frame was cited most frequently (figure 24): the release of the ICID report, the prosecutor's application for arrest warrants against Ahmed Harun and Ali Kushayb, and the application for and the issuing of an arrest warrant against President al-Bashir. The reporting of destruction of livelihood and displacements, in contrast, showed steady declines barely interrupted by judicial interventions.

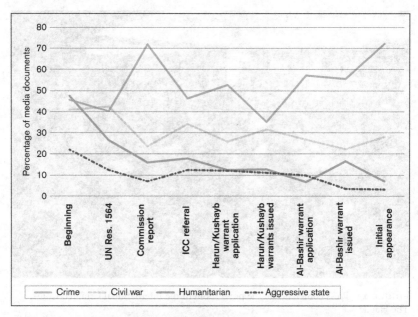

FIGURE 23. Percentage of newspaper documents on Darfur using the crime, civil war, humanitarian emergency, and aggressive-state frames, by time period.

Modest exceptions are minor upticks in reporting the destruction of livelihood after the release of the commission report and the charging of al-Bashir, as well as in reporting about displacements after the issuing of arrest warrants against Harun and Kushayb.

What exactly does the changing intensity of applying the crime frame and of reporting specific types of victimization mean, and how can it be explained? The first major peak in citations of the crime frame followed the release of the ICID report in January 2005 (figure 23), and was paralleled by a peak in intensity of reporting about killings and rapes (figure 24). This may not be surprising, as the commission had cited instances of war crimes and crimes against humanity (but not genocide). Thus, not only did all papers intensify reporting about Darfur after February 1, 2005, the day of the report's release to the public, as we saw earlier, but they also now stressed the crime frame and reminded readers of the suffering of the population. An article written by Warren Hogue of the *New York Times* (2/1/2005) illustrates how a US paper described the ICID report to its readers: "A United Nations commission investigating violence in the Darfur region of Sudan reports Monday that it had found a pattern of mass killings and forced displacements of

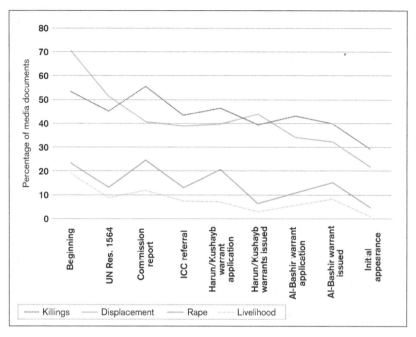

FIGURE 24. Percentage of newspaper documents referencing different types of suffering, by time period.

civilians that did not constitute genocide but that represented crimes of similar gravity that should be sent to the International Criminal Court for prosecution" (p. 3).

The article was followed, on February 2, 2005, by an op-ed by Nicholas Kristof entitled "Why Should We Shield the Killers," critiquing the initial inclination of the Bush administration to challenge a UNSC referral of the Darfur situation to the ICC. Also on February 2, 2005, Lydia Polgreen of the *NYT* wrote an article headlined "Both Sides of Conflict in Darfur Dispute Findings in U.N. Report." On February 9, 2005, Warren Hogue reported again, this time about Sudanese attempts to prevent international prosecution. On February 10, 2005, Samantha Power, then a "lecturer at the Kennedy School of Government at Harvard," used an op-ed in the *NYT* to offer strong support for the ICC as a "court of first resort" and for a referral of Darfur to the court. The paper's February 11, 2005, edition featured the following "quotation of the day," which it attributed to "Mohammed": "'We will take care of the child. It is very difficult to love a janjaweed, but we will try to accept him as one of our own.' MOHAMMED, whose sister Ashta gave birth after being raped by a janjaweed militia fighter in Darfur, Sudan." More than a dozen articles and editorials followed in the remainder of February 2005, supplemented by numerous letters to the editor.

Other in-depth journalistic examinations are telling. As a first example, one of the prominent German papers, the *Süddeutsche Zeitung*, featured, on February 2, 2005, an article by Arne Perras about the ICID report. The article, entitled "Crimes in Darfur: The United Nations Charge the Sudanese Power Holders [*Machthaber*] and Demand They Be Punished" and "The Masters of the Death Riders" [*Die Herren der Todesreiter*], included this summary: "A UN report proves that the government in Khartoum positioned the militias in West Sudan" (author's translation). Another dozen articles followed in the *SZ* in February alone. Those that included opinions expressed clear support for a referral of the case to the ICC. In France, on February 2, 2005, *Le Monde* reprinted segments of the commission report under the headline "'Action Is a Matter of Urgency': The UN Does Not Determine Genocide but Denounces Crimes against Humanity in Darfur" (author's translation). On the same day, correspondent Corine Lesnes contributed a lengthy report on the commission's conclusions. Some ten articles followed in February. In the United Kingdom, the *Guardian*'s February 1, 2005, report by "diplomatic editor" Ewen MacAskill was entitled "Sudan's Darfur Crimes Not Genocide, Says UN Report." But MacAskill followed up on February 2, 2005 with a piece headlined "Sudan Risks Sanctions as UN Lists Atrocities." The editorial begins: "The Sudanese government could be hit by UN sanctions after the publication yesterday of a 244-page report on the Darfur crisis which detailed horrific and widespread crimes against humanity, including the systematic use of rape as a weapon of terror" (p. 15). The number of subsequent articles was smaller than in the other papers, while several reviews of the film *Hotel Rwanda* built bridges between the Rwandan genocide and events in Darfur. On February 16, 2005, for example, Africa correspondent Jeevan Vasagar, writing from Kigali, quoted Paul Rusesabagina, the former manager of Mille Collines (the real-life model for Hotel Rwanda), as saying at the time of the genocide: "What happened in Rwanda is now happening in Darfur, in the Congo, in all of these places they are butchering innocent civilians" (p. 3).[11]

For a second example, consider the rise in the number of crime frame citations after the Office of the Prosecutor applied for an arrest warrant against Sudan's sitting president, Omar al-Bashir (figure 23). Use of the crime frame stabilized at this new, high level after the warrant was issued, and it increased further in the final reporting period, after the initial appearance of a rebel before the ICC. Again, a closer look at patterns of reporting in specific media sheds light on the meaning of this peak.

In the United States, the *New York Times* featured on July 15, 2008, one day after Moreno-Ocampo's application for an arrest warrant against al-Bashir, a long report by staff journalists Marlise Simons (Paris), Lydia Polgreen (Dakar), and Jeffery Gettleman (Nairobi). Their 1,446-word article reviewed the mass violence in Darfur. It also reminded the reader of Slobodan Milošević and Charles Taylor, two previous sitting presidents who had been tried before international tribunals. The authors further quoted chief prosecutor Moreno-Ocampo: "Mr. Bashir had 'masterminded and implemented' a plan to destroy three ethnic groups. . . . Using government soldiers and Arab militias, the president 'purposefully targeted civilians'" (p. 1). An editorial of the same day, entitled "Charged with Genocide," opens with this sentence: "The truth can be difficult. That doesn't make it any less true. And so we support the decision by the prosecutor of the International Criminal Court to bring charges of genocide against Sudan's president, Omar Hassan al-Bashir, for his role in masterminding Darfur's horrors" (*NYT* 7/15/2008, p. 18). Also on the same day, an opinion piece by Richard Goldstone, former chief prosecutor of the ICTY and ICTR, strongly supported the arrest warrant against al-Bashir. Both the editorial and Goldstone's piece challenged critics who pointed at an indictment's problematic consequences for aid delivery and diplomatic efforts. Some twenty additional articles and editorials follow in the *New York Times* in the remainder of July 2008 alone. The editorials uniformly supported the prosecution.

But attention to the prosecutor's decision to charge al-Bashir and to the crimes committed in Darfur does not *necessarily* imply a paper's support for the prosecutor. The German *Frankfurter Allgemeine Zeitung* may serve as an example. Following the date of the application, July 14, 2008, the *FAZ* published a flood of articles, beginning with an 883-word front-page report on July 15 entitled "Arrest Warrant against Sudanese President Applied For: Prosecutor at Criminal Court Charges al Bashir with Genocide in Darfur." (author's translation) The article was accompanied by a front-page editorial by editor-in-chief Günther Nonnenmacher entitled "Law against Violence" (*Recht gegen Gewalt*). Nonnenmacher expressed sympathy with those who welcomed the pending prosecution, and spelled out the suffering al-Bashir had brought to so much of his country. Although he clearly did not deny that violence and suffering had occurred, he sympathized with critics of prosecution and their political objections. He wrote about inadequate attempts to compensate for political failure by judicial means, and he anticipated that the situation on the ground would deteriorate as a consequence of the prosecutor's action. Comparable to the number of items in the *New York Times,* in the remaining two weeks of July, the *FAZ* published almost twenty more reports and editorials following these first items.

In the wake of the prosecutor's decision to charge al-Bashir, the *FAZ*'s attention thus clearly returned to Darfur, and the criminal nature of the violence was confirmed. Yet Nonnenmacher's editorial critique did not appear in isolation. Several subsequent pieces expressed doubt about the political wisdom of prosecution. For example, a July 20, 2008, article by Hans Christian Rössler was entitled "Rather Vote Out of Office [*Lieber abwählen*]: Even Some Opponents of Sudan's Head of State al Bashir Do Not Approve of the Arrest Warrant against Him" (author's translation). A July press agency report published in the *FAZ* cited doubts against the prosecutions expressed by Amr Mussa, president of the Arab League. A brief piece by Rössler on July 22 was entitled "Peace Process at Risk: Sudan Warns against Charging Bashir" (author's translation) A book review on July 23 discussed Harald Welzer's work on the ecological causes of violence, reflecting one of the arguments that opponents of criminalization had previously used to challenge judicial responses. And on July 28 an article by Rössler, "Risks of Failure in Sudan" (author's translation) warned that prosecutions would endanger the North-South process.

In short, comparing reporting and commentary in the *NYT* and the *FAZ* sheds light on the meaning of peaks in crime frame citation frequency. First, ICC interventions refocused the world's attention on the violence in the conflict zone. Second, the criminal nature of the violence was confirmed. And third, refocused attention and use of the (diagnostic) crime frame was in some cases associated with support for the prosecutor's decision—but with challenges to judicial responses in others. Strategies deemed appropriate against criminal violence thus may or may not correlate with the use of the crime frame. The (prognostic) frame, referring to preferred solutions, may well not be aligned with the diagnostic frame, and it is indeed not aligned in reporting about Darfur by papers such as the *FAZ*.[12]

THE JOURNALISTIC FIELD, THE HUMANITARIAN FIELD, AND THE COLORING OF REPORTS

Descriptions of *FAZ* reporting following the application for an arrest warrant against President al-Bashir reveal that news media that cite the crime frame do not necessarily support criminal justice interventions. While acknowledging the criminal nature of the violence, such reports may nevertheless highlight the need of mediation or military intervention. At other times media recognize violence as criminal but opine that aid should trump justice in the light of human suffering. In the statement quoted above, Günther Nonnenmacher from the *FAZ* even sympathized with the call for justice, but he eventually pleaded against penal responses in anticipation of a deterioration of the humanitarian situation on the ground and challenges to the peace process as a consequence of an indictment against al-Bashir.

Previously we encountered skepticism toward the judicial field in humanitarian aid organizations. Chapter 4 on MSF provides manifold examples. It is not surprising, given the relationship between the humanitarian and journalistic fields analyzed above, that such skepticism is reflected in media reports. Interviews with humanitarian NGO experts reveal their often close contact with correspondents in crisis regions, for example, as hosts in relatively safe compounds within often challenging natural and social environments. Likewise, journalists also report about their contacts with humanitarian NGOs. For instance, both German correspondents I interviewed listed aid organizations as important sources of information. One mentioned MSF in particular (as did an American journalist). Three British journalists referred to either aid agency reports, humanitarian organizations on the ground, or just INGOs as crucial sources of information. One French journalist told about NGOs based in Chad whose representatives served him as crucial informants. He too mentioned MSF by name. Another French correspondent also referred to MSF, not incidentally when she stressed her paper's avoidance of the term *genocide,* in line with MSF policies. Here the policy and framing of an aid organization corresponds with journalistic vocabulary, and may have inspired it.[13]

Despite the centrality of aid NGOs as sources of information, however, citations of the humanitarian emergency frame, as figure 23 shows, faded compared to uses of the crime frame. While they started at the same high levels, making an appearance in almost every other article published in the initial period, references to the humanitarian frame dropped to below 30 percent in the second period. They declined further to between 10 and 20 percent in the later periods. What might explain this rapid decline in the number of humanitarian representations to a relatively low level? Evidence suggests that here, too, media markets and political forces are causal contributors. We know that the government of Sudan evicted humanitarian NGOs from Darfur, including three sections of MSF, as early as 2007 and as late as 2014. Those who remained grew cautious in their statements to the news media (and to the court). The actions of the Sudanese state thus likely contributed to declining use of the humanitarian frame in media reports. In addition, a humanitarian emergency is a state more than an event. It lingers. It is news for a brief period, after which it becomes old information and thus of little value in media markets.

Yet some newsworthy events do occur in the humanitarian realm. Consider the release of spectacular reports by INGOs such as the often-cited Amnesty report on rape and the two MSF reports "No Relief in Sight" and "The Crushing Burden of Rape." Release of "No Relief in Sight" coincided with an extraordinary opportunity to reach a world audience. In the words of one MSF interviewee:

> Well, I was the crisis communications manager in June and July in Khartoum, Darfur, and Paris. And this was right at the moment when we released epidemiological data. . . . The actual press release that I helped write in the field with the president of MSF-France and the head of mission was called "No Relief in Sight."[14] And it accompanied an epidemiological report. And the basic premise of that was to say, "Without a massive humanitarian response lots of lives would be lost." . . . And Colin Powell came to visit Khartoum. . . . [The respondent was in Murnei refugee camp in West Darfur,] and there was a big scramble to get me back to Khartoum because there was going to be the entire press corps, following with Colin Powell. And I remember coming into the press room, just walking from one person to the other and handing out our press release, the "No Relief in Sight." And I believe it was quoted in a lot of those initial stories.

Is the MSF staffer right in his perception of the effect of the news release? The document is dated June 21, 2004, and the opportunity to distribute it to the press corps following US secretary of state Colin Powell's visit offered itself on Wednesday, June 30. A look at our newspaper data does show intense media attention to Darfur around these dates. On July 1, 2014, the NYT featured a front-page article on the situation in Darfur. Earlier, on June 24, the Swiss *Neue Züricher Zeitung* had reported on a visit of the Swiss foreign minister to Sudan, including its refugee camps. In portraying the violence, the paper did cite the MSF report: "No one knows exactly how many civilians were killed by the Janjawiid. One probably has to assume several tens of thousands of dead as a minimum. This conclusion is suggested by a survey that Médecins Sans Frontières conducted in the refugee camps of Murnai and Zalingei in West Darfur—the most comprehensive study of this kind thus far" (author's translation). Information about the methodology of the survey leads the journalist to conclude: "Should this percentage be representative of the entire rural population of Darfur, then we would calculate a number far above 120,000 dead. To be added to those are the persons who now perish in the refugee camps, because the government restricts the delivery of urgently needed aid" (author's translation). For the remainder of June, I found one more reference to MSF, but not to the report itself.

In the United Kingdom, the *Times* of London featured Secretary Powell's visit in an article of July 1, 2004. The report recounted the history of violence and suffering in Darfur without, however, citing the MSF release. The *Times'* left-liberal competitor the *Guardian*, however, featured a lengthy June 25 article authored by Jeevan Vasagar entitled "There Is No Hunger Says Sudan As Children Die." It was reported from Khartoum and from the Murnei refugee camp, from which my interviewee rushed to Powell's press conference just a couple of days later. From within the camp, Vasagar reported about an MSF feeding center, and cited MSF president Jean-Hervé Bradol's grave accusations against the government in Khartoum for impeding the delivery of aid.

In France on June 25, 2004, *Le Figaro* featured an 804-word article on the violence in Darfur. The report, entitled "Darfur under the Pain of Hunger and 'Arab Cavalries [*cavaliers arabes*]'" (author's translation), cites MSF, though without mentioning the specific report. No other *Figaro* piece in June returned to any MSF source. *Le Figaro*'s left-liberal competitor *Le Monde* paid closer attention. On June 25 it featured a detailed report by its staff reporter Jean-Philippe Rémy. The article's title is a quotation of MSF's Jean-Hervé Bradol: "Khartoum has maintained a ferocious repression on Darfur" (*Khartoum a mené une repression féroce au Darfour*). Another piece on June 25, published under the same title, summarized the events and provided a count of those killed and displaced. Almost a half-dozen articles followed in the final days of June and at least one, a June 30 article on Colin Powell's visit, again cited patterns described by MSF.

Other papers too reported about Darfur on the days following the report's release and Colin Powell's visit, and several of these cited the MSF study. Clearly, the INGO's campaign was reflected in the world press. Reports like "No Relief in Sight" in all likelihood contributed to the substantial media attention in mid-2004. They helped advance the humanitarian crisis frame in the early stages of reporting. Yet they neither prevented the decline in reporting nor did they secure the application of the humanitarian emergency frame in the long run. This finding is all the more remarkable as the MSF press release was part of a flood of pronouncements during the summer of 2004. Both Colin Powell and Secretary-General Kofi Annan visited Sudan and Darfur and addressed the humanitarian catastrophe. Many other aid organizations were active and spoke up as well. A report from the German Evangelical Press Service (EPD), published on the front page of the *FAZ* on June 28, 2004, and supplemented by a report on page 6 by Thomas Scheen, the paper's Africa correspondent, makes this point quite clear: "The assistant foreign minister [*Staatsministerin im Auswärtigen Amt*], Kerstin Müller (Green Party), has reproached the Sudanese government for continuing to impede the delivery of humanitarian aid for the Darfur region. Organizations such as the Technisches Hilfswerk and the Malterser Hilfsdienst attempt in vain to transport goods into the region, reports Müller at the end of an African journey in Nairobi. Also, the truce in the west of Sudan was not respected, contrary to statements from Khartoum, she added" (author's translation).

In short, humanitarian emergencies are news for a short period of time. Relatively close contact between aid workers and journalists helps bring them to the attention of newspaper readers in the early stages of a crisis. In long-lasting emergencies, however, news media lose interest. Sudanese state repression of media and aid organizations further contributes to the observed decline of the humanitarian frame in reporting. Unlike the criminal court process, which also drags out over a long time, at least from a journalistic perspective, humanitarian work does not even produce spectacular events along the way such as an indictment against a country's president. Media do report the occasional release of NGO reports, but such releases do not produce the same cascade of articles and editorials that an ICC decision evokes.

THE JOURNALISTIC FIELD, THE DIPLOMATIC FIELD, AND THE COLORING OF REPORTS

Journalistic citations of the civil war and aggressive-state frames provide initial information about the role of the diplomatic field and about how news media communicate that field's mode of framing the conflict to a broad public. The civil war frame is important for diplomatic activity, even if diplomats expressed little sympathy for the term itself in the context of Darfur. Diplomats whom I interviewed, after all, gave as their primary purpose the settling of armed conflict, and the civil war and aggressive-state frames (which our coding scheme measured) come closest to a broader notion of armed conflict.

Citations of the civil war frame show a particular pattern in at least two ways (see figure 23). First, for most time periods, they are less numerous than crime frame citations but more frequent than humanitarian frame citations. Second, citations of the civil war frame over time contrast remarkably with references to the crime frame. The two frames develop over time in opposite directions: the civil war frame increases when the crime frame declines and vice versa. The graph thus seems to display a conflict between the uses of these contrasting frames, in line with the opposing institutional logics of the criminal justice and diplomatic fields discussed above. Again, while criminal law is interested in stigmatization and exclusion and oriented toward procedure, diplomacy is concerned with including power holders and oriented toward substantive outcomes. When one perspective reigns, it seems to do so at the expense of the other. This tension between the two frames does not explain, however, why the armed conflict theme throughout fares more prominently than the humanitarian emergency trope but less so than the crime frame. What characteristics of the diplomatic field and its relationship with the journalistic field may explain this pattern?

Journalists draw on diplomats as sources of information with some regularity. A German correspondent mentioned "embassy people" as informers; a US journalist referred to "UN people"; an Austrian correspondent reported about her conversations with "diplomats"; three British interviewees spoke, respectively, about sources among "UN and embassy people," especially from the United States and the United Kingdom; "Western diplomats"; and more generally, "diplomats in Khartoum"; a French journalist told me that diplomats in Paris provided information. In short, the majority of journalists I interviewed explicitly listed actors from the diplomatic field as important sources of information. This should help explain why diplomatic concerns with Darfur, framed as an armed conflict, and concerns with the establishment of peace appear relatively frequently in journalistic reports.

Yet journalists also frequently cite humanitarian agencies as informers. Why, then, do frames that focus on armed conflict appear more often in media reports than the humanitarian frame does (and why less often than the crime frame)? Part of the answer lies in the nature of diplomacy and its value for media organizations. Much diplomatic work, similar to that of aid agencies, is tedious and drawn-out from a journalistic perspective. Even so, diplomatic proceedings occasionally yield spectacular moments that may not be comparable to an indictment by the ICC, but are newsworthy nevertheless. The openings and the conclusions of peace negotiations are such instances. While not "media events" as Dayan and Katz (1992) describe them for the live broadcasting of history, they are still events, rituals that attract media attention. Subsequent news reporting should reflect with particular clarity the logic and framing of diplomacy. In the case of Darfur, the signing of the Abuja Peace Agreement on May 5, 2006, and the beginning of the Doha peace process in February 2009 are such moments (see figure 17, chapter 6). Both events fall into the time frame of our analysis. A close look at figure 23 reveals potential consequences for the framing of the conflict in media reports. We note that, at the time of the signing in Abuja, the crime frame lost ground against the civil war and aggressive-state frames. How, specifically, was the signing of the Abuja treaty on May 5, 2006, represented in the media?

In Switzerland, the *Neue Züricher Zeitung* (NZZ) paid close attention to the Abuja peace negotiations in the days before and after the treaty's signing. A May 4 article reported about an extension of the deadline ("Deadline for Darfur Agreement Again Extended" [*Frist für Darfur-Abkommen erneut verlängert*]). The following day the paper ran the article "Pressure from the USA on Parties in Darfur" (*Druck der USA auf die Parteien in Darfur*). It told readers that Assistant Secretary of State Robert Zoellick was sent to Abuja to pressure the negotiating parties. The article interpreted this intervention as a reflection of the Bush administration's domestic concerns. The highly mobilized US public perceived that its government's deeds had not lived up to its rhetoric. Finally, on May 6, 2006, the NZZ featured a lengthy article by Kurt Pelda from Nairobi about the signing of the Abuja agreement. Entitled "Convergence among Conflict Parties in Darfur" (*Annäherung der Konfliktparteien in Darfur*), the article detailed the agreement and spelled out reasons for skepticism about its effectiveness. Other Darfur-related articles in May reported primarily about ongoing efforts to send a UN peacekeeping mission into the region. Additional information on Abuja, specifically about two rebel groups' continuing refusal to sign the agreement, appeared in two brief pieces on June 2.

In France, *Le Monde* reported on Abuja on May 6, 2006, the day after the signing, but the report focused more on the rebel factions' refusal to support the agreement than on the signing itself. One day later a 253-word front-page notice was followed by a lengthy article in which Philippe Bernard offered a more detailed assessment of Abuja. A few more references on the following days culminated in a May 9 editorial entitled "Hope in Darfur" (*Espoir au Darfour*). The title and text spoke of hope, but hope modulated with substantial cautionary notes. Only on June 3 did *Le Monde* report about Abuja again, and this time the focus returned to the continuing refusal of two major rebel factions to sign the agreement.

Elsewhere, the *Guardian* of London also published two informative pieces on Darfur on May 6 and 8, 2006, respectively. These articles were followed, a full week later and again during the second half of May, by reports on the continuing violence and the refusal of two rebel groups to sign. Similarly, the *Süddeutsche Zeitung* of Munich printed several brief press agency reports released just before and after May 5, 2006 (AP, Reuters, Agence France Presse). The paper supplemented these reports with a portrait of a central diplomatic actor, Salim Ahmed Salim, chief negotiator for the AU in Abuja. This string of articles finally culminated in a May 8 editorial by then–Africa correspondent Arne Perras entitled "A Bit of Peace for Darfur: Treaty between Government and Rebels Provides First Hope for West Sudan" (*Ein bischen Frieden für Darfur: Das Abkommen zwischen Regierung und Rebellen gibt erstmals Hoffnung für den Westsudan*). A few subsequent Darfur-related articles, appearing in May, focused on other themes, especially the planned UN deployment of a peacekeeping force.

In short, the culmination of the prolonged diplomatic efforts in Abuja was clearly reflected in news media reporting. At least for the period following the ceremonial signing of the treaty, it used the war and aggressive-state frame at the expense of the crime frame (figure 23). Yet, over the long haul, the effect of diplomatic negotiations was weaker than the resonance of ICC decisions examined above.

Data on the beginning of the Doha peace negotiations confirm this observation. This event too was noted in our sample of newspapers, but it did not leave profound traces. Consider the following examples. On February 18, 2009, almost two weeks after the signing, the *Irish Times* offered the following Reuters message under "News in Short": "Warring sides in Sudan agree to peace talks. Dubai: Sudan's government and a leading Darfur rebel faction agreed yesterday to meet for peace talks and signed a deal with concessions from both sides. The Qatari mediator urged all other rebels and Chad to come to the table. The agreement included measures to aid and protect refugees in Darfur and a commitment by the two sides to continue negotiations in Doha. Rebel group Justice and Equality Movement also wants a prisoner swap."

In Canada, the *Toronto Globe and Mail* published a front-page article by Geoffrey York on February 26, 2009, that, while mentioning the Doha negotiations, was entitled "Historic Arrest Warrant for Sudan's Leader Sparks Global Debate"—and indeed, for this paper, the court action obviously overshadowed the diplomatic event. In the United Kingdom, I found no contributions by which the *Guardian* marked the beginning of the Doha negotiations in February 2009. Yet, on March 2, correspondent Xan Rice reported from Nairobi in a short article on page 18: "Fierce Fighting after Darfur Ceasefire Deal." The failure appeared to be more newsworthy than the beginning of talks. In France, *Le Monde* printed a brief note (*"lettre d'information"*) on page 6 of its February 13, 2009, edition entitled "Meeting between Khartoum and Rebels in Doha" (*Rencentre entre Khartoum et les rebelles à Doha*). On the same day, the paper featured a front-page article entitled "The President of Sudan Will be Subject to an Arrest Warrant" (*Le president du Soudan va être l'objet d'un mandate d'arrêt*). Obviously, new information about an upcoming major ICC decision overshadowed the beginning of peace negotiations. It pushed them onto the back pages.

Diplomatic events are thus noted in the media, but they do not make the same splash as do ICC decisions against high-level actors. Compared to the humanitarian aid field, however, the diplomatic field occupies a stronger position vis-à-vis the media as it does produce newsworthy and highly ritualized events. Its position is further strengthened as routine encounters between journalists and diplomats and newsworthy events are supplemented by repeated interventions by highly visible foreign policy and diplomatic actors. If we pick any month—say, August 2007—and consider any single paper—take Germany's *FAZ*—we find reports about (or quotes by) the following high-profile diplomatic actors: Peter Schumann, leading the UN delegation to southern Sudan and Ali Karti of the Sudanese Foreign Ministry (8/1/2007); the UNSC

(8/1); the German minister for development, Heidemarie Wieczorek-Zeul (8/2 and 8/13); Africa experts from the Christian-Democratic and Green factions of the German *Bundestag* (8/2); UN secretary-general Ban Ki Moon (8/2, 8/18, and 8/29); German foreign minister Walter Steinmeier (8/3); Jan Eliasson, the UN special envoy for Darfur (8/4); several German legislators (8/5); AU commission president Alpha Dumar Konaré (8/14); and in the United States, a White House spokesperson (8/25). Clearly, statements by these actors with national and often international visibility stand a good chance of being transmitted to a broad public by the news media.

In short, representations of mass violence produced in the diplomatic field fare prominently in media reporting about Darfur. This diplomatic media presence is partly due to journalists' routine encounters with diplomats as informants, relatively rare but noteworthy events produced in the diplomatic field, and the high public visibility of some actors in this field. The latter two factors appear to secure the diplomatic field's better representation in the news media than is granted the humanitarian field. Yet diplomatic framing still declines over time as compared to citations of the judicial frame. Events produced by the ICC demonstrate a particular ritual power (Durkheim [1912] 2001) or legitimacy that is based on their communicative quality (Osiel 1997) or on their procedure (Luhmann 2004) and that secures them news value. And such news value, reflective of the market forces to which media are exposed, contributes to explaining the dominant position of the crime frame in reporting about Darfur. Finally, the mirror image of trend lines for the crime frame and those frames that speak to armed conflict, where one increases when the other declines (and vice versa), reflects conflicts between the criminal justice and diplomacy fields and their opposing institutional logics.

PATTERNS IN MEDIA: COUNTRY AND REGIONAL CONTEXT, IDEOLOGY, AND GENDER

Different newspapers, all relatively close to the autonomous pole of their social field, show some degree of homogeneity, in line with expectations; but it would be wrong to deny the variation within the sample of newspapers under study here. As already observed in this book, there are nationally distinct patterns of reporting, even within our group of relatively comparable Northern countries. Larger differences should be expected for Northern versus African countries. And distinctions at lower levels of analysis are likely to add to differences in cross-national and cross-regional comparison. Examples of such differences include the paper's ideological orientation and categories of journalists—for example, men versus women. Here I address patterns that bring variety to journalistic representations of the mass violence in Darfur.

Country Patterns in Representations of Darfur

Nation-specific patterns of media reporting about Darfur are to be expected given our findings in previous chapters. Chapter 3 addresses the exceptional character of American media reports, with their strong allegiance to a criminalizing frame, and chapter 5 shows the affinity of Irish media with the dominant humanitarian approach of their country. While these cases are outliers, variation in reporting along a number of analytic dimensions can be observed across all countries. Figure 25 offers but one illustration for the use of the crime frame across periods by country. While it may be difficult to decipher and explain each country line (not my intention here), and while all countries similarly respond to specific interventions, it is obvious that they do so at different levels.

In short, while I offer a detailed exploration of media reporting for exceptional cases in previous chapters, analyses of the Darfur media

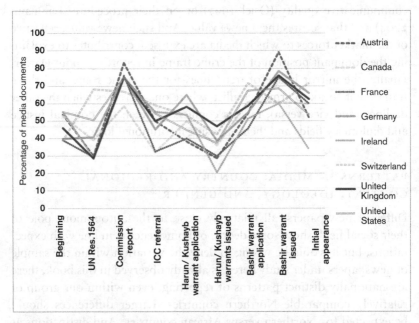

FIGURE 25. Percentage of newspaper documents citing the crime frame across periods by country.

data set also reveal country-specific patterns as a general feature of news reporting. I spell out three explanations for such patterns, and I provide illustrative evidence from my interviews with journalists. The first explanation for the fact that reporting varies by country lies in broad structural and cultural differences, even within our group of Northern democracies. The second concerns the specific strength and shape of the fields that supply journalism with information within each country. The third explanation is the varying shape of media fields themselves in cross-country comparison.

First, journalism—even if practiced by expat correspondents in Africa—is imbedded in national contexts. Chapters 3 and 5 show how US and Irish particularities in reporting may be explained by distinct potentials for civil society mobilization and government responsiveness to such mobilization in the United States, and by a humanitarian and development aid focus in Irish foreign policy. Both mobilization and policy foci are themselves driven by carrier groups and national collective memories. Differences were relatively pronounced when the application of interpretative frames and evaluative labels (e.g., *genocide*) with strong normative implications were at stake, while the reporting of suffering was more homogeneous. Importantly, country-specific differences in reporting indicate an overlap between the journalistic field and cultural and structural features of the national context.

Examples from interviews abound. One Belgian interviewee among the Africa correspondents was greatly inspired by his family's ties with Congo, his homeland's former colony. A journalist with a Sri Lankan family background told me that he is, in light of his family's history, more empathetic with those in the Periphery who express grievances against the Center. A French interviewee spoke about the particular concern of the French state and society with issues of former French colonies, which in the Darfur crisis center on Chad and the risk that the conflict might spill over.[15] Clearly, journalists are themselves products of national contexts. Their educational experience and cultural sensitivities differ from country to country, and that likely affects their sympathy with particular topics and frames.

Second, national differences within specialized fields such as humanitarian aid and diplomacy play into media reporting, as these fields provide journalists with information. This chapter has demonstrated how criminal justice, humanitarianism, and diplomacy interpenetrate the journalistic field. And they do so with more or less force depending on the country. Examples from interviews point to the anchoring of humanitarian concerns in the churches in Germany; close ties between government aid and humanitarian NGOs in Ireland; and the headquarters of the International Committee of the Red Cross and the particular intensity of diplomatic mediation programs in Switzerland. Given the centrality of these fields as sources of information, journalists are likely to be affected by such particularities of fields in their countries of origin. Indeed, my analysis indicates that media reporting is colored by the particular national features of the fields from which journalists draw information.

Third, the journalistic field itself takes distinct shapes in different countries.[16] The size of the market differs across countries, and with it the resources available to the media. In addition, publicly subsidized media are stronger in one country (e.g., Germany), while commercial television is more dominant in another (e.g., United States). In addition to structural characteristics of the field, journalistic traditions vary, for example between the "political/literary" press tradition in France and the "objective/informational" model in the United States (Benson 2006:197–198; 2013). Also my interviews spoke to national particularities in the journalistic field. Respondents reported, for example, the reluctance of a major French paper to have journalists on the ground in Africa; the incomparably large market of a paper such as the *NYT*, which provides it with vast resources and many more journalists in Africa than any other paper could afford; and, at the other end of the spectrum, the small size of media markets in countries with less than 5 percent of the US population. Such media depend especially on press releases in reporting about Africa. Their content is consequently less detailed, and some nuances will not be provided. In addition, competitive pressure varies by country and with it the contest for market share. Providing what audiences perceive as sensational and, in reporting about conflicts, offering starker depictions of opposing groups tend to be comparatively more attractive in more competitive national media fields. The Darfur media data set suggests that differences caused by national particularities of the journalistic field are not limited to style, but extend to topical foci and framing as well.

In short, three types of national forces result in nation-specific patterns of reporting: broad structural and cultural distinctions between countries; country-specific shapes of fields that supply media with information; and finally different shapes that media fields themselves take in each country. Topical choices, framing, and styles of reporting are affected, as a comparative analysis of the uses of the term *genocide* and of analogical bridging to the Holocaust illustrates.

Using "Genocide" and Holocaust Bridges in International Comparison

The varying use of the term *genocide* across countries illustrates how the three nation-specific forces outlined above affect country patterns of reporting. As noted earlier, the genocide label and bridging to the Holocaust are especially prominent features of reporting about Darfur in US media. This pattern corresponds closely not only with the centrality of the genocide theme in American civil society and its massive Save Darfur campaign, but also with the use of the term *genocide* by high-ranking government actors. A French journalist stationed in the United States spoke to this difference: "In the US you had Colin Powell, who said that [word *genocide*]. If you have an official using that term, then the media will pretty much follow it. . . . But then, in France nobody did that. And the media then started to wonder about it. So the UN is the umpire of this, arbiter of this. So the UN didn't do it. . . . And then I remember Doctors Without Borders not using it."

Figure 26 shows that this journalist's assessment is reflected in the statistics of my news media analysis. Indeed, we find the United States and France to be the outliers at both ends of the distribution. The figure also again confirms the reluctance of media in Ireland and Germany to use the genocide label.[17]

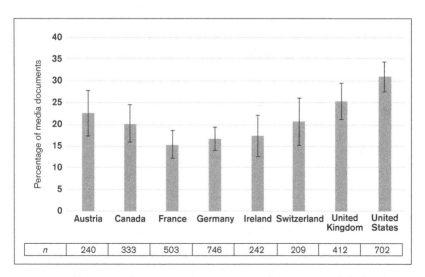

FIGURE 26. Percentage of newspaper documents using the term *genocide* for Darfur, by country.

While it is likely that social movements, leading politicians, and news media reinforced each other's preferred terminology, the causal arrow from civil society to the media in the United States is likely to have been strengthened by the competitiveness of the American media market. Here the third condition of nation-specific media reporting identified above is at work: the particularity of the national media field. But broader cultural sensitivities matter also. In Germany a journalist talked about his reluctance to subsume Darfur under the same category (genocide) under which the Holocaust is categorized. In addition to this cognitive impediment, we also encountered normative constraints among German respondents, indicating the standing of the Shoah as a "sacred evil" especially in that country (Alexander 2004a). Consider also Ireland, where a humanitarian complex is firmly established, associated with the country's foreign policy and collective memory, thus contributing to a general hesitance to use strong vocabularies vis-à-vis the Sudanese state. Consequently, the term *genocide* is used cautiously here too. Irish media reporting shows an elective affinity with the national particularity of the humanitarian field, even if we cannot make out the precise causal path. The first factor identified above, general national cultural characteristics, is here at work. In Ireland it is supported by the strength of the humanitarian field as a source of information—the second force working toward national particularities identified above.

In short, country-specific uses of *genocide*—as well as metaphorical bridging to the Holocaust—confirm what an examination of Darfur reporting in news media shows more generally: that the journalistic field overlaps with national conditions pertaining to a country's larger structural and cultural characteristics, nation-specific strengths of fields that supply media with information, and particularities of national media fields themselves (see also Benson 2013).

Northern versus African Countries and Group Identification

Patterns of national distinction in news reporting identified across Northern countries suggest that comparisons between Northern and African news media should be especially pronounced. After all, cultural and structural differences between both regions, differences in the role of specialized fields, and particularities of the media field itself are substantial. A brief examination for one issue must suffice here: the categorization of perpetrators and victims of human rights violations in the conflict. Some media scholars are highly critical of the use of ethnic categories in Northern press representations of African conflicts. They charge that Western journalists "swallowed the ethnic interpretation of conflict promoted by interested parties locally" (e.g., McNulty 1999:283). Also Wall (2007) observes a tendency in Western media to attribute African violence to tribalism. She argues that reference to long-standing ethnic or tribal affiliations allows Western media to avoid references to the contributions of colonial powers in planting the seeds of conflict. Interviews that Wahutu Siguru, a doctoral student at the University of Minnesota, conducted with African journalists from Kenya and South Africa show that they expressed similar critical sentiments regarding the ethnicization of conflicts in Africa by their Northern colleagues (Siguru and Savelsberg 2013; see also Mamdani 2009b).

Yet one of the most scathing critiques of simplified uses of ethnic categories in debates about Darfur was written by Rob Crilly (2010), a British journalist. Also, many of my interviews with Africa correspondents from the Global North reveal considerable sensitivity toward oversimplified depictions of conflicting parties along ethnic lines. Further, systematic analyses of African media reporting disclose astonishingly small differences in the use of vocabulary. One of the few content analyses of African newspapers and their reporting about Darfur in fact finds astounding similarities with Northern media reports: "a tendency to report on the violence in an oversimplified racialized way" whereby "fault lines in this conflict are often the same as those used by western media" (Ray 2009:172, 176).

We are thus confronted by a double paradox: that Northern journalists speak critically of ethnicized or racialized descriptions of African conflicts—exactly the practice for which they are reproached—and that African media do not seem to differ fundamentally from their European and North American counterparts—despite the disdain with which their journalists speak about Northern media. Part of the explanation lies in the nature of journalistic genres. Space constraints lead to simplified narratives that do not live up to the differentiations and elaboration of insights into the historical construction of group identities that we might encounter in interviews with journalists. But further, if major Northern newspapers—leaders in the world of journalism in countries such as the United Kingdom, France, Germany, and Canada—suffer from a shortage of resources and resulting constraints in inner-African travel, African journalists suffer these limitations even more. This shortage of resources results in restrictions on investigative journalism and creates, instead, dependency on news agencies or reports

TABLE 3. REPRESENTATIONS OF DARFUR IN CONSERVATIVE (C) VERSUS LIBERAL (L) NEWSPAPERS, BY PERIOD.

	Conflict begins		Resolution 1565		Commission Report		ICC referral		Midlevel warrants app.		Midlevel warrants issued		Al-Bashir warrant app.		Al-Bashir warrant issued		Initial appearance	
	% C	% L	% C	% L	% C	% L	% C	% L	% C	% L	% C	% L	% C	% L	% C	% L	% C	% L
Victimization																		
Killing	44.1	60.5	40.2	50.4	53.7	57.6	35.6	46.9	42.4	49.6	37.2	42.0	39.5	45.0	42.7	35.0	28.9	32.1
Rape	12.2	30.9	11.8	15.4	20.4	27.3	11.7	13.1	22.0	19.7	6.6	5.6	9.2	14.4	13.3	16.3	4.8	4.3
Displacement	62.0	76.2	47.2	56.0	33.3	41.4	34.4	40.9	37.3	41.0	43.2	40.3	26.1	35.0	33.3	28.8	22.1	20.7
Frames																		
Crime frame	34.9	52.9	27.6	46.2	74.1	73.7	41.7	46.6	50.9	53.9	36.6	36.8	54.6	59.4	72.0	76.3	58.7	59.3
Humanitarian frame	47.6	57.5	24.4	32.9	13.0	16.2	16.0	21.3	17.0	11.1	14.2	16.9	6.7	13.1	17.3	22.5	7.7	8.6
Civil war frame	42.4	47.3	43.3	51.3	24.1	23.2	38.0	38.4	27.1	25.6	38.3	32.5	35.3	31.3	29.3	23.8	29.8	32.1
Genocide	14.4	15.4	12.6	23.9	22.2	19.2	17.8	22.9	20.3	22.9	24.6	22.9	41.2	45.0	21.3	17.5	19.2	17.9

issued by international organizations or INGOs. The dependency of African journalists, in particular, on such sources must be considered at least one explanation for the relatively small difference in patterns of media reporting between Global North and African papers. A thorough comparative investigation of African and Northern journalistic work on mass violence in African countries goes beyond this book's purposes, but a first promising effort is under way (Siguru, in progress).

Below the Level of Nation-States: Media Ideological Orientation

This book has paid little attention to patterns below the level of the nation-state, as such an effort would distract from its central arguments. Yet here I briefly highlight two such forces, and I recommend them for future investigation. My choice of a liberal and a conservative paper in each country lends itself to a comparison along ideological lines. Table 3 depicts differences across a number of central dimensions used to describe the violence in Darfur. Interesting patterns emerge, patterns that also speak to the cultural strength of the institutional interventions I am concerned with here.

The data in table 3 reveal that a substantially greater percentage of articles on Darfur appearing in liberal-leaning newspapers were inclined to report the victimization of Darfur in the first period of the conflict. At that stage they were also much more likely to use the crime and the humanitarian frame than they were the civil war frame or the genocide label. Yet, interestingly, differences between conservative and liberal papers diminished as international organizations and eventually the ICC intervened. Both the reporting of victimization and the framing of the conflict became more similar across the ideological spectrum.

Why the initial overrepresentation of the recognition of suffering and use of crime labels in articles about Darfur in liberal-leaning media, an overrepresentation that multivariate analyses prove to be significant for the entire reporting period (Savelsberg and Nyseth Brehm 2015)? A necessarily speculative answer points to the left-liberal tendency to speak on behalf of weaker members of society, those suffering from oppression. But why the growing similarity in reporting after the judicial interventions? Again, I can only speculate at this point, but it appears as though such assimilation across ideological lines may result from the ritual power or procedural legitimacy, or both, that media, including and possibly especially conservative media, attribute to formal institutions of law. Remember that previous literature on the legal processing of Auschwitz at the Frankfurt trial detected an affinity between judicial and journalistic narratives, identifying a close correspondence between judicial depictions of mass atrocities and journalistic accounts (Pendas 2006). Above I also cite work that finds a closer resemblance of media and textbook narratives of the My Lai massacre to the judicial account than to the accounts of the Peers Commission and Seymour Hersh's Pulitzer Prize–winning book (Savelsberg and King 2011).

In short, a brief comparative analysis of conservative and liberal news media across intervention periods suggests that ideological orientation matters, but that its weight diminishes over time. Again, judicial interventions do not just contribute to the intensity of reporting but also shape the quality of journalistic narratives. Importantly, they at least partially neutralize the ideological orientation of media organizations.

Below the Level of News Media: Journalist Gender

Much feminist literature has documented that even in scholarly work the observer's standpoint colors his or her depiction of social reality (e.g., Harding 1996; D. Smith 1992). What applies in academia likely also holds true in the world of journalism. I thus expect gender to matter in media reporting about Darfur, especially in light of the gendered nature of mass violence and genocide (Burkhardt 2005; Hagan 2003; Kaiser and Hagan 2015). What gender-specific patterns might be hidden in the Darfur media data set? Patterns should be most pronounced in reporting about rape, which I examine here.

Comparing the reporting of rape in articles written by male and female journalists across our time periods indicates that females were more likely to speak to the issue of rape than males in their reports about Darfur, at least in the majority of periods (see figure 27). Multivariate analyses show that this difference holds up when we consider the entire time period and when we control for other variables (Savelsberg and Nyseth Brehm 2015). This pattern may reflect female reporters' greater empathy with female victims. Note, though, that the overrepresentation of rape reporting by female journalists applies especially in the first period, when most media accounts were still based on INGO and IO reports, and in the periods around the ICC decisions concerning President al-Bashir, when much reporting came from The Hague. This may indicate the prevalence of female reporters writing about Darfur

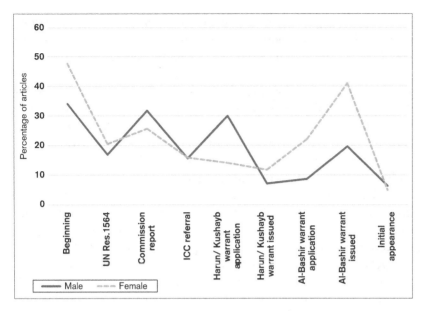

FIGURE 27. Percentage of newspaper documents referencing rape, by period and gender of journalist.

from Europe or North America. In addition, however, female corre-spondents who do report out of Darfur may have easier access to infor-mation about rapes. Male journalists certainly face greater challenges in interviewing female rape victims, a challenge noted in more than one of the interviews I conducted.

Additional analyses, not shown here, indicate for the macro level that media from countries with a larger percentage of females among their correspondents were substantially more likely to include issues of rape in their reports about Darfur.

In short, the gender of journalists mattered in reporting about Dar-fur, at least with regard to the issue of rape. More generally, patterns below the level of the nation-state, such as the newspaper's ideological leaning and the gender of its journalists, merit future investigation.

CONCLUSIONS: JOURNALISTIC REPRESENTATIONS AND WHY THEY MATTER

Analysis of the Darfur media data set shows that the first wave of mass violence in Darfur in 2003 was almost completely neglected by news media. Massive suffering is not a sufficient condition for media to report an event. During the second stage, immediately following the second wave of the violence, however, reporting experienced the first of two major peaks. During this period UN secretary-general Kofi Annan addressed the violence in his speech before the General Assembly on the tenth anniversary of the Rwandan genocide. The high visibility of his statements, and the weight added by his analogical bridging to the horrific and, by 2004, widely recognized Rwandan genocide, was a major contributor to this first outburst of reporting. Also, in national contexts, interventions by politicians of high standing who were engaged with the Sudan conflict and human rights issues contributed to this first peak. The German story of former justice minister Gerhart Baum and his interaction with one of the newspapers under analysis provided an example. Political initiatives were accompanied, and partly preceded, by initiatives from civil society groups, including the USHMM and evangelical Christian groups in the United States. While the intensity of reporting declined somewhat during the subsequent two years, it still remained at a relatively high level. These years were filled with UN and ICC interventions, including the ICID report, the UNSC's referral of the Darfur case to the ICC, intense campaigns by human rights INGOs, and substantial engagement by humanitarian aid organizations.

The second peak of reporting occurred after the ICC issued the first indictments, without which it certainly could not be explained. Yet it was followed in subsequent years by a dramatic decline in the intensity of reporting about Darfur, despite the continuing deprivation of the population in refugee and IDP camps, as well as continued killings, rapes, and displacements, albeit at a reduced level. After this point, Bourdieu's observation proves true: media tend to raise one episode of mass violence, only to drop it when its newsworthiness declines. They moved on from Darfur to South Sudan and then to the Central African Republic, soon dropping those cases to turn to northern Nigeria, Syria, Ukraine, and elsewhere, and so the journey of migrating attention continued. Such processes reflect the declining market value of prolonged suffering in the media field, a factor strengthened by growing restrictions on journalistic work imposed by the government of Sudan. But we also saw that judicial interventions delayed this decline in the case of Darfur and continued to affect the framing of news reports in later stages, albeit at a lower incidence of reporting. Bourdieu's thesis is thus partly confirmed, but it warrants modification: interventions by civil society, states, and the judicial field have the capacity to delay the drop-off in coverage, keeping journalistic attention alive over several years and coloring interpretations of mass violence.

My analysis shows in fact that interventions by the judicial field, specifically the ICC, colored reporting about Darfur. Several intervention points were followed by substantial increases in citations of the crime frame as a lens through which journalistic sources of information interpreted the violence. Advanced statistical analyses presented elsewhere confirm these patterns (Savelsberg and Nyseth Brehm 2015). Judicial interventions are also followed by increases in reporting about some forms of violence such as killings and rapes, albeit much less about displacements and the destruction of livelihood. These judicial intervention effects might be surprising, given the major obstacles Africa correspondents experience in terms of geographic distance from the court, the distinctiveness of legal language, and the mismatch between the time horizon of legal proceedings and the fast pace of journalistic work. But these impediments, it seems, are partially overcome by the particular ritual force of judicial interventions and the legitimacy that court proceedings enjoy, as previous studies on the journalistic processing of mass violence have suggested (Pendas 2006, Savelsberg and King 2011). Impediments are further overcome as most news media send specialists for judicial affairs and international institutions to The Hague to cover dramatic legal pronouncements. Indictments of a minister and certainly of a head of state such as Omar al-Bashir are among these events.

A word of caution is warranted, though, for judicial interventions did not succeed in the long run in keeping the case of Darfur on the radar of public and media attention. They did, however, lead to new peaks in the number of narratives that applied the crime frame to the mass violence in Darfur, even in the late stages of the period under study.

Proponents of a humanitarian emergency frame find less comfort in the information from the Darfur media data set. It is true that Africa correspondents highlighted the importance of the humanitarian aid field in informing journalistic work. Accordingly, the humanitarian emergency frame manifested most prominently in the initial phases of reporting. Yet it declined quickly and dramatically. This decline, it seems, resulted from several forces. First, continued suffering soon stops being news. Notions of newsworthiness and market forces trump victims' need to get the story of suffering before the public. Second, the government of Sudan barred many humanitarian aid organizations from Darfur, especially after it began suspecting them of being sources of information on which charges against Sudanese state actors were based. The third factor is self-censorship of the remaining aid organizations, whose representatives feared that they too would be forced to leave the country for speaking out about the violence. Fourth and finally, humanitarian aid delivery is continuous. It does not produce dramatic moments. Here it differs from both the judicial and the diplomatic field.

Indeed, citations of the civil war frame appeared more prominently (and declined less rapidly) than references to the humanitarian emergency frame. Remember that ending the fighting usually dominates the diplomatic agenda. Diplomatic activities should thus correspond to war frames. But why should they affect media reporting? On the one hand, diplomacy, just like humanitarian aid, proceeds continuously and hidden from public view. On the other hand, diplomatic work differs from aid delivery in its display of performative, often dramatic moments. Examples are the beginnings and conclusions of peace negotiations, often opened or sealed by prominent actors from the world of politics and diplomacy who carry more newsworthiness than doctors, nurses, logistics experts, or truck drivers who deliver food or medicine to devastated areas (see figure 17, chapter 6).

In short, all three fields examined in this book, judicial (especially), humanitarian (initially), and diplomatic (intermittently) leave their traces in journalistic reporting. And so do the political field and media markets. While the types of media analyzed here, and the journalists who serve as Africa correspondents, enjoy a relatively high degree of autonomy compared to other news outlets, the intensity and interpretive implications of reporting cannot be understood without reference to such forces. Suffering and its causation alone certainly are insufficient conditions for journalistic attention or choices of interpretive frames.

While this chapter focuses on patterns of reporting over time and along intervention points, it also examines the global versus national controversy and confirms many previous observations in this book. In line with globalization arguments (e.g., Boyle 2002; Boyle and Meyer 1998; Frank, Hironaka, and Schofer 2000; Meyer, Ramirez, and Soysal 1992), patterns of reporting, its intensity, the acknowledgment of diverse forms of suffering, and the uses of various frames across periods follow similar paths in all countries. Yet they do so at different levels. The likelihood of reporting about Darfur, of speaking about the killings, and of using the crime frame or the genocide label is more pronounced in some countries than in others. As analyzed throughout this book, the country-specific mobilization of civil society; the relative weight of different fields in a country; cultural sensitivities and policy practices, often rooted in the type and intensity of national memories; and the nature of the media field—all are decisive forces. Thus, for example, the frequency of reporting is especially high in the United States and Germany and—if controlled for the smaller number of papers—in Ireland, compared to the other five countries; the use of the crime frame is pronounced in the United States and Germany; and the humanitarian frame is privileged in Ireland.

Below the level of the nation-state, the ideological orientation of newspapers matters, with left-liberal papers having been more likely to address the Darfur issue in the early stages of the mass violence—a difference that became neutralized with the onset of formal interventions. Finally, individual-level variables also affect reporting. Female journalists are more likely, for example, to address issues of rape. Again, both ideology and gender effects are confirmed in multivariate analyses (Savelsberg and Nyseth Brehm 2015). In addition, gender effects translate to the macro level as media in some countries made more use of female journalists in reporting about Darfur than their counterparts in others.

What do these patterns mean for a sociology of the journalism field? Journalism's relationship to other fields is obviously crucial to understanding patterns of reporting on mass violence. This finding is in line with efforts by Pierre Bourdieu (1998) and his followers (Benson 1998, 2006) to develop a sophisticated model of journalism vis-à-vis other fields. Remember, Bourdieu depicts the world of fields in a spatial model, defined by a vertical axis representing increasing volumes of diverse forms of capital, and by a horizontal axis depicting the proportion of cultural-to-economic capital owned by specific actors (with cultural capital concentrated at the left and economic capital at the right end of this continuum). Bourdieu places media in the upper half of that space, as a dominating force. On the horizontal axis he locates media on the left side of the spectrum, as cultural producers, dominated in this respect. But Bourdieu also differentiates between types of media. Represented on the far left of the horizontal axis, where cultural capital reigns, are highly autonomous media with little or no economic prowess (e.g., small literary journals). The center and, even more, the right side of the horizontal dimension are inhabited by institutions in which concern with economic capital trumps engagement with cultural capital (e.g., commercial TV networks). Prestigious newspapers analyzed in this book would be found toward the left side of the horizontal axis; my interview data provide insights into the relative autonomy that Africa correspondents experienced when reporting about mass violence in an African context.

Future work should examine media in other places on the horizontal axis, media with stronger emphases on either cultural or economic capital than applies to the newspapers under examination here. I suggest, though, that the present papers' simultaneous attention to cultural and economic forces secures them prestige as well as access to policy makers and to those societal groups that pay special attention to foreign and international events. In this realm they exercise a force Bourdieu (1998:46) attributes to actors in the journalistic field generally: as "controllers of means of public expression" who "sanctify" events. Indeed, past research has shown that newspapers can directly influence public opinion, especially on foreign and international issues far removed from citizens' lifeworlds (McCombs and Shaw 1976; Wanta and Hu 1993). Partly mediated through public opinion, they also appear to affect foreign policy (Walgrave, Soroka, and Nuytemans 2008), the allocation of foreign aid (Rioux and Van Belle 2005), and presidential actions (Wood and Peake 1998).

The above analysis warrants a word of caution against exaggerated theses regarding the mediatization of politics (Strömbeck and Esser 2014). Journalism itself may depend on the sanctification of events by political actors, as it did in the case of Darfur. Further, this chapter shows that it is not sufficient to locate the journalistic field vis-à-vis economic forces. In this the chapter supports recent comparative work on media fields by Rodney Benson (2013). Adding to Benson's insights, I argue that journalism also depends on informational and interpretive input from the fields of diplomacy and humanitarian aid and—of particular weight according to the data analyzed in this chapter—the judicial field. Finally, no matter the causal direction between the journalistic field and the fields of politics, humanitarianism, diplomacy, and law, only through media reporting do national civil societies and a global public become "spectators" of suffering in distant lands (Boltanski 1999). And spectators they have to be before they can mobilize to demand or contribute to aid, peacemaking, and justice.

CHAPTER 10

Conclusions

Fields, the Global versus the National, and
Representations of Mass Violence

In this book I have invited the reader on a journey through the competing representations of mass violence in distinct social fields and countries. Examining responses to the violence endured by the inhabitants of the Darfur region of Sudan during the first decade of the twenty-first century, I was especially interested to learn how the interventions of the UN Security Council and International Criminal Court, both part of the justice cascade, colored representations of mass violence. I also examined what distinct images of suffering and of responsible actors arose from the humanitarianism and diplomatic fields. I was, finally, concerned with the ways in which mass media in different countries communicated these competing perspectives to the public. I stress again that it is not assumed that news media will be receptive to the court's decisions or messages, much less that court events will prevail over those staged by competing institutions. Indeed, patterns of receptivity show considerable variability.

Answers to these questions matter for scholarship and for practice. In scholarly terms they provide insights into the generation of knowledge and representations at the intersection of fields, countries, professions, and biographies. They respond to crucial questions raised in branches of scholarship as varied as sociology (and its subfields of crime and law, culture and knowledge, political and mass communication), criminology and criminal justice, political science, and media studies, as well as globalization research, which cuts across disciplines.

Answers also matter for practice, as representations of mass violence, including genocide, affect—structure, inhibit, or propel—responses and interventions.[1] Finally, they are important in normative terms as the international community, in the 1948 Convention on the Prevention and Punishment of Genocide, drafted in the immediate aftermath of the Shoah, began its campaign to intervene against the crime of crimes. Any intervention depends on overcoming denial (Cohen 2001), and appropriate interventions depend on appropriate definitions of the situation (Thomas 1928). What definition is appropriate, though, depends on the position of actors in the social structure, as we have seen throughout this book.

Zooming in on the mass violence in Darfur in the early twenty-first century, I provide answers to the above questions comparatively for eight Western countries, the United States and Canada for North America, and France, the United Kingdom, Ireland, Germany, Austria, and Switzerland for Europe. My analysis of 3,387 news reports and opinion pieces, constituting the Darfur media data set, and in-depth interviews with Africa correspondents of leading newspapers, NGO experts from Amnesty International and Doctors Without Borders, and foreign ministry officials provides much of the evidence. I describe how representations of mass violence vary, at times substantially, across social fields. I demonstrate that judicial interventions color the representation of mass violence in all countries, and that they eventually do so more effectively than humanitarian and diplomatic responses. But I simultaneously document that the inclination to subscribe to the criminalizing frame and use the genocide label differs significantly from country to country. I offer explanations for these patterns, thereby contributing to our understanding of how the world, especially the Global North, acknowledges and frames violence in the Global South, specifically in Africa.

As this journey through the competing representations of the mass violence in Darfur and their communication to an international public draws to a close, I summarize central empirical insights. I conclude with a summary of theoretical contributions and insights for practice along the themes laid out in the introduction.

FINDINGS: PATTERNS OF REPRESENTING MASS VIOLENCE

This book's four parts raise a series of themes and questions: justice in lieu of impunity? Aid versus justice? Peace versus justice? And finally, mediating competing representations. Insights gained from the analyses presented in the chapters speak to each of these themes.

From Impunity to Justice: The Justice Cascade, ICC, and the Human Rights Field

Analyzing responses to the Darfur conflict shows that reactions by the international community were propelled by the justice cascade—that is, the replacement of impunity by the pursuit of individual criminal accountability against perpetrators of grave human rights violations—and these reactions simultaneously constituted a part of the cascade. The broader patterns, powerfully described by political scientist Kathryn Sikkink (2011), were thus confirmed for Darfur. I also found confirmed that driving forces of the justice cascade are international organizations and human rights NGOs, often interconnected in transnational activist networks (TANs) (Keck and Sikkink 1998). Simultaneously, the case of Darfur provided insights into strengths and limits of the justice cascade. A report by the International Commission of Inquiry on Darfur (ICID) and the ICC charges, reaching up to Sudan's president, Omar al-Bashir, powerfully depicted central political actors as criminal perpetrators. They squarely produced representations of the Darfur conflict within the crime frame. Yet the judicial account also illustrates the narrative constraints of criminal law (in addition to obvious enforcement constraints). While it is true that the ICID, part of the Darfur proceedings, was mindful of the social and political conditions of the conflict, it relegated such insights to a "background" section. The logic of criminal law attributes mass violence to a small number of individuals. Structural conditions and organizational contexts are underappreciated in the judicial field's representation of mass violence. The court's indictments focus yet further on a select number of individuals and their actions as conditions of the violence. This finding is consistent with previous research on judicial responses to mass violence, including the Mauthausen trial (Jardim 2012); the "Doctors' Trial," one of the subsequent Nuremberg trials (Marrus 2008); the Frankfurt Auschwitz trial (Pendas 2006); and war crimes trials against perpetrators of massacres in My Lai, Vietnam, and Haditha, Iraq (Savelsberg and King 2011).

The ICC of course does not act alone. A crucial condition of the justice cascade is the mobilization of human rights NGOs. I look closely at Amnesty International and its fight to end impunity in the case of Darfur. Interviews show that Amnesty's narrative resembles and supports the judicial field's. Here too the focus is on the goal of justice and on individual perpetrators, at the expense of larger structural patterns. Respondents insisted that justice, once achieved, would help actors reach other goals such as peace.

Respondents' relative unanimity in representing the violence as criminal supports the strength of the globalizing forces highlighted by the World Polity School (Meyer, Ramirez, and Soysal 1992; Boyle and Meyer 1998). This is expected for an international NGO that closely coordinates actions with other INGOs. It should be especially unsurprising in the case of Amnesty, with its strong International Secretariat in London and its relatively hierarchical organizational structure. Yet even in the case of Amnesty, national conditions also color narratives. Examples include the strong pacifist roots of NGO volunteers in a country such as Germany and pressure on Amnesty in the United States to cooperate with members of the massive civil society movement gathered under the umbrella of the Save Darfur campaign. In all countries, Amnesty workers are aware of their government's traditions, interests, and policy foci when they seek to influence government policies. Without such awareness they surely could not communicate effectively with pubic officials. They are also mindful of nation-specific carrier groups and their cultural sensitivities when they attempt to mobilize volunteers and the public and raise funds. Such mindfulness, a precondition for effective work at the national level, resulted—as we saw—in varying criminalizing representations of mass violence in Darfur. In addition, workers for international NGOs are themselves shaped by the national contexts in which they were socialized and educated.

But not only INGOs and TANs supported the justice cascade in the case of Darfur; national governments were also crucial actors, albeit to different degrees. I pay particular attention to the United States, its civil society, and government, as this country stood out in international comparison. It sought, more strongly than other members of the international community, to advance a criminalizing frame for Darfur and a definition of the violence as genocide. Crucial contributors were civil society groups, especially evangelical Christians, African Americans, and Jewish organizations, organized in the Save Darfur campaign. The George W. Bush administration followed suit, despite its opposition to the ICC, but under the pressure of civil society. Conditions for this transmission included the porousness of boundaries between civil society and the state in the United States (Bendix 1949 [1974]; Roth 1987; Savelsberg 1994). Articles in the *New York Times* and the

Wall Street Journal, especially opinion pieces, reflected and reinforced the consensus between civil society and the state. They highlighted the crime frame, labeled the violence as genocide, and used dramatic bridging metaphors to shed light on the violence of Darfur by referencing past genocides, including the Holocaust.

Nation-specific patterns are in line with recent literature on national contexts within which INGOs work (Stroup 2012), and with a long tradition of historicizing neo-Weberian scholarship (Bendix 1949 [1974]; Kalberg 1994, 2014; Savelsberg and King 2005). Some national sections of INGOs find stronger resonance in their respective country's governments than others, depending on the institutionalization of civil society–government relations. Nevertheless, this finding should not distract from the fact that national sections of human rights INGOs are characterized by a common denominator: the pursuit of human rights and some degree of consistency in their criminalizing narratives.

Justice or Humanitarianism? Aid NGOs and the Humanitarian Complex

Responses by the UNSC, human rights NGOs, and some countries, including the United States, thus advanced the justice cascade and the representation of mass violence in Darfur within a criminalizing frame. But to focus only on these actors would be misleading. Examining representations of Darfur in other fields reveals at times sharply competing definitions of the situation in the besieged region of Sudan. One potential competitor of the judicial field and its supporters is the humanitarian aid field, here explored with specific attention to one NGO, Doctors Without Borders (MSF). I show that humanitarian representations differ significantly from those of the human rights field. Humanitarian organizations highlight those aspects of suffering that can best be addressed by aid programs. Displacements and the conditions for IDPs and refugees in camps are privileged over the fate of others who lose their lives during massacres, in rape campaigns, and on death marches into the camps. Humanitarian narratives treat the government of Sudan cautiously. They emphasize long-term conditions such as the desertification of the Sahel zone and long-standing center-periphery conflicts, and soft-pedal government actions that are immediate precursors, and likely conditions, of the violence. The humanitarian catastrophe frame is privileged over the crime frame, and actors shy away from the genocide label. My analysis identifies the powerful position of the government of

Sudan vis-à-vis the humanitarian aid field as a crucial condition for this representation, in line with earlier examinations of the humanitarian field (de Waal 1997; Hagan, Schoenfeld, and Palloni 2006).

My analysis of the humanitarian field also displays global-national tensions similar to those diagnosed for the human rights field. Yes, a global humanitarian representation can be identified, and here too international NGOs and aid organizations are major contributors, confirming arguments from globalization theory. Yet, as in the human rights field, cross-national variation in representations is pronounced. In the humanitarian field, too, activists have to speak effectively to reach government actors with specific policy preferences and volunteers and potential donors within civil society who are motivated by distinct collective memories and cultural sensitivities. Again, the validity of historicizing neo-Weberian arguments is demonstrated, and Stroup's observations (2012) on national boundaries within the international NGO movement find further support.

Cross-national patterns themselves are complicated by distinctions between members of diverse professions that inhabit the humanitarian field. Lawyers working in this field are less immune to the logic of the justice cascade than members of other professions such as physicians. Educational backgrounds and professional trajectories thus intersect with field and national context conditions and produce patterns of knowledge and habitus far less homogeneous than a focus on the field alone would suggest. Conflicts between human rights and humanitarian fields should thus not be conceived of as zero-sum. This conclusion is all the more important as conflict gives way at times to a division of labor, as when humanitarian organizations produce evidence of suffering and victimization that justice institutions may later use to assign criminal liability.

While the intersection between fields, national contexts, and professional backgrounds may lead to a weakening of the ideal-typical humanitarian narrative, other conditions move the humanitarian representation closer to the master narrative. I illustrate this hardening of the narrative for Ireland, a country with a strong humanitarian aid orientation and with a close network of state organizations, aid NGOs, and the Irish Catholic Church, all rooted in policy practices that mutually reinforce a humanitarian orientation and associated representation of Darfur. I refer to the structural basis of this constellation as a humanitarian complex. Interviews, supported by many conversations and observations of the cityscape of Dublin, with its numerous and moving memorials to Irish suffering, reveal some of the cultural foundations of this humanitarian complex. This evidence suggests that collective memories of poverty and famine were crucial driving forces of NGO humanitarianism, aid- and development-focused foreign policy, and supportive public opinion.[2] In Ireland, the memory of famine and poverty is supplemented by additional memories that raise skepticism against humanitarianism's challenger, the human rights and associated judicial narratives. Irish interviewees interpreted the Northern Ireland conflict as supporting the notion of amnesties in the context of politically motivated violence. This memory in fact proved to be institutionalized in Dublin's Department of Foreign Affairs, where a working group drew lessons from the Northern Ireland conflict in developing foreign policy principles.

And, as in the case of MSF, the representation of mass violence in a humanitarian-complex situation such as Ireland's takes a particular shape. Here too aspects of suffering were highlighted that could be addressed by aid programs, and the responsibility of the government of Sudan was downplayed. The crime frame and the genocide label were used cautiously. This pattern, identified through interviews, is confirmed by media analysis. The causal mechanism was the same as for humanitarian NGOs, given the government of Sudan's role as gatekeeper for the delivery of aid.

Nevertheless, despite such national particularities and, again, as in the human rights field, globalization theory is not to be discarded. Irish government officials still considered their policies aligned with the rest of Europe and the United Nations. And Ireland is indeed among the many European countries that have ratified the Rome Statute, without which the ICC prosecution against President al-Bashir and others would not be possible. While such allegiance thus supports warnings against essentializing a country, its culture and institutions, positions, representations, cultural patterns, and policy practices are simultaneously well suited to illustrating and indeed confirming neo-Weberian concerns regarding national carrier groups and cultural sensitivities.

Peace or Justice? Diplomacy across Countries

In addition to representations from the humanitarian field, narratives of the mass violence in Darfur generated in the diplomatic field also differed sharply from judicial and human rights representations. Interviews revealed a diplomatic master narrative or ideal type of diplomatic representation of mass violence. We saw that diplomacy focuses, even more than the humanitarian aid field, on long-term and structural causes of conflicts. It tends to avoid naming responsible actors, using the crime frame, or applying the genocide label. Information provided by interviewees suggests a similar causal mechanism. Again, the role of the Sudanese state is decisive. Humanitarian aid organizations depend on permits by lower-level government bureaucracies, where boundary-crossing professional solidarity may at times be at work. But in the diplomatic field dependency is yet more pronounced. Here actors depend on active participation by high-ranking politicians of the country in which mass violence unfolds. Clearly the bar is higher and the pressure to take account of the Sudanese state more intense.

Another distinction between the human rights and diplomatic fields is decisive. Unlike judicial actors and their allies, diplomats are less oriented toward procedure than toward substantive outcomes. They seek to advance their respective countries' material and ideal interests, which were tied—in the Darfur case—to the pursuit of peace and political stability in the region. Diplomats have internalized their field's institutional logic and its doxa, its matter-of-course assumptions about the world. The analysis relativizes arguments by Samantha Power (2002) for the United States and Karen Smith (2010) for Europe, according to which cautious language in the foreign policy field, even in the face of genocide, indicates the reluctance of rational actors to get involved, lest they incur potentially high political costs. I suggest that much of this hesitation must be attributed instead to the habitus of diplomats and its rootedness in the structural conditions of their field.

The diplomatic field thus generates a particular representation of Darfur, distinct from the humanitarian account and in stark contrast to the human rights narrative. Interviewees from foreign ministries generally applied great caution about using dramatizing labels, especially *genocide,* when they described the violence, and about attributing direct responsibility, especially criminal responsibility, to central actors in the Sudanese state. Even so, national contexts matter here even more than in the human rights and humanitarian fields, as my evidence suggests. This may be surprising at first, given that all countries under analysis are members of major international organizations and all but the United States have ratified the Rome Statute. It is also true that all interviewees from foreign ministries insist that their countries are aligned. Yet foreign policy and associated diplomatic work are primarily the domain of national governments, and my evidence suggests that the diplomatic master narrative is pulled in different directions by the national contexts in which it is cultivated.

Strong mobilization of civil society in combination with porous state-society boundaries contributed to dramatizing narratives, including in the diplomatic field. My analysis shows this pattern especially for the United States. A government's intense interactions with the Sudanese state, in contrast, resulted in representations that stuck close to the diplomatic ideal type. Such interactions may have been fostered through various mechanisms. The Austrian case showed the effects of Sudan's lobbying efforts. Another factor may be a country's reputation for neutrality and associated expertise and involvement in mediation, a force visible in the case of Switzerland. Consider also effects of the close interaction with Sudanese officials in the humanitarian field on display in the case of Ireland. In addition, a country's status as a former colonial power—with the regional expertise, presence of expatriate groups, and normative commitment that this entails—plays into the way its policy makers and diplomats speak about and respond to mass violence occurring in a former colony. The United Kingdom served as an example, and France was particularly concerned with a potential destabilization of Chad, its former colony and immediate neighbor of not just Sudan but the Darfur region specifically. Finally, Germany exemplified the complex effects of the "cultural trauma of perpetrators" (Giesen 2004a) of the Holocaust. Throughout the German responses, national carrier groups and memorial normativities—those commitments implicated in and emerging from collective memories—affected responses to Darfur. While especially pronounced, the German case has one characteristic in common with other countries: communicative memories, embedded in specific carrier groups, matter. The weight of collective memory in the representation of mass violence and the fight for human rights thus confirms observations Daniel Levy and Natan Sznaider (2010) make in their sociohistorical work on memory and human rights; however, my observations challenge their position regarding the declining weight of communicative memories tied to particular carrier groups.

Not to be misunderstood: as in the case of the human rights and humanitarian fields, I seek to essentialize neither field nor nation in the foreign policy and diplomatic realms. For nations, civil society organization, carrier groups, memories, aid programs, and ties to the Sudanese state are all variable. And here too fields overlap with their actors' diachronic experiences such as educational socialization and professional career trajectories, and with synchronic contexts such as organizational settings. We saw that it matters, for example, if diplomats work in a legal department, especially a human rights unit, or in a political department of their foreign ministry. Also, despite the distinction between judicial and diplomatic representations of Darfur, resulting tensions do not constitute a zero-sum conflict. In some cases diplomats may even use the threat of criminal sanctions as a tool in diplomatic negotiations (Savelsberg and King 2011: ch. 3). In addition, diplomats are involved where international treatises are being promulgated, including the Rome Statue, on which the ICC is based and from which the prosecutions against President al-Bashir and others were launched (Scheffer 2012). Nevertheless, as abundant evidence in this book shows, diplomatic representations are highly distinct from human rights narratives, albeit variable across countries, and—like humanitarian narratives—they pose one potential challenge to the unfolding of the justice cascade.

This book's analysis thus shows that fields, national contexts, and actors' educational and professional trajectories intersect as they generate patterns of representation of mass violence. What applies to Darfur should also apply to other cases. We are thus one step closer to understanding the cacophony of voices that observers of world events encounter when they seek to make sense of distant suffering (Boltanski 1999).

Communicating Suffering to Civil Society: The Journalistic Field

The final question raised in this book addresses the communication of competing narratives to civil society. While NGOs involved in human rights and humanitarian activism seek to reach the public through their own campaigns, most members of civil society learn about instances of mass violence through news media. Also, foreign ministries and institutions of criminal justice depend on media to take seriously their press releases, their ceremonies marking the opening and closing of negotiations (diplomacy), and their hearings (court actions) when they seek to reach a broad public.

Based on interview data and supported by ideas from Bourdieuian sociology applied to the journalistic field, I show how Africa correspondents who reported on Darfur submitted to their field's rules of the game. Their habitus was shaped by their positions in the semiautonomous journalistic field, albeit mediated by the trajectories by which they reached their positions. All interviewees strongly identified with the journalistic profession, appreciated the work of writing, were highly educated in a diverse range of fields (though most lacked an Africa-specific background), shared some dose of adventurism, were relatively independent from their editors (but variably so), and depended heavily on external sources of information, including IO and INGO reports; other news sources, especially guiding media ("*Leitmedien*") such as BBC and CNN; and networks of colleagues in the field. I refer to the last-named sources as local cosmopolitan media networks, partially clustered by nationality. This mix of features entails some elements that strengthen journalistic autonomy (e.g., education and identification with journalistic work) and others that weaken it (e.g., dependency on IOs and INGOs as sources). It is in light of this relative autonomy that the relationship between journalism on the one hand and politics, diplomacy, human rights law, and humanitarianism on the other affects media reporting.

Interviews and analysis of the Darfur media data set indeed highlight the varying influences of distinct fields on media representations of mass violence. After initial neglect, a first—and massive—rise in reporting followed political initiatives, especially Kofi Annan's analogical bridging before the UN General Assembly from the Rwandan genocide (on its tenth anniversary) to Darfur. Also, initiatives by domestic politicians, especially ones affiliated with international organizations, ignited media attention.

After the initial wave of media reporting was at risk of taking the typical nosedive (see Bourdieu 1998), steps by the UN to initiate judicial proceedings, followed by the ICC's interventions, pulled Darfur back into the limelight of media attention. Several judicial interventions were followed by new peaks of reporting, drawing attention to killings and rapes and framing the violence as criminal. Analysis of the Darfur data set shows that the crime frame appeared more prominently in media reporting than any other frame, and its prominence intensified even when overall media attention to Darfur declined. In the case of Darfur, the justice cascade with its supporting forces—human rights NGOs, TANs, IOs, and the new, permanent International Criminal Court—thus significantly weakened the chances of abusers of human rights to go unnoticed or even to enter world history with a reputation as heroes (Giesen 2004b). Arguments about the discursive nature of court proceedings (Osiel 1997), their legitimacy by virtue of procedure (Luhmann 2004), and their ritual power (Durkheim [1912] 2001) may help explain the pronounced impact of court interventions on the intensity of media reporting and its coloring of the violence as crime.

The humanitarian field and its distinctive representations also turned out to be a crucial source of information for journalists, and the humanitarian emergency frame initially manifested prominently. Yet use of this frame declined quickly and dramatically. At least two reasons appear to account for this pattern. Most important, suffering in refugee camps that lasts for long periods loses newsworthiness. This feature of the media market was augmented by actions of the government of Sudan that increasingly barred humanitarian aid organizations from Darfur or made their continued presence contingent on "good behavior," that is, on refraining from criticism and from any agenda of bearing witness. MSF sections were thus among the first organizations to be expelled from Sudan.

The diplomatic field affected media reporting more enduringly than the humanitarian field did, but less intensely than the judicial field. Like the latter it can produce dramatic moments. Its chances are even better the more its actions involve prominent political actors who themselves are considered newsworthy, enhancing the attractiveness of news from the field of diplomacy for mass media. But diplomatic negotiators usually do not have the same level of legitimacy as courts. Negotiations are not public, do not follow strict procedure, and lack a trial's ritual force. Also, the outcomes of negotiation, even when an accord is reached, are more uncertain and lack the drama of an indictment against a head of state. In line with these considerations, the analysis reveals that the war or armed conflict frame, with its elective affinity to the diplomatic field, fared less noticeably and less enduringly than the crime frame in reporting about Darfur.

Finally, this analysis adds to insights from recent international comparative research on media reporting (Benson 2013). It shows that not only general structural and cultural features of the media's home country affect reporting, including the relative strength of competing fields, but also national particularities of the media field itself.

THEORETICAL CONTRIBUTIONS AND INSIGHTS
FOR PRACTICE

The foregoing chapters present theoretical themes outlined in the introduction, and the empirical observations speak to those themes. These include concerns from the sociology of knowledge and collective representations, especially the role of legal rituals and procedures as well as carrier groups, their cultural sensitivities and memories; field theory, with its focus on actors and the web of ties in which they are embedded, marred by power imbalances; and debates between globalization theorists versus scholars who highlight national forces even in a globalizing world. Simultaneously, empirical observations in this book speak to issues of practice and policy: the justice cascade and the forces that advance this cascade and its effects, as well as the strategies of different fields and how they relate to, support, or challenge other fields. Many messages appear throughout the review of empirical findings offered above. A brief summary of policy and theoretical themes in this final section of the book will nevertheless be helpful.

The justice cascade is at the center of massive debates, waged at once in scholarship and in practice. Increasing attribution of individual criminal liability in cases of grave human rights violations in domestic, foreign, and international courts is powerfully documented in the work of political scientist Kathryn Sikkink (2011; see also Neier 2012). The story of Darfur supports many of those arguments, even if the struggle to end impunity has not yet resulted in arrests and trials. The criminalization of human rights violations follows the story of past criminalizations of other behaviors, explored in a long tradition of constructivist criminology following the classical contributions of Turk (1969), Chambliss (1964), and Gusfield (1967). Yet, in contrast to these classics, the concern today is less with status group politics or the politics of class and race at the level of nation-states than with the diffusion of norms across national boundaries (Jenness 2004) and from global institutions down to nation-states. Also, recent literature on the justice cascade replaces conflict theory's critical stance toward criminalization (of the weak) by a supportive stance toward criminalization (of the powerful).

While questions remain regarding the endurance of the justice cascade as a short-term versus secular trend, the fiercest debates have focused on its consequences. In general, and in the Darfur case, critics argue that threatening sanctions motivates powerful perpetrators to resist a transfer to a more democratic and human rights–respecting regime (Goldsmith and Krasner 2003, Snyder and Vinjamuri 2003–2004; Pensky 2008). Sikkink (2011) instead argues, and she provides statistical evidence for her position, that the justice cascade will not harm, and may possibly improve, democracy and human rights records. In seeking to explain supporting correlations, she stresses the effectiveness of deterrence. Mindful of past punishments, potential perpetrators will shy away from committing human rights crimes. But the deterrence mechanism does not—and it cannot—stand alone. It is accompanied by potential cultural effects that work through the capacity of criminal proceedings to represent violence as a form of criminal offending—and thus to contribute to a collective memory of violent repression as a form of human rights crime. In fact, deterrence presumes this cultural effect as it envisions actors who are conscious of acts committed and penalties paid in the past. Here too the story of Darfur provides evidence. UNSC and ICC interventions contributed to a depiction of leading actors of the Sudanese state, all the way up to its mighty president, Omar al-Bashir, as criminal perpetrators. Media communicated this image to a broad public across national boundaries. The justice cascade seems to have worked in an important way even though no arrests have been made (yet) and even if no trial is under way.

Linking ideas from field theory to debates about the justice cascade reveals reasons for both the cultural effectiveness and constraints associated with the cascade, the judicial field, and institutions such as the ICC. For all fields on which I focus—judicial, humanitarian, diplomatic, and journalistic—the crucial role of actors becomes apparent, in line with arguments by Bourdieu (1987, 1988, 1998) and his followers (Benson 1998, 2006; Hagan 2003; Hagan and Levi 2005), but also consistent with the conception of strategic action fields (Fligstein 2001; Fligstein and McAdam 2011). Actors in these fields pursue specific goals such as justice, humanitarianism, and peace while they also seek to strengthen their own position within their respective field. Interviews with humanitarians, human rights workers, diplomats, and journalists alike provide abundant evidence. But actors are both enabled and constrained by their field's rules of the game. They become carriers of a habitus, a set of relatively fixed dispositions. They have little choice but to incorporate into their habitus their field's dominant institutional logic, a notion borrowed from Weber (1976) and elaborated by Luhmann (2004). They thus buy into the field's doxa, its matter-of-course assumptions about the world.

In criminal law this consistency between habitus and the surrounding field and the logic of its institutions means a focus on specific individual actors (as opposed to the social structures or broad cultural patterns that social scientists might stress) and on those rules of evidence compatible with the law's procedural requirements (not those rules deemed relevant by historians). It also implies application of a binary logic whereby clear distinctions between "guilty" and "not guilty" leave little room for the recognition of "shades of grey" (Levi 1988) and allow for a "decoupling" (Giesen 2004a) of bystanders, more or less passive supporters of the violence, and others from the guilt determined against a few in criminal trials. While the field thus enables its actors to pursue specific goals, it constrains them and the representations to which they contribute. Important aspects of social reality are left out when it is constructed through the lens of a particular field, aspects that actors in other fields alert us to.

Further, the representation of mass violence by the global human rights field is not just complicated, for better or worse, by the contributions of surrounding fields to the social construction of the reality of mass violence (Berger and Luckmann 1966). The story of fields examined here is further complicated by their simultaneous operation at national and international levels (see also Dezalay and Garth 1997; Hagan 2003). Bourdieu's study of academic life, but also much of his work on journalism, examines fields at the nation level, specifically for the case of France. This national focus produces two shortcomings. First, it buys into national conditions of fields without explicating their particularities. It runs the risk of exaggerating external validity, of overgeneralizing. Second, it misses complex interactions between global fields and national subfields, characterized by the structural, institutional, and cultural particularities of each country. Actors in national subfields are also confronted with (or are themselves members of) national carrier groups with specific historical experiences, collective memories, and cultural sensitivities. These scholarly insights likely have consequences for practice, even if it is a matter for further debate whether the application of national filters constitutes an advantage or a problem for the justice cascade or the pursuit of humanitarianism or peace. It is clear, though, that mobilization on behalf of any of these goals, including human rights, has to take nation-level forces into account.

Revelation of such intersectionality between global and national fields contributes insights into debates between globalization theorists and others who highlight national contexts. The World Polity School of John Meyer and his followers (e.g., Meyer, Ramirez, and Soysal 1992; Boyle and Meyer 1998; Frank, Hironaka, and Schofer 2000), suggesting that fields in which multiple global actors are involved should produce global representations and scripts, finds significant confirmation in my research. Indeed, I identify common denominators in the human rights, humanitarian, and diplomatic narratives across national boundaries. Yet empirical patterns also suggest caution. Nation-specific factors, carrier groups, interests, institutions, and cultural sensitivities clearly affect representations, in support of a different, historicizing brand of neo-Weberian scholarship (Bendix [1949] 1974; Gorski 2003; Roth 1987; Rueschemeyer 1973; Kalberg 1994, 2014; Savelsberg and King 2005, 2011). My findings confirm and elaborate on Halliday and Carruthers's conclusion (2010) that cultural distance from the global affects national adaptations of global models. Not just cultural distance matters, though, but also the substance of national cultures, their qualitative particularities. My findings do not stand alone. They are supported by recent work on the impact of national contexts on cross-national variation in responses to mass violence by Western governments (K. Smith 2010) and by INGO actors (Stroup 2012). Even work inspired by the World Polity School found nation-specific patterns in the implementation of human rights law (Boyle 2002). Still other scholars write about cosmopolitanism, especially in the realm of human rights (e.g., Levy and Sznaider 2010). They too take the nation level seriously, while insisting that international and global concerns are increasingly incorporated into national ideas, memories, and practices. My analysis sheds light on the relative weight of the global, the national, and the cosmopolitan and their interactions.

Interpenetration not only between the global and the national but also between national society and fields is further supplemented by systemic interpenetration between fields, for example, when diplomats use the threat of criminal sanctions in negotiations or when actors in the humanitarian field produce medical evidence that may later be used by criminal justice actors. A concrete example for the interpenetration of fields and national backgrounds is provided by the director of an operational center of a humanitarian aid agency in Europe. While working in the humanitarian field, he was trained as a lawyer (with affinities to the rights narrative) and his roots were in the United States (a strong supporter of judicial intervention against Sudan). His position in the organizational field, his educational background, and his national upbringing simultaneously contributed to his distinctive knowledge and habitus. Instead of harmonizing, biographical trajectory and field demands often produce contradictions that create room for improvisation. Recognizing such intersectionality across fields potentially provides actors with powerful tools for collaboration.

In short, complications (as well as opportunities) arise for the human rights field and its associated institutions, including the ICC, from their competition with other fields, from the global-national tension, and from complex interpenetrations with trajectories of professional socialization and national upbringing. Added to this is a final challenge, the need to communicate representations of mass violence to a global public. Again, few members of Western societies have direct experience with mass violence in places such as Darfur, even if the cultural trauma of mass violence in their own regions persists. In contrast to other policy fields, they learn about those events primarily through media messages. Through them they become subject to distant suffering (Boltanski 1999) and cultural trauma (Alexander et al. 2004). To the degree that policy decisions are informed by public perceptions of international issues—and scholarship shows that they are (see note 1)—media thus become an important social force. In line with historical and sociological literature on the processing of judicial narratives in media reports (Pendas 2006; Jardim 2012; Savelsberg and King 2011), my analysis documents compatibilities between the logic of the judicial field and the journalistic rules of the game. The need for dramatization and a focus on individual actors are among them. Criminalizing representations in the Darfur case thus more strongly and more enduringly affected media reporting across countries than representations from other fields.

To conclude, in the complex intersection of overlapping and conflicting fields there emerge consequential representations of mass violence. Building on a long tradition of ideas from the sociology of knowledge, rooted in the classical works of Emile Durkheim ([1912] 2001), Max Weber (1976), Karl Mannheim (1952), and leading to the work of Peter Berger and Thomas Luckmann (1966) and Pierre Bourdieu (1998), this volume further contributes to our understanding of how competing fields, at national and global levels, interact to produce collective representations of mass violence that news media communicate selectively. Collective representations then constitute a cultural repertoire (Swidler 1986) on which creators of collective memory of cruelty and suffering (Halbwachs 1992; Olick 1999; Osiel 1997; Savelsberg and King 2011) and cultural trauma (Alexander et al. 2004) eventually draw. Making sense of these patterns is a critical precondition for understanding, explaining, and predicting how civil societies and governments respond to mass violence. And such responses affect chances of breaking those "cycles of violence" (Minow 1998) that have tortured humanity throughout its history, with Darfur being one of the recent chapters of such suffering (Hagan and Rymond-Richmond 2008). Nation building succeeded in dramatically reducing civil violence within modernizing societies (Elias 1978; Johnson and Monkkonen 1996; Cooney 1997; Eisner 2001). Will the building of global institutions, especially in the justice field, lead to a similar degree of pacification worldwide? This book suggests that the building of global judicial institutions has the potential of contributing to global pacification at the international and national levels, especially if the builders tolerate, and learn to creatively manage, substantial conflicts between fields and nations; if they are mindful of the potential for division of labor and cooperation; if they are not bogged down by inevitable failures and frustrations; and if they prevail against massive resistance by those with an interest in the exercise of brute force.

Postscript

Neither the legal case against those charged with the gravest of crimes in the mass violence in Darfur, nor the armed confrontation, nor the humanitarian emergency had ended or been resolved as I was writing the final pages of this book. This text, then, presents not just a history of a recent and devastating past but also a history of a cruel present in Darfur. And, again, what applies to Darfur also applies to many more situations around the globe. In this situation, it is disconcerting, irrespective of the observer's field, to witness signs of weakness in the very institutions set up to respond to the situation in Darfur and to others like it.

In December 2014, Fatou Bensouda, the second chief prosecutor of the ICC and successor to Luis Moreno-Ocampo, announced to the United Nations that she had decided to "hibernate" the prosecution of those charged with crimes in Darfur: "Given this [UN Security] Council's lack of foresight on what should happen in Darfur, I am left with no choice but to hibernate investigative activities in Darfur as I shift resources to other urgent cases, especially those in which trial is approaching. It should thus be clear to this Council that unless there is a change of attitude and approach to Darfur in the near future, there shall continue to be little or nothing to report to you for the foreseeable future."[1] Bensouda expressed considerable frustration over the court's inability, and the world powers' unwillingness, to bring those charged before the court. Accordingly, in a February 12, 2015, article, "Is the

War Crimes Court Still Relevant?" *New York Times* journalist Somini Sengupta and a correspondent at the UN wrote of a growing pile of cases, defiant government authorities, and the Security Council's call for investigations but negligible effort to advance them. And the Darfur case is not the only one for which the court's lack of direct access to an enforcement staff comes in full and, for those in pursuit of criminal justice, painful display.[2]

The court's weakness is often attributed to the hostility from the world's superpowers, their defensiveness against incursions into their sovereignty, and their geopolitical and economic interests across the globe. The court has faced stiff resistance whenever it addresses issues in which the Great Powers have vested interests. Examples include current plans to investigate US military personnel for engaging in torture in Afghanistan and to take on the grave human rights violations in North Korea, China's ally. Growing resistance from the African continent constitutes another hurdle, as illustrated most recently by Omar al-Bashir's June 2015 escape from South Africa—despite a South African court order for his arrest. I do not disagree with such causal attributions, but my data point to another challenge to criminal justice and the ICC: the competition the legal field experiences from others, including the humanitarian and diplomatic fields. This competition is associated with considerable, at times cautiously worded, at other times aggressively presented, ambivalence toward the court and its rationales. This undercurrent of doubt has, just like the resistance of countries such as China, Russia, and—beyond the Darfur case—the United States, similarly contributed to frustrations and to the ICC prosecutor's recent decision. We have seen throughout this book that rationales of diplomats and humanitarians differ substantially from those of criminal justice actors and those involved in the justice cascade. Their definition of the situation on the ground varies with their respective fields' strategic interests and the web of power relations in which they are embedded. Here the court faces a resistance that is not limited to the obvious interests of major powers but that pervades the international community and seeps into the very mindsets of a multitude of actors outside the justice system who are involved in situations such as Darfur.

And not only the ICC's position has been weakened. Humanitarians appear to be facing increasing need with declining resources, even though no good data on the ratio of the displaced and wounded to resources in Darfur are available. And diplomatic efforts on behalf of the search for peace in Darfur have subsided. Diplomats' interests have shifted to new situations, of which there is no shortage. As of this writing, in the past year alone, crises appeared in the Central African Republic, Syria, Northern Iraq (ISIS), Northern Nigeria, South Sudan, and Ukraine. Meanwhile, in Sudan, the UN–African Union military force UNAMID, created to protect civilians in Darfur, is being dismantled or substantially reduced.[3]

Meanwhile, the suffering in Darfur continues. Activists find no shortage of ever new reports of atrocities (see, for example, the sites of academic-activist Eric Reeves, Radio Dabanga, and the *Sudan Tribune*).[4] Millions continue to be confined to refugee camps in Chad and IDP camps in Sudan; 2014 alone added some 400,000 Darfuris to those stranded in camps. At times, desperate villagers seek refuge in the vicinity of UNAMID compounds,[5] housing the very forces that are to be substantially reduced. In February 2015 Human Rights Watch issued a report about recent actions of members of the Sudanese Armed Forces. In their pursuit of rebels, soldiers again committed atrocities against civilians: "Sudanese army forces raped more than 200 women and girls in an organized attack on the north Darfur town of Tabit in October 2014, Human Rights Watch said in a report released today. The United Nations (UN) and African Union (AU) should take urgent steps to protect civilians in the town from further abuses. The 48-page report, 'Mass Rape in Darfur: Sudanese Army Attacks Against Civilians in Tabit,' documents Sudanese Army attacks in which at least 221 women and girls were raped in Tabit over 36 hours beginning on October 30, 2014."[6]

Are all actors examined in this book, and the fields in which they are embedded, thus losing to those who pursue their political interests with brute force? As far as the ICC is concerned, the finding of this book still stands: the court has, mediated by news reports and commentaries, ingrained in much of the world's collective conscience a notion of the violence in Darfur as criminal. Also the observation of one of my journalist interviewees may still be valid, and I paraphrase: After the foundation of the ICC, militia leaders who would in the past have boasted by pointing to piles of corpses they left behind in a nearby village, or have shown off their child soldiers, no longer do so. The ICC is a young organization, a historical novelty, and any resignation now would be premature.

Humanitarian organizations continue to struggle to find pragmatic middle ground between witnessing and securing access to those in misery. And those who dedicate their careers and lives to the pursuit of peace continue to negotiate and to build institutions. Journalists report about their efforts and the violence against which they are directed. Scholars monitor the process, take stock, seek to depict and explain. They continue to provide an interpretive understanding of the actions of those who work toward relief, peace, and justice—and of those who incite and execute violence—in the social contexts in which they act. Resulting explanations may advance appropriate responses.

Many may be tempted to give up in light of ever recurring mass violence. Yet, just as Sisyphus keeps pushing his rock up the hill in the existentialist work of Albert Camus, humans will continue their desperate fight for humanitarianism, peace, and justice. They will do so despite the tensions between the fields in which they are embedded and the mighty forces with which they have to contend. They will continue to act in the mode of Bernard Rieux, the physician in Camus's novel *La Peste*, even in the face of a seemingly hopeless struggle. They will be driven by the forces of the field in which they are embedded and the habitus they have acquired, following the road signs of those institutions to which they are dedicated.

In closing I remind the reader of legal scholar Martha Minow's famous words, cited above, that the twentieth century distinguished itself from its predecessors not by amassing a record of grave violations of human dignity and destruction of human lives, but by setting up—for the first time in human history—institutions that seek to respond to and prevent mass violence. The twenty-first century provides multiple tragic opportunities to put these institutions to a test. Their future is highly contingent, and forecasting their chances of success—writing a history of their future—may go beyond the capacity of contemporary social science. But observe these institutions' operations and their consequences for those affected by mass violence we must. Distant suffering is not quite so distant any more. Observing it will continue to advance the search for remedies.

Photo Credits and Copyright Information

Figure 1: Map of Darfur within Sudan and neighboring countries. Source: U.S. Department of State, http://www.state.gov/p/af/ci/su/

Figure 2: The Building of the International Criminal Court in The Hague. Reprinted with permission: © ICC-CPI.

Figure 3: Title page of indictment against President Omar al-Bashir. Source: ICC website, http://www.icc-cpi.int/iccdocs/doc/doc279860.PDF

Figure 4: Village in Darfur attacked and destroyed by Janjawiid (supplied by Amnesty International). Reprinted with permission © WFP/Vincenzo Sparapani.

Figure 5: Young Darfuri Refugees in Goz Amir Refugee Camp in Eastern Chad (Image and following text supplied by Amnesty International). Reprinted with permission by © Amnesty International. 'One of a series of photographs taken by Alex Neve, Secretary General, Amnesty International Canada, during his mission to Chad in November 2013. Alex and his colleagues spent time during the visit interviewing Darfuri refugees who fled from Sudan to eastern Chad in 2013. Most came in April after a surge in fighting and grave human rights abuses in Central Darfur State – some of the worst violence in the region in years. At least 50,000 refugees have arrived in Chad in 2013, joining 250,000 who have already been here for the past decade. It is the highest refugee exodus out of Darfur since 2006. Interviewing dozens of refugees at Goz Amir camp, numerous common themes emerged. Amnesty International has documented the eyewitness testimonies from survivors of a massive armed attack on the town of Abu Jeradil and several surrounding villages in early April. Together they tell a story of tremendous chaos and indiscriminate violence. More information on Alex's Livewire blog: 'Will there be hell here also?' – Darfuris experience endless displacement.'

Figure 6: Save Darfur Demonstration in Washington DC. Reprinted with permission by United to End Genocide, formerly Save Darfur.

Figure 7: Save Darfur Demonstration in Washington DC. Reprinted with permission by United to End Genocide, formerly Save Darfur.

Figure 8: Percent of US American articles that address killings, rapes and displacements (US versus other media). Author's figure.

Figure 9: Percent US American articles on Darfur citing the crime frame, using the genocide label, and bridging to the Holocaust (US versus other media). Author's figure.

Figure 10: Rendering of genocidal violence in Washington DC by artist Naomi Natale (Million Bones Project), depicted on Save Darfur web site. Reprinted with permission by Naomi Natale (artist) and Teru Kuwayama (photographer).

Figure 11: Displaced Darfuris and their "housing" (from MSF website). Reprinted with permission © Dominique Bernard/MSF.

Figure 12: Darfuri women and children at MSF medical service site (from MSF website). Reprinted with permission © Juan Carlos Tomasi/MSF.

Figure 13: Famine Memorial in Dublin, Ireland. Licensed under CC-BY 3.0. Attribution: Chmee2, 2010.

Figure 14: Percentage of Irish articles that address killings, rapes and displacements (Irish versus all others). Author's figure.

Figure 15: Percentage of Irish articles citing the crime frame and using the genocide label (Irish versus all others). Author's figure.

Figure 16: Ambassador Tomas Ulicny, head of the EU delegation to Sudan, and Dr. Hassan El Turabi, head of the Popular Congress Party, engage in peace negotiations, Khartoum, February 3, 2015. Reprinted with permission © Jan Lucas, European Union 2015.

Figure 17: Doha peace negotiations (July 14, 2011 signing of treaty). Reprinted with permission, Oliver Chassot (photographer), UNAMID (organization).

Figure 18: Journalist Rob Crilly in North Darfur. Reprinted with permission by Rob Crilly.

Figure 19: Journalist Rob Crilly after interview with SLA commander Ibrahim Abdullah al "Hello" (far left) and a rebel in En Siro, North Darfur. Reprinted with permission by Rob Crilly.

Figure 20: Africa-correspondent Thomas Scheen interviewing rebels in Darfur. Reprinted with permission: F.A.Z.-Foto / Wolfgang Eilmes.

Figure 21: Number of articles on Darfur in 14 Northern newspapers by country over time. Author's figure.

Figure 22: Press conference at the International Criminal Court (press room). Reprinted with permission: © ICC-CPI.

Interview Guidelines

The guidelines vary somewhat for interviews with journalists versus NGO experts. Some terms appear in bold type to aid the interviewer.

- Introduction of my work/me/my project
- Consent form

QUESTIONS

- What in **your life course** has contributed to your working on issues of Sudan/ Darfur today? (education, socialization, career, position)
- In your position, with whom do you cooperate on the issue of Darfur (**hierarchy, division of labor**)?
  - Coordination; conflicts
- The topic of **Darfur itself.** Please summarize your own personal understanding of the developments in Darfur, especially during the past decade.
  - **First, what happened?** [Wait, then follow up.]
  - Follow-up
    - Victimization (kind and degree)
    - Local actors
      - Sudanese government
        - Al-Bashir
      - Janjawiid
      - Rebel groups
      - Others
    - Changes over time?

- **What are the underlying causes of the conflict?** (Follow up on desertification; old ethnic conflicts; late effects of colonialism; intervention by other countries [e.g., Libya, Chad]; strategies of Sudanese government; center-periphery conflict.)
- In addition to basic facts, there are different ways of **framing** the conflict. I'll mention a number of frames and ask you to tell me if they suggest an appropriate interpretation of the conflict (or did so in specific phases).
  - Rebellion/"insurrection"
  - Civil war
  - Humanitarian catastrophe
  - Aggressive state
  - State crime (which type[s]—war crimes, crimes against humanity, genocide?)
  - Other(s)?
- A related question concerns the appropriate reaction. **Which goals** are most important? **What means** are best suited to achieve those goals? How did goals and appropriate means change over time?
  [Wait, then follow-up]
  - Securing Sudanese state — by fighting insurgents
  - Securing peace — through negotiations
  - Survival of those affected — through aid delivery and cooperation
  - Justice — through court intervention (ICC)
- Follow-up on **arrest warrants by ICC**
  - Contribution to achieving different goals?
  - Impediment toward goal attainment?
  - By phases?
  - How have you communicated with the ICC? What was helpful? What caused problems? Any miscommunication?
- Position of (interviewee's country's) **government?**
  - Role of shifts in governing coalitions/ministers
  - Role of ICC intervention—official position of ministry?
  - Conflicting positions within government/ministry?
  - Difference between (country) positions and those of other Western countries?
- Position of (your country's) **NGOs**
- **Role of (your country's) history for position** (your personal position and possibly that of [your country's] government)?
  - Special responsibility in light of (country's) history?
  - Other aspects of history/reaction to previous atrocities?
- **Convergence across countries?** When? How?
- Inquiry into **sources of information** (not confidential ones). What types of sources are especially influential as you acquire information and interpretations? Problems?
  [Wait for reply, then follow up]
  - Own investigations on site?
  - Scholarship?
    - Institutions (university scholarship, think tanks)
    - Specific actors

- Specific books
- Journalism
- NGOs/civil society
- Films
- Justice (ICC)
- Other
- **Other contacts** for me?
  - Foreign ministries in neighboring countries
  - NGO reps
  - Scholars
- **Archives/Documents** (analysis of positions over time)?

Excerpts from Coding Manual for Newspaper Articles

The coding manual was developed in close collaboration with Hollie Nyseth Brehm. The following excerpt focuses on variables used in this book. Editorial comments are marked by brackets. The full code book is available on the author's website.

TABLE OF CONTENTS

[GENERAL] DIRECTIONS [FOR CODERS]

[Omitted here; for key information, see chapter 1]

EXPLANATIONS OF VARIABLES

PART 1. INFORMATION REGARDING SOURCE

Var. 1:   Source.
          Write the number that corresponds to the type of document in the
          blank.

Var. 2:   Title.
          Write the title of the document in the "Notes" section that corre-
          sponds to this variable. If there is no title, leave it blank.

Var. 3:   Date of Publication.
          Document the date of publication. Please note that it should be writ-
          ten in the following order: year-month-day. Use 4 numbers to iden-
          tify the year and 2 for both the month and the day. E.g.: February 23,
          2004 would be 2004–02–23.

Var. 4:   Length of Document.
          Note the number of words in the document. This may be listed
          somewhere on the page. If not, you can either find the document
          electronically and obtain the word count that way or provide an
          estimate. Also include the number of words spent on Darfur if it is a
          minor aspect of the document. If the majority of the article focuses
          on Darfur, there is no need to do this.

Var. 5:   Code the number that corresponds to the type of newspaper contri-
          bution. If the type is not listed, please write it in the "Notes" section.

Var. 6:   Write the number that corresponds to the section of the newspaper
          where the article was printed; if the section is not listed, please write
          it in the corresponding "Notes" portion of the coding form. Leave
          this variable blank if the section is not provided.

Var. 7:   Write the page number where the article appears. Leave this variable
          blank if the page number is not provided.

Var. 8:   Write the first author's name in the "Notes" section.

Var. 9:   Enter "1" if this first author is a female and "0" if he is male. If you
          are uncertain, you could perform a quick search online.

Var.10:   Write the number that corresponds to the first author's profession.
          If more than one profession is listed, chose the one listed first. If no
          profession is listed, assume the author is a journalist.

[Vars. 11–20: same for additional authors—omitted here.]

PART 2. HISTORIC EVENTS/ ROOTS OF THE CONFLICT

Var. 21: Enter a "0" if desertification or resource scarcity is not mentioned,
          "1" if it is mentioned, and "2" if it is mentioned as a cause of the
          current conflict.

Var. 22: North/South Sudanese Civil War [coding as for Var. 21].

Var. 23:   Imperialism (colonialism/postcolonialism) [coding as for Var. 21].
Var. 24:   1989 al-Bashir coup [coding as for Var. 21].
Var. 25:   2003 rebellion by the Sudan Liberation Army (SLA) and the Justice
           and Equality Movement (JEM) [coding as for Var. 21].
Var. 26:   Neglect of the Darfur region [coding as for Var. 21].
Var. 27:   North-South Peace agreement [coding as for Var. 21].
Var. 28:   Abuja Peace Talks (2004–2006) [coding as for Var. 21].
Var. 29:   United Nations Security Council reports or resolutions on Darfur
           [coding as for Var. 21].
Var. 30:   International Criminal Court charges/warrants [coding as for Var. 21].

PART 3: INFORMATION REGARDING FORM AND AMOUNT OF
VIOLENCE/ACKNOWLEDGMENT VS. AVOIDANCE
Please note: If the particular incidents mentioned seem especially relevant or
interesting, please make note of them in the "Notes" section. (There is a blank
by the "yes" option, but it is up to you as a coder to decide if the incident is
noteworthy or not.) Also, note that there is a separate section for aid workers,
peacekeepers, and other neutral parties who may have been harmed in the context of the conflict.

For "overall" variables, "thousands" = 1, "tens of thousands" = 2, "hundreds of thousands" = 3, "millions" = 4, and a rate = 5. For specific incidents,
"dozens" should be coded as 50; "hundreds" should be coded as 500, and
"thousands" should be coded as 5000. For all other numeric values expressed
in vague words, make your best educated guess to translate them into numbers.

KILLINGS AND DEATH
Var. 31:   Killing
           Code as a "1" if killings, deaths, or lives lost are mentioned any-
           where in the document. If not, code it as "0."
Var. 32:   Overall Killings
           If the document mentions the total number of people killed due to
           the conflict to date, write it on the coding sheet. You should write
           exactly what appears in the document, so you will enter either a
           numeric value or a word like "thousands" or "hundreds of thou-
           sands." If no number is provided, leave it blank.
Var. 33:   Specific Incident [omitted from this appendix]
Var. 34:   Specific Number of Killings [in incident; omitted here]
Var. 35:   Detailed Depiction [of incident; omitted here]
Var. 36:   Deaths from "Natural" Causes [omitted here]
Var. 37:   Number of Deaths from "Natural" Causes [omitted here]

TORTURE
Var. 38:   Torture
           Code this variable as "1" if torture is mentioned in the context of
           the conflict. If it is not mentioned, code it as "0."

[Vars. 39–42 are equivalent to list of variables under "killings"—omitted from this appendix.]

WOUNDS/INJURIES
Var. 43: Wounds or Injuries
Code this variable as "1" if the document mentions that people were wounded or injured (though not fatally) as a result of the conflict, and "0" otherwise.

[Vars. 44–47 are equivalent to list of variables under "killings"—omitted here.]

RAPES
Var. 48: Rapes
Enter a "1" if rapes are mentioned as an aspect of the conflict. If rape is not mentioned, code this as "0."

[Vars. 49–52 are equivalent to list of variables under "killings"—omitted here.]

KIDNAPPING
Var. 53: Kidnapping
Assign this variable a "1" if kidnapping is mentioned, and "0" if it is not.

[Vars. 54–57 are equivalent to list of variables under "killings"—omitted here.]

LIVELIHOOD
Var. 58: Destruction of Livelihood
Code this variable as "1" if destruction of livelihood is mentioned as part of the conflict, and "0" if it is not. Livelihood could include food, water, livestock, wells, etc. Please note that there is a separate variable for the destruction of homes and villages.

[Vars. 59–62 are equivalent to list of variables under "killings"—omitted here]
Var. 63: Code this variable as "1" if the destruction of homes or villages is mentioned. Often, burning homes will be mentioned. This variable should also receive a "1" if "arson" is mentioned. If neither the destruction of homes or villages is mentioned, code this variable as "0."

SHORTAGE OF FOOD OR WATER
Var. 64: Shortage of Food or Water
Assign this variable a "1" if hunger, starvation, or food/water shortage is mentioned in the context of the violence. A shortage of water also includes shortages of *clean/potable* water. Assign it a "0" if it is not mentioned or if it is mentioned but it in a different context.

[Vars. 65–68 are equivalent to list of variables under "killings"—omitted here.]

RESETTLEMENT ISSUES

Var. 69: If issues of resettlement, refugees, internally displaced persons (IDPs), or IDP or refugee camps are mentioned in the context of the conflict, code this variable as "1." If these issues are not mentioned, assign it a "0."

[Vars. 70–73 are equivalent to list of variables under "killings"—omitted here.]

DISEASE

Var. 74: Assign this variable a "1" if disease or illness related to the conflict is mentioned. Otherwise, assign it a "0."

[Vars. 75–78 are equivalent to list of variables under "killings"—omitted here.]

AID WORKERS/PEACEKEEPERS

Var. 79: Assign this variable a "1" if an aid worker, peacekeeper, or other neutral party was killed or wounded in the context of the violence. If not, assign it a "0."

Var. 80: Assign this variable a "1" if an aid worker, peacekeeper, or other neutral party was kidnapped or threatened in the context of the violence. If not, assign it a "0."

RACE/ETHNIC CONFLICT

Var. 81: Motive
Assign this variable a "1" if race or ethnicity is suggested as motivating aggressors. This variable should also receive a "1" if the presence of racial epithets is mentioned or illustrated. If not, assign it a "0."
A reference to "ethnic conflict" or a conflict between Arabs and Africans *does not* indicate racial motivation; it must be more explicit.

Var. 82: Construction
Code this variable as a "1" if race or ethnicity is depicted as constructed, or "0" if it is not depicted as constructed.

Var. 83: Skip this variable if race or ethnicity is not depicted as constructed. If it is, choose the number that corresponds to *whom* race/ethnicity is constructed by. If multiple actors are depicted as constructing race/ethnicity, please make notes in the corresponding "Notes" section.

Var. 84: Code this variable as "1" if the conflict is specifically described as following decades of conflict in Darfur, a "2" if it is specifically described as an age-old ethnic conflict, or as "0" otherwise.

PART 4. FRAMES

Please note: The "diagnostic" variable under each frame does not have to be coded as "1" in order for the prognostic or motivational variables to be assigned a "1." Furthermore, several frames could be present in one article. Please refer to the social movement piece by Benford and Snow 2000 for further reference and explanation of diagnostic, prognostic, and motivational frames.

TERRORISM/VIOLENT GANGS/INSURGENTS

Var. 85: Diagnostic

Code this variable as a "1" if the actors and actions in the conflict are explicitly described as "terrorists," "terrorism/terrorist acts," "violent gangs," or "insurgents." If not, assign it a "0."

Var. 86: Prognostic

Code this variable as "1" if the document suggests as a solution killing and arresting "terrorists"/gang members or intimidating the population in which they seek refuge.

Var. 87: Motivational

Code this variable as "1" if maintenance of the integrity of the Sudanese state is mentioned as a goal. If it is not mentioned as a goal, assign it a "0." Essentially, the idea is that the state has a legitimate right to defend itself; and the motivation is defending itself against terrorists/other aggressors.

Var. 88: Author's Voice

Assign this variable a "0" if the author clearly rejects this frame, a "1" if the author of the document clearly subscribes to this frame, and a "2" if it is not clear. If the document has two authors (like a debate from a state department source), code it as "2." Otherwise, leave this variable blank (i.e. if the frame is not mentioned or used in the article).

CIVIL WAR FRAME

Var. 89: Diagnostic

Assign this variable a "1" if the violence is explicitly referred to as a civil war or a tribal war. You should also assign this a "1" if any source describes events that would definitely be classified as a civil war. A civil war is a *war* between organized groups within a single nation-state or, less commonly, between two countries created from a formerly united nation-state. The aim of one side may be to take control of the country or a region, to achieve independence for a region, or to change government policies. It is a high-intensity conflict, often involving *regular armed forces*, that is sustained, organized, and large-scale. Civil wars may result in large numbers of casualties and the consumption of significant resources (Wikipedia).

Var. 90: Ethnic War

Assign this variable a "1" if the conflict is described as an ethnic conflict, or a "0" if it is not. Any reference to "Arab vs. African" would necessitate a "1" in this category. Both the civil war diagnostic and this variable could receive a "1," but the violence may also be described as "ethnic violence" without the specification of a civil war. Likewise, it could be described as a civil war without an ethnic component.

Var. 91: Prognostic
Code this variable as "1" if the document suggests that peace negotiation is the appropriate solution, or "0" otherwise.

Var. 92: Motivational
Code this variable as "1" if achieving peace is mentioned as a goal. If it is not mentioned as a goal, assign it a "0."

Var. 93: Author's Voice
Assign this variable a "0" if the author clearly rejects this frame, a "1" if the author of the document clearly subscribes to this frame, and a "2" if it is not clear. If the document has two authors (like a debate from a state department source), code it as "2." Otherwise, leave it blank.

CRIME AND STATE CRIME FRAME

Var. 94: Diagnostic
Code this as "0" if the violence is not described as criminal and if no acts that are criminal are noted. Assign this variable a "1" if acts that are considered criminal in most criminal codes (rape, torture, murder, pillaging, robbery, kidnapping, etc.) are mentioned. Please note that killing is not necessarily considered a crime in the context of war, but an explicit reference to "murder" is a crime. Assign this variable a "2" if the acts are explicitly referred to as "criminal" or as "crimes." This variable would also receive a "2" if a source suggests that someone in Sudan should be charged for war crimes, crimes against humanity, genocide, etc., or reports that someone was charged with these or similar crimes.

Var. 95: War Crimes
Code this variable as "1" if acts included in the violence are specifically labeled "war crimes" by any source, or "0" if they are not.

Var. 96: Crimes Against Humanity
Code this variable as "1" if acts included in the violence are specifically labeled as "crimes against humanity" by any source, or "0" if they are not.

Var. 97: Genocide
Code this variable as "1" if any source specifically refers to the violence as "genocide," or "0" if they are not. "Genocidal acts" should also receive a "1," but "characteristics of genocide" or "worse than genocide" should not.

Var. 98: Genocide Debated [omitted here]
Var. 99: Genocidal Intent [omitted]
Var. 100: Destruction of Groups [omitted]
Var. 101: Types of Destruction [omitted]

TYPES OF CRIMINAL PERPETRATORS

Var. 102: Assign this variable a "1" if the Sudanese State is explicitly referred to as a criminal perpetrator or participating in murder, torture, or rape. If not, assign it a "0."

Var. 103: Assign this variable a "1" if the Janjawiid/Arab militias are explicitly referred to as criminal perpetrators or as perpetrating rape or torture. If not, assign it a "0." Please also note that "Janjawiid" are often referred to as "Arab militias" and should be treated as the same entity throughout this coding.

Var. 104: Assign this variable a "1" if rebels are explicitly referred to as criminal perpetrators or as perpetrating rape, torture, or murder. If not, assign it a "0."

Var. 105: Please note if there are other actors who are described as criminal perpetrators or as perpetrating rape, torture, or murder.

LEVEL OF CRIMINALS

Var. 106: President of Sudan [omitted here]
Var. 107: Sudanese Cabinet Ministers [omitted]
Var. 108: Tribal Leaders [omitted]
Var. 109: Sudanese Military Officers [omitted]
Var. 110: Sudanese Soldiers [omitted]
Var. 111: General Support/Tolerating [omitted]
Var. 112: Material Support [omitted]
Var. 113: Armed Action [omitted]
Var. 114: Prognostic [omitted]
Var. 115: Motivational [omitted]

CONSEQUENCES OF ICC INTERVENTION

Var. 116: Prolonged Conflict [omitted]
Var. 117: Isolation of President or Country [omitted]
Var. 118: Peace [omitted]
Var. 119: Justice [omitted]
Var. 120: Other Outcomes [omitted]
Var. 121: Author's Voice [omitted]

HUMANITARIAN EMERGENCY FRAME

Var. 122: Diagnostic
Code this variable as "1" if hunger, illness, lack of (clean) drinking water, or encampment of the civilian population is depicted as a main aspect of the conflict or if the conflict is explicitly called a "humanitarian emergency." If not, assign it a "0."

Var. 123: Prognostic
Code this variable as "1" if delivery of aid to civilians affected by the violence and by internment is suggested or praised. Assign it a "0" if it is not mentioned, or a "2" if it is rejected.

Var. 124:   Motivational
            This variable should receive a "1" if any source suggests that
            near-term survival is the primary concern toward which several
            or all sides of the conflict, including the Sudanese state, should
            cooperate.
Var. 125:   Author's Voice [omitted here]

AGGRESSIVE STATE FRAME
Var. 126:   Diagnostic
            Assign this variable a "1" if the Sudanese state is depicted as ag-
            gressive but not criminal. If the state is not portrayed as aggres-
            sive, assign it a "0." Aggressive behavior is disproportional or
            inappropriate use of force not depicted as criminal. We really want
            to capture acts that are seen as "going too far" but not criminal.
               Also, note that a state could be seen as both aggressive and
            criminal. If one person in a document says that the Sudanese state
            is criminal, do not assign it a "1" for this category based on that
            statement, because the criminal acts involved in Darfur are always
            aggressive. However, often another voice in the document will
            speak about Sudan as aggressive but not criminal even though oth-
            ers see it as criminal; and then both the diagnostic in the aggressive
            state frame and the criminal frame would be coded as "1."
Var. 127:   Prognostic 1 [economic, political]
            Code this variable as a "1" if international pressure, economic
            sanctions, isolation, or other similar responses to the aggression
            are suggested. If one of these actions is not suggested, assign this
            variable a "0." If one or more is rejected, assign it a "2."
Var. 128:   Prognostic 2 [military]
            Code this variable as a "1" if humanitarian intervention (by any
            actor, such as the UN, NATO, or a specific country) is suggested,
            a "0" if it is not suggested, or a "2" if it is rejected. Humanitarian
            intervention is the use of force across state borders by a state or
            group of states aimed at preventing widespread violations of hu-
            man rights of individuals other than its/their own citizens. It is *not*
            aid/disaster relief.
Var. 129:   Motivational
            Assign this variable a "1" if reduction of the aggression of the
            Sudanese state is mentioned as a goal. If not, assign it a "0."

AGGRESSORS
In this section, we want to know who is blamed as an aggressor. A group that is
portrayed as a victim responding to aggression is *not* an aggressor. Rather, we
are interested in pro-active action (not defensive action) that is seen as dispro-
portional. Also, please note that if you coded someone as "criminal" based on
a statement, do not code this actor as aggressive based on that same statement.
It is possible that separate statements by different people (or the same person

about different incidents) characterize the same actor in the conflict as both criminal and aggressive, in which case this actor would be coded as a criminal and as an aggressor.

Var. 130: Janjawiid/Arab militia [omitted here]
Var. 131: Sudanese Military [omitted here]
Var. 132: Rebels/ "Africans" [omitted here]
Var. 133: Please make a note of any other actors who are depicted as aggressors.
Var. 134: Author's Voice [omitted here]

PART 5. COMPLICITY/SUPPORT OF SUDAN BY OTHER COUNTRIES
[omitted here]

PART 6. REFERENCES TO PAST ATROCITIES
Var. 143: Reference
This variable should receive a "1" if past atrocities are mentioned in the document *in the context of a discussion about Darfur.* Sometimes atrocities are mentioned in a different context (e.g., in connection with the Sudanese civil war), and in this case you would not code the atrocity here. Also note that we are interested in genocide and similar atrocities. There is no need to note the mention of humanitarian emergencies or to include these in the bridging section. If this variable receives a "0," skip to Variable 153.

Var. 144–151: Specific Atrocities [e.g., Holocaust, Rwanda, Bosnia]
Any atrocities that are mentioned in the document should receive a "1."

Var. 152: Please note any other atrocities (aggressive war, war crimes, crimes against humanity) mentioned in the corresponding "Notes" section on the coding sheet.

Var. 153: Responsibility
Explicit reference to the source country's (i.e., country in which the paper is produced or which the state department represents) responsibility to act against violence [omitted here].

Var. 154: History
Explicit reference to source country's responsibility to act due to its history [omitted].

Var. 155: Place in World
Source country's responsibility to act due to its place in the world [omitted].

Var. 156: Genocide Convention
Source country's responsibility to act due to Genocide Convention [omitted].

BRIDGING METAPHORS

Please note: We are interested in the violence itself, not reactions to it.

Var. 157: Mimetic Bridging
Code this variable a "1" if Darfur violence is mentioned as equal or equivalent to past atrocity. If not, assign it a "0." Also, please make note of the atrocity in the "Notes" section.

Var. 158: Contextual Bridging
Assign this variable a "1" if the violence in Darfur is mentioned as having similar contextual conditions (type of war, weak command structure, etc.) as another conflict or event, and note the conflict/event in the "Notes" section. Otherwise, assign it a "0."

Var. 159: Prognostic Bridging
Assign this variable a "1" if the author forecasts that the violence in Darfur will produce an outcome (loss, victory, loss of legitimacy, public support, etc.) similar to that of a past event, and make a note of that event. Otherwise, assign it a "0."

Var. 160: Bridging Challenge
Assign this variable a "1" if the author contrasts the conflict in Darfur with another atrocity, and make a note of the atrocity. If not, assign it a "0."

[PARTS 7–9 (VARS. 161–179) CONCERN USE OF OTHER FACTORS, PHOTOGRAPHS, AND REFERENCES TO SOURCES OF INFORMATION—OMITTED FROM THIS APPENDIX.]

[CODE SHEET OMITTED FROM APPENDIX]

Notes

INTRODUCTION

1. Dana Hughes, "Bill Clinton Regrets Rwanda Now (Not So Much in 1994)," *ABC News*, February 28, 2014, http://abcnews.go.com/blogs/politics/2014/02/bill-clinton-regrets-rwanda-now-not-so-much-in-1994/ (last retrieved May 4, 2014).

2. Military, literary, religious, and other fields could of course be added. For the treatment of the Darfur conflict in the field of environmentalism, see chapter 8 in Smith and Howe (2015). A focus on the three fields selected here seems reasonable given their prominence in discourses on Darfur. Only 2 percent of media articles, for example, cite the desertification of Darfur as a cause of the mass violence, despite the prominence of this theme among environmentalists.

3. Both groups draw on Weberian ideas, but they highlight different aspects of Weber's work. World polity scholars see world-level scripts as oriented toward rational models; they also adopt from Weber the notion of an iron cage, but not as a result of rational organizational action but of normative pressures to which individual, organizational, and nation-state actors are exposed. The competing group of neo-Weberians is instead sensitive to Weber's historicizing claims.

4. Targets of these attacks are members of the Fur, Massalit, and Zaghawa peoples, identified as "Blacks." To be sure, Hagan and Rymond-Richmond do not essentialize these groups. Recognizing that racial and ethnic identities are being created and manipulated by actors in the conflict, they attribute major responsibility to the Sudanese state. Once created, however, the affected groups adapt these identifiers. Again, definitions become "real in their consequences" (Thomas 1928).

5. Around 2005, major U.S. newspapers, activists, and UN secretary general Kofi Annan cited similar numbers.

6. In the Yugoslav wars of the 1990s, for example, Serbian leaders stressed the history (and myths) of long-ago suffering and victimization. Highlights were military humiliation under the Ottoman Empire and, more recently, Croatian-assisted atrocities committed during Nazi Germany's occupation of World War II. The time dimension also matters in judicial contexts. It was thus that the International Military Tribunal at Nuremberg (IMT) focused primarily on crimes committed after the outbreak of the war in 1939 to thereby avoid sovereignty-based legitimacy challenges.

7. Flint and de Waal (2008) further use the example of Sheik Hilal, father of the infamous Janjawiid leader Musa Hilal. The sheik reports on desertification and how this ecological process pushed the nomadic camel herders south and intensified conflict with sedentary Darfuri agriculturalists. Closer to the present, but yet long preceding the violence of 2003, Flint and de Waal (2008) describe a 1985 trip of the Sudanese minister of defense "to Kordofan and Darfur to mobilize Arab tribes against the SPLA" (23).

8. Hagan and Rymond-Richmond (2008) report that many ADS interviewees quote attackers as yelling racial epithets when they attacked villages, demanding: "Kill all the black people" (1). Their statistical analysis of the geographic distribution of killings shows that attackers spared villages identified as "Arab," even in the immediate vicinity of "Black" villages. Further, the death toll was especially high in places where racial epithets were more often heard during attacks. They conclude that racial intent joins other elements of the definition of genocide and that the violence in Darfur is indeed to be diagnosed as the first genocide of the twenty-first century.

9. For Mamdani (2009), both insurgency and counterinsurgency "were driven by an intermeshing of domestic tensions in the context of a peace-averse international environment defined by the War on Terror" (145–46). In addition to splits within the political elite and, locally, between nomads and settled farmers, imperial political interests are implicated. They benefit, Mamdani argues, from a depoliticized interpretation of the conflict in three ways: being granted the moral high ground; unifying otherwise contending forces, from "the Christian right and the Zionist lobby . . . [to] a mainly school- and university-based peace movement" (150); and legitimizing intervention, directly or through proxy forces. "A large part of the explanation . . . lies in the international context of the War on Terror, which favors parties who are averse to taking risks for peace" (152–53). As one major pillar of his causal model, Mamdani uses a postcolonial frame to interpret the violence in Darfur.

10. Just as cosmopolitan sensitivities, and the memories supporting them, are distinct from national scripts, they also differ from abstract principles of universalism. In cosmopolitanism the particularities of others remain relevant, while only a "universalistic minimum" is postulated; the contradiction between particularism (and associated "feeling") versus universalism (with its abstract Kantian principles) thus arrives at a new synthesis.

11. I sought to interview at least one journalist from each paper, one representative of the Sudan desk at each foreign ministry, and one Darfur expert each from the national sections of the two NGOs. Logistics of interviewing were

challenging, requiring travel to Berlin, Munich, Frankfurt, Bielefeld, Vienna, Bern, Geneva, Paris, The Hague, London, Dublin, Washington, DC, and New York City. Africa correspondents were only on occasional and brief visits in their home countries (in one case the correspondent had to leave the country [for Libya] on short notice on the day preceding the interviewer's arrival). Still, almost all interviews were conducted in person (only five over the phone, via Skype, or by mail), which is far superior as it allows the interviewer and interviewee to establish trust in the context of a sensitive theme.

12. I had co-organized the Bellagio conference together with my colleagues Jens Meierhenrich from the London School of Economics and John Hagan from Northwestern University and the American Bar Foundation.

13. Only one of our fourteen papers, the *Toronto Sun* does not fit this profile. Canada experts suggested we include this paper as a conservative contrast to the *Globe & Mail*.

14. Here I relied on librarian experts who assured me that all articles that appeared in print were available in LexisNexis and ProQuest Newsstand. Random checks supported that assessment.

15. Sudan also experienced a civil war between 1983 and 2005, pitting the North and the South against each other. We did not code articles that focused only on that civil war. In addition, violence in Darfur often crossed the border into Chad. We coded Darfuri refugees in Chad as victims; otherwise, we did not code the violence that took place outside Sudan's borders.

16. The *New York Times, Le Monde,* and the *SZ* were slightly oversampled for a few weeks of analytical work as we were solidifying the sampling scheme.

17. Cohen's Kappa was used in its form that allows for the pairwise assessment of coders in a team of coders. See "The Content Analysis Guidebook Online: An Accompaniment to *The Content Analysis Guidebook* by Kimberly A. Neuendorf," http://academic.csuohio.edu/kneuendorf/content/reliable/pram.htm (last retrieved May 11, 2015).

CHAPTER I

1. The ICC, however, cannot yet exercise its jurisdiction over crimes of aggression.

2. Once established, doxa diffuse through the international legal system, even if names shift, as Meierhenrich (2006) has shown for the notions of "conspiracy" (US law), "criminal organization" (IMT at Nuremberg), and "joint criminal enterprise" (ICTY).

3. http://www.icc-cpi.int/iccdocs/doc/doc639078.pdf (last retrieved December 23, 2013).

4. On ICC efforts to shape public opinion locally, see, for the case of Northern Uganda, Golden 2013.

5. In support of these arguments, see also the comprehensive literature review in Nobels 2010.

6. Multiple contributions at two conferences, one titled "Legal Frames of Memory," held in Warsaw in fall 2013, and the other "Contested Past, Contested Present: Social Memories and Human Rights in Post-Communist

Europe," held in Minneapolis in March 2015, provided evidence (see, e.g., Cercel 2013; Stan 2013; Nedelsky 2013; Czarnota 2015)

7. See Alexander 2004b:16–17; Osiel 1997. On the selectivities of Holocaust trials, see Douglas 2001.

8. Carla Del Ponte (2006, 2008), former chief prosecutor of the International Criminal Tribunal for the former Yugoslavia and for Rwanda, highlights the gaps of the judicial record even within the legal frame. She notes, among other factors, the lack of an enforcement agency to allow for more thorough investigations, the lack of cooperation with states that have vested interests in the outcomes, and the destruction of documents and disappearing witnesses. In short, despite best efforts, the material gathered and admissible at trials is often a fraction of the historical record.

9. "Conspiracy" refers to an agreement between two or more individuals entered into for the purpose of committing an unlawful act.

10. This tension is discussed by Max Weber (1978) in his sociology of law. Weber's arguments have been updated in more recent literature on technocratization (Stryker 1989), substantivation (Savelsberg 1992), responsive law (Nonet and Selznick 1978), and postliberal law (Unger 1976).

11. On the emergence and solidification of a semi-autonomous transnational legal field, see Dezalay and Garth 1997.

12. Those actors failed, however, who sought to allow *only* the UNSC to refer cases to the ICC.

13. http://legal.un.org/icc/statute/romefra.htm (last retrieved on January 22, 2014).

14. The court is further weakened by the fact that rich and powerful countries seek to protect themselves against potential ICC interventions. The United States, for example, has entered numerous bilateral immunity agreements that reward smaller countries for guarantees that they will not extradite American citizens to the ICC.

15. While court trials are limited by the logic of criminal law, the paper trails they leave behind also serve as sources for future and differing narratives. See, for example, Browning 1998, on "ordinary men," and Goldhagen 1996, on "Hitler's willing executioners," both based on court archives from the Hamburg Police Battalion trial.

CHAPTER 2

1. Amnesty International, 2013 entry, http://www.amnesty.org/en/library/asset/AFR54/007/2013/en/9233d37f-a7da-45d5-9e34-d4523289fb88/afr540072013en.pdf (last retrieved December 21, 2013).

2. "Sudan: Darfur: 'Too Many People Killed for No Reason,'" Amnesty International, February 3, 2004, http://www.amnesty.org/en/library/info/AFR54/008/2004/en (last retrieved January 23, 2014).

3. "Sudan: Darfur: Rape as a Weapon of War: Sexual Violence and Its Consequences," Amnesty International, July 18, 2004, http://www.amnesty.org/en/library/info/AFR54/076/2004/en (last retrieved January 23, 2014).

CHAPTER 3

1. UN Security Council, "Security Council Refers Situation in Darfur, Sudan, to Prosecutor of International Criminal Court" (press release), United Nations, March 31, 2005, http://www.un.org/News/Press/docs/2005/sc8351. doc.htm (last retrieved on January 15, 2014).

2. Media documents comprise all news articles or reports plus all opinion pieces. The total of reports or articles plus opinion pieces does not exactly add up to the total of documents, because coders in a few cases were not able to unambiguously categorize a media document as being of one or the other type.

3. The "whiskers" around the bars show confidence intervals, i.e., potential deviations of the value for the population from that of the sample. For "killings" and "rapes" we find no overlap, either for all documents or for opinion pieces. We can thus conclude with certainty that the differences apply to the population from which the sample was drawn. For news reports we find a small overlap. It is thus possible, though unlikely, that differences shown would not apply to the entire population of news reports. For "displacements" we find substantial overlap. Here the difference identified for the sample may thus not apply to the population of articles.

4. See note 3 for an explanation of confidence intervals, indicated by the "whiskers" around the bars. Results show that we may assume with certainty that citations of the genocide label apply to the full population of articles from which the sample was drawn. For uses of the crime frame we can conclude with certainty that the differences apply to all documents and to opinion pieces. We find a small overlap for news reports, for which there is thus a small chance that the patterns may not apply to the whole population.

5. An analysis of confidence intervals shows that there is a very small risk that these patterns would not hold up for the entire population of articles. The risk is somewhat larger for news articles (see note 3 for an explanation).

6. "The Crisis in Darfur," Secretary Colin L. Powell, Testimony before the Senate Foreign Relations Committee, September 9, 2004, US Department of State Archive, http://2001–2009.state.gov/secretary/former/powell/remarks/36042.htm (last retrieved January 23, 2014).

7. See also Ambassador Richard Williamson, President Bush's special envoy to Sudan, on the continuing justification of the policy to the US House of Representatives Subcommittee on International Monetary Policy and Trade of November 30, 2010. "The Need to Stand Up to Atrocity Crimes and the Sudan Accountability and Divestment Act" (testimony), Brookings Institution, http://www.brookings.edu/research/testimony/2010/11/30-sudan-divestment-williamson#. While expressing skepticism toward divestment policies generally, Williamson supported the current law in light of the situation on the ground and the uncompromising stance of the al-Bashir government.

8. Within the world of social movements the Save Darfur campaign was not the only force Amnesty activists had to contend with. Save Darfur wanted a somewhat different campaign, but others protested the Darfur campaign from the beginning: "I went to talk at Harvard and I was protested. Now, why are you supporting the capitalists who want oil in Sudan, why are you targeting

Muslims." It is in this context that the Amnesty interviewee referred to the post-colonialism position of Mahmood Mamdani discussed above, and to challenges resulting from previous US engagements, especially in Iraq with the human rights violations American personnel committed there, legally dubious imprisonment (e.g., at Guantanamo), and torture practices.

9. Research for this paper was funded by an REU (Research Experience for Undergraduates) grant from the National Science Foundation, supporting work by Meghan Zacher and supplementing my research grant (No. SES-0957946).

10. We selected documents published between January 1, 2003, and December 31, 2010, on each organization's website, including but not limited to press releases, reports from NGO workers in the field, interview transcripts, and position statements. We performed searches in subsections dedicated entirely to Sudan because these issue-specific sites best illustrate the intended representation each organization sought to convey through its website.

We viewed each document listed in these sections of the websites to ascertain which ones substantively engaged with the issue of Darfur. We compiled documents that discussed at least three of the variables in the coding scheme (discussed below), and randomly selected for coding one out of every three documents. Because of the small initial sample sizes, we randomly sampled additional documents from MSF and Save Darfur. In total, we sampled 65 documents from AI, 66 from MSF, and 62 from Save Darfur.

11. "Give ICC Jurisdiction to Prosecute Perpetrators of Atrocities in Sudan, Amnesty International Urges," Amnesty International, February 1, 2005 (no longer available on website).

12. "ICC Arrest Warrants," Save Darfur Coalition, May 2, 2007, http://ww20.savedarfur.org/index.php/pages/press/icc_arrest_warrants (last retrieved May 19, 2012), now archived at http://www.webcitation.org/67lcwnB4B.

CHAPTER 4

1. This is not accidental, as Ireland is characterized by a foreign policy focused on humanitarian and development aid. It is for this reason that Ireland, while not a heavyweight in international relations, provides valuable insights, as we shall see.

2. Again, for lawyerly-versus-technocratic patterns of knowledge generally, see Stryker 1989.

3. See International Red Cross and Red Crescent Museum 2000: especially 122–225 (highlighting the organization's humanitarian benefits with regard to the Nazi concentration camps).

4. "Founding of MSF," MSF USA, n.d., http://www.doctorswithoutborders.org/about-us/history-and-principles/founding-of-msf (last retrieved May 23, 2015). For a competing account, see Weissman 2011. Fabrice Weissman of MSF argues that the witnessing mission was introduced only in 1977, a contradiction that indicates internal mnemonic struggles over the appropriate definition of MSF's history and identity.

5. This decision prompted a split-off of some of its founders, who then established Médecins du Monde as a new association of doctors that maintained the early informality of MSF.

6. www.doctorswithoutborders.org/founding-msf (last retreived July 15, 2015).

7. Included in this study are interviews with members of two of the operational centers (France and Switzerland) and three supportive sections (Austria, the United Kingdom, and the United States).

8. "Charter," MSF USA, n.d., http://www.doctorswithoutborders.org/about-us/history-and-principles/charter (last retrieved March 8, 2014).

9. In one case an interview request was declined with the argument that "MSF Ireland is a very new MSF office (opened in 2006) and does not have an operational role within the MSF movement."

10. June 21, 2004, http://www.doctorswithoutborders.org/article/emergency-darfur-sudan-no-relief-sight (last retrieved March 6, 2014).

11. Lacking the counterfactual, we do not know if such "transparency" affects the content of the reports and press releases through which the humanitarian aid organization informs the wider public of the violence and suffering in the area of conflict.

CHAPTER 5

1. At 0.081% of GNI, Ireland's aid budget is around four times higher than the respective values for Austria, Canada, France, and the United States, and about twice as high as those for the United Kingdom and Switzerland.

2. The *Irish Times* correspondent who originally agreed to an interview had to leave Dublin the day before our meeting to report about the dramatic events unfolding in Libya in March 2011. In her place, she recommended the correspondent I in fact interviewed, a person with substantial knowledge whose understanding of Darfur corresponded well with her own.

3. In the words of the organization's website: "Irish Aid is the Irish Government's programme for overseas development. The programme is managed by the Development Co-operation Division of the Department of Foreign Affairs and Trade. The work we do in fighting global poverty and hunger is integral to Ireland's foreign policy" (https://www.irishaid.ie/about-us/ [last retrieved May 24, 2015]).

4. "About Trócaire," http://www.trocaire.org/whatwedo/who-we-are (last retrieved March 19, 2014).

5. "About Concern," Concern Worldwide, https://www.concern.net/about (last retrieved March 19, 2014).

6. "About Us," GOAL, http://www.goal.org/about-us/our-story (last retrieved May 24, 2015).

7. On its website, however, GOAL declares that it is a nondenominational, nongovernmental, and apolitical organization.

8. The "whiskers" around the bars show confidence intervals, i.e., potential deviations of the whole-population value from that of the sample. For "displacements" we find no overlap for any of the document types. We can thus conclude with certainty that the differences apply to the population from which the sample was drawn. For "killings" we find substantial overlap and for "rapes" some. Here the difference identified for the sample may thus not apply to the population of articles.

9. Confidence intervals are relatively large because of the comparatively small number of Irish articles for which the crime frame and genocide label could be identified. There is thus a statistical chance that patterns identified may not hold up for the entire population of articles. Note, however, that patterns measured for the sample all point in the same direction and perfectly correspond with the qualitative findings. This may give us substantial confidence that the patterns identified for the sample also apply for the entire population of news reports and opinion pieces.

10. References to the Holocaust were too rare to allow for a quantitative comparison.

CHAPTER 6

1. Karen Smith (2010) follows Finnemore (2000) in arguing that the social (as opposed to the legal) norm against genocide is particularly consequential. It entails a strong commitment to act.

2. Such differences between the rationales of diplomats versus criminal justice officials have previously been depicted in studies on international responses to the civil wars in the former Yugoslavia (Hagan 2003; Savelsberg and King 2011: ch. 4).

3. We identified 210 press releases that focused on Darfur from foreign ministries in Austria, Canada, Germany, Ireland, Switzerland, the United Kingdom, and the United States, dated 2003–2012 (for Germany, 2008–2012; France omitted due to coder language constraints). Each document was coded for suggested solutions (judicial interventions, diplomatic negotiations, humanitarian aid delivery, peacekeeping operations, and military intervention) and framing (crime, humanitarian, conflict/war). Less suited for cross-country comparisons (each country's foreign ministry follows its own styles and policies, and inclusion of a theme has country-specific meaning), this analysis indicates which frames and types of solutions are privileged *within* each country. Suzy McElrath, a graduate research assistant whose work was supported by funding from the Center for German and European Studies at the University of Minnesota, conducted this analysis.

4. Intuition may of course be misleading. Autesserre (2009) shows, in her detailed study of international peace builders in the Democratic Republic of Congo, how deeply internalized frames that disregard the centrality of local conflict definitions contribute to failure.

5. The same respondent similarly critiqued the estimates of victimization numbers from the North-South conflict in Sudan.

6. Percentages do not add up to 100, because not every press release allows for the identification of a frame, but each may suggest more than one solution.

CHAPTER 7

1. Even the People's Republic of China (PRC) implemented policy changes, for example, by ceasing to resist the establishment of a UN peacekeeping force. Yet China certainly did not use strong rhetoric against the government of Sudan.

2. Some of the forces cited here are the same that affect nation-specific patterns within the civil society branches of the human rights and humanitarian aid fields, documented in the analyses of Amnesty International and MSF, in confirmation of Stroup's (2012) findings. Causal factors examined there should also apply to foreign policy, some even more directly.

3. Paul Slatin is a descendent of "Slatin Pascha," a nineteenth-century Austrian military officer who served in the British colonial administration as *mudir* (governor) of Dara, the southwestern part of Darfur, and, after 1881, as governor-general of Darfur, a role in which he led bloody campaigns against the Mahdist Revolt in the "Anglo-Sudan War."

4. Germany's sense of obligation may, in this case, have been helped by the fact that it was less involved in the Sudanese North-South negotiations and thus less concerned about the risks that the Darfur case would pose for the talks.

5. My interviewee characterized Steinmeier's successor, Guido Westerwelle, as more proactive. Westerwelle instituted a task force on Sudan, especially in response to the expected separation between North and South and the potential consequences for other African countries.

CHAPTER 8

1. Bourdieu (1998) recognizes the weight of this distinction. He argues in fact that the division of media between television and elite newspapers reinforces a bifurcated public (18).

2. Niklas Luhmann (1971) would characterize autonomy as the ability of a system to steer and filter input from other systems.

3. The objectivity rule dominates in the journalism world in most of the countries under investigation. Only France constitutes something of an exception.

4. Revers (2013) analyzes the risk of "pollution" by political forces to which those journalists are especially exposed who report on legislatures. These journalists engage in struggles to negotiate the boundaries between their own journalistic field and that of politics.

5. As pointed out in the introduction, this characterization applies only partially to the Canadian media selection.

6. Travel logistics, given here as the primary reason, contribute to this underrepresentation. But consider also the following comment by the (not French) journalist just quoted: "In 2005, after these civil war–like troubles in Côte d'Ivoire, . . . I moved to Johannesburg, also quite simply because the logistics broke down in Abidjan. Air connections became irregular. Several embassies—African embassies, that is—left Abidjan, which made it very difficult for me to still get visas. The situation became untenable" (author's translation).

7. One senior editorialist I interviewed is a notable exception to this rule. But he works out of his home country. Having worked for his paper first in Scandinavia and later as the US editor based in Washington, DC, he returned to his capital city, where he became the foreign editor of his paper and in 2004 the paper's foreign affairs columnist ("the [paper's] voice"). "And at that time, the first time, I personally began to write on issues such as of Darfur."

8. There are exceptions, of course, as in most fields of professional work. One journalist for a British paper conceded that the social ties exist (that are "historical among correspondents, people who travel together and socialize together"), but characterized his own style as that of a "loner . . . I think I'm probably more in line with the sort of lonely foreign correspondent image. And certainly, previously in Darfur. . . . I was completely on my own." A German correspondent displayed more of the competitive traits that Bourdieu (1998) associates with the journalistic field: "I avoid such contact for one very simple reason. I had very bad experiences with colleagues in Abidjan. The civil war in Côte d'Ivoire began; simultaneously war raged in neighboring Liberia. I had contacts. I knew how to move around. And many colleagues exploited this shamelessly, without me receiving anything in return. And since then I have been avoiding journalists" (author's translation).

CHAPTER 9

1. On the correlation between Western coverage of African conflicts and the scale of involvement by Western countries, see also McNulty (1999:269).

2. Chaon (2007) investigates this delay for the Rwandan genocide. She attributes responsibility primarily to the media, in particular those in positions of authority in news departments, rather than to journalists themselves.

3. In her analysis of a different, albeit overlapping, set of news media, Mody (2010) confirms this peak.

4. On the intense spate of editorial writing on Darfur for the months of April–September 2004, see Murphy (2007).

5. This warrant was put on hold in January 2015 by ICC chief prosecutor Fatou Bensouda, in part to protest the lack of enforcement action by the international community.

6. Generally, military conflicts alone prompt restrictions on journalistic work, as exemplified by several commentators at the Asser Institute conference "On the Frontline of Accountability: War Reporting and Related Contemporary Issues in International and Humanitarian Law," held in January 2011 in The Hague, on the issue of journalistic reporting from war zones. Journalists commonly depend on militarized parties in the conflict for access and face threats from the contending military forces.

7. In addition to impediments and dependencies arising from the political field, journalists are always at risk of being instrumentalized. At the 2011 Asser Institute conference, reports from war correspondents and others working on war journalism abounded about risks of "military censorship" (Geoffrey Robertson, former judge for the Special Court for Sierra Leone [SCSL]), "weaponization of information" (Julia Hoffmann, Amsterdam) and "information warfare" (Robert Heinsch, Leiden). The risk is enhanced by dangers that correspondents are exposed to and aware of, even though Western journalists enjoy better protections than local ones (Blake Evans-Pritchard, The Hague).

8. Also, the newspaper industry witnessed a massive decline in revenue in the years after 2008 (especially in the United States, where print media depend heavily on advertisement). Correspondents (foreign more than domestic) are

4 4 4

often the first to whom staff cuts apply, a factor possibly contributing to the decline of coverage on Darfur from 2008 to 2010. I thank Matthias Revers, sociologist of journalism, for alerting me to this potential cause for declining media attention. Future research should pay attention.

9. A study of media representations of a massive factory fire that killed many workers showed that news reporting was most intense immediately after the tragedy occurred and, at the other end of the process, when the criminal court made public its decisions against responsible actors (Wright, Cullen, and Blankenship 1995).

10. Human rights talk may, alternatively, be denounced as a "tool of intellectual combat" in the hands of enemies of democracy—rhetoric used by Michael Chertof, US secretary of homeland security during the George W. Bush administration (Gordon 2014).

11. Interestingly, Vasagar's source for this quote is the US-based *People Magazine*.

12. This seeming paradox is, of course, not unique to the types of crime at stake here (nor is it unique to issues of crime and punishment). In debates about drug crimes, to pick just one example, acceptance of the criminal nature of the action may be associated with pleas for public health strategies as superior to criminal justice responses.

13. Close relationships do not guarantee against mistrust, however. One German correspondent warned that NGO victim counts were inflated because high numbers enhanced the organizations' appeals to potential donors.

14. See Doctors Without Borders, June 21, 2004, http://www.doctorswithoutborders.org/news-stories/press-release/emergency-darfur-sudan-no-relief-sight (last retrieved May 31, 2015).

15. Conversely, a journalist's Africa experience may change his or her view of his or her country's own history. A British correspondent with part–Catholic Irish roots told me: "I see it more from both sides now" JJS: "Has your view of Irish history changed?" "It pretty much has over time. . . . Certainly my work in Africa overall has; maybe I've become more cynical. . . . I used to think that Irish Republicanism had all the answers, and I think I am now much more reluctant to listen to the ideologists battling it out. I believe much more in compromise and negotiation and quiet diplomacy than I used to."

16. What applies to the journalistic field is true for all others. The fields overlap with national conditions. Bourdieu, in his work, typically examines distinct fields in the French national context, and in all cases the shape of fields differs from that in their counterparts in other countries. The reader of *Homo Academicus* (Bourdieu 1984), for example, needs an introduction to the French academic system to fully comprehend the book. In short, while fields may be characterized by quasi-universal laws, an appropriate understanding of patterns of production requires specification of national contexts. For important steps in that direction, see Benson (2013) for his analysis of immigration news in France and the United States.

17. Confidence intervals show that outliers overlap somewhat with countries in the middle field of the distribution. There is, however, no overlap between low-end outliers and the high-end outlier.

CHAPTER 10

1. On the impact on foreign policy, see Hawkins 2002; Walgrave, Soroka, and Nuytemans 2008; on public opinion, see McCombs and Shaw 1972; Wanta and Hu 1993; on allocation of foreign aid, see Van Belle and Hook 2000; Rioux and Van Belle 2005; and on presidential actions, see Wood and Peake 1998.

2. Such causal ties between memory and policy are in line with findings from previous comparative research on the effects of national memories of hate-driven violence on hate crime law and its enforcement (Savelsberg and King 2005, 2011).

POSTSCRIPT

1. "Security Council Inaction on Darfur 'Can Only Embolden Perpetrators'—ICC Prosecutor," UN News Centre, December 12, 2014, http://www.un.org/apps/news/story.asp?NewsID=49591#.VNzuuS6zmxY (last retrieved June 3, 2015). The *New York Times* reported a "hibernation" of the "case against Sudan's President Omar al-Bashir on charges of genocide"—with wording that, in line with observations made in chapter 3) focuses on the top of Sudan's political and military hierarchy and on the gravest of charges.

2. In the fall of 2014, the prosecutor's decision to withdraw charges against President Kenyatta of Kenya provided a poignant example of high-level diplomacy interacting with the judicial field.

3. "UNAMID Facts and Figures," UNAMID: African Union/United Nations Hybrid Operation in Darfur, http://www.un.org/en/peacekeeping/missions/unamid/facts.shtml (last retrieved February 25, 2015).

4. Eric Reeves, "Sudan: Research, Analysis, and Advocacy," http://sudanreeves.org/ (last retrieved June 3, 2015); Radio Dabanga: Independent News from the Heart of Darfur and Sudan, https://www.dabangasudan.org/en (last retrieved June 3, 2015); "Plural News and Views on Sudan," *Sudan Tribune,* http://www.sudantribune.com/ (last retrieved June 3, 2015).

5. "Newly Displaced Seek Protection and Humanitarian Assistance Outside UNAMID Base in North Darfur," UNAMID—African Union–United Nations Mission in Darfur, http://unamid.unmissions.org/Default.aspx?tabid=11028&ctl=Details&mid=14215&ItemID=24406&language=en-US> (last retrieved June 3, 2015).

6. "Sudan: Mass Rape by Army in Darfur" Human Rights Watch, http://www.hrw.org/news/2015/02/11/sudan-mass-rape-army-darfur (last retrieved June 3, 2015).

References

Alexander, Jeffrey C. 2004a. "On the Social Construction of Moral Universals: The 'Holocaust' from War Crime to Trauma Drama." Pp. 196–263 in *Cultural Trauma and Collective Identity*. Edited by J. C. Alexander et al. Berkeley: University of California Press.

———. 2004b. "Toward a Theory of Cultural Trauma." Pp. 1–30 in *Cultural Trauma and Collective Identity*. Edited by J. C. Alexander et al. Berkeley: University of California Press.

Alexander, Jeffrey C., Ron Eyerman, Bernhard Giesen, Neil J. Smelser, and Pjotr Sztompka, eds. 2004. *Cultural Trauma and Collective Identity*. Berkeley: University of California Press.

Allen, Tim, and Jean Seaton, eds. 1999. *The Media in Conflict: War Reporting and Representations of Ethnic Violence*. New York: St. Martin's Press.

Annan, Kofi. 2004. "UN Secretary-General Kofi Annan's Plan to Prevent Genocide." Address to the UN General Assembly, April 7. http://www.preventgenocide.org/prevent/UNdocs/KofiAnnansActionPlantoPreventGenocide-7Apr2004.htm. Last retrieved May 13, 2015.

Autesserre, Séverine. 2009. "Hobbes and the Congo: Frames, Local Violence, and International Intervention." *International Organization* 63(2):249–280.

Baechler, Günther. 2011. "Darfur in the Middle of Crisscrossing Fault Lines That Shape the Sudan: Can Switzerland Help to Promote Peace?" Pp. 79–94 in *The Politics of Peace: From Ideology to Pragmatism?* Edited by Laurent Goetschel. Berlin: LIT.

Baer, Alejandro. 2011. "The Voids of Sephard: The Memory of the Holocaust in Spain." *Journal of Spanish Cultural Studies* 12(1):95–120.

Barkan, Elazar. 2013. "Justifying Atrocities: Contested Victims." Lecture presented at Legal Frames of Memory conference, Warsaw, Poland.

Bass, Gary Jonathan. 2000. *Stay the Hand of Vengeance: The Politics of War Crimes Tribunals*. Princeton, NJ: Princeton University Press.

Beck, Ulrich, and Natan Sznaider. 2006. "Unpacking Cosmopolitanism for the Social Sciences: A Research Agenda." *British Journal of Sociology* 57(1):1–23.

Bendix, Reinhard. [1949] 1974. *Higher Civil Servants in American Society*. Westport, Conn.: Greenwood Press.

Benford, Robert D, and David A. Snow. 2000. "Framing Processes and Social Movements." *Annual Review of Sociology* 26:611–639.

Benson, Rodney. 1998. "Field Theory in Comparative Context: A New Paradigm for Media Studies." *Theory and Society* 28(3):463–498.

———. 2006. "News Media as a 'Journalistic Field': What Bourdieu Adds to Neo-Institutionalism, and Vice Versa." *Political Communication* 23(2):187–202.

———. 2013. *Shaping Immigration News: A French-American Comparison*. New York: Cambridge University Press.

Benson, Rodney, and Erik Neveu, eds. 2005. *Bourdieu and the Journalistic Field*. Cambridge: Polity Press.

Berger, Peter, and Thomas Luckmann. 1966. *The Social Construction of Reality: A Treatise in the Sociology of Knowledge*. New York: Anchor Books.

Black, Donald. 1993. *The Social Structure of Right and Wrong*. San Diego, CA: Academic Press.

Boltanski, Luc. 1999. *Distant Suffering: Morality, Media and Politics*. Translated by Graham Burchell. Cambridge: Cambridge University Press.

Bortolotti, Dan, 2010. *Hope in Hell: Inside the World of Doctors Without Borders*. Buffalo, NY: Firefly Books.

Bourdieu, Pierre. 1987. "The Force of Law: Toward a Sociology of the Juridical Field." Translated by R. Terdiman. *Hastings Law Journal* 38(5): 805–853.

———. 1988. *Homo Academicus*. Stanford: Stanford University Press.

———. 1998. *On Television*. New York: New Press.

Boyle, Elizabeth Heger. 2002. *Female Genital Cutting: Cultural Conflict in the Global Community*. Baltimore: Johns Hopkins University Press.

Boyle, Elizabeth Heger, and John Meyer. 1998. "Modern Law as a Secularized and Global Model: Implications for the Sociology of Law. *Soziale Welt* 49(3):275–294.

Browning, Christopher Robert. 1998. *Ordinary Men: Reserve-Police Batallion 101 and the Final Solution in Poland*. New York: HarperPerennial.

Burkhardt, Sven-Uwe. 2005. *Vergewaltigung als Verbrechen gegen die Menschlichkeit: Sexualisierte Gewalt, Makrokriminalität und Völkerstrafrecht*. Münster: LIT Verlag.

Cercel, Cosmin S. 2013. "Anxieties of the Nomos: Fascism, Communism and Discontinuity on Post-war Romania." Paper presented at Legal Frames of Memory conference, Warsaw, Poland.

Chambliss, Bill. 1964. "A Sociological Analysis of the Law of Vagrancy." *Social Problems* 12(1):67–77.

Chaon, Anne. 2007. "Who Failed in Rwanda, Journalists or the Media?" Pp. 160–166 in *The Media and the Rwanda Genocide*. Edited by Allen Thompson. London: Pluto Press.

Cohen, Stanley. 2001. *States of Denial: Knowing about Atrocities and Suffering*. Cambridge: Polity Press.

Cooney, Mark. 1997. "From Warre to Tyranny: Lethal Conflict and the State." *American Sociological Review* 62(2):316–338.

Crilly, Rob. 2010. *Saving Darfur: Everyone's Favourite African War*. London: Reportage Press.

Czarnota, Adam. 2015. "Law as Mnemosyne Married with Lethe: Quasi-judicial Institutions and Collective Memories." Paper presented at Contested Past, Contested Present: Social Memories and Human Rights in Post-Communist Europe conference, Minneapolis, 2015.

Dayan, Daniel, and Elihu Katz. 1992. *Media Events: The Live Broadcasting of History*. Cambridge, MA: Harvard University Press.

Degomme, Olivier, and Debarati Guha-Sapir. 2010. "Patterns of Mortality Rates in Darfur Conflict." *The Lancet* 375:294–300.

Deitelhoff, Nicole. 2009. "The Discursive Process of Legalization: Charting Islands of Persuasion in the ICC Case." *International Organization* 63:33–65.

Del Ponte, Carla. 2006. "Investigation and Prosecution of Large-Scale Crimes at the International Level: The Experience of the ICTY." *Journal of International Criminal Justice* 4:539–555.

———. 2008. *Madame Prosecutor: Confrontations with Humanity's Worst Criminals and the Culture of Impunity*. Milan, Italy: Feltrinelli Editore.

de Waal, Alex. 1997. *Famine Crimes: Politics and the Disaster Relief Industry in Africa*. Bloomington: Indiana University Press.

———, ed. 2007. *War in Darfur and the Search for Peace*. Boston: Global Equity Initiative.

Dezalay, Yves, and Bryant G. Garth. 1997. *Dealing in Virtue: International Commercial Arbitration and the Construction of a Transnational Legal Order*. Chicago: University of Chicago Press.

Douglas, Lawrence. 2001. *Making Law and History in the Trials of the Holocaust*. New Haven: Yale University Press.

Durkheim, Emile. [1912] 2001. *The Elementary Forms of Religious Life*. Translated by Carol Cosman. Oxford: Oxford University Press.

Edelman, Murray J. 1985. *The Symbolic Uses of Politics*. Urbana: University of Illinois Press.

Eisner, Manuel. 2001. "Modernization, Self-Control and Lethal Violence." *British Journal of Criminology* 41(4):618–638.

Elias, Norbert. 1978. *The Civilizing Process*. 1st American ed. New York: Urizen Books.

Emirbayer, Mustafa, and Victoria Johnson. 2008. "Bourdieu and Organizational Analysis." *Theory and Society* 37(1):1–44.

Fichtelberg, Aaron. 2005. "Crimes beyond Justice—Retributivism and War Crimes." *Criminal Justice Ethics* 24:31–46.

Finnemore, Martha. 2000. "Are Legal Norms Distinctive?" *Journal of International Law and Politics* 32:699–705.

Fligstein, Neil. 2001. "Social Skill and the Theory of Fields." *Sociological Theory* 19(2):105–125.

Fligstein, Neil, and Doug McAdam. 2011. "Toward a General Theory of Strategic Action Fields." *Sociological Theory* 29(1):1–26.

Flint, Julie, and Alex de Waal. 2008. *Darfur: A New History of a Long War.* London: Zed Books.

Fourcade, Marion, and Joachim J. Savelsberg. 2006. "Introduction: Global Processes, National Institutions, Local Bricolage: Shaping Law in an Era of Globalization." *Law and Social Inquiry* 31:513–519.

Frank, David John, Ann Hironaka, and Evan Schofer. 2000. "The Nation-State and the Natural Environment over the Twentieth Century." *American Sociological Review* 65(1):96–116.

Galanter, Marc. 1974. "Why the Haves Come Out Ahead: Speculations on the Limits of Legal Change." *Law and Society Review* 9(1):95–160.

Gans, Herbert J. 2005. *Deciding What's News: A Study of* CBS Evening News, NBC Nightly News, Newsweek *and* Time. Evanston, IL: Northwestern University Press.

Geertz, Clifford. 1973. "Ideology as a Cultural System." Pp. 193–233 in *The Interpretation of Cultures: Selected Essays by Clifford Geertz.* New York: Basic Books.

Giesen, Bernhard. 2004a. "The Trauma of Perpetrators: The Holocaust as the Traumatic Reference of German National Identity." Pp. 112–154 in *Cultural Trauma and Collective Identity.* Edited by J. C. Alexander et al. Berkeley: University of California Press.

———. 2004b. *Triumph and Trauma.* Boulder, CO: Paradigm.

Goffman, Erving. 1986. *Frame Analysis: An Essay on the Organization of Experience.* Boston: Northeastern University Press.

Golden, Shannon. 2013. "After Atrocity: Community Reconstruction in Northern Uganda." PhD dissertation, University of Minnesota.

Goldhagen, Daniel Jonah. 1996. *Hitler's Willing Executioners: Ordinary Germans and the Holocaust.* New York: Knopf.

Goldsmith, Jack, and Stephen D. Krasner. 2003. "The Limits of Idealism." *Daedalus* 132(1):47–63.

Gordon, Neve. 2014. "Human Rights as a Security Threat: Lawfare and the Campaign against Human Rights NGOs." *Law and Society Review* 48(2):311–344.

Gorski, Philip S. 2003. *The Disciplinary Revolution: Calvinism and the Rise of the State in Early Modern Europe.* Chicago: University of Chicago Press.

Gusfield, Joseph 1967. "Moral Passage: Symbolic Process in Public Designation of Deviance." *Social Problems* 15(2):175–188.

Hafner-Burton, Emilie M., and Kiyoteru Tsutsui. 2005. "Human Rights in a Globalizing World: The Paradox of Empty Promises." *American Journal of Sociology* 110(5):1373–1411.

Hagan, John. 2003. *Justice in the Balkans: Prosecuting War Crimes in the Hague Tribunal.* Chicago Series in Law and Society. Chicago: University of Chicago Press.

Hagan, John, and Ron Levi. 2005. "Crimes of War and the Force of Law." *Social Forces* 83(4):1499–1534.

Hagan, John, and Alberto Palloni. 2006. "Death in Darfur." *Science* 313(5793):1578–1579.

Hagan, John, and Wenona Rymond-Richmond. 2008. *Darfur and the Crime of Genocide.* Cambridge: Cambridge University Press.

Hagan, John, Heather Schoenfeld, and Alberto Palloni. 2006. "The Science of Human Rights, War Crimes, and Humanitarian Emergencies." *Annual Review of Sociology* 32:329–349.

Halbwachs, Maurice. 1992. *On Collective Memory.* The Heritage of Sociology. Chicago: University of Chicago Press.

Halliday, Terence C., and Bruce G. Carruthers. 2007. "The Recursivity of Law: Global Norm Making and National Lawmaking in the Globalization of Corporate Insolvency Regimes." *American Journal of Sociology* 112(4):1135–1202.

———. 2009. *Bankrupt: Global Law Making and Systemic Financial Crisis.* Stanford: Stanford University Press.

Hannerz, Ulf. 2004. *Foreign News: Exploring the World of Foreign Correspondents.* Chicago: University of Chicago Press.

Harding, Sandra. 1996. "Standpoint Epistemology (a Feminist Version): How Social Disadvantage Creates Epistemic Advantage." Pp. 146–160 in *Social Theory and Sociology.* Edited by Stephen P. Turner. Oxford: Blackwell.

Hawkins, Virgil. 2002. "The Other Side of the CNN Factor: The Media and Conflict." *Journalism Studies* 3(2):225–240.

ICID (International Commission of Inquiry on Darfur). 2005. *Report of the International Commission of Inquiry on Darfur to the Secretary-General of the United Nations.* Geneva, January 25. http://www.un.org/news/dh/sudan/com_inq_darfur.pdf. Last retrieved May 13, 2015.

International Red Cross and Red Crescent Museum. 2000. Exhibition catalogue. Geneva: International Red Cross and Red Crescent Museum.

Jardim, Tomaz. 2012. *The Mauthausen Trial: American Military Justice in Germany.* Cambridge, MA: Harvard University Press.

Jenness, Valerie. 2004. "Explaining Criminalization: From Demography and Status Politics to Globalization and Modernization." *Annual Review of Sociology* 30:147–171.

Johnson, Eric A., and Eric H. Monkkonen, eds. 1996. *The Civilization of Crime: Violence in Town and Country since the Middle Ages.* Urbana: University of Illinois Press.

Kaiser, Joshua, and John Hagan. 2015. "Gendered Genocide: Rape, Murder, and Forced Displacement in Darfur." *Law and Society Review* 49(1):69–108.

Kalberg, Stephen. 1994. *Max Weber's Comparative-Historical Sociology.* Chicago: University of Chicago Press.

———. 2014. *Searching for the Spirit of American Democracy: Max Weber's Analysis of a Unique Political Culture, Past, Present, and Future.* Boulder, CO: Paradigm.

Keck, Margaret E., and Kathryn Sikkink. 1998. *Activists beyond Borders: Advocacy Networks in International Politics.* Ithaca, NY: Cornell University Press.

Kennedy, David. 2004. *The Dark Sides of Virtue: Reassessing International Humanitarianism.* Princeton, NJ: Princeton University Press.

Khagram, Sanjeev, James Riker, and Kathryn Sikkink. 2002. *Restructuring World Politics: Transnational Social Movements, Networks, and Norms.* Minneapolis: University of Minnesota Press.

Kim, Hunjoon, and Kathryn Sikkink. 2010. "Explaining the Deterrence Effect of Human Rights Prosecutions for Transitional Countries." *International Studies Quarterly* 54(4):939–963.

King, Ryan D. 2005. "When Law and Society Disagree: Group Threat, Legacies of the Past, and the Organizational Context of Hate Crime Law Enforcement." PhD dissertation, University of Minnesota, Minneapolis.

Krause, Monika. 2014. *The Good Project: Humanitarian Relief NGOs and the Fragmentation of Reason.* Chicago: University of Chicago Press.

Kydd, Andrew H. 2006. "When Can Mediators Build Trust?" *American Political Science Review* 100(3):449–462.

Landsman, Stephan. 2005. *Crimes of the Holocaust: The Law Confronts Hard Cases.* Pennsylvania Studies in Human Rights. Philadelphia: University of Pennsylvania Press.

Lanz, David. 2009. "Save Darfur: A Movement and Its Discontents." *African Affairs* 108(433):669–677.

Lenoir, Remi. 1994. "La Parole est aux juges: Crise de la magistrature et champs journalistique." *Actes de la Recherche en Sciences Sociales* 101–102:77–84.

Levi, Primo. 1988. *The Drowned and the Saved.* New York: Simon and Schuster.

Levy, Daniel, and Natan Sznaider. 2010. *Human Rights and Memory.* Essays on Human Rights. University Park: Pennsylvania State University Press.

Luhmann, Niklas. 1971. "Soziologie des politschen Systems." Pp. 154–177 in *Soziologische Aufklärung.* Köln/Opladen: Westdeutscher Verlag.

———. 2004. *Law as a Social System.* Oxford: Oxford University Press.

Mamdani, Mahmood. 2009a. *Saviors and Survivors: Darfur, Politics, and the War on Terror.* New York: Doubleday.

———. 2009b. "The Politics of Naming: Genocide, Civil War, Insurgency." Pp. 145–153 in *Darfur and the Crisis of Governance in Sudan: A Critical Reader.* Edited by Salah M. Hassan and Carina E. Ray. Ithaca, NY: Cornell University Press.

Mannheim, Karl. 1952. *Essays on the Sociology of Knowledge.* London: Routledge and Kegan Paul.

Marrus, Michael. 2008. "The Nuremberg Doctors' Trial and the Limitations of Context." Pp. 103–122 in *Atrocities on Trial.* Edited by Patricia Heberer and Jürgen Matthäus. Lincoln: University of Nebraska Press.

Mason, Simon J. A., and David Lanz. 2009. "Mehrwert oder Leerlauf? Der 'Whole of Government'-Ansatz der Schweiz im Sudan." *Bulletin zur Schweizerischen Sicherheitspolitik* 2009:57–82.

Matsueda, Ross L., Derek A. Kreager, and David Huizinga. 2006. "Deterring Delinquents: A Rational Choice Model of Theft and Violence." *American Sociological Review* 71(1):95–122.

Mazzoleni, Gianpietro, and Winfried Schulz. 1999. "'Mediatization' of Politics: A Challenge for Democracy?" *Political Communication* 16(3):247–261.

McCarthy, Bill. 2002. "New Economics of Sociological Criminology." *Annual Review of Sociology* 28:417–442.

McCombs, Maxwell E., and Donald L. Shaw. 1972. "The Agenda-Setting Function of Mass Media." *Public Opinion Quarterly* 36(2):176–187.

McNulty, Mel. 1999. "Media Ethnicization and the International Response to War and Genocide In Rwanda." Pp. 268–286 in *The Media in Conflict: War Reporting and Representations of Ethnic Violence*. Edited by Tim Allen and Jean Eaton. New York: St. Martin's Press.

Mead, George Herbert. 1918. "The Psychology of Punitive Justice." *American Journal of Sociology* 23(5):577–602.

Meierhenrich, Jens. 2006. "Conspiracy in International Law." *Annual Review of Law and Social Science* 2(1):341–357.

———. 2014. "The Evolution of the Office of the Prosecutor at the International Criminal Court: Insights from Institutional Theory." Pp. 97–127 in *The First Global Prosecutor*. Edited by Martha Minow, Alex Whiting, and Cora True-Frost. Ann Arbor: University of Michigan Press.

Meyer, John W., Francisco O. Ramirez, and Yasemin Nohoglu Soysal. 1992. "World Expansion of Mass Education, 1870–1980." *Sociology of Education* 65(2):128–149.

Minow, Martha. 1998. *Between Vengeance and Forgiveness: Facing History after Genocide and Mass Violence*. Boston: Beacon Press.

———. 2002. *Breaking the Cycles of Hatred: Memory, Law, and Repair*. Introduced and with commentaries by Nancy L. Rosenblum. Princeton, NJ: Princeton University Press.

Mody, Bella. 2010. *The Geopolitics of Representation in Foreign News: Explaining Darfur*. Lanham, MD: Lexington Books.

Murphy, Deborah 2007. "Narrating Darfur: Darfur in the U.S. Press, March–September 2004." Pp. 314–336 in *War in Darfur and the Search for Peace*. Edited by Alex de Waal. Cambridge, MA: Harvard University Press.

Mutua, Makau. 2002. *Human Rights: A Political and Cultural Critique*. Philadelphia: University of Pennsylvania Press.

Nedelsky, Nadya. 2013. "Transitional Justice and Civil Society in Slovakia." Paper presented at Legal Frames of Memory conference, Warsaw, Poland.

Neier, Aryeh. 2012. *The International Human Rights Movement: A History*. Princeton, NJ: Princeton University Press.

Nobels, Melissa. 2010. "The Prosecution of Human Rights Violations." *Annual Review of Political Science* 13:165–182.

Nonet, Philippe, and Philip Selznick. 1978. *Law and Society in Transition: Toward Responsive Law*. New York: Octagon Books.

Olick, Jeffrey K. 1999. "Genre Memories and Memory Genres: A Dialogical Analysis of May 8, 1945 Commemorations in the Federal Republic of Germany." *American Sociological Review* 64:381–402.

Olick, Jeffrey K., and Daniel Levy. 1997. "Collective Memory and Cultural Constraint: Holocaust Myth and Rationality in German Politics." *American Sociological Review* 62(6):921–936.

Osiel, Mark. 1997. *Mass Atrocity, Collective Memory, and the Law*. New Brunswick, NJ: Transaction.

———. 2014. "The Demise of International Criminal Law." *Humanity Journal*, June 10. http://www.humanityjournal.net/blog/the-demise-of-international-criminal-law/. Accessed May 13, 2015.

Pendas, Devin O. 2006. *The Frankfurt Auschwitz Trial, 1963–65: Genocide, History and the Limits of the Law.* Cambridge: Cambridge University Press.

Pensky, Max. 2008. "Amnesty on Trial: Impunity, Accountability, and the Norms of International Law." *Ethics and Global Politics* 1(1–2):1–40.

Power, Samantha. 2002. *A Problem from Hell: America and the Age of Genocide.* New York: Perennial.

Prunier, Gérard. 2007. *Darfur: The Ambiguous Genocide.* Ithaca, NY: Cornell University Press.

Ray, Carina. 2009. "Darfur in the African Press." Pp. 170–198 in *Darfur and the Crisis of Governance in Sudan: A Critical Reader.* Edited by Salah Hassan and Carina Ray. Ithaca, NY: Cornell University Press.

Redfield, Peter. 2013. *Life in Crisis: The Ethical Journey of Doctors Without Borders.* Berkeley: University of California Press.

Reeves, Eric. 2011. "On the Obstruction of Humanitarian Aid." *African Studies Review* 54(3):165–174.

———. 2013. "Humanitarian Conditions in Darfur: A Climate of Violence and Extreme Insecurity." Sudan: Research, Analysis, and Advocacy. August 5. http://sudanreeves.org/2013/08/05/humanitarian-conditions-in-darfur-a-climate-of-violence-and-extreme-insecurity-2/. Last retrieved October 3, 2014.

Revers, Matthias. 2014. "Journalistic Professionalism as Performance and Boundary Work: Source Relations at the State House." *Journalism* 15(1):37–52.

Rioux, J. S., and D. A. Van Belle. 2005. "The Influence of *Le Monde* Coverage on French Foreign Aid Allocations." *International Studies Quarterly* 49(3):481–502.

Roth, Günther. 1987. *Politische Herrschaft und Persönliche Freiheit: Heidelberger Max Weber Vorlesungen.* Frankfurt: Suhrkamp.

Rueschemeyer, Dietrich. 1973. *Lawyers and their Society.* Cambridge, MA: Harvard University Press.

Rummel, R. J. 1994. *Death by Government.* New Brunswick, N.J.: Transaction.

Savelsberg, Joachim J. 1992. "Law That Does Not Fit Society: Sentencing Guidelines as a Neoclassical Reaction to the Dilemmas of Substantivized Law." *American Journal of Sociology* 97(5):1346–1381.

———. 1994. "Knowledge, Domination, and Criminal Punishment." *American Journal of Sociology* 99(4):911–943.

———. 2016. "Legal Culture as Memorial Normativity." Forthcoming in *The Normative Complex: Legal Cultures and Normativities.* Edited by Werner Gephart et al. Frankfurt: Vittorio Klostermann Verlag.

Savelsberg, Joachim J., and Ryan D. King. 2005. "Institutionalizing Collective Memories of Hate: Law and Law Enforcement in Germany and the United States." *American Journal of Sociology* 111(2):579–616.

———. 2007. "Law and Collective Memory." *Annual Review of Law and Social Science* 3:189–211.

———. 2011. *American Memories: Atrocities and the Law.* New York: Russell Sage Foundation.

Savelsberg, Joachim J., and Hollie Nyseth Brehm. 2015. "Global Justice, National Distinctions: Criminalizing Human Rights Violations in Darfur." *American Journal of Sociology* 121(2) (in press).

Schabas, William. 2004. "United States Hostility to the International Criminal Court: It's All about the Security Council." *European Journal of International Law* 15(4):701–720.

Scheffer, David. 2012. *All the Missing Souls: A Personal History of the War Crimes Tribunals*. Princeton, NJ: Princeton University Press.

Schofer, Evan, and Marion Fourcade-Gourinchas. 2001. "The Structural Context of Civic Engagement: Voluntary Association Membership in Comparative Perspective." *American Sociological Review* 66(6):806–828.

Schofer, Evan, David John Frank, Ann Hironaka, and Wesley Longhofer. 2012. "Sociological Institutionalism and World Society." Pp. 57–68 in *New Blackwell Companion to Political Sociology*. Edited by Edwin Amenta, Kate Nash, and Alan Scott. Oxford: Blackwell.

Schwartz, Barry. 2009. "Collective Forgetting and the Symbolic Power of Oneness: The Strange Apotheosis of Rosa Parks." *Social Psychology Quarterly* 72(2):123–142.

Seekers of Truth and Justice. 2003. *The Black Book*. (No place or publisher.)

Siguru, Wahutu. In progress. "Social, Field and Regional Conditions of Knowledge: News on Darfur in Africa and the Global North." PhD dissertation, University of Minnesota.

Siguru, Wahutu, and Joachim J. Savelsberg. 2013. "Regional versus Field Conditions of Knowledge: News on Darfur in Africa and the Global North." Paper presented at the 2013 Annual Meetings of the American Sociological Association.

Sikkink, Kathryn. 2011. *The Justice Cascade: How Human Rights Prosecutions Are Changing World Politics*. New York: W. W. Norton.

Smith, Dorothy. 1992. "Sociology from Women's Experience: A Reaffirmation." *Sociological Theory* 10(1):88–98.

Smith, Karen. 2010. *Genocide and the Europeans*. Cambridge: Cambridge University Press.

Smith, Philip. 2008. *Punishment and Culture*. Chicago: University of Chicago Press.

Smith, Philip, and Nicolas Howe. 2015. *Climate Change as Social Drama*. New York: Cambridge University Press.

Snyder, Jack, and Leslie Vinjamuri. 2003–2004. "Trials and Errors: Principle and Pragmatism in Strategies of International Justice." *International Security* 28:5–44.

Stan, Livia. 2013. "Civil Society and Post-Communist Transitional Justice." Paper presented at Legal Frames of Memory conference, Warsaw, Poland.

Strömbeck, Jesper, and Frank Esser. 2014. "Mediatization of Politics: Towards a Theoretical Framework." Pp. 3–28 in *Mediatization of Politics: Understanding the Transformation of Western Democracies*. Edited by Frank Esser and Jesper Strömbäck. Basingstoke, Hampshire, UK: Palgrave Macmillan.

Stroup, Sarah S. 2012. *Borders among Activists: International NGOs in the United States, Britain, and France.* Ithaca, NY: Cornell University Press.

Stryker, Robin. 1989. "Limits on Technocratization of Law." *American Sociological Review* 54(3):341–358.

Swidler, Ann. 1986. "Culture in Action—Symbols and Strategies." *American Sociological Review* 51(2):273–286.

Thomas, William Isaac. 1928. *The Child in America: Behavioral Problems and Programs.* New York: A. A. Knopf.

Thompson, Allan, ed. 2007. *The Media and the Rwanda Genocide.* Ottawa, Canada: Pluto Press.

Tsutsui, Kiyoteru, and Christine Min Wotipka. 2004. "Global Civil Society and the Human Rights Movement." *Social Forces* 83(2):587–620.

Turk, Austin. 1969. *Criminality and Legal Order.* Chicago: Rand McNally.

Unger, Roberto M. 1976. *Law in Modern Society.* New York: Free Press.

Van Belle, Douglas A., and Steven W. Hook. 2000. "Greasing the Squeaky Wheel: News Media Coverage and US Foreign Aid." *International Interactions* 26(3):321–346.

Walgrave, Stefaan, Stuart Soroka, and Michiel Nuytemans. 2008. "The Mass Media's Political Agenda-Setting Power—A Longitudinal Analysis of Media, Parliament, and Government in Belgium (1993 to 2000)." *Comparative Political Studies* 41(6):814–836.

Wall, Melissa. 2007. "An Analysis of News Magazine Coverage of the Rwanda Crisis in the United States." Pp. 261–275 in *The Media and the Rwanda Genocide.* Edited by Allan Thompson. London: Pluto Press.

Wanta, Wayne, and Yu-Wei Hu. 1993. "The Agenda-Setting Effects of International News Coverage: An Examination of Different News Frames." *International Journal of Public Opinion Research* 5(3):250–264.

Weber, Max. 1978. *Economy and Society.* Berkeley: University of California Press.

———. 2009. *Max Weber: "The Protestant Ethic and the Spirit of Capitalism" and Other Writings on the Rise of the West.* Translated and edited by Stephen Kalberg. New York: Oxford University Press.

Weissman, Fabrice. 2011. "Silence Heals . . . From the Cold War to the War on Terror, MSF Speaks Out: A Brief History." Pp. 177–198 in *Humanitarian Negotiations Revealed: The MSF Experience.* Edited by Claire Magone, Michael Neuman, and Fabrice Weisman. New York: Columbia University Press.

Whitman, James Q. 2005. *Harsh Justice: Criminal Punishment and the Widening Divide between America and Europe.* Oxford: Oxford University Press.

Williamson, Richard S. 2009a. "Darfur: The U.N. and the Responsibility to Protect: A Study in Failure." Pp. 309–322 in *America's Mission in the World: Principles, Practices, and Predicaments.* Chicago: Prairie Institute for Economic Growth and Freedom.

———. 2009b. "The Options for U.S. Policy on Darfur." Pp. 323–332 in *America's Mission in the World: Principles, Practices and Predicaments.* Chicago: Prairie Institute for Economic Growth and Freedom.

Wood, B. D., and J. S. Peake. 1998. "The Dynamics of Foreign Policy Agenda Setting." *American Political Science Review* 92(1):173–182.

Wright, John P., Francis T. Cullen, and Michael B. Blankenship. 1995. "The Social Construction of Corporate Violence: Media Coverage of the Imperial Food Products Fire." *Crime and Delinquency* 41(1):20–36.

Zacher, Meghan, Hollie Nyseth Brehm, and Joachim J. Savelsberg. 2014. "NGOs, IOs, and the ICC: Diagnosing and Framing Darfur." *Sociological Forum* 29(1):29–51.

Zelizer, Barbie. 1993. "Journalists as Interpretive Communities." *Critical Studies in Mass Communication* 10(3):219–237.

Index

CPSIA information can be obtained
at www.ICGtesting.com
Printed in the USA
FSOW03n2050151215
14319FS